Edition 2006

Kuwait
The Complete **Residents'** Guide

Dedicated to the memory of Simon White, May 1960 to July 2005.
Without his dedication, passion and enthusiasm this book would not have been possible.
May he rest in peace.

Passionately Publishing...

EXPLORER

Kuwait Explorer 2006 ISBN 13 - 978-976-8182-46-3 ISBN 10 - 976-8182-46-6

Reprinted in 2007

Front Cover Photograph – Victor Romero

Printed and bound by Emirates Printing Press, Dubai, United Arab Emirates.

Explorer Publishing & Distribution
PO Box 34275, Zomorrodah Bldg, Za'abeel Rd, Dubai
United Arab Emirates
Phone   (+971 4) 335 3520
Fax   (+971 4) 335 3529
Email   Info@explorerpublishing.com
Web   www.explorerpublishing.com

Kuwait Explorer
The Complete Residents' Guide

Also available in this series:
Abu Dhabi, Bahrain, Dubai, Geneva, Hong Kong, London, New York, Oman, Qatar, Singapore, Sydney

Forthcoming titles in this series (2007):
Amsterdam, Barcelona, Dublin, New Zealand, Paris, Shanghai

Contributing Authors
Sheena Smith, Susan Corner,
Ulrika Thor, Simon White

Publisher
Alistair MacKenzie

Editorial
Managing Editor Claire England
Lead Editors David Quinn, Jane Roberts, Matt Farquharson,
Sean Kearns, Tim Binks, Tom Jordan
Deputy Editors Helen Spearman, Jake Marsico, Katie Drynan,
Rebecca Wicks, Richard Greig, Tracy Fitzgerald
Editorial Assistants Grace Carnay, Ingrid Cupido, Mimi Stankova

Design
Creative Director Pete Maloney
Art Director Ieyad Charaf
Senior Designers Alex Jeffries, Iain Young
Layout Manager Jayde Fernandes
Designers Hashim Moideen, Rafi Pullat,
Shefeeq Marakkatepurath, Sunita Lakhiani
Cartography Manager Zainudheen Madathil
Cartographer Noushad Madathil
Design Admin Manager Shyrell Tamayo
Production Coordinator Maricar Ong

Photography
Photography Manager Pamela Grist
Photographer Victor Romero
Image Editor Henry Hilos

Sales and Marketing
Area Sales Manager Stephen Jones
Marketing Manager Kate Fox
Retail Sales Manager Ivan Rodrigues
Retail Sales Coordinator Kiran Melwani
Corporate Sales Executive Ben Merrett
Digital Content Manager Derrick Pereira
Distribution Supervisor Matthew Samuel
Distribution Executives Ahmed Mainodin, Firos Khan, Mannie Lugtu
Warehouse Assistant Mohammed Kunjaymo
Drivers Mohammed Sameer, Shabsir Madathil

Finance and Administration
Administration Manager Andrea Fust
Financial Manager Michael Samuel
Accounts Assistant Cherry Enriquez
Administrators Enrico Maullon, Lennie Maugaliuo
Driver Rafi Jamal

IT
IT Administrator Ajay Krishnan R.
Senior Software Engineer Bahrudeen Abdul
Software Engineer Roshni Ahuja

Contact Us
Reader Response
If you have any comments and suggestions, fill out
our online reader response form and you could win prizes.
Log on to **www.explorerpublishing.com**

General Enquiries
We'd love to hear your thoughts and answer any questions
you have about this book or any other Explorer product.
Contact us at **info@explorerpublishing.com**

Careers
If you fancy yourself as an Explorer, send your CV (stating
the position you're interested in) to
jobs@explorerpublishing.com

Designlab and Contract Publishing
For enquiries about Explorer's Contract Publishing arm
and design services contact
designlab@explorerpublishing.com

PR and Marketing
For PR and marketing enquiries contact
marketing@explorerpublishing.com
pr@explorerpublishing.com

Corporate Sales
For bulk sales and customisation options, for this book or
any Explorer product, contact
sales@explorerpublishing.com

Advertising and Sponsorship
For advertising and sponsorship, contact
media@explorerpublishing.com

Explorer Publishing & Distribution
Office 51B, Zomorrodah Building, Za'abeel Road
PO Box 34275, Dubai, United Arab Emirates
Phone: +971 (0)4 335 3520, **Fax:** +971 (0)4 335 3529
info@explorerpublishing.com
www.explorerpublishing.com

GROWING STRONGER

Strength can be measured by reputation and Salhia Real Estate Company since 1974 has grown to be regarded as a truly solid, reliable and professional operation in Kuwait.

Salhia Real Estate Company portfolio of properties comprises some of Kuwait's most impressive hotels, shopping centers and office towers.

Built on a foundation of quality, commitment and mission to be a leader in its domain, Salhia Real Estate Company's vision is to serve its customers, business travelers, tourists and local residents with excellence.

LHIA COMPLEX • SALHIA COMPLEX RESTAURANTS & PLAZA • AL SAHAB TOWER • JW MARRIOTT KUWAIT HOTEL • ARRAYA CENTRE • ARRAYA SHOPPING CENTER • ARRAY

AYA OFFICES • ARRAYA BALLROOM • COURTYARD MARRIOTT HOTEL • ARRAYA OUTDOOR RECREATIONAL PLAZA • ARRAYA CENTRE - PHASE II • AL ASIMA PROJECT • JW M

SALHIA COMPLEX

JW MARRIOTT.
KUWAIT CITY

Arraya Centre

COURTYARD
Marriott
KUWAIT CITY

شركة الصالحية العقارية ش.م.ك.

They Mean the World to You

We understand the importance of making your relocation experience as smooth as possible. After all, we're not just relocating your possessions, we are helping to relocate the most precious things in your life. Crown Relocations is a leading provider of domestic and international moving and settling-in services with over 100 locations in more than 45 countries.   ***Well Connected. Worldwide.*** ™

Dubai
Tel: (971) 4 289 5152
Fax: (971)4 289 6263
Email: dubai@crownrelo.com

Abu Dhabi
Tel: (971)2 674 5155
Fax: (971)2 674 2293
Email: abudhabi@crownrelo.com

Bahrain
Tel: (973)17 227 598
Fax: (973)17 224 803
Email: bahrain@crownrelo.com

Egypt
Tel: (202) 580 6628
Fax: (202) 580 6601
Email: cairo@crownrelo.com

Kuwait
Tel: (965) 299 7850
Fax: (965) 299 7800
Email: kuwait@crownrelo.com

Qatar
Tel: (974) 462 1115/1170/1439
Fax: (974) 462 1119
Email: doha@crownrelo.com

Turkey
Tel: (90) 212 347 4410
Fax: (90) 212 347 4413
Email: istanbul@crownrelo.com

Please Visit **www.crownrelo.com**
for details.

CROWN
RELOCATIONS

LEADERSHIP THROUGH EXCELLENCE

AT THE CORE.

Through years of dedicated and personalized customer care, rentalmulla carved a clear path for its service standard. To augment customer value, a wide vehicle selection boasting of the latest models was invested in and coupled with rentalmulla's customary free car collection and delivery. All through, offering the most flexible and attractively priced long and short-term car rentals backed by a 24-hour roadside assistance and reservation system. It is not surprising then to find that rentalmulla's leadership stems from emphasis on excellence from the core outwards.

Visit our branch at Kuwait International Airport (GF 78)
or call 4738410, 4738205

AL MULLA RENTAL & LEASING
OF VEHICLES & EQUIPMENT CO. WLL

☎ 4848195, 4838153, 3980566

Hashim MM
AKA: Speedy Gonzales
They don't come much faster than Hashim – he's so speedy with his mouse that scientists are struggling to create a computer that can keep up with him. His nimble fingers leave his keyboard smouldering (he gets through three a week), and his go-faster stripes make him almost invisible to the naked eye when he moves.

Jane Roberts
AKA: The Oracle
After working in an undisclosed role in the government, Jane brought her super sleuth skills to Explorer. Whatever the question, she knows what, where, who, how and when, but her encyclopaedic knowledge is only impressive until you realise she just makes things up randomly.

Helen Spearman
AKA: Little Miss Sunshine
With her bubbly laugh and permanent smile, Helen is a much-needed ray of sunshine in the office when we're all grumpy and facing harrowing deadlines. It's almost impossible to think that she ever loses her temper or shows a dark side... although put her behind the wheel of a car, and you've got instant road rage.

Jayde Fernandes
AKA: Pop Idol
Jayde's idol is Britney Spears, and he recently shaved his head to show solidarity with the troubled star. When he's not checking his dome for stubble, or practising the dance moves to 'Baby One More Time' in front of the bathroom mirror, he actually manages to get some designing done.

Henry Hilos
AKA: The Quiet Man
Henry can rarely be seen from behind his large obstructive screen but when you do catch a glimpse you'll be sure to get a smile. Lighthearted Henry keeps all those glossy pages filled with pretty pictures for something to look at when you can't be bothered to read.

Kate Fox
AKA: Contacts Collector
Kate swooped into the office like the UK equivalent of Wonderwoman, minus the tights of course (it's much too hot for that), but armed with a superhuman marketing brain. Even though she's just arrived, she is already a regular on the Dubai social scene - she is helping to blast Explorer into the stratosphere, one champagne-soaked networking party at a time.

Ieyad Charaf
AKA: Fashion Designer
When we hired Ieyad as a top designer, we didn't realise we'd be getting his designer tops too! By far the snappiest dresser in the office, you'd be hard-pressed to beat his impeccably ironed shirts.

Katie Drynan
AKA The Irish Deputy
Katie is a Jumeirah Jane in training, and has 35 sisters who take it in turns to work in the Explorer office while she enjoys testing all the beauty treatments available on the Beach Road. This Irish charmer met an oil tycoon in Paris, and they now spend the weekends digging very deep holes in their new garden.

Ingrid Cupido
AKA: The Karaoke Queen
Ingrid has a voice to match her starlet name. She'll put any Pop Idols to shame once behind the mike, and she's pretty nifty on a keyboard too. She keeps us all ticking over and was a very welcome relief for overworked staff. She certainly gets our vote if she decides to go pro; just remember you saw her here first.

Ivan Rodrigues
AKA: The Aviator
After making a mint in the airline market, Ivan came to Explorer where he works for pleasure, not money. That's his story, anyway. We know that he is actually a corporate spy from a rival company and that his multi-level spreadsheets are really elaborate codes designed to confuse us.

Kiran Melwani
AKA: Bow Selector
Like a modern-day Robin Hood (right down to the green tights and band of merry men), Kiran's mission in life is to distribute Explorer's wealth of knowledge to the fact-hungry readers of the world. Just make sure you never do anything to upset her – rumour has it she's a pretty mean shot with that bow and arrow.

Abdul Gafoor
AKA: Ace Circulator
After a successful stint on Ferrari's Formula One team Gafoor made a pitstop at our office and decided to stay. He has won our 'Most Cheerful Employee' award five years in a row – baffling, when you consider he spends so much time battling the traffic.

Andrea Fust
AKA: Mother Superior
By day Andrea is the most efficient manager in the world and by night she replaces the boardroom for her board and wows the pants off the dudes in Ski Dubai. Literally. Back in the office she definitely wears the trousers!

Ahmed Mainodin
AKA: Mystery Man
We can never recognise Ahmed because of his constantly changing facial hair. He waltzes in with big lambchop sideburns one day, a handlebar moustache the next, and a neatly trimmed goatee after that. So far we've had no objections to his hirsute chameleonisms, but we'll definitely draw the line at a monobrow.

Cherry Enriquez
AKA: Bean Counter
With the team's penchant for sweets and pastries, it's good to know we have Cherry on top of our accounting cake. The local confectioner is always paid on tin so we're guaranteed great gatea for every special occasion.

Claire England
AKA: Whip Cracker
No longer able to freeload off the fact that she once appeared in a Robbie Williams video, Claire now puts her creative skills to better use – looking up rude words in the dictionary! A child of English nobility, Claire is quite the lady – unless she's down at Jimmy Dix.

Ajay Krishnan R
AKA: Web Wonder
Ajay's mum and dad knew he was going to be an IT genius when the found him reconfiguring his Commodore 64 at the tender age of 2. He went on to become the technology consultant on all three Matrix films, and counts Keanu as a close personal friend.

David Quinn
AKA: Sharp Shooter
After a short stint as a children's TV presenter was robbed from David because he developed an allergy to sticky back plastic, he made his way to sandier pastures. Now that he's thinking outside the box, nothing gets past the man with the sharpest pencil in town.

Alex Jeffries
AKA: Easy Rider
Alex is happiest when dressed in leather from head to toe with a humming machine between his thighs – just like any other motorbike enthusiast. Whenever he's not speeding along the Hatta Road at full throttle, he can be found at his beloved Mac, still dressed in leather.

Enrico Maullon
AKA: The Crooner
Frequently mistaken for his near-namesake Enrique Iglesias, Enrico decided to capitalise and is now a regular stand-in for the Latin heartthrob. If he's ever missing from the office, it usually means he's off performing for millions of adoring fans on another stadium tour of America.

Alistair MacKenzie
AKA: Media Mogul
If only Alistair could take the paperless office one step further and achieve the officeless office he would be the happiest publisher alive. Wireless access from a remote spot somewhere in the Hajar Mountains would suit this intrepid explorer – less traffic, lots of fresh air, and wearing sandals all day – the perfect work environment!

Firos Khan
AKA: Big Smiler
Previously a body double in kung fu movies, including several appearances in close up scenes for Steven Seagal's moustache. He also once tore down a restaurant with his bare hands after they served him a mild curry by mistake.

Ladies and Gentlemen - the Explorer has landed! Blown in on a warm desert shamal, the Kuwait Explorer is the be all and end all of fact-filled guidebooks.

Written and researched by resident experts on the ground (and with maps photographed by resident satellites in space!) we can proudly claim that no other guide contains as much vital information and advice as this one. Whether you're visiting friends and family, you're in town on business, you've just arrived to set up home or you've been in the country for years, the Kuwait Explorer is for you.

A General Info chapter fills you in on Kuwait's geography and eventful history, has lots of useful facts and figures, and lists places where the weary traveller can rest his or her head. The Residents chapter is for those who plan to make Kuwait their home, with advice on visas and vital documents, housing, healthcare, education and work. The Exploring chapter gives you the info you need to get out and about and discover the country, while Activities has details of every imaginable club, group or society to ensure you make the most of your valuable free time. Talking of free time, the Shopping chapter is like a dream come true for eager shopaholics, and Going Out will leave you spoilt for choice with hundreds of reviews of Kuwait's restaurants, cafés and entertainment venues.

The ultimate insider guide, with the trusty Kuwait Explorer by your side you'll never be lost for an answer, lost for somewhere to go, lost for something to do, or just lost, ever again.

Ciao for now! The Explorer Team.

Now it's over to you…

Just because you didn't get involved in the making of this book doesn't mean you can just sit on your laurels. We've done our best to uncover all the facts about living in Kuwait, but we accept – and it hurts to say this – that we might have left

things out. Which is where you come in. We want to know what we've done wrong, who we've missed out and where we can improve. Have we left out your ice-sculpting club or dissed your favourite restaurant? Tell us! And don't forget that compliments are also gratefully received, so feel free to send in as many expressions of unadulterated praise as you want.

Visit our website to fill in our Reader Response form, and tell us exactly what you think of us.

www.explorerpublishing.com

Bods Behind the Book...

A lot goes into the production of our Complete Residents' Guides. Sweat, tears, late nights, laughter, talents, tantrums, dedication, prayers, moral support and a colourful collection of vocabulary have all been offered selflessly by members of the Explorer family over the last few months. They all deserve a shake of the hand, a pat on the back, and copious air kisses for their contributions.

Our creative genius aside, there's a whole extended Explorer family to thank. A big shout goes out to the tireless efforts of our roving reporters and backstage hands. These are the people who work just as hard as us (sometimes harder), and yet still manage to hold down their day jobs. Thank you to everyone who had a hand in the creation of this masterpiece – here they are:

Our principal authors, Sheena Smith, Susan Corner, Ulrika Thor and Simon White as well as Alan England, Brian Cummingham, David Plowman, Jeff Delange, John Morley, Mark Bloemers, Simon Balsom – who deserve medals for their contributions to food and drink research.

Thanks also to the following for lending a hand: Anand and Tony from Emirates Printing Press, Maher and Peter (maps), Mr. Saed Al Darmaki (Director of Censorship – Abu Dhabi), Mr. Ahmed Al Shamsi, Ms. Maha Shams Al Kelani, Ms. Lamiya Ali Al Shamsi, Mr. Ibrahim, Mr. Nadawi, Mr. Juma Obaid Alleem (Director of Censorship – Dubai).

Extra special thanks to long-suffering partners Alan, Alex, Arnel, David, Dominik, Felicitas, Fraser, Grace, Greg, Justin, Jodie, Marjan, Nijula, Peter, Raihanath, Raji, Robert, Sadanand, Sadhiya, Sajithkumar and Sunitha: well done for putting up with our bad moods, late nights and general deadline frenzy. And to the youngest Explorers – Caitie, Dylan, Fiza, Hannah, Kanyon, Lauren E, Lauren G, Louise-Alodia, Lourdes-Amely, Mohammed Shaaz, Peter-Vincent, Sean, Shahaha, Shahhina, and Shahinsha – your mummies and daddies will be home soon!

Come on then if you think you work hard enough...
If you fancy yourself as an Explorer and want a piece of the action send your details to Jobs@explorerpublishing. com and mark the email subject with one of the following: Food Reporter (if you want to write for your supper), Freelance Writer (if you think you have insider info to contribute), Editorial (if you want to join the ranks of our esteemed production team), Design (if you have professional creative skills), Research (if you think you could be an Explorer investigator).

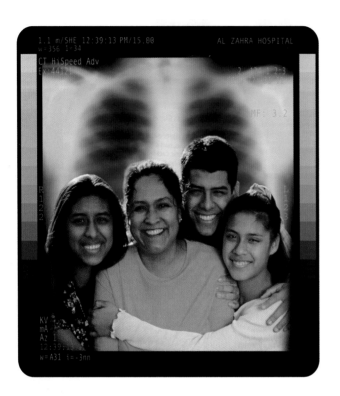

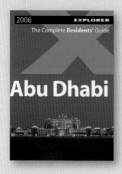

Residents' Guides

Activity Guides

Practical Guides

Lifestyle Guides

Map Guides

Visitors' Guides

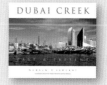

Photography Books

Contents   General Info

Residents

An in-depth look at the areas worth exploring in Kuwait and all the attractions to be found there, including museums, heritage sites, parks, beaches and amusement centres, and what can be found in Kuwait's neighbouring countries.

Activities

With enough to keep everyone busy, from beach lovers and theatre players up to even the most ardent extreme sports enthusiasts, Kuwait has a variety of sports and activities to keep you busy. Comprehensive listings for all the sports, activities, clubs and relaxation available.

From large and flash malls to traditional, atmospheric souks, there's a massive range of shopping opportunities in Kuwait. There are reviews on each mall and shopping area and sections on where to find whatever you want to buy.

Whether you love fine dining or street-side shawarma, this chapter opens up Kuwait's culinary delights with independent reviews of all the 'must-do' places. There's also a rundown of cinemas and theatre options.

Importing electronics from China?

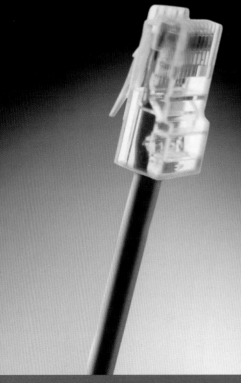

We've got the connections.

No one knows China like we do.

Whatever you're importing, plug into DHL. With more experience, more offices and more commercial flights a week than any other operator, nobody knows China like we do. Not just the geography but the people and their way of working. So if you're doing business in China, remember there's one network with all the right connections.
Call 800 4004 now and ask about our fantastic "takeaway" offer.
Offer valid only in UAE from 15th October to 31st December 2005.
Don't miss out, call NOW.

Deutsche Post 🦅 World Net
MAIL EXPRESS LOGISTICS FINANCE

General Information

EXPLORER

General Information

Highlights...

A Modern City in the Making
[p.6]

Kuwait's skyline is currently undergoing a dramatic transformation with new architectural wonders popping up all over the city. From state-of-the-art shopping malls and a sports stadium of gigantic proportions to gigantic residential and commercial towers that will literally scrape the sky, the developments currently planned or already under construction are set to change the face of Kuwait forever.

Geography

Strategically located at the northern end of the Arabian Gulf, Kuwait is bordered by Iraq to the north and west, Saudi Arabia to the south-west and south, and the Arabian Gulf to the east. Kuwait shares 240km of border with Iraq and 222km of border with Saudi Arabia.

The country covers an area of approximately 17,820km², including nine islands; Bubiyan, Failaka, Warba, Miskan, Oha, Kubbar, Qaruth, Umm Al Maradem and Umm Al Namil. Bubiyan is the largest of the islands, measuring 863 square kilometres, and will soon be home to a large container port which will be linked to Kuwait's road network. Failaka Island played an important role in Kuwait's history with settlements dating back to the Stone Age.

The geographical coordinates for Kuwait are 29°30 N, 45°45 E.

Kuwait's local authorities are split into six separate governorates; Kuwait City, Ahmadi, Farwaniya, Hawalli, Jahra and Mubarak Al Kabeer.

Kuwait City is the capital and is the commercial and financial heart of the country. The skyline is dominated by the Liberation Tower, a telecommunications tower completed in 1996 and the Kuwait Water Towers, located on the Ras Ajooza promontory in Dasman, which are the country's most famous landmark. At 372m the Liberation Tower is the fifth highest telecommunications tower in the world. Ahmadi, Kuwait's oil town, is located approximately 35km south of Kuwait City and is home to the Kuwait Oil Company (KOC).

Kuwait's topography is characterised by little more than flat, gravelly desert with a few sabkhah (salt flats) and marshes. The highest point in the country is near Al Salmi in the western region where the elevation is approximately 300m. Ahmadi Hill in the south has an elevation of 137m, and Jal Azzor (Mutla Ridge), north of Kuwait Bay, an elevation of 145m. The somewhat uninteresting 290km of mainland coastline comprises predominantly mudflats from the north to Kuwait Bay, and sandy beaches from Kuwait Bay to the Saudi Arabian border. Shallow depressions found throughout the country fill with water after the heavy seasonal rains and attract birdlife. Kuwait has no rivers or mountains.

History

Kuwait was once controlled by various dynasties that originated from Mesopotamia and Persia. The Safavids, a Persian dynasty based in the region around AD 1500, were the most influential. They established a powerful commercial empire along the eastern parts of the Arabian Peninsula. This area later became part of the Turkish Ottoman Empire and remained so until the Al Sabah family took administrative control towards the end of the 19th century and guided the country towards semi-autonomy. In an agreement that would afford them protection from the Turks, the Kuwaitis allowed the British to take control of foreign affairs. The Turkish threat ended with the collapse of the Ottoman Empire at the end of World War One. However, the British retained control of Kuwait until independence was gained on 19th June 1961. At the time of independence, the head of state was Sheikh Abdullah.

Towering example of liberation

General Info

Kuwait Overview

Independence was shortly followed by threats from the Iraqi leader, Abdullah Karim Qassim. Stating that all of Kuwait belonged to Iraq, he intimated that Iraq would invade by gathering troops on the Kuwaiti borders. The arrival of international troops to protect Kuwait saw him back down.

The Emir of Kuwait, Sheikh Abdullah, died in 1965 and was succeeded by his younger brother, Sheikh Sabah Al Salim, who died 12 years later, in 1977. Sheikh Jaber Al Ahmed Al Sabah, the former Crown Prince, then became Emir and Sheikh Sa'ad Abdulla Salim became Crown Prince.

Kuwait's large oil revenues enabled the country to develop a strong economic infrastructure, and education and social welfare systems were introduced. However, threats from Iraq continued, this time under Saddam Hussein, and when Iraq raised unrealistic demands relating to oil production and outstanding debt (Kuwait had backed Iraq in the 1970-74 Iran-Iraq war, to the tune of approximately US$50m), Kuwait's fate was sealed. Iraqi forces invaded Kuwait in the early hours of 2nd August 1990.

Senior government officials fled the country and Kuwait was incorporated into Iraq as a 19th province. Seven months of looting and destruction all but destroyed Kuwait's infrastructure. Thousands of Kuwaitis and expatriates were taken hostage and many were never seen alive again.

The US led a UN coalition, in an operation known as Desert Shield, to limit further expansion by the Iraqi occupiers. Under Desert Shield there was a massive build-up of military might from the coalition, that culminated in Operation Desert Storm. After five weeks of air strikes against Iraqi positions, liberating forces entered Kuwait on 23 February 1991 and the entire country was liberated in four days.

The legacy of the occupation was considerable, and Kuwait spent five billion dollars alone on repairing and replacing oil infrastructure damaged during 1990 and 1991. There was however a deeper legacy in the mindset of the Kuwaitis who, for the following twelve years, still lived in some degree of fear that Saddam Hussein would mount another Iraqi invasion.

This period between the Gulf wars was a subdued period for Kuwait from an economic perspective, with much Kuwaiti money invested offshore, and cross-border trade to Iraq (which was historically significant) not possible.

The second Gulf war in 2003, staged predominantly by US-led coalition forces based in Kuwait, represented a watershed in the psyche of the Kuwaitis who were finally freed from the threat of their northern neighbour. Increased investment of private sector money into Kuwaiti projects is one tangible benefit of this. At the same time the opening of cross-border trade with Iraq, and the large presence of military customers in both Kuwait and Iraq, has led to an economic boom in the country.

Economy

Kuwait Overview

Kuwait's wealth is based largely on oil production. Oil and petroleum accounted for almost 50% of the gross domestic product (GDP) and 89% of Kuwait's annual revenue in the 2003/2004 fiscal period. Kuwait's GDP in 2003 was US$39.8 billion. The country had a record surplus of KD 1.5 billion (US$5 billion) at the start of 2004, approximately 12% of the 2003 GDP. Although initially predicted to be a deficit, the 2004/2005 period is likely to show at least a KD 1 billion surplus, based on prevailing oil prices.

Although historically any surplus has been used to accumulate further foreign assets, the Kuwaiti government is now seeking to increase spending. Budget expenditure for the 2003/2004 fiscal period was up by approximately 10%, almost 45% of the 2003 GDP.

Total oil production capacity currently stands at almost three million barrels per day. With a proven 10% of the world's total crude oil reserves, Kuwait is pushing ahead with a plan to provide four million barrels per day by 2020.

With most of the national reserves of approximately US$100 billion spent on rebuilding efforts following the first Gulf War, Kuwait's economy has fully recovered thanks to huge UNCC (United Nations Compensation Committee) damage claims and high world oil prices. With the recent regime change in Iraq, Kuwait's economy is moving full-speed ahead.

The positive changes to economic regulations, including the amendments to regulations governing foreign investments (FDI), continue to create positive sentiment. A number of international banks are in the process of receiving operating licences.

No Taxes

Kuwait is largely a tax-free economy. Although corporate income tax is levied on foreign companies operating in Kuwait, there is no personal income tax on salaries, or on income from commercial activities, and no sales tax or estate tax.

Although there are still restrictions, the FDI law allows for the possibility of 100% foreign ownership and a 10 year tax exemption. Kuwaiti shareholders are not taxed, while foreign shareholders are currently taxed up to 55%. There is no personal income tax in Kuwait.

The Kuwait Towers

Non-oil activities, including services and trade, continue to contribute to the growing GDP. Kuwait is used as a gateway to Iraq, and the increase in demand for hotel accommodation since the 2003 war has been considerable. Occupancy has averaged 60%, with some hotels reporting 100%. Property development has increased private sector investment considerably and a number of foreign companies operating in Iraq have based themselves in Kuwait, creating an increased demand for work-related services. Optimism has been bolstered by the prospect of the renewal of ties, particularly in business, between the two countries.

Over 90% of the national workforce is employed in the public sector, primarily due to the high salaries, generous benefits and short working hours. In order to get more of the Kuwaiti workforce to move into the private sector the government is implementing measures such as 'Kuwaitisation', whereby private businesses are required to employ a specific percentage of Kuwaiti staff, depending on the business sector. This can range from 2% to 50%. Expatriate workers contribute over 80% of the country's total workforce.

Per capita income for 2004 was approximately KD 5,000 (US$17,000), the third highest in the region after Qatar and the UAE. However, this figure disguises the fact that the unskilled labourers, who make up a high percentage of the expatriate workforce, continue to receive wages of as little as KD 40 (US$140) per month.

Kuwait exports oil and refined products, as well as a number of by-products (including fertilizer). The country's main export partners are Japan, South Korea, USA, Taiwan and Singapore. Imports include construction materials, clothing, and vehicles and parts, with the main import partners being the USA, Japan, Germany, China, UK, Saudi Arabia, Italy and France. Kuwait's climate prevents large-scale agriculture practices, meaning the majority of foodstuffs, excluding fish, have to be imported.

Kuwait's credit rating was ranked A2 for 2003 by Moody's, the leading investor-services resource. Kuwait has no external debt.

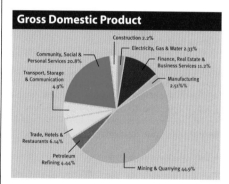

Gross Domestic Product

Construction 2.2%
Electricity, Gas & Water 2.33%
Finance, Real Estate & Business Services 11.2%
Community, Social & Personal Services 20.8%
Transport, Storage & Communication 4.9%
Manufacturing 2.51%%
Trade, Hotels & Restaurants 6.14%
Petroleum Refining 4.44%
Mining & Quarrying 44.9%

Tourism Developments

Historically Kuwait has been a difficult country to visit. Bureaucratic immigration procedures have always been somewhat lengthy, primarily due to security concerns. However, the government has embarked on a long-term plan to increase tourism and is in the process of expanding the current infrastructure to attract foreign visitors.

Tourism is currently an infinitesimal part of the country's revenue. Most people coming to Kuwait do so on business, or to visit their relatives. For those who do visit, there is a wide range of hotels to choose from; from the five star deluxe to budget hotels.

A number of substantial projects are under way as part of the country's 20 year tourism masterplan, driven by the desire to diversify the source of national income.

Key Kuwait City Projects

Kuwait is investing large amounts of capital in major commercial, residential, and tourism projects. The top development ventures are listed below. Additional projects in the planning stage include a 1,100 bed hospital in South Surra, a national library, a cardiac hospital, a dedicated maternity hospital and a number of major facilities for the oil industry and government organisations.

360° Kuwait

Proposed for completion in 2007, 360° Kuwait will be a huge circular shopping mall with an impressive 59,000 square metres of retail space to be anchored by a large hypermarket and two well-known department stores. Leisure facilities such as a 15 screen cinema with an IMAX theatre, a bowling alley and plenty of restaurants will share the space. It will be located at the intersection of King Faisal Highway and the 6th Ring Road.

Al Khiran Pearl City

Work has begun on phase one of this US$138 million development. Located adjacent to the Saudi border, the 6,500 hectare project will be developed in a number of stages and will ultimately be home to 50,000 residents.

Bubiyan Island Port

Feasibility studies are under way as part of the project to build a container port on the 530 square-kilometre island. The development of the port is expected to progress over a period of 20 years, at an estimated cost of over US$1 billion.

Failaka Island Project

There are plans to develop Failaka Island into a multi-billion-dollar tourist attraction. The project would comprise a complete holiday resort with accommodation and entertainment facilities. Construction is expected to take up to ten years and will cost up to US$3 billion.

Golf Course

A 6,600 yard, par 70 golf course is currently being completed at the Hunting & Equestrian Club off the 6th Ring Road, with thirteen of the 18 holes located within the race track. The result will be a challenging, contoured course with three lakes, 12m high hills and over 5,000 trees. Facilities will include a clubhouse, pro-shop, spa, health club, restaurants, a driving range and a golf academy.

Gulf University for Science & Technology (GUST)

The Gulf University is scheduled to open in 2006. Located on a 10 hectare site in Mishref, the long-term plan is to accommodate 5,500 students. The Community Development & Training Centre will hold a 500-seat auditorium and a 200 seat lecture hall in addition to exhibition and conference spaces.

Heritage Village

This 40 storey commercial tower, five-storey mall and 1,400 bay carpark will be located in Sharq. Cinema and entertainment facilities will also be available. The project is valued at US$155 million and is due for completion at the end of 2007.

Kuwait Business Town (KBT)

Featuring nine luxurious office towers, shopping malls, and a new luxury hotel, Kuwait Business Town will create a business community in Kuwait City along the lines of similar projects in Dubai and Qatar. The project is being developed on more than 11,000 square metres of prime real estate.

Kuwait International Airport (KIA)

There are plans to upgrade and expand the airport, including the building of a second terminal. With KIA currently handling five million passengers a year, it has been suggested that a new terminal could accommodate a further 15 million a year. Further plans will see the construction of a third terminal for use by private aircraft.

Kuwait University

Plans have recently been drawn up for a major project to develop a new University City, complete with a medical campus. Although still in the planning stage, this US$3 billion project is expected to be completed within three years, when all campuses run by Kuwait University will be relocated to the new site.

Madinat Al Fahaheel

The pride and joy of Tamdeen Real Estate, Madinat Al Fahaheel hopes to become the new city centre of Fahaheel. Combining modern design with traditional Arabian architecture, the development is already home to the Al Kout Mall (see [p.182] in Shopping) while Al Mahnsar is currently under construction. The latter will feature a shopping mall, entertainment centre, four residential towers, one office tower and a large convention centre as well as a five-star hotel. Al Manshar is due for completion in 2006.

Sheikh Jaber Al Ahmed International Stadium

This 60,000 seat stadium covering an area of 130,000 square metres will comprise a full-size football field and an Olympic standard athletics track. The project is due for completion in 2006. Project value is US$189 million.

Subiya Causeway

The 36 km Subiya causeway will cross the expanse of Kuwait Bay, linking Kuwait City to Subiya in the north. The expected cost of this project is a whopping $1,500 million.

The Avenue Shopping Mall

Construction has begun on 'The Avenue', on the 5th Ring Road in Al Rai. The two-storey mall will cover an area of 100,000 square metres and have a 2,000 vehicle car park. The project is valued at US$189 million, and completion is anticipated within two years. French hypermarket chain Carrefour is expected to open a new store here.

Watya Complex

The Watya complex is a US$101 million project to construct a three-tower complex comprising two commercial/residential towers, and a hotel.

International Relations

Kuwait has maintained excellent relations with the US and UK since the liberation from Iraqi occupation in 1991. This was illustrated when Kuwait allowed the US led coalition to use the country as a springboard for the 2003 war in Iraq. In addition to these special relationships, Kuwait has close ties with other European and East Asian powers as well as with its GCC partners.

A number of countries, including Cuba, Jordan, Sudan and Yemen, supported Iraq during the invasion of Kuwait, and relations were subsequently strained. The Palestine Liberation Organisation, led by Yasser Arafat, also supported Saddam Hussein, causing a great deal of bitterness. All Palestinian workers in Kuwait were ordered out of the country, and it was only in 2001 that restrictions against workers from these countries were finally lifted.

As well as allowing use of its land, Kuwait donated hundreds of millions of dollars, primarily in fuel, to the 2003 war effort. Kuwait has subsequently provided huge sums of money for the rebuilding of Iraq.

Kuwait has been a member of the Arab League (League of Arab States) since 1961, the United Nations since 1963 and the GCC (also known as the Arab GCC) since its inception in 1981.

As a member of the Arab League, Kuwait participates in the Arab boycott against Israel, and as such, trade between the two countries is non-existent. Kuwait maintains an Israeli Boycott Office.

The National Assembly Building

Kuwait is a member state of a number of Arab and international organisations including the Arab Monetary Fund (AMF), International Monetary Fund (IMF), Organisation of Petroleum Exporting Countries (Opec) and the World Trade Organisation (WTO).

Kuwait's maritime boundary is 12 NM (nautical miles). There is currently no maritime boundary with Iraq. Negotiations concerning a joint maritime boundary are being conducted by Kuwait and Saudi Arabia with Iran.

A number of countries have embassy/consulate representation in Kuwait (see table on [p.23]).

Government & Ruling Family

The late Emir (ruler) of Kuwait, Sheikh Jaber Al Ahmad Al Sabah, passed away on January 15, 2006 to the deepest sorrow of the Kuwaiti people, both locals and expats, as well as those in Kuwait's neighbouring GCC countries. Sheikh Jaber rose to power in 1977 succeeding his cousin Sheikh Sabah Al Salim. The period of his rule was eventful to say the least, with an assassination attempt in 1985 followed by a period of rule in exile during the Iraqi occupation. More recently his rule saw the liberation of Iraq, transforming the economic conditions in the country whilst closing a difficult chapter in Kuwait's history once and for all. Initially the Crown Prince Sheikh Sa'ad Al Abdullah Al Sabah took over as ruler, however, his questionable health lead to him abdicating and the Prime Minister, Sheikh Sabah Al Ahmad Al Sabah then became the 15th Emir of Kuwait.

Kuwait's constitution, as a nominal constitutional monarchy, was approved in 1962 after the country gained independence from British rule. Kuwait has an elected parliament of 50 members, known as the National Assembly or Majlis Al Umma.

The Beloved Sheikh

When the late Emir of Kuwait, Sheikh Jabir Al Ahmad Al Jabir Al Sabah died in January 2006 the nation mourned for the loss of a unique, steadfast and determined leader who took Kuwait through some of its toughest years in history. The magnitude of condolences that flooded in from around the GCC, Middle East and world was testiment to the international standing of this pioneer.

In practice the National Assembly has spent long periods in dissolution during this period, notably from 1986 through to the first Gulf War in 1990. As part of the negotiation to be restored to power the Emir agreed to re-instate the National Assembly, which he duly did in 1992. The National Assembly has been sitting regularly ever since, although the relationship between parliament and cabinet is often a rocky one. Notably, in 1999 the National Assembly was once again dissolved by the Emir, due to continued issues of conflict between them and the government, and therefor early elections were held.

Whilst political parties do not exist in Kuwait, the current political make-up of the National Assembly is the Islamists with 21 seats, followed by government supporters with 14 seats, independents with 12 seats and liberals with three seats.

Kuwait is divided into 25 constituencies with the top two candidates in each electorate elected to the National Assembly. Campaigning is generally conducted via the traditional meeting-place or diwaniya.

After years of campaigning, and following a narrow defeat in 1999, parliament finally passed a legal amendment in May 2005 granting Kuwaiti women the right to vote and stand in elections. The electoral law previously allowed only men to vote and run for office, but this was seen as being out of step with the country's constitution which promotes sexual equality. The new ruling had the full backing of the Emir and the Prime Minister, although it was opposed by more conservative Islamists and tribal legislators.

Kuwaiti Women In Politics

Just one month after the Kuwaiti government granted full political rights for women, liberal academic Maasuma Al Mubarak was named as the first woman minister. As the Minister of Planning and Administration her appointment marked a new era, not only for women in politics in Kuwait, but also in high level positions across all industries.

Elections are held every four years with the next election scheduled for 2007. Members of the police and armed forces are not eligible to vote, to ensure these bodies remain apolitical.

The Emir appoints the government, generally from members of the ruling family. The key positions are as follows: Deputy Emir and Crown Prince, Prime Minister and Foreign Minister, Deputy Prime Minister and Defence Minister.

Facts & Figures

Population

The local population has increased dramatically since 2003, primarily due to the large number of companies that have based themselves in Kuwait to support their operations in Iraq.

By the end of 2004 the expatriate population had increased by 11.1% over 2003's figure. Expatriates now number almost 1.8 million and account for around two thirds of the population, which stood at 2,753 million at the end of 2004. The indigenous population of 956,000 accounts for 34.7% of the total population.

Population by State

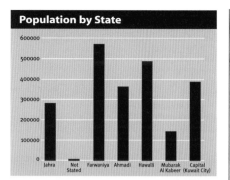

Population Age Breakdown

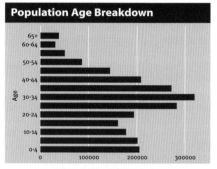

Education Levels

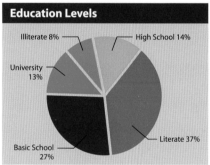

Illiterate 8%
High School 14%
University 13%
Literate 37%
Basic School 27%

Source: Ministry of Planning; The Public Authority for Civil Information

Asians, who number over one million, make up the largest contingent in Kuwait. Europeans number 9,000, Americans 12,000 and Australians approximately 1,000.

The last available official figures are those issued by the Ministry of Planning following the 1995 census. A population census is undertaken once every 10 years. The 2005 statistics are scheduled to be released in the third quarter of the year.

Average size of local family household: 10

Ratio of men to women: 1.37:1

Highest life expectancy: 77.86 (female 2004 est)

Population growth rate: 8.1% (2004) – according to PACI (NBK report)

National Flag

Designed in 1961 and based on the Arab revolt flag of the first world war, the national flag of Kuwait has three horizontal stripes starting with green at the top, then white and red. A black trapezoid runs the length of the hoist side and protrudes into the white horizontal stripe.

The colours of the national flag are common to most of the Arab nations and, in the case of Kuwait, are derived from a poem by Sadie Al Deen Al Hali;

'White for our work, Black for our struggles, Green for our spring homes, Red for our past.'

The Kuwaitis are very patriotic and the national flag is seen flying almost everywhere you go. On National Day and Liberation Day the flag flies from lamp posts, the tops of houses, hotels, public buildings, and most vehicle aerials. Patriotism becomes even more evident at night when many government and private buildings are adorned with a multitude of coloured lights representing the colours of the flag.

When foreign heads of state visit Kuwait they are welcomed by the sight of their own country's flag flying alongside that of Kuwait on roads to and from the airport, prominent meeting places and palaces. During all national celebrations one will often see a white flag, upon which is placed a black fingerprint and a small representation of the Kuwait national flag. This flag stands as a tribute to all those lost as POWs in the first Gulf War.

Local Time

Kuwait is three hours ahead of UCT (Universal Coordinated Time, formerly known as GMT). Daylight saving is not used. When it is 12:00 midday in Kuwait, it is 04:00 in New York, 09:00 in London, 14:30 in Delhi and 18:00 in Tokyo (not allowing for daylight saving in any of these countries).

Social & Business Hours

Friday is the holy day, and everywhere closes. From 1 September 2007, the official weekend will be Friday and Saturday. Until then, some places will have a Thursday / Friday weekend. Some employers work a five and a half day week.

General Info

Facts & Figures

Private sector office hours vary between split shifts and straight shifts. Split shifts begin between 08:00 and 09:00 and close for lunch around 12:00 or 13:00, re-opening any time between 15:00 and 17:00, and closing between 18:00 and 20:00. Straight shifts tend to commence at 08:00 or 09:00 and finish at 17:00 or 18:00.

Major shopping centres open at 10:00 and work a straight shift through to 22:00. You will find that some outlets within major shopping centres operate on a split-shift basis and close for lunch for an hour or two.

Ministries operate from 07:00 to 14:00, Saturday to Wednesday during the summer months and from 07:30 to 14:30 during the winter months. During the holy month of Ramadan, Ministry working hours are considerably reduced; usually only from 10:00 to 13:00. Banks operate Sunday to Thursday and tend to open at 08:00 and will close at either 13:00 or 14:00. A few of the major banks open specific branches in the evenings. Schools have a five-day week, from Saturday to Wednesday.

Corner shops (known as bakalas) often open at 06:00 and close at 22:00, although these times do vary, and a number close at prayer times for about fifteen minutes.

Most major government co-operatives (supermarkets) operate 24 hours a day, as do most of The Sultan Centre supermarkets. This is really helpful for when you are trying to avoid busy periods. Most hours change during the holy month of Ramadan.

Public Holidays

Kuwait follows the Hijra calendar and all Muslim festivals are therefore timed according to sightings of specific moon phases. Kuwait celebrates two major religious holidays; Eid Al Adha (the Festival of the Sacrifice) celebrates Prophet Abraham's willingness to offer his son in sacrifice, and Eid Al Fitr (the Festival of the Breaking of the Fast) is observed at the end of the holy month of Ramadan. Dates are calculated from the lunar calendar, which is 11 days shorter than the Gregorian calendar, although the Gregorian calendar is used in day to day business.

A National Assembly cabinet resolution, passed in 2001, states that, should a holiday fall in the middle of a working week, it will be moved to the following Saturday. Should any of these holidays fall on a Thursday no additional day will be given.

Public Holidays – 2006

2006	
New Year's Day (1)	Jan 1[Fixed]
Eid Al Adha (4)	Jan 10[Moon]
Islamic New Year (1)	Jan 31[Moon]
National Day (1)	Feb 25[Fixed]
Liberation Day (1)	Feb 26[Fixed]
Prophet Mohammed's Birthday (1)	Apr 11[Moon]
Ascension Day (1)	Aug 22[Moon]
Eid Al Fitr (3)	Oct 26[Moon]

Electricity & Water

Other options → Electricity & Water [p.72]

Electricity and water services are provided by the Ministry of Electricity & Water (MEW), sometimes referred to as the Ministry of Energy (MoE). Power cuts and water shortages are very rare in Kuwait.

Electricity is 240v at 50Hz. Wall sockets are primarily of the three-pin square variety, while electrical appliances are sold with either two-pin or three-pin plugs. You may therefore need a number of adapters, resulting in your plug sockets looking a little over-laden.

Kuwait's unusual water tanks

Temperature (°C) / Humidity

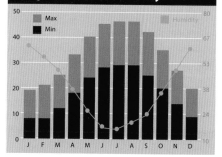

Average Number of Days With Rain

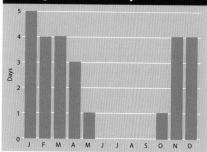

Tap water is desalinated seawater mixed with about 10% brackish water to provide extra taste and minerals. It is considered safe to drink. Although the majority of kitchens have water filters fitted and most people seem to prefer bottled water.

Photography

Tourist photography is acceptable to a point, but care should be taken. For instance, it is illegal to photograph government and public buildings, including ports, airports, palaces and oil installations. Military areas are obviously off limits, and are usually marked with large red signs. Photography in public places, such as shopping malls and museums, is often prohibited as well; if in doubt, ask first. Never take photos of the local people without first obtaining their approval. You will not usually be asked for money in exchange for taking someone's picture.

Environment

Climate

Kuwait's summer climate can be compared to the dry heat omitted from an oven when you are cooking your Sunday roast! It is extreme. Temperatures will reach in excess of 50°C (122°F) in the sun. Fortunately the country does not experience the same levels of humidity as that found in other areas of the Gulf.

Winters can be cold with temperatures of 15°C (59°F) during the day, dropping to single digits at night. Cloudbursts between October and April can result in severe flooding.

The Shamal, the north wind that blows from Iraq, occurs primarily during the spring months and coats all of Kuwait in a fine dust. When it blows in summer it raises the temperature considerably and the sky takes on a dusty hue.

The wonderful weather during the short spring and autumn periods, with average daily temperatures of 25°C (77°F), is very pleasant. Annual rainfall tends to be between one and seven inches (25 - 180mm), although recent years have seen increased rainfall during particular periods resulting in annual rainfall exceeding 13 inches (350mm).

For up to date weather reports, log on to www.bbc.co.uk/weather and choose Kuwait as your destination.

Summer temperatures soar in the city...

General Info

Environment

Flora & Fauna

Kuwait's natural environment was devastated by the oil pollution resulting from the destruction of oil wells during the Gulf War in 1991. However, the flora and fauna has proved to be remarkably resilient, although the impact of unrestricted hunting and encroaching urban development is creating new problems.

Kuwait is home to a surprising number of species, all of which have adapted to the temperature extremes. There are some 400 species of indigenous plants and flowers, including the purple Desert Iris, Desert Hyacinth and Rimth. The best time to view these plants and flowers is from January to March, after the rains, when the desert comes to life. Only one species of tree, the Talha (Acacia), is native to Kuwait.

Indigenous fauna includes 38 species of reptiles and 28 species of mammals. On rare occasions you will find gazelles, the Honey Badger, Fennec Fox,

Date Palms

Kangaroo Rat and Dhub – a spiny tailed lizard. Further desert life includes snakes (some harmless, some extremely venomous), lizards, geckos, hedgehogs, skunks, wild cats, wild hares and a number of invertebrates.

Almost 300 species of bird have been recorded in Kuwait, the majority of which are migratory. Kuwait has a number of Middle East IBAs (Important Bird Areas), eight of which play a significant role in bird conservation. Bird species

visible in Kuwait, although not regularly, include the Greater Spotted Eagle, Imperial Eagle, Lesser Kestrel, Houbara Bustard and Socotra Cormorant. All are listed as VU (Vulnerable). The Basra Reed-Warbler is listed as EN (Endangered) due to the extensive draining of its breeding habitat, as is the Saker Falcon as numbers have fallen considerably due to the unregulated capture for the falconry trade across the region.

Migrating species include the Golden Oriole, House Sparrow and Rose-ringed Parakeet. Species common to Kuwait include the Desert Lark, Hoopoe Lark, Flamingo and Brown-necked Raven.

Kuwait's marine environment plays host to a wide range of sea life, some of which is seasonal, including a variety of fish, whales, dolphins, sharks, turtles, sea snakes and 21 species of coral unique to the Arabian Gulf.

The turtle species are under threat as a result of urban expansion and pollution from ballast dumped by oil tankers. Kuwait has suffered from wide-scale fish deaths as a result of toxic algal bloom and bacteria. The fishing season is restricted to allow for specific species to breed successfully.

The Municipality spends a great deal of time beautifying the landscape by planting grass, flowers and trees in urban areas. It is a very common sight to see hordes of municipality employees working on the roadsides, maintaining flower beds and watering plants and trees from huge water tankers. It is still difficult to understand why most watering is done during the day in the summer when a large percentage of the water must be lost to evaporation. Most of the older areas of the city and it surrounds have wonderful gardens full of old trees. Kuwait has a large number of well-kept public parks, although it is best to steer clear of them the day after a weekend or public holiday when the vast amounts of litter are being cleared.

Protection

There is poor environmental awareness in Kuwait. The daily sight of littering and dumping shows that the country has some way to go in educating the wider population about the importance of protecting the environment.

That said, the approach to conservation and the environment is slowly improving. There are a number of local organisations passionate about the environment who are working hard to protect their natural surroundings and educate the community.

Beautiful Cities, Beautiful Sights

From Dubai's dreamy deserts to Geneva's joie de vivre, our photography books have captured the beauty of the world's most captivating cities. Whether you buy one as a gift or as a souvenir for your own coffee table, these books are packed with images that you'll want to view again and again.

Phone (971 4) 335 3520 · **Fax** (971 4) 335 3529
Info@explorerpublishing.com · www.explorerpublishing.com
Residents' Guides · Visitors' Guides · Photography Books · Activity Guidebooks · Maps

EXPLORER

Passionately Publishing...

Nature reserves include the Jahra Pools Nature Reserve, the Doha Peninsula Nature Reserve in Sulaibikhat (Kuwait Bay) and the Sheikh Sabah Al Ahmed Nature Reserve in Subiya. There are no marine reserves, although there continues to be interest in protecting a number of the islands, Kubbar in particular.

Kuwait has extremely limited natural fresh water resources and therefore operates some of the world's largest desalination plants.

Air pollution is on the increase thanks to the increased traffic levels, and the emissions from local oil refineries and oil wells. Air quality is continually recorded by the six monitoring stations located throughout the country.

The region's marine environment has been under considerable pressure from the effects of the dumping of oil and by-products during the Gulf War, as well as from the significant industrial and urban growth. A third factor is the discharge from tankers and oil platforms.

Official bodies include ROPME (Regional Organisation for the Protection of the Marine Environment, formerly know as the Kuwait Action Plan), KEPS (Kuwait Environment Protection Society), KISR (Kuwait Institute for Scientific Research) and the EPA (Environment Public Authority). NGOs actively involved in protecting the environment include the Kuwait Volunteers Centre, Kuwait Dive Team and the Kuwait Bird Monitoring and Protection Team. There is an annual reef clean-up, usually held in September.

Kuwait is party to international agreements on biodiversity, climate change, desertification, endangered species, environmental modification, hazardous wastes, law of the sea (1986) and ozone layer protection, and has signed two treaties prohibiting the development and use of weapons modifying the environment. A marine dumping agreement has not been ratified. The only people who seem 'interested' in recycling are the poorly paid, unskilled labourers who are often seen collecting cardboard and tin cans in order to supplement their income.

Culture & Lifestyle

Culture

Kuwait's culture and traditions are deeply rooted in the religion of Islam. Religion provides structure to daily living, from prayers before sunrise to those at the end of the day. Family is extremely important; it is common for up to four generations of one family to live under the same roof. Networks based on the 'clan' are very strong and form the basis of social relationships.

Unlike Saudi Arabia, women are at liberty to drive and walk around freely, and a recent change in the law means women can now vote in elections and run for office.

The AWARE Centre, a non-profit NGO, is a cultural centre that was established to promote relations between Westerners and Arabs through dialogue, friendship and cultural exchange.

Diwaniyas

It is traditional for most Kuwaiti men to spend their evenings after work in their diwaniya; a room either in the house or purpose-built in the garden. Activities within the diwaniya include talking with friends and family, playing cards, drinking coffee and watching television.

During the winter months diwaniyas are often found outdoors (in tents or open areas of a garden). Many important contacts and business deals are made at diwaniyas and invitations are generally for men only. It is customary to remove ones shoes before entering.

Hospitality

Kuwaitis are very generous people and enjoy welcoming guests to their homes. Should a man be invited to a Kuwaiti's home it is wise to check whether the invitation is for him alone, or also for his wife. Socialising with strangers is different to socialising with friends and the sexes often socialise separately.

When entering a home make sure to take off your shoes if you notice other people's shoes outside the front door; this shows respect to your host. On entering the seating area it is customary for everyone in the room to rise and for you to give the polite greeting of 'Assalam A'laikum (Peace be with you)' Replies of 'A'laikum Assalam (and Peace be with you)' will be made. Always stand for greetings. It is at this time that you will know whether the women will sit apart from the men.

Out of respect, Kuwaitis say a number of greetings when meeting friends and business acquaintances. These greetings include asking after family, although it is considered impolite to specifically ask after women and children unless one knows the family very well.

It is customary for Kuwaitis of the same sex to kiss one another on the cheek when greeting; this can be a single kiss or up to four kisses depending on the relationship. A kiss on the forehead is usually given by a junior member of a family to a senior member (such as a grandson kissing his grandfather). This is a gesture of deep respect. Extremely conservative men will not shake hands with a woman, and conservative women will not shake hands with men, apart from relatives.

At weddings and funerals men and women will sit in separate rooms/areas. Visitors are expected to do the same.

Out of respect for Muslim hosts, don't show the soles of your shoes when seated. It is also considered extremely impolite to turn your back on anyone.

Female visitors should always dress modestly. Never wear very short skirts, sleeveless outfits or plunging necklines. Always ensure that knees are covered when seated.

Language

Other options → Language Schools [p.152]
Learning Arabic [p.85]

Arabic is the official language of Kuwait, although English, Hindi and Urdu are widely spoken. English is the language of business and is widely understood, although it can be beneficial to speak some Arabic when dealing with ministries. Street signs are written in both Arabic and English, as are the majority of shop signs.

Arabic has many dialects and the language spoken in Kuwait is different to that spoken in Egypt or Morocco, and is different again to classical Arabic.

It is worth learning a few words of the language, even if it just to say hello or to pay for your petrol. Trying to speak Arabic is a wonderful way to break the ice and always results in a smile, particularly if you are visiting a ministry or are stopped at a police road block. Most people will be impressed that you are making an effort, and will happily help you out with pronunciation.

Religion

Islam is the official religion of Kuwait. Muslims make up approximately 85% of Kuwait's total population, with Christians, Hindus, Parsi and other religions accounting for the remaining 15%.

Most Muslims today belong to one of two major sects, Sunni or Shi'a, which share most rituals but are divided on principals. The majority of Kuwaitis are Sunnis. Kuwait has almost 1000 mosques, from the simple to the elaborate, with the Grand Mosque, located in Kuwait City, covering an internal area of 20,000 square metres.

Muslims are required to carry out formal prayer five times a day (facing Mecca) according to the position of the sun; before dawn, at noon, during the afternoon, after sunset and in the evening. Calls to prayer emanate from loudspeakers at every mosque, reminding the faithful of prayer times.

The numerous mosques throughout Kuwait ensure that all Muslims have easy access to somewhere to pray, although women generally tend to pray at home. However, it is not uncommon to see the faithful praying at the side of the road or in the desert, and in prayer rooms located in shopping malls, hospitals and offices. Friday is the Islamic holy day and Muslims make a special effort to ensure that they pray at a mosque for the lunchtime congregational prayers.

There are five formal aspects of worship, known as the Five Pillars of Islam. Testimony of Faith, Prayer, Fasting, Almsgiving and Pilgrimage. Every Muslim who is financially and physically able is expected to make the pilgrimage (Hajj) to Mecca (Makkah), in Saudi Arabia, at least once in their lifetime.

Kuwait is tolerant of many other religions, a number of which are allowed to practise freely (see the box below). Kuwait is the only Gulf country to maintain a strong relationship with the Vatican.

Places of Worship

Church of Our Lady of Arabia, Holy Family Cathedral, the Chapel at the Indian School, Salmiya (all Roman Catholic), St Paul's Anglican Church (Ahmadi), National Evangelical Church, also known as the American International Church (Qibla). Catholic and Protestant services are also carried out in the Chapel at Camp Doha Military Base.

Churches are located throughout the country to serve the Catholic, Protestant, Greek Orthodox, Maronite (Lebanese) and Ecumenical communities. Many other denominations, including Seventh-Day Adventist, the Church of Jesus Christ of Latter-Day Saints, Marthoma, and the Indian Orthodox Syrian Church, although not recognised legally, are allowed to operate in private homes or in the facilities of recognised churches. Members of religions not sanctioned in the Quran, including Hindus, Sikhs, Baha'is and Buddhists, may not build places of worship but are allowed to worship privately in their homes without interference from the Government.

Basic Arabic

General

(If you) **Please**	Lauw sammaht
God willing	Inshaa'a l-laah
No	La
Please (in offering/invitation)	Tfadhal
Praise be to God	Al hamdu l-illah
Thank you	Shukraan / Mashkoor
Thank you very much	Shukraan jazeelan
Yes	Naam / Aiwa

Greetings

Fine, thank you	Al hamdu l-illah bikhair
Good Evening	Masaa al khair
Good Evening (in reply)	Masaa an-noor
Good Morning	Sabaah al khair
Good Morning (in reply)	Sabaah an-noor
Goodbye	Maa as-salaama
Goodbye (in reply)	Allah yisullmak
Goodnight	Tisbah ala khair
Greeting (Peace be upon you)	As-salaam alaykum
Hello	Marhaba
Hello (in reply)	Marhabteyn
How are you?	Kayf haalak? (m) / Kayf haalik (f)
Welcome	Hala
Welcome (in reply)	Hala / Hayak'allah

Introduction

I am from...	Anaa min...
America	Amreekee (m) / Amreekeeyah (f)
Britain	Breetaanee (m) / Breetaaneeyah (f)
Europe	Orobeeyah (m) / Orobeeyah (f)
India	Hindee (m) / Hindeeyah (f)
Kuwait	Kuwayti / Kuwaitiyah
South Africa	Janoob afreekee (m) / janoob afreekeeyah (f)
My name is...	Ismi...
What is your name?	Shismik (m) / Shismich (f)
Where are you from?	Min wayn inta?

Questions

Also	kamaan
And	Wa
From	Min
How many / much?	Chem / Kem
How?	Kayf? / Eshloon?
In / at	Fee
There isn't	Ma fee / Ma koo
This/that	Haatha
To / for	Eila
What?	Shinu?
When?	Mata?
Where?	Weyn?
Which?	Aywho?
Who?	Miyn? Miynoo?
Why?	Lesh?

Taxi / Car Related

Airport	Mataar
Behind	Wara / khalf
Between	Beyn
Close to	Qareeb min
Corner	Zaawya
Desert	Al Barr
East	Sharq
First	Ewwil
Hotel	Finduk
In front of	Jiddaam
Left	Yisaar
Next to	Jamb
North	Shemaal
On top / Upstairs / Up	Fowg
Opposite	Mugaabil
Petrol Station	Mahattat banzeen
Restaurant	Mataam
Right	Yimeen
Road	Tareeg
Roundabout	Dawwaar
Sea / beach	Bahr / Shaatee
Second	Thaani
Signal(s)	Ishaara(at)
Slow down	Bateea / Eshway eshway
South	Janoob
Stop	Kif
Straight ahead	Seeda
Turning	Leff
West	Gharb

Accidents

Accident	Haadeth
Insurance	Ta'meen
Licence	Roksaht al qiyadah
Papers	Waraq al seyaara
Police	Poolîs / Makhfar Shurta
Policeman	Shurti
Policemen	Shurtiyyin
Sorry	Aasif (m) / Aasifa (f)

Numbers

Zero	Sifir
One	Waahid
Two	Ithnayn
Three	Thalaatha
Four	Araba'a
Five	Khamsa
Six	Sitta
Seven	saba'a
Eight	Thamaanya
Nine	Tiss'a
Ten	Ashra
Fifty	Khamseen
Hundred	Miyya
Thousand	Alf

Ramadan

The Holy Month of Ramadan is the ninth month of the Islamic calendar and the month during which it is believed the Koran was revealed to the Prophet Muhammad (PBUH). Special night-time prayers throughout Ramadan ensure that the mosques are particularly active.

Ramadan is a period of fasting during which all Muslims abstain from eating, drinking, smoking and sexual activity during daylight hours. Pregnant women, children, the sick, and those travelling are the only exceptions. Westerners are expected, as a matter of respect, to comply with the requirements of the fast. It is a punishable offence to be caught breaking the fast between dusk and dawn; the penalty is jail for the remainder of Ramadan.

Each day at sunset the fast is broken with 'Iftar', traditionally consisting of dates and water or sweet laban, a type of drinking yoghurt. Iftar times are published in the newspapers and are announced by mosques. The main meal of the day (Ghabgha) is enjoyed later in the evening. Many of the five-star hotels erect Ramadan tents specifically for this feast, and lay out a traditional buffet. This is a meal to be enjoyed slowly, followed by Arabic coffee, dates and shisha smoking. It is a time to sit with family and friends and enjoy a game of cards, or a round or two of backgammon.

Office and Ministry hours change during Ramadan, as do the timings for all retail outlets. The roads become extremely congested at 1pm, when the Ministries and government organisations tend to close, and are eerily quiet at sunset when all Muslims are at home breaking the fast.

Ramadan culminates in a three-day celebration called Eid Al Fitr (feast of the breaking of the fast). This celebration is always a national holiday, much the same as Christmas is for Christians and Diwali for Hindus.

National Dress

Kuwaiti men always look elegant in their traditional garment, the dishdasha or khandura. This white, full-length, long-sleeved 'robe' usually has a Nehru-type collar with a few buttons, and covers a loose fitting pair of trousers.

There are three elements to the headress. A white skullcap known as a gahfiya is first placed on the head and is then covered by the gutra, a white square of fabric, folded diagonally and usually made of cotton or polyester. The final part of the headress is the agal, a double circle of black cord which is placed over the gutra to hold everything in place. The manner in which the headress is worn varies from person to person. The more formal manner sees the gutra centred on the head, with two of the corners hanging evenly on either side of the head and the third corner neatly placed at the back. The agal tilts ever so slightly from front to back. You will often see young men paying special attention to their headress in an effort to position every element perfectly. The final aspect of a Kuwaiti man's dress is a pair of leather sandals, or a pair of Western-style lace-up or slip-on shoes for more formal occasions or the corporate environment. Accessories will often include the latest mobile phone, a pair of sunglasses and, most importantly, prayer beads.

The winter months sees a change from the white, cotton dishdasha to one which is darker and made from lightweight wool, and the gutra is either made from a slightly heavier white fabric, or is sometimes red and white checks.

On special occasions the bisht, a semi-transparent garment with gold braiding, is worn as a robe over the dishdasha.

Kuwait's National Dress

General Info

Culture & Lifestyle

Kuwaiti women traditionally wear an abaya, a black, long-sleeved floor-length robe usually made of silk or polyester. The abaya, which covers the outfit underneath, may be embellished with small areas of ornamentation from plain stitching to black sequins and beading. All traditional Kuwaiti women wear hijab, the Islamic headscarf, to cover their hair and neck. Some also wear the burqa, a short black veil that covers the entire face.

National Weddings

Most weddings in Kuwait are elaborate affairs. Houses will be adorned with row upon row of lights and the festivities usually last about 14 days. The celebrations are often held in hotel ballrooms or sports clubs, and men and women always celebrate separately. The bride and her entourage will spend many hours in the beauty salon having their hair and make-up done before arriving at the venue. The bride takes to the stage where she will sit for about two hours, receiving her guests prior to the arrival of her husband. Both the bride and guests will be wearing new dresses; the more detailed the better. The women will be free of their abayas whilst participating in traditional dancing and refreshments, but once the groom arrives (dressed in a dishdash and a bisht) they cover themselves again from head to toe. The bride and groom will receive congratulations from their close relatives before departing.

Food & Drink

Other options → **Eating Out [p.197]**

It is possible to eat all that your heart desires, with the exception of 'haram' products, those forbidden by Islam. Kuwaitis are passionate about their food and there is a huge range of eateries throughout the country. From Lebanese and Indian to Japanese and Polynesian, you can get it all. All major fast-food companies are present too, and most of them deliver! Restaurants are generally well priced, although eating in major hotels will always cost you an extra 15% due to the service charge.

Supermarkets and cooperatives (co-ops) offer a varied range of imported products and almost all are open 24 hours a day. Co-ops are slightly cheaper for some products as the prices are subsidised. Corner shops (bakalas) carry all basic foodstuffs and are open from about 06:00 – 22:00, Saturday to Thursday. Some do close during prayer times for approximately 15 minutes.

There are a small number of markets in Kuwait selling fish, meat, fruit and vegetables, both local and imported, without the supermarket price tags. In addition to the fish and clams, local prawns are available seasonally. During the closed season prawns are fished in Iranian waters. Fish is cleaned and filleted at no extra charge. Meat sold at the markets is primarily lamb, mutton and chicken although beef does appear from time to time. All the vendors lay their wares out quite artfully. Shopping at the market next to Souq Sharq in Kuwait City, and the market at Al Kout shopping mall in Fahaheel, is a very pleasant experience. Both are scrupulously clean.

Local Cuisine

Kuwait's native cooking is a fusion of Bedouin, Indian, Persian and Eastern Mediterranean influences. The country's long association with India is reflected in the ways in which spices are used; Bedouin influences include laban (yoghurt), dates and mutton, and Eastern Mediterranean (Lebanese) influences include hummus, tabbouleh and fattoush. Kuwait's fishing heritage ensures that seafood plays a very important role in the traditional diet. Hammour, zubaidi, sboor and nagroor are often served with chopped parsley and onion, sometimes mixed with dill.

Traditional meals include Khouzi (baked lamb stuffed with rice and nuts), but influences from other cuisines have created something of a change in local eating habits. Foods from other Arabic countries are prepared regularly and include hummus (ground chickpeas and sesame seeds infused with lemon juice and garlic), tabbouleh (a finely chopped parsley, tomato and onion salad mixed with bulgar wheat), fattoush (a green salad with mint, tomato, cucumbers, green pepper, radishes and onion served with a tart vinegar and oil dressing), crispy pitta bread and the wonderful herb, sumac. Dolma are rolled vine leaves stuffed with flavoured rice and meat mixtures. Desserts are usually a variety of fruits or prepared sweets such as Umm Ali, a crème-caramel type desert very popular with the locals. There is a multitude of shwarma and kebab shops, all of which serve delicious food at very reasonable prices.

Alcohol is prohibited and may not be imported. It is not served in restaurants and is not available to buy in bottle stores.

Muslims are forbidden from eating pork and laws in Kuwait state that no person, Muslim or otherwise, may import or eat pork or any pork by-products. Like alcohol, it cannot be purchased anywhere in Kuwait.

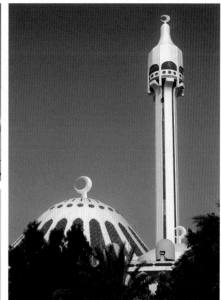

Kuwait's many mosques

Eating Etiquette

Refreshments are served as a matter of course, no matter how long or short the visit, and it is considered good manners to partake. Dinner is always served very late in Kuwaiti homes and meals are usually elaborate affairs. Food is eaten using the right hand on informal occasions; on formal occasions Western-style dining takes place. Cleanliness is very important and hands are always cleaned prior to eating and the word 'Bismillah (in the name of God) precedes the beginning of a meal. At the end of the meal hands are washed and coffee (or tea), with sweets, is usually served in a separate room. Tea is served in small glasses on saucers, Arabic coffee in small china/porcelain cups. Should you not wish to have your cup refilled simply twist the cup between thumb and forefinger to show that no more coffee is required. It is very important not to outstay your welcome after dinner. A good host will always try to tempt you to stay; however, this is a gesture of politeness and it is not expected for you to agree to stay on!

Entering Kuwait

Visas

Other options → Entry Visa [p.48]
Residence Visa [p.48]

Visit visas are now processed on arrival at Kuwait International Airport for passport holders from the 34 countries listed below. The cost is KD 3, except for citizens of the UK, USA, Italy, Norway and Sweden, for whom there is no charge.

No Visa Required

Andorra, Australia, Austria, Belgium, Brunei, Canada, China, Denmark, Finland, France, Germany, Greece, Hong Kong, Iceland, Ireland, Italy, Japan, Lichtenstein, Luxembourg, Malaysia, Monaco, the Netherlands, New Zealand, Norway, Portugal, San Marino, Singapore, South Korea, Spain, Sweden, Switzerland, UK, USA, the Vatican

All other visitors to Kuwait, other than GCC citizens, require a visa and need to be 'sponsored'. Sponsorship may only be provided by a Kuwaiti citizen or a Kuwaiti company. Foreigners with a valid residence permit are permitted to sponsor dependants. Five-star hotels are able to arrange visas for their guests.

Visit visas are valid for entry into Kuwait 30 days from the date of issue, and allow a maximum stay of 30 days from the date of entry. Remaining in Kuwait for longer than the permitted period will result in a fine of KD 10 for every day or part thereof, and the possible 'black-listing' of the sponsor. Any fines incurred have to be paid at the Immigration Department in Shuwaikh prior to departure; you are not able to pay the fines at the airport.

Should you know that you will not be able to leave Kuwait at the end of the permitted 30 day period, it is possible to obtain a visa extension, although this can only be done prior to the expiry of the original visa. Visitors are allowed a maximum of two one-month extensions.

Business Visas

In order for a business visa to be issued the visitor will require sponsorship by a Kuwaiti sponsor or company.

Multi-entry Visas

Multi-entry visas are essentially visit visas; however, the holder of the multi-entry visa may enter and exit Kuwait any number of times over a given period. Multi-entry visas tend to be given for three or six months. A business visa may be converted to a multi-entry visa whilst the holder is in Kuwait, but a visit visa processed on arrival may not.

Transit Visas

Transit visas may be obtained from a Kuwaiti Embassy or from the Kuwait Port Authority should you arrive by sea. They are valid for a period of seven days. You must be able to show a confirmed onward ticket when arriving in Kuwait by air, and have a valid visa, if required, for you next destination.

Work Permits

Work permits may be obtained under Articles 17 (public sector) or 18 (private sector) of the Kuwait Labour Law (see Labour Law, [p.55]). A summary of the process follows;

• The employment offer is made and accepted.

• The sponsor/employer applies for the work permit at the MSA&L (Ministry of Social Affairs & Labour).

• Private sector employers obtain an NOC (No Objection Certificate) from the Criminal Investigation Department after submission of the employee's particulars (copy of passport). In addition, a certificate of good conduct may be required by the police for certain nationalities.

- On receipt of the work permit from the MSA&L the employer sends a copy to the employee in his country of origin. This copy is then to be submitted to the Kuwaiti Embassy for endorsement, after which an entry visa is applied for. In addition to completing the necessary paperwork all employees are to obtain a medical certificate from a clinic or doctor recognised by the Kuwait Embassy, confirming that the employee is fit to work and is free from specified diseases such as Tuberculosis and HIV/AIDS. Should there not be a Kuwaiti Embassy in the employee's country of origin, the employer will obtain the necessary entry permit from the Ministry of Interior in Kuwait and pass a copy on to the employee.

Should the employee be in Kuwait on a visit visa when his work permit is being applied for, it is then necessary to leave Kuwait and return on the entry visa. In addition, the necessary medical certificate will have to be obtained whilst outside Kuwait. It is common practice for employees, if they cannot proceed to their home country, to travel to Bahrain to undergo the necessary medical tests.

- On arriving in (or returning to) Kuwait the employee is obliged to undergo further medical tests. If any person is found to be carrying or suffering from HIV/AIDS, Tuberculosis, Hepatitis (B&C), Typhoid or Malaria, they are immediately deported. All employees, irrespective of where they reside in Kuwait, are required to have the medical tests carried out at the Ports & Borders Health Division, Ministry of Health, Gamul Abdul Nasser Street, Shuwaikh. It is recommended, if at all possible, that you have the company representative (or 'mandoub') guide you through this procedure as it can be confusing and stressful.

- Fingerprinting and security clearance are mandatory for all expatriates arriving in Kuwait and must be carried out at one of the four fingerprinting departments (Ahmadi, Farwaniya, Jahra and Sharq) depending on the location of your residence.

- Application for the residence permit is to be made at the Immigration & Passport Department in Shuwaikh. A maximum period of five years will be granted at a cost of KD 10 per year. Employees working in the public sector are to pay this cost whilst it is a matter of negotiation as to whether private sector employees or their employers pay.

There are a number of companies who, on completion of immigration procedures, still insist on holding employees passports for 'safekeeping'. This is not advisable, especially as it means you will not be able to travel at short notice in an emergency. Should you have handed your passport to an employer and have difficulty getting it back, you are advised to contact your embassy immediately.

Kuwait pays tribute to its allies

Always make a copy of your work visa (permit) and keep it in a safe place. Only two copies of the work visa are ever issued; one is given to the Immigration Department to process a residency application and the other is retained by the sponsoring company. Should the sponsoring company misplace their copy it cannot be replaced.

The Airport

Kuwait International Airport has undergone something of a facelift in the last few years. The compact building and facilities are more modern and include a number of shops and eateries. There are two duty free outlets selling jewellery, books, electronics, perfumes, etc, although prices are not that cheap. A number of smoking rooms can be found in the departures area, but that doesn't seem to stop people smoking where they like. The immigration booths have been replaced by less intimidating desks, and the staff are now polite. All baggage is x-rayed prior to leaving the reclaim area; only rarely will an item be searched by hand. The rest rooms, although clean, are still looking a little tired and the children's play area in departures is not always open.

Transferring to Another Sponsor

Transfer from one sponsor to another can be a fraught and complicated process and it is known for companies to refuse to transfer sponsorship, resulting in work and residence permits being cancelled. To ensure a smooth transfer it is vital that your current sponsor agrees to it. This agreement needs to take the form of a signed 'letter of release' which should be accompanied by a copy of the current sponsor's commercial licence.

The formalities for obtaining a new work permit will then apply, although a medical test will not be necessary. The fee for the new work permit is KD 2 and there may be a transfer charge of KD 10.

Laws relating to the transfer of residence permits are complex and do vary so it's prudent to check the current status completely before commencing the process. At the time of writing it is possible to transfer from one sponsor to another, without too much difficulty, if an expatriate has resided in Kuwait for a minimum of two years.

Meet & Greet

Hala Kuwait (842 842 ext. 304) is a collection of services offered to arriving, departing, transit and VIP guests by National Aviation Services. Bookings must be made at least 24 hours in advance.

Arriving visitors will be met at the aircraft gate and escorted through immigration and baggage reclaim. Departing passengers will be provided with check-in assistance and then escorted through immigration and to the departure gate. A limousine service to and from the airport is available.

VIP services include the use of the Hala Lounge for departing and transit passengers, and special escort services for passengers arriving and departing on private (chartered) flights.

Costs vary according to the service required. The cost for Arrivals Meet & Assist is KD 7 for one person and KD 12 for two. Group rates of KD 5.500 per person are available for parties of 10 or more arriving on the same flight. Departure Meet & Assist costs is KD 7 for one person, KD 14 for two, and KD 5.500 per person for parties over 10 departing on the same flight.

A Fast Track service is also available for departing passengers. This includes separate check-in and use of the Hala Lounge.

The walk from any of the arrivals gates to the immigration area takes a maximum of two minutes, depending on how many children or company brochures you are carrying! A further 10 seconds will get you into the baggage claim area. There are two duty-free shops located in the area between the arrivals gates and the immigration desks. Cash machines are only available in the arrivals hall after you have cleared immigration and collected your baggage. Queues for immigration can be fairly long, depending on the time that you arrive. Be patient; they do move fairly quickly. There are many porters in the baggage reclaim area who will take your bags from the carousel and wheel them to your vehicle. A small trolley costs 500 fils and a large trolley costs KD 1. The porters will often try to squeeze more money out of you, at which point you should politely remind them that the signs on the trolley clearly indicate the cost of porterage.

The arrivals area of the airport is located on the ground floor. It is a very clean and well laid out area although it becomes extremely busy at peak times. Should the flight for which you are waiting be delayed there are a number of shops that you can wander around, as well as a number of eateries. The Starbucks in the arrivals hall is one of the busiest in the country.

Customs

No taxes are levied on used personal effects imported into Kuwait. However, it is possible that the customs officials may apply a maximum duty of 5% on inspected items that they deem to be new. 500 cigarettes or 2lb of tobacco may be imported into Kuwait without incurring any customs duty.

There are no set restrictions on the amount of perfume that may be imported. However, if someone attempts to bring in a large quantity of unopened perfumes the customs officials, at their discretion, may charge a 5% import duty.

All forms of alcohol, including beer, wines and spirits, and alcohol manufacturing kits are strictly prohibited, as are pork products. These items will be confiscated on arrival and, depending on the quantities recovered, legal action may be taken.

On arrival at Kuwait International Airport all baggage passes through X-ray machines prior to leaving the arrivals hall, affording the customs officials an opportunity to check for banned items. Any questionable items including CDs, DVDs, videos, books and magazines may be retained for inspection, but will be returned if found to be inoffensive. Make sure that you obtain a receipt for these items.

Kuwait has extremely strict laws regarding drugs and they are actively enforced. Anyone found importing narcotics will be prosecuted, and anyone convicted of drug trafficking could face the death penalty.

All items manufactured by companies that appear on the Israeli Boycott list will be confiscated.

Any political and religious items which may be deemed offensive to the Kuwait Government and Islam will be confiscated and the likelihood is that the consignee will be detained pending legal action.

Additional import restrictions pertain to wireless transmitters and communications equipment, firearms and ammunition, weapons (including decorative pieces) and explosives, and any items made from ivory or an endangered species.

There are no restrictions on the import or export of currency.

Health Requirements

No health certificates are required for entry into Kuwait, but if you've travelled to an area affected by cholera or yellow fever you may have to produce a vaccination certificate. It's recommended that you confirm prior to arrival in Kuwait if any new restrictions have been imposed. There is no risk of malaria in Kuwait.

Health Care

Other options → General Medical Care [p.76]

Kuwait has excellent medical care, but at a price – visitors are strongly advised to arrange private medical insurance before arriving. There are six large government hospitals in Kuwait and they are all recommended in case of an emergency.

All residents of Kuwait have access to public healthcare, and most private companies have some sort of medical insurance for their employees which gives access to all private hospitals and clinics.

The ambulance service is not for the faint-hearted. If you have an accident and it is at all possible, make your own way to the hospital.

There are no specific heath risks to visitors. However, during the summer months it does take some time to adjust to the hot climate and the consequent air-conditioning. It is vital to avoid prolonged exposure to the sun, particularly during the summer when outdoor temperatures reach as high as 56C. Make sure that you drink plenty of fluids and choose early morning or late afternoon for outdoor exercise. Always try to wear a hat outside and make sure you use an appropriate sunscreen. Polarised lenses in sunglasses are recommended if you are going to be spending a lot of time driving.

Embassies and Consulates

Australia	257 0391	4-A3
Bahrain	531 8530	12-A2
Canada	256 3025	7-B1
China	533 3340	11-C1
Denmark	534 1005	11-E2
Egypt	251 9955	4-B4
France	257 1061	3-E4
Germany	252 0756	6-D1
India	253 0600	4-C4
Iran	256 0694	4-B4
Italy	535 6010	12-C2
Japan	531 2870	12-D1
Jordan	253 3261	6-E3
Lebanon	256 2103	4-B4
Malaysia	255 0394	4-C4
The Netherlands	531 2650	12-C2
Oman	256 1956	11-E1
Pakistan	532 7649	12-E1
Philippines	534 9099	12-E1
Qatar	251 3606	4-B4
Saudi Arabia	240 0250	3-E1
South Africa	561 7988	13-C4
Spain	532 5827	12-B2
Sri Lanka	533 9140	12-E1
Switzerland	534 0172	11-E2
Syria	539 6560	18-B1
Thailand	531 7530	12-D1
United Arab Emirates	535 5764	4-B4
United Kingdom	240 3334	3-E1
United States of America	259 1001	13-A4

Travel Insurance

Full travel insurance, including medical cover, is recommended. Ensure that you choose a reputable firm and, should you wish to participate in sports such as scuba diving or kite surfing, make sure these are specifically covered in your policy.

Female Visitors

Harassment of women in Kuwait has increased over the past ten years or so, and ranges from trying to start a conversation, to attempts to get you to 'go somewhere quiet'. It would be in a woman's best interests to dress conservatively, not respond to being approached in the street, and avoid direct eye contact with anyone trying to attract attention.

Women can travel alone at night although remote areas are not recommended. Keep to the areas frequented by Westerners if you are on your own, or go in a group if you plan on going elsewhere. As with all cities in the world, common sense is required.

If you ever feel intimated make your way to the safety of a police station or public place frequented by Westerners. Should this not be possible your best bet is to make a lot of noise which will more than likely cause your intimidator to silently retreat. The way in which foreign women are treated in Kuwait has a lot to do with how they are portrayed in the media in the West. It is worth noting that the unwanted attention is not from Kuwaiti men alone; there are a number of nationalities responsible for this behaviour. You will find most Kuwaiti men will be quite upset to hear of a visitor to Kuwait being threatened in such a manner.

Travelling with Children

Kuwait offers a wide range of entertainment for children, whether fun-filled or educational.

Amusement and water parks are located throughout the country, but check before visiting as a number of them are only open seasonally. Kuwait has a well-kept zoo, a wonderful aquarium with a Discovery area, and a number of museums.

A wide range of sporting activities are available, from horse-riding to ice-skating to kite surfing. Most expatriate families tend to join a beach club where they will spend most of their weekends. There are a few mother and child groups for those with younger children.

Most restaurants cater for children and some will provide colouring sheets and crayons, but not all will have a children's menu or even highchairs.

There has always been a serious lack of baby-changing facilities but the situation has recently improved. The range of baby foods is quite limited.

Babysitting services are limited to major hotels. Most resident expatriates have a maid who carries out this function when required. A few of the hotels and shopping centres have play areas, but this is not the norm.

Physically Challenged Visitors

Wheelchair facilities in Kuwait are very limited. There are parking spaces for disabled people at the airport and big shopping centres, but these are invariably taken up by ignorant, able-bodied drivers who don't like to walk too far. Facilities in Kuwait are improving, but slowly.

Hotels catering for disabled visitors include the Carlton Tower Hotel, Crowne Plaza Kuwait, Four Points by Sheraton, Hilton Kuwait Resort, JW Marriott, Kuwait Continental Hotel, Le Meridien Kuwait, Le Meridien Tower (Art + Tech), Marina Hotel, Mövenpick, Radisson SAS, Safir International Hotel and Sheraton Kuwait Hotel & Towers.

Kuwait International Airport provides a wheelchair service to passengers, and has lifts. Passengers requiring special assistance should inform their airline prior to arrival.

Dress Code

Expatriate women in Kuwait are not required to wear the abaya (black gown) over their clothing. It is possible for men and women to dress as they are used to back home, but a certain amount of sensitivity and respect should always be considered if you would like to avoid unwanted attention.

Lightweight clothing is recommended for the summer months, although you may find that you need an extra layer when you are inside an air-conditioned building. Warmer clothing is required for the winter period when it is surprisingly cold.

Local designer threads

It is common to see young Kuwaiti girls dressed in the latest designer gear from head to toe. However, this is usually confined to shopping centres and restaurants where they are with like-minded individuals. One aspect of their dress that is common to all is that they never expose their upper arms or ankles.

Although there are a number of public beaches where swimming is permitted, the sight of an expatriate woman in a swimming costume would draw a considerable amount of staring. It is best to keep revealing attire for beach clubs. Sunbathing topless is forbidden and the consequences of being caught don't bear thinking about. Entry to your local supermarket is restricted if you are wearing shorts (men and women), short skirts and sleeveless tops. You should cover up when visiting markets, suburban shops and rural areas.

The general evening dress code for restaurants and hotels is smart casual.

Dos and Don'ts

Alcohol is forbidden. Customs carry out checks at all points of entry into the country and will confiscate contraband on sight. Depending on the amounts involved you may be liable to prosecution and a stint in prison.

Drug possession, and/or dealing, is taken very seriously and will almost certainly result in a custodial sentence. Drug smuggling/trafficking may possibly carry the death penalty.

Dress appropriately and don't venture into shops and markets wearing shorts (men and women), short skirts or sleeveless tops. Visitors to mosques will have to have arms and legs covered and women will be required to cover their heads with a scarf.

It is illegal for unmarried men and women to live together, unless members of the same family.

Ensure that you carry identification with you at all times; Civil ID for residents and passport/visa for visitors. If you drive make sure that you carry your driving licence and that the vehicle's paperwork is in order and kept in the car. Road blocks, manned by the Ministry of Interior (Police), pop up at a moment's notices. Should you be stopped, and not have the required paperwork, the police have the right to take you into custody and will keep you at a police station until your sponsor shows up with the relevant documentation.

It is considered extremely impolite to ask an Arab man about his wife and children (read 'daughters')

if you do not know him very well. Other taboo subjects include religion and politics.

Don't get caught drinking, eating or smoking between sunrise and sunset during the holy month of Ramadan. You could be put in prison until the end of the month.

In summary, remember that you are a guest in Kuwait. Respect the local way of life and customs and you will enjoy your stay.

Safety

Kuwait is considered to be a very safe country. However, as with anywhere in the world a degree of common sense is required. Violent crime, although rare, does occur. One of the greatest things about living in Kuwait is that the country is considered a safe environment in which to raise children.

Kuwait has a dreadful record for traffic accidents. Driving laws are generally not enforced with the result that, for a population of almost 2.5 million, there were in excess of 45,376 traffic accidents in 2003. It is vital for your safety that you are very aware of your surroundings when driving. If you are a passenger in a taxi being driven too fast tell the driver to slow down; they usually do. Not all taxis have seat belts. Flash flooding occasionally occurs during the rainy season and can cause havoc on the roads. When driving in rural areas, stick to roads or known tracks. Unexploded ordnance left behind after the 1990-91 Gulf War is still found in the desert from time to time. Never pick up any suspicious item lying in the desert.

The extreme summer temperatures can cause sunstroke, heatstroke and severe dehydration. When driving, particularly if you decide to go into the desert, make sure that you have plenty of water, in case of a flat tyre or breakdown. It is also wise to carry extra water for your vehicle to top up the radiator. Hats and a high-factor sun cream are a prerequisite for going outside and you would be ill-advised to allow children outside in the summer for extended periods. Never leave children in the car in the sun, particularly if you don't have air-conditioning.

Petting stray cats and dogs is not always a good idea due to the prevalence of rabies.

Police

There is one police force which carries out all policing duties. There is no tourist police.

All police are armed and wear the same uniform; a khaki shirt and long trousers with black and silver epaulettes, a black belt and hat. Police vehicles range from khaki 4WDs and grey sedans to the latest American-style traffic police vehicles.

There is a good police presence, although it doesn't always seem so, particularly if you have been involved in a traffic accident and are waiting for them to arrive. If you have had the misfortune of being involved in a traffic accident you will need to advise the police immediately. No vehicles may be moved, irrespective of whether they are blocking four lanes of rush-hour traffic. Failure to comply may result in your insurance becoming invalid and you may be considered to have fled the scene.

The police are accommodating if you need to ask for directions, although you will not always find an officer who speaks good English.

The police are called by dialing 777.

Lost/Stolen Property

Losing a passport and visa copy in Kuwait is problematic to say the least, particularly if you are in Kuwait on a short visit. It makes a lot of sense to photocopy your documentation and keep it in a safe place, away from the originals.

Should you lose your passport, you will need to advise your embassy/consulate immediately. The loss of a visa copy will need to be reported to your sponsor immediately, so that they may in turn advise the Department of Immigration. Loss of airline tickets needs to be reported to the relevant airline office.

If you have lost an item in your hotel or in a taxi, call them to see if it has been handed in. There are many honest people in Kuwait who will be pleased to reunite you with your lost property. Stolen property should be reported to the police immediately, who will advise on what action may be taken.

Kuwait City Tourist Info Abroad

Please refer to the Tourism Offices Overseas. There is no government organisation or local company with representation in major cities worldwide to promote Kuwait.

Kuwait City Tourism Offices Overseas		
India	Delhi	+9111 4100791
UK	London	+44207 2351787
USA	Washington DC	+12023 380211

Places to Stay

Accommodation is pretty varied although generally not cheap. The Kuwait Hotel Owner's Association has a fixed price for its five-star hotels. There are currently over 50 hotels in Kuwait, including resorts, with licences issued for a further 100, although it remains to be seen whether all of them will actually be constructed.

Hotel apartments vary tremendously in quality and price. Guesthouses, as they are known in the west, are non-existent. Youth hostels seem to have fallen off the radar, and camping sites are little more than open areas in the desert where the local population spend time enjoying the cool weather between December and March.

Hotels

Other options → Weekend Breaks [p.122]

Hotels range from KD 24 to KD 500 a night. Although there is a concentration of hotels within the Kuwait City limits, a number of hotels and resorts are located along the entire length of the coast south of Kuwait City, and within the residential areas. Hotel occupancy has averaged 60% over the past two years, with some hotels reporting 100% for the same period. Kuwait has outperformed all regional markets, including Dubai. A rating system does exist although a number of establishments seem to be a little too highly rated. The Kuwait Hotel Owner's Association controls the room rate at a number of the five-star hotels.

Traditional Architecture

Hotels

Five Star	Beach Access	Phone	Map	KD	Web/Email
Crowne Plaza Kuwait	–	477 2000	16-C2	72	www.kuwait.crowneplaza.com
Hilton Kuwait Resort P.213	✔	3725500	1-D3	99	www.hilton.com
JW Marriott Kuwait City Hotel P.209	–	245 5550	3-C4	85	www.marriott-middleeast.com
Kempinski Julai'a Hotel & Resort	✔	84 4444	1-D4	100	www.kempinski-kuwait.com
Kuwait Regency Palace Hotel	✔	572 8000	12-D1	75	na
Le Meridien	–	251 0999	4-A3	77	www.lemeridien.com/kuwait
Le Meridien Tower (Art + Tech)	–	83 1831	3-B4	77	www.tower.lemeridien.com
Marina Hotel Kuwait	✔	224 4970	8-B2	95	www.marinahotel.com
Mövenpick	–	461 0033	5-B2	55	www.moevenpick-hotels.com
Palms Beach Hotel & Spa, The	✔	82 4060	13-D3	90	www.thepalms-kuwait.com
Radisson SAS Hotels & Resorts P.217	✔	5756000	13-D3	77	www.kuwait.radissonsas.com
Rester Palace	–	390 8630	1-D3	150	www.refad.com
Safir International Hotel Kuwait P.xiii	–	253 0000	4-A2	78	www.safirhotels.com
Sheraton Kuwait Hotel & Towers	–	242 2055	3-B4	77	www.starwoodhotels.com

Four Star					
Carlton Tower Hotel	–	245 2740	3-B4	45	na
The Courtyard by Marriott Kuwait P.209	–	299 7000	3-E2	60	www.marriott-middleeast.com
El Goan Resort	✔	328 1897	1-D4	na	na
Four Points by Sheraton Kuwait	–	241 5001	3-B4	65	www.fourpoints.com/kuwait
Ghani Palace Hotel	–	571 0301	8-D2	45	www.ghanipalace.com
Holiday Inn	–	84 7777	8-E2	55	www.holiday-inn.com
Khalifa Resort	✔	328 0144	1-D4	na	www.jfkw.com
Kuwait Continental Hotel	–	252 7300	4-A3	35	www.kcontl.net
Kuwait Palace Hotel	–	572 5773	8-D2	45	www.ghanipalace.com
New Park Hotel	–	563 4200	7-D2	58	www.newpark-hotel.com
Safir Al Bastaki Hotel	–	255 5081	3-E3	69	www.safirhotels.com
Safir Al Dana Resort	✔	390 2760	1-D3	na	www.safirhotels.com
Safir Heritage Village	✔	252 0600	1-D2	na	www.safirhotels.com
Safir Palace Hotel	–	82 1111	10-C2	52	www.safirpalace.com
Shiik Flamingo Hotel & Resort	✔	572 5050	8-D4	65	www.shiik-flamingo.com
Swiss Inn Kuwait Plaza Hotel	–	243 6686	3-C4	48	www.swissinnkuwait.com

Three Star					
Imperial Hotel	–	252 8766	4-B3	39	na
Oasis Hotel	–	246 5489	3-D3	35	www.oasis.com.kw
Safari House Hotel	–	244 3136	3-C3	25	na
Second Home Hotel	–	253 2100	4-A3	20	na
Spring Continental Hotel	–	574 2410	4-A3	24	na

Two Star					
International Hotel	–	574 1788	8-C2	30	na
Kuwait Residence Hotel	–	246 7560	3-E1	25	na

General Info

Places to Stay

Kuwait Main Hotels

Al Manshar Rotana Hotel & Suites   Map Ref → 1-C4

Opening mid 2006, the Al Manshar Rotana Hotel & Suites is part of the Al Manshar Complex. Located in walking distance from the breathtaking waterfront Al Kout Shopping Centre and Fahaheel's beach, the hotel will stand at 18 stories with views of the Arabian Gulf. The hotel will have a spectacular roof-top pool and 200 luxurious rooms and suites.

Crowne Plaza Kuwait   Map Ref → 16-C2

The Crowne Plaza is located a five-minute drive from the airport and 15 minutes from Kuwait City. There are 310 rooms and suites. Emphasis is placed on the restaurants, of which there are seven. Recreational facilities include a health club, outdoor swimming pool, five squash courts and a sauna.

Four Points by Sheraton   Map Ref → 7-C3

This new addition to the Sheraton complex is located in the heart of Kuwait City and within the city's business and industrial hub. The hotel has a number of amenities and facilities including adjoining rooms, babysitting services, fitness facilities, business centre and an outdoor pool. This modern hotel is perfect for families or business travellers.

Hilton Kuwait Resort   Map Ref → 1-C3

Located in Mangaf, this resort has one of the best beaches and health clubs in the country. There are 143 rooms, four suites, 80 chalets, 61 studios and apartments, 52 Presidential Villas and 12 Royal Villas, plus four restaurants, two cafes, one coffee shop and two poolside bars. The resort also has a water sports pavilion and a dive centre.

JW Marriott Kuwait City Hotel   Map Ref → 7-C3

The JW Marriott is located in the heart of Kuwait City, 15km from the airport and has 240 rooms and 75 suites over 16 floors. There are three restaurants including the well-known La Brasserie, and two lounges. Club Elite boasts a pool, whirlpool and gym. It was voted Business Traveller Hotel of the year in 2004 but also attracts its fair share of leisure guests.

Kempinski Julai'a Resort   Map Ref → 6-D1

Located approximately 100km south of Kuwait City, the Kempinski resort has 77 villas and elegant chalets and 56 hotel rooms, all of which overlook one of the spacious swimming pools. Facilities include three restaurants, two cafes, a cinema, health club, Ayurvedic Centre, entertainment centre, water sports and bike hire.

Le Meridien Kuwait   Map Ref → 7-A4

Not to be confused with Le Meridien Tower, all rooms in this hotel are about to undergo refurbishment, promising to bring them up to Kuwait's newfound luxury standards. Leisure facilities are limited to a small outdoor swimming pool and a gym but there are a number of excellent restaurants popular with visitors and expats.

Le Meridien Tower (Art + Tech)   Map Ref → 6-B2

Built in 2003, the Art + Tech hotel takes modern hospitality to another level with cutting edge amenities perfect for business travellers. All of the 70 rooms feature interactive Plasma screen TVs, DVD, VCD and CD facilities, and high speed Internet access. Hotel facilities include a restaurant, lobby lounge, health club and outdoor swimming pool.

Marina Hotel Kuwait
Map Ref → 11-E2

Located in the Marina development in Salmiya, between the marina and the beach, the Marina Hotel is 20km from the airport and includes 91 rooms and seven suites. There is a restaurant and lounge, and easy access to additional restaurants and cafes in Marina Crescent and Marina Mall. This is a low-rise boutique style hotel.

Mövenpick Kuwait
Map Ref → 6-D2

Located in the Free Trade Zone on the waterfront overlooking Shuwaikh Bay, this hotel consists of 100 rooms including 57 deluxe rooms, 41 Executive Club rooms and two Executive Suites. Facilities include three restaurants, a lounge, an outdoor pool, with a fantastic lazy river, and a fully equipped gym. Perfect for both business and family visitors.

Radisson SAS
Map Ref → 14-A1

This 'grand dame' of Kuwait's hotels is located in Salwa and has 200 rooms including 12 suites, six deluxe apartments and 49 Royal Club rooms on the executive floor. The Kuwaiti Village features the largest dhow in the world, the Al Hashemi III, which is used for banquets and conferences. The hotel has three restaurants and comprehensive health club facilities.

Safir International Hotel
Map Ref → 4-A2

Located in Bneid Al Gar, the Safir International has 146 rooms and suites, almost all of which have stunning views overlooking the tranquil Arabian Gulf. There are three restaurants, including one on the 19th floor commanding wonderful views across Kuwait Bay. Recreational facilities include a gym and swimming pool.

Safir Al Bastaki Suites
Map Ref → 4-A2

Minutes from the Safir International hotel these luxurious suites are blessed with the same breathtaking views of the city and coastline. Each of the guest rooms, some of which are connected, have a balcony and the on-site facilities include a health club, swimming pool and a beauty salon. Also available are a number of executive suites.

Sheraton Kuwait Hotel & Towers
Map Ref → 7-C3

Located in Kuwait City, this modern hotel has 310 rooms and suites and is easily accessible from the airport. Catering largely to business travellers, the hotel's leisure facilities include a fully equipped health club, an outdoor swimming pool and a golf simulator. There are five restaurants, a lobby lounge and Kuwait's best tea lounge.

The Courtyard by Marriott
Map Ref → 3-E2

Located in the heart of the business and banking district, The Courtyard Kuwait City is part of the Arraya Complex and is a modern hotel with eclectic decor. There's a large atrium with magnificent views of The Liberation Tower and The Kuwait Towers. The 297 rooms are split between the two towers and are spacious, modern and equipped with the latest technology.

The Palms Beach Hotel & Spa
Map Ref → 6-D1

The Palms is the latest five star hotel to open in Kuwait. It overlooks the Arabian Gulf and has a small beach area with a number of swimming pools, as well as a health club. The 128 suites overlook either the sea or the gardens. There are seven cafes and restaurants, and the Orchid Spa offering a wide range of health and beauty treatments.

Hotel Apartments

Hotel apartments can be rented weekly, monthly or annually and are fully furnished. Facilities such as parking, a gym and a swimming pool are often available but not always included in the price – check your agreements before signing and negotiate for these facilities if they are not covered. A rating system is in operation, although it is fair to say that one or two operations seem to be rated a little too highly!

Hostels

There was once a number of youth hostels in Kuwait however at present none of them are operational.

Campsites

Other options → Camping [p.132]

A favourite pastime of the Kuwaiti people is to spend time camping in the desert during the spring. Large areas are taken over and semi-permanent camps erected. No campsite is complete without a couple of large water tanks, satellite dish and a couple of off-road vehicles parked outside the tent. Campsites are not regulated, although the Municipality is currently campaigning to reduce the annual camping period from 1st December to 31st March, thereby reducing the impact on the environment. Camping accounts for 6% of Kuwait's desertification problem.

After the Iraqi invasion, camping in the desert was a risky business because of the landmines left behind. By 1993, some 'safe areas' had been cleared, and today there is virtually no danger of happening upon abandoned landmines or other munitions.

Getting Around

Other options → Exploring [p.95]
Maps [p.251]

Primary modes of transport are the car, taxi or bus.

Kuwait's road network is a radial grid design. Comprised of seven major 'Ring Roads' and a number of major dual-carriage expressways, the road network links Kuwait City to every area of Kuwait, as well as to the Iraqi and Saudi Arabian borders.

Kuwait has an excellent road infrastructure which has taken something of a beating over the last two years due to the demands made on it by the ever-increasing urban population. A number of roads suffer from excessive use by heavy loads. Subsequently there are now restrictions as to when heavy vehicles are permitted to use certain roads. The government is currently spending hundreds of millions of dollars upgrading a number of roads including the 1st Ring Road, 4th Ring Road and 5th Ring Road.

The ring roads radiate out from Kuwait City, with the 1st Ring Road hugging the downtown area, and the 7th Ring Road located approximately 28km south. The major expressways running approximately from north to south and starting with the most easterly road first, are the Abdulaziz Bin Abdulrahman Al Saud Expressway (also known as the Istiqlal Expressway, Fahaheel Expressway, and Road 30), the King Fahd Custodian of the Two Holy Mosques Expressway (also known as the Maghreb Expressway, Ahmadi Expressway, and Road 40). Road 30 merges with Road 40 approximately 50km south of Kuwait city near the area of Ad Dubaiyah. The road then becomes the King Fahd Expressway. Further west is the King Faisal Expressway (also known as the Riyadh Expressway, Road 50 and the Magwa Road further

Hotel Apartments

Deluxe	Phone	Area	One B/room Apts (Weekly)	Two B/room Apts (Weekly)	Email
Dream House	255 5650	Safat	4	196	na
El Noray Executive Apartments	573 8085	Salmiya	4	175	www.elnoray.net
Flowery Holiday Suites	573 2605	Salmiya	4	245	na
Frost Real Estate	564 3149	Salwa	4	196	www.frost-realestate.com
Hala Motel	256 2303	Bneid Al Gar	3	123	na
Kuwait Residence Hotel	246 5860	Safat	3	105	na
Lighthouse International	261 1342	Salwa	4	90	www.lighthouseint.com
Mirage Hotel Apartments	575 0001	Salmiya	3	105	na
Royal Suite Hotel Apartment	253 0700	Bneid Al Gar	5	560	na
The Viewpoint	261 3640	Bneid Al Gar	5	280	na

south), the Airport Road (Road 55), and the Ghazali Expressway (Road 60) which runs north to Shuwaikh Port.

The coastal road, which runs from the east of Kuwait City all the way to the western-most intersection with the 6th Ring Road, and then picks up at the western-most intersection with the 7th Ring Road and travels all the way down to Al Kout Shopping Mall in Fahaheel, is known as the Gulf Road, Arabian Gulf Street or Coastal Road. It is also known as Road 15 between Kuwait City and the intersection with the 2nd Ring Road, and as Road 25 from the intersection with the 2nd Ring Road to the intersection with the 6th Ring Road! It may all seem a little overwhelming at first, but it doesn't take too long to get used to the road network!

It used to be said that the 4th Ring Road was the one to avoid during the rush hour, but the increase in traffic throughout the country now means that most main roads are congested.

Most road signs are in Arabic and English, although be aware that not all roads are marked. When entering a suburban area on a main road you will often see a blue sign with a series of misshapen white and yellow blocks containing numbers. These are the areas into which the suburb is divided, and the yellow blocks show the areas that you are driving through.

When asking for an address, particularly in the outlying suburban areas, you will be told a variant of the block/area, Street, and House number. A word of warning – street numbers are not consecutive!

When driving, be sure to remain in the right-hand lane if you are anticipating a turning as junctions are not indicated very far in advance. There are a number of intersections where roads are only marked at the actual turning; very frustrating if you are in the wrong lane. If you do happen to miss your turning you will often have to travel quite some distance to find a u-turn to bring you back. Manoeuvering your way around a u-turn is akin to running the gauntlet; a challenge at the best of times!

Two reliable bus services operate in the country. Kuwait Public Transport Company (KPTC) operates large, air-conditioned buses on 32 different routes and tends to be used by expatriate workers at the lower end of the income scale. Citybus, owned by The Transport & Warehousing Group Co, runs city hopper-style buses on all major routes. The first two rows of seats in any bus are usually reserved for female passengers. Bus services also operate between Kuwait City and a number of Middle Eastern capitals.

Cycling tends to be limited to low-income labourers who save every fil to send home. Cycling is not recommended on major roads due to the extremely dangerous manner in which cars are driven. However, it is common to see cyclists, without helmets, navigating their way through traffic.

Kuwait has no trams or trains.

Traffic accidents are a common occurrence in Kuwait. For a population of almost 2,5 million, there were in excess of 45,878 traffic accidents in 2004.

Air

Other options → Meet & Greet [p.22]

Air fares from Kuwait are not particularly cheap, although airlines will have special offers during low-season periods (outside of religious and school holidays). A number of airlines operate a direct service to Kuwait. Other airlines, represented by local agents, have ticketing and reservation offices in Kuwait. Most of these airlines operate a code share service to or from the host country via Dubai. Whenever you enquire about flights to and from Kuwait it is worth asking if there are any stops en route. There are no domestic flights within Kuwait.

Kuwait Airways, the national carrier, flies to 39 destinations worldwide. The airline continues to be troubled by a substantial debt, primarily due to the purchasing of a fleet of aircraft following losses of 85% of its assets as a result of the 1991 Gulf War. Jazeera Airways, Kuwait's private no-frills carrier, (www.jazeeraairways.com), offers 30 flights a week to key destinations within the Middle East and the Indian subcontinent and has a number of promotional deals.

Located approximately 16km south of Kuwait City, Kuwait International Airport has undergone something of a facelift in the last four years. The once drab terminal building has been modernised and includes a number of shops and eateries, as well as banks. The Immigration desks are less intimidating than they once were.

The airport currently handles five million passengers a year and the plan is to increase this figure by constructing a second terminal. Although the size is yet to be confirmed, the existing runway would allow for a new terminal to handle a further 15 million passengers per year. Further plans will see the construction of an additional terminal for private aircraft.

Duty free shopping is available on a small scale. As Kuwait is a tax-free country there are no reimbursements from customs on departure.

Lounges in the departures area are being upgraded. The only dedicated play area for children is in the recently completed Pearl Lounge, operated by National Aviation Services (NAS). Entrance is KD 12 per person. Smoking rooms are located in the departures area; there is a small Nursery Room desperately in need of updating, a number of prayer areas and a medical centre. Assistance for passengers with special needs is available.

Flight information: 181

Airlines

Air Arabia	244 9824	www.airarabia.com
Air China	243 8568	www.air-china.co.uk
Air France	247 1356	www.airfrance.com.kw
Air India	243 8184	www.airindia.com
Air Slovakia	243 4346	www.airslovakia.sk
Al Jazeera	433 9436	na
Ariana Afghan Airlines	244 1041	www.flyariana.com
Balkan Bulgarian Airlines	241 6474	www.balkan.com
Biman Air Airlines	244 1041	www.bimanair.com
British Airways	242 5635	www.britishairways.com
Czech Airlines	243 3141	www.czechairlines.com
Egypt Air	243 9576	www.egyptair.com
Emirates	242 5566	www.emirates.com
Gulf Air	245 0180	www.gulfairco.com
Indian Airlines	245 6700	www.indian-airlines.nic.in
Iran Air	245 1228	www.iranair.com
Iran Aseman Airlines	241 4161	www.iaa.ir
JAT Airways	242 6846	www.jat.com
Jet Airways	241 2742	www.jetairways.com
KLM	243 8142	www.klm.com
Kuwait Airways	434 5555	www.kuwait-airways.com
Lufthansa	242 2493	www.kuwait.lufthansa.com
Middle East Airlines	242 3073	www.mea.com.lb
Olympic Airways	242 0003	www.olympicairlines.com
Oman Air	241 2284	www.oman-air.com
PIA	242 1044	www.piac.com.pk
Qatar Airways	242 3888	www.qatarairways.com
Royal Jordanian	241 8064	www.rja.com.jo
Saudi Arabian Airlines	242 6310	www.saudiairlines.com
Shaheen Airlines	241 1368	www.shaheenair.com
Syrian Arab Airlines	242 3117	www.syrianair.com
Turkish Airlines	245 3820	www.turkishair.com
Ukraine Int'l Airlines	249 9994	www.ukraine-international.com
Yemen Airways	240 8933	www.yemenia.com

Airport Bus

There are two air-conditioned bus services which run from Kuwait International Airport to the main bus terminal located in the area of Mirqab in Kuwait City. One bus is operated by Kuwait Public Transport Company (KPTC) and the other is operated by Citybus. Both buses follow the same route (Route 501) in both directions and the cost for the entire journey one way is 250 fils. There are five main stops along the route, although the drivers will stop almost anywhere if flagged down. The 16km journey takes anywhere between 20 and 45 minutes, depending on the time of day and traffic. The first bus departs the airport at 05:15 and the last bus departs at 22:35.

Unless you are on a budget, if you need to head directly to Kuwait City, the use of a taxi would be preferable. For KD 5 you can travel from the airport to most locations within a radius of about 17 kms, including Kuwait City, Salmiya and Fintas. An additional KD 2 will get you to Jahra, Ahmadi and Mangaf. Alternative transport is available in 'limousines' which will cost between KD 7 and KD 18 to Kuwait City, depending on whether you opt for a station wagon or a stretch limo.

Boat

Kuwait Public Transportation Company (KPTC) operates a daily ferry service from Ras Al Ardh in Salmiya to Failaka Island. Departure times vary and the return journey costs KD 2.500 per person, with additional charges for vehicles. Call for more info (574 2664). Dhows can be hired from any dhow harbour for a daily charge of about KD 100. Boats and yachts are available to hire from most of the yacht clubs.

Bus

Two reliable bus services are in operation. Kuwait Public Transport Company (KPTC, Tel: 88 00 01) operates large, air-conditioned buses on 32 different routes and tends to be used by expatriate workers at the lower end of the income scale. Citybus (Tel: 88 22 11), owned by The Transport & Warehousing Group Co. runs air-conditioned, city hopper-style buses on 12 of the routes covered by KPTC. Fares on both services range from 150 fils to 250 fils. KPTC does offer a travel-card ticket for regular travels – these are available from any of the main stations. The first two rows of seats in any bus are usually reserved for female passengers.

KPTC route information can be obtained by calling into their office at the Mirqab terminal in Kuwait City, or by visiting their website at www.kptc.com.kw. Maps of Citybus routes are available on the buses themselves.

Bus services also operate between Kuwait City and a number of Middle Eastern capitals.

Car

Other options → **Transportation [p.85]**

Driving Habits & Regulations

Kuwait has an excellent road infrastructure but a poor standard of driving. Laws, including the mandatory use of seatbelts, are generally not enforced. For a population of almost two and a half million, there were in excess of 45,376 traffic accidents in 2003. It is vital for your safety that you are very aware of your surroundings when driving. Habits to look out for include high-speed, aggressive driving, tailgating, constant lane changing without indication and overtaking on all sides. The best advice is never assume what your fellow drivers are about to do, and expect the unexpected. The use of a cell/mobile phone whilst driving is legal. Right turns at red traffic lights are not permitted, unless there is a flashing green or amber arrow indicating otherwise.

Speed Limits

Speed limits are indicated by roadside signs. The limit for driving on expressways is 100 or 120kph, depending on whether you are leaving or entering a built-up area. The limit on city and suburban roads is 45kph or 60kph, depending on the location. A minimum speed of between 40 to 80kph is required on some major routes. Speed cameras are permanently located on all major roads, and additional temporary cameras operate from the back of parked police vehicles. It is rare for a speeding fine to be issued on the spot, and they are not sent by post either. Instead, fines must be paid before you can renew your vehicle

> **Absolute Zero**
>
> *A policy of zero tolerance applies to driving under the influence of drugs and/or alcohol. It is an extremely serious offence and, based on your level of intoxication, will invariably result in a custodial sentence or deportation. Repeat traffic violations will have the same result.*

registration, or before your residency can be cancelled. If a fine is incurred whilst driving a hire car, the company will deduct the amount from your credit card.

Driving Licence

Driving in Kuwait is only permitted for holders of a GCC licence, or an International Driving Permit (IDP) for visitors for the duration of their visa period. Those applying for, or who have received their residence permits in Kuwait may not drive on either a GCC licence or an IDP. Residents from the UK, US and France may obtain a Kuwait driving licence on the strength of their national licence. All other nationalities will have to apply for a learner's licence and take a driving test. Driving without the correct licence and vehicle documentation is a serious offence. If you are stopped by the police and cannot present the required documentation you may be taken into custody until someone brings it on your behalf. This could become a rather tricky situation if your family is away and you're the only one with keys to your home!

> **Blood Money**
>
> *Should a person die in a vehicle accident in Kuwait, his/her heirs are entitled to file a claim for death compensation (blood money) of KD10,000, or more. Should the fatal accident have been due to the negligent driving of the deceased, no amount is payable. All claims should be filed within three years of the date of the accident.*

Accidents

If you do have the misfortune of being involved in a traffic accident, however big or small, it is a requirement of law that the accident is reported to the police immediately, by dialling 777. Failure to do so will invalidate your insurance. Do not leave the scene unless it is imperative that you get to a hospital. If you do leave the scene, you may end up taking the blame, even if the accident wasn't your fault. The ambulance service is not for the faint-hearted. If you have an accident and it is at all possible, make your own way to the hospital.

Non Drivers

Pedestrians and cyclists are a hazard to drivers. Jay walking is common and you'll often encounter cyclists coming towards you on a main road. Paths for pedestrians and cyclists are found on the corniche, and all major parks have walking/cycling tracks. Cycling on main roads is not recommended.

Traditional professions such as fishing still flourish in modern Kuwait

Parking

Parking can be a problem in built-up areas. There are a number of parking garages and uncovered, controlled parking areas in the heart of Kuwait. Payment is usually 100 fils per hour but does vary, and is payable to the man in the booth as you exit. Long-term contracts for parking are available, particularly for people working in the city. Shopping centres, co-ops and beach clubs usually have their own parking areas, although the number of spaces varies considerably. There are a number of open desert areas located within the city and the suburbs in which one is able to park for free. Both long and short term parking is available at Kuwait International Airport. Parking against any pavement painted black and yellow is prohibited.

Petrol/Gas Stations

All petrol stations, of which there are about 90, are owned by Kuwait National Petroleum Company. Open 24 hours a day, they are located along main roads and expressways. The set-up is pretty basic; they offer a refilling service and will also carry out an oil change. They don't have 24 hour shops or automatic car wash facilities, and don't do windscreen washes. Most are self-service although women will generally be assisted by the forecourt staff. The fuel price is generously subsidised by the government; expect to pay 60 fils for a litre of unleaded premium and 65 fils for super premium. Diesel is around 55 fils a litre.

Kuwait's national pride remains steadfast

PetroNet, a prepaid fuel card has recently been introduced and is available in various denominations, from KD 15. As with a phone card, the PetroNet card can be used any number of times until the credit is used up.

Car Hire

Visitors to Kuwait may hire a car on presentation of an International Driving Permit (IDP). All IDPs must be validated by a local insurance company (the rental company will arrange this) at a charge of between KD 10.500 and KD 11.500 for one month, and between KD 17 and KD 20 for a maximum three-month period. If you intend to visit Kuwait repeatedly, have your IDP validated for three months; it will save you having to pay every time you hire a car. Residents of Kuwait must have a Kuwaiti licence. Vehicles are leased on both short and long-term agreements. If you have the time, try to shop around to get a good rate. Check to see if any form of accident assistance is provided. As a guide, a Toyota Corolla with unlimited mileage will cost KD 9 per day, KD 55 for a week and KD 135 monthly. A Toyota Prado, also with unlimited mileage, will cost KD 30, KD 175 and KD 400 respectively.

Car Rental Agencies	
Al Babtain Car Rental	476 9353
Al Mulla Rental & Leasing of Vehicles & Equipment Co. W.L.L P.ix	482 3731
Al Sayer Car Rental & Leasing	244 1425
Avis Rent a Car	246 5082
Budget Rent a Car	431 0064
Europcar Alghanim Rent a Car	473 5626
Hertz Rent a Car	483 1616
National Car Rental	249 2145
Sixt Rent A Car P.87	84 3843

Taxi

For non-drivers, taxis are the preferred mode of transport in Kuwait. Taxi companies are not regulated; most do not have meters and a large number do not have seat belts. The majority operate 24 hours. Negotiate the price before you get in and don't feel intimated if the driver then tells you the price is higher than agreed; just threaten to get out, it usually works. Fares are usually a minimum of KD 1 and will increase slowly depending upon the destination. From the airport to Kuwait City (16km) will cost KD 5, and from the airport to Fintas (22km) the cost will be KD 6. A surcharge may be payable at night.

The best way to arrange a taxi is to call a company in advance. State your destination and check the price before the car is dispatched. The drivers have a fair knowledge of the city and surrounds. If possible show a map of your destination or give them a landmark such as a hotel or shopping centre to aim for.

Orange taxis, which you can hail from the side of the road, are as scruffy inside as they look outside. The drivers are likely to drop off and collect further passengers along the route. Fares range from 150 fils to KD 1, depending on how far you travel. They will transport single passengers to a destination of choice, for the right price. Pickup trucks (wanettes) also act as a taxi service, although they are only authorised to carry goods and passengers accompanying goods. Neither of these services are recommended, particularly for western women.

The airport operates a taxi and limousine service. For this well-maintained, clean service you will pay a premium.

Taxi Companies

Al Jameheer Taxi	573 3100
Al Mulla Call Taxi	244 4486
Al Osta Taxi	241 0538
Al Remal Al Dahabia Taxi	572 7444
Al Tahreer Taxi	575 5035
Kuds Taxi	241 3414
Meshwar Taxi	575 5888
Salwa Taxi	565 8219
Sixt Rent a Car P.87	84 3843

Train

There is no train or tram service in Kuwait, although there continues to be talk among GCC countries to set up a regional rail network.

Walking

Travelling by car is the preferred method of getting around in Kuwait City and its environs. Extreme summer temperatures confine most people to the interior of an air-conditioned vehicle. That being said, the city is accessible by foot, although uneven pavements have resulted in many a twisted ankle and prove problematic for those pushing prams or wheelchairs. Pedestrian bridges are found on major roads and expressways, although some are positioned in rather inconvenient locations. 'Zebra crossings' are found at a number of intersections and traffic lights. However, don't rely on the traffic stopping to let you cross.

Money

Cash is the preferred method of payment although credit cards are generally accepted. Traveller's cheques are widely accepted although it is recommended that you take travellers cheques in US dollars or UK pounds sterling to avoid additional exchange rate charges. The use of cheques is not common.

Foreign currencies can be changed at any of the numerous foreign exchange offices, hotels and banks. A passport is not always required in order to affect a currency exchange, although it would make sense to have it with you just in case.

Some hotels and major supermarkets will accept payment in foreign currencies, such as sterling, US dollars and other GCC currencies.

There are no current restrictions on the import and export of local and foreign currency.

Local Currency

The Kuwaiti Dinar (KD) is the official currency of Kuwait. The KD (international currency code is KWD) is accepted worldwide and complies with International Monetary Fund regulations. KD 1 is equal to 1000 fils. Notes are issued in denominations of KD 20, KD 10, KD 5, KD 1, KD 0.500 and KD 0.250. Coins are in denominations of 100 fils, 50 fils, 20 fils, 10 fils and 5 fils.

In May 2007, the dinar dropped its pegging to the US Dollar, which had been in place since 2003.

Currency exchange in the souk

Now, it is linked to a basket of currencies, of which the US Dollar makes up 75%.

Exchange rates are published daily in all major Arabic and English newspapers.

Exchange Rates

Foreign Currency (FC)	1 Unit FC = X KD	KD 1 = X FC
Australia	0.221	4.51
Bahrain	0.774	1.29
Bangladesh	0.005	220.03
Canada	0.231	4.31
China	0.035	28.34
Cyprus	0.636	1.57
Denmark	0.049	20.27
Euro	0.367	2.72
Hong Kong	0.037	26.64
India	0.006	149.08
Iraq	0.00021	5,279.45
Japan	0.0027	368.69
Jordan	0.412	2.42
Lebanon	0.00019	5,184.93
Malaysia	0.076	13.01
New Zealand	0.207	4.81
Oman	0.758	1.31
Pakistan	0.005	204.22
Philippines	0.005	186.40
Qatar	0.080	12.46
Saudi Arabia	0.077	12.84
Singapore	0.176	5.67
South Africa	0.044	22.42
Sri Lanka	0.002	342.06
Sweden	0.040	24.99
Switzerland	0.237	4.20
Thailand	0.007	134.29
UAE	0.079	12.57
UK	0.533	1.872
USA	0.292	3.42

Banks

Kuwait has an excellent, internationally recognised banking system with a wide range of commercial and personal services including money exchanges and transfers. A number of the banks have first-class online facilities.

The majority of banks are located in the central area of Kuwait City, with branches throughout the country. Kuwait is in the process of granting licences to a number of international banks to open branches in Kuwait, including BNP Paribas, National Bank of Abu Dhabi, Citibank and HSBC.

Banking hours are from 08:00 – 14:00, Sunday to Thursday. Some do open for one evening a week but this varies from bank to bank.

Main Banks

Al Ahli Bank of Kuwait (ABK) P.163	89 9899	www.eahli.com
Bank of Bahrain & Kuwait (BBK)	241 7140	www.bbkonline.com
Bank of Kuwait and the Middle East	80 2000	www.bkme.com
Burgan Bank	243 9000	www.burgan.com
Central Bank of Kuwait	244 9200	www.cbk.gov.kw
Commercial Bank of Kuwait	241 1011	www.cbk-online.com
Gulf Bank	80 5805	www.gulfbank-online.com
Industrial Bank of Kuwait (IBK)	245 7661	www.ibkuwt.com
Kuwait Credit & Saving Bank	241 1311	na
Kuwait Finance House (KFH)	80 3333	www.kfh.com
Kuwait Real Estate Co.	245 8177	www.kuwait_toplist.com/krec
National Bank of Kuwait (NBK) P.IFC	80 1801	www.nbk.com

ATMs

24-hour ATMs are located throughout Kuwait. It is common to see roadside signs indicating the location of a bank and therefore an ATM machine, whether you are driving on an expressway or a main road. Each area of Kuwait has a major co-operative (supermarket) which usually has either an ATM machine or a bank in the vicinity.

A small charge is applied if you draw money from an ATM of another bank. International visitors will also pay a small fee for this service.

Visa, Visa Electron, Maestro, Cirrus, KNet (local), GCCNET (Gulf-wide) and PLUS systems operate in Kuwait.

Money Exchanges

In addition to the services offered by the banks, there are a number of reputable independent money exchanges in Kuwait. Rates are better than those you would be given at major hotels. These exchanges will also transfer money to an international account for a fraction of the price that a bank will charge. The majority of the exchanges operate Saturday to Thursday, from 08:30 – 13:00 and 16:00 – 19:00. A limited number of exchanges open on Friday afternoons.

Exchange Centres

Al Mulla International Exchange Co.	246 3220
Bahrain Exchange Co. (BEC)	82 4000
City International Exchange Co.	244 1845
Dollarco Exchange Co.	241 2767
Express Money Services	80 8880
Kuwait Bahrain International Exchange	242 1971
Kuwait India International Exchange Co.	242 2677
Security Exchange Co.	243 8203

Credit Cards

Major credit cards (American Express, Diners Club, MasterCard and Visa) are accepted in hotels and at retail outlets and restaurants throughout Kuwait. Co-operatives and corner shops, as well as local markets, prefer to deal in cash. You may be expected to pay a surcharge if you wish to pay by credit card in the smaller establishments. The benefit of paying in cash at the traditional markets is that you will be able to negotiate discounts. Your credit card will work in most of the ATMs and can be used to obtain cash from a bank.

Tipping

Tipping in Kuwait is entirely discretionary. Should you wish to acknowledge good service an appropriate amount would be 10%. An increasing number of restaurants will include a service charge in the bill although this does not usually make its way to the waiting staff.

The attendant who fills your car at the petrol station will be very happy to receive a tip of a maximum of 250 fils, as will the man who wheels your shopping trolley to your car. A recommended maximum tip of 10% may be paid to a taxi driver.

Media & Communications

Newspapers/Magazines

There are seven daily newspapers printed in Kuwait. Two are in English (150 fils each): *Arab Times* and *Kuwait Times*. The remaining five Arab papers (100 fils each) are *Al Anbaa*, *Al Qabas*, *Al Rai*, *Al Seyassah* and *Al Watan*.

Regional and international newspapers are available and usually arrive in Kuwait up to two days after the date of publication. International newspapers are available in supermarkets and hotel shops and some bookshops. They are up to three times the price that one would pay at home.

A wide range of magazines covering subjects including computing, crafts and hobbies, fishing and photography can be found at all bookshops and supermarkets. Foreign magazines are usually received in shops two to four weeks after they are published (due to shipping and censorship delays) and they often have a number of pages removed, depending on the content. It is also common to see 'indecent' photos blacked out with a large felt-tip pen. Magazines are expensive and cost up to three times what they would at home. A number of English-language magazines are published locally, including *Kuwait This Month* and *Kuwait Life*.

Further Reading

Other options → Websites [p.40]

Free monthly publications include *Kuwait Zoom*, *Student Talk* and *Airport*. Other magazines including *Kuwait This Month* and *Kuwait Life* provide details on forthcoming events and cost KD 1.

Guidebooks include the *Lonely Planet* series and the *Kuwait Pocket Guide*. Numerous coffee table books have been published, including *Footsteps in the Sand* by Anne Al Bassam, *Glimpses from the Last 50 Years* by Tareq S. Rajab, and *Welcome Visitors Guide to Kuwait* by Eric Tan.

Post & Courier Services

Other options → Postal Services [p.74]

The Ministry of Communication is responsible for the postal system. Delivery of post to residential addresses is not as reliable as delivery to a work address or a post box, which may be rented for KD 4 annually after an initial payment of KD 7 (including key charge). All incoming post is subject to customs inspection. Post to and from the USA, Europe and Australia can take anything from three days to six weeks as delays are often incurred in Kuwait. Deliveries within the GCC should take approximately three days. Letters (up to 20g) cost 25 fils to Kuwaiti addresses, 50 fils to GCC countries and 150 fils to the rest of the world.

Post should be handed in at any of the post offices operating throughout Kuwait. To ensure delivery it is recommended that all items be registered, although it is not possible to register express

Websites

Business/Industry

www.baladia.gov.kw	Arabic site of Kuwait Municipality
www.britishcouncil.org	British Council Kuwait
www.cbk.gov.kw	The Central Bank of Kuwait
www.fasttelco.net	Internet service provider
www.gulfdirectory.com.bh	Gulf Directory
www.gulftelecom.com	Internet service provider
www.kcci.org.kw	Kuwait Chamber of Commerce & Industry
www.kuwait-airport.com.kw	Kuwait International Airport
www.kuwait-airways.com	Kuwait Airways
www.kuwaitdutyfree.com	Kuwait Duty Free
www.qualitynet.net	Internet service provider
www.zajil.com	Internet service provider

Embassies

www.embassyworld.com	Embassies abroad

Kuwait Information

www.arabicnews.com	News of the Arab World
www.arabtimesonline.com	Local newspaper
www.aware.com.kw	Cultural centre
www.baytlothan.org	Cultural centre
www.deraradio.com	Dera Radio
www.dpm.gov.kw	Diwan of the Prime Minister
www.e.gov.kw	Gateway to government services
www.expatexchange.com	Forum for expatriates
www.explorer-publishing.com	Our site!
www.gis.baladia.gov.kw	Great interactive map site
www.indiansinkuwait.com	Portal for the Indian community
www.kif.net	Exhibition listings
www.kubbar.com	Weather
www.kuwait.kw	The official website of the State of Kuwait
www.kuwaitiah.net	Unofficial guide to Kuwait
www.kuwait-info.com	Kuwait Information Office in India
www.kuwaitinfo.org.uk	Kuwait Cultural Office in the UK
www.kuwaitmission.com	Permanent Mission of the State of Kuwait to the UN
www.kuwaitpocketguide.com	Informative Site on all aspects of living and working in Kuwait
www.kuwaittimes.net	Local newspaper
www.kuwait-toplist.com	Comprehensive information on Kuwait business
www.kuwait-yellow-pages.com	Kuwait Yellow Pages
www.mockw.net	Kuwait Ministry of Communication
www.moi.gov.kw	Arabic site of the Ministry of Information
www.paci.gov.kw	Civil ID enquiry service
www.q8directory.com	Directory

Wheels

www.q8car.com	Buy a vehicle online

letters or packages. Parcels may be sent from the main post office, located in Fahad Al Salem Street in Kuwait City, or from any of the larger post offices. An express service, Mumtaz Post, has priority in both Kuwait and the country of delivery. Stamps are available at all post offices.

A slightly more expensive option for getting an item delivered urgently is the use of a courier service.

Courier Companies	
Aramex	434 5444
DHL	80 8345
Express Post	241 8204
FedEx	80 2233
Gazelle	243 3288
OCS	474 2444
TNT	461 0888
UPS	434 4822

Radio

Local radio stations broadcast in Arabic, English, Persian, Tagalog and Urdu.

Superstation (FM99.7) plays predominantly Top 40 music but does have weekly shows dedicated to rock and other styles. Regular news bulletins are transmitted, along with limited sports news and weather reports. Easy FM (FM92.5) plays easy listening music, FM103.7 plays modern Arabic music and FM87.9 plays classical Arabic music. The MW English service broadcasts from 963 KHz for 6 hours a day, from 08:00 – 11:00 and 21:00 - 24:00. The American Forces Network (FM104.3) and British Forces Broadcasting Service (FM102.0) broadcast a wide range of modern music.

Television/Satellite TV

Other options → Satellite TV & Radio [p.74]
Television [p.74]

Kuwait has five channels, all of which are run by the state. KTV2 is the only English channel, broadcasting a selection of programmes for a limited period, from early afternoon to midnight.

Satellite services are available and are generally provided by Orbit and Showtime. They offer a varied selection of programmes including sport, entertainment, cartoons, movies, documentaries and news channels. In addition to the cost of the decoder and satellite dish, the service costs from KD 5 per month depending on the selection of channels.

Local coffee shops will show football games on TV, particularly if the Kuwaiti team is playing. All major hotels have a satellite service.

Telephones

Other options → Telephone [p.73]

The excellent landline telephone service in Kuwait is provided by the Ministry of Communication. All local calls are free. An international line will require a substantial deposit, usually KD 500. To avoid having to pay this deposit, an alternative is to use a phone card when making international calls. Sold in various denominations at corner shops and supermarkets, these cards can only be used on telephones with tone dialing. Phone boxes are not easily accessible. Should you need to make a local call, most shops will allow you the use of their phone for a minute or two. Hotels add their usual percentage onto any calls made.

Area Codes & Useful Numbers	
Citybus Route Enquiries	88 2211
Civil ID Enquiries	88 9988
Coastguard	574 3333
Emergency Services – Police, Ambulance, Fire	777
KPTC Route Enquiries	88 0001
Kuwait Airport Information	181
Kuwait Country Code	+965
Ministry of Communication	481 9033
MTC Vodaphone Enquiries	80 8045
Operator - International Calls (Subscribers)	022
Talking clock (in Arabic)	113
Telephone Billing Enquiries	123
Telephone Complaints	117
Telephone Directory Enquiries	101
Wataniya Telecom Enquiries	121
Weather (in Arabic)	104

Internet

Other options → Internet [p.73]
Internet Cafes [p.222]

The internet is accessible in internet cafes, and most hotels have access in guests' rooms or the Business Centre.

Internet cafes are found throughout Kuwait although their locations are not always obvious. They charge anything from 250 fils to KD 1 per hour. All of the internet service providers (ISPs) in Kuwait have some sort of censorship. This censorship often extends to perfectly

General Info

Media & Communications

reasonable sites. If you require access to a particular site, and feel that it has been blocked incorrectly contact your ISP. Local domain names usually end in .com.kw

ISPs include QualityNet (Tel: 80 4444), Fastelco (Tel: 88 6666), Gulf Telecom (Tel: 246 8111) and Zajil-Kems (Tel: 820 820). Some ISPs sell pre-paid internet cards, in denominations ranging from KD 1 to KD 10, providing you with access for up to 150 hours.

Annual Events

Kuwait Annual Events

A national assembly cabinet resolution, passed in 2001, states that, should a holiday fall in the middle of a working week, it will be moved to the following Saturday. Should any of these holidays fall on a Thursday no additional day will be given.

Eid Al Adha/Eid Al Fitr

The festival of Eid Al Adha is held on the 10th day of Dhu Al Hijjah, the pilgrimage month, while Eid Al Fitr marks the end of the holy month of Ramadan. Each lasts three or four days, with Eid Al Fitr being a particularly festive event. People dress up in new clothes, houses are decorated with lights, and there are fireworks and great feasts. It is a time for visiting friends and family, and children usually receive gifts of money.

Camel Racing

The season for camel racing, a sport which is undergoing something of a revival, is from late winter to early spring. It is a popular cultural pastime with up to sixty camels taking part in a single race of up to six kilometres in distance. Races usually take place on Thursdays and Fridays, the timings of which are printed in the local newspapers. Al Atraf Camel Racing Club (Tel: 539 4014).

Hala February Shopping Festival

Hala February, which literally translated means 'Welcome February', is an annual festival of cultural and entertainment events during which many retail outlets offer considerable discounts to shoppers. The festival has something for all the family, and allows people to sample real Arabian hospitality.

National Day

National Day, although celebrated on 25th February, is actually on June 19th. It marks Kuwait's independence from Britain in 1961, prior to which Kuwait was a protectorate of the Empire. The occasion is celebrated with fireworks and festivities, with residents wearing their national dress.

Liberation Day

Liberation Day (February 26) marks the end of the Gulf War and Iraqi aggression in Kuwait in 1991. It is not officially a holiday in Kuwait although most people treat it as one. The occasion is marked by public get-togethers, but there is a sombre overtone as people remember those that died during the occupation, and the 605 prisoners of war that were captured.

Regional Environment Day

ROPME, the Regional Organisation for the Protection of the Marine Environment, observes 24th April as the region's Environment Day in order to increase public awareness and renew the importance of protecting the environment, particularly the marine environment. There are regular themed art competitions with which the local schools get involved.

Exhibitions

Kuwait International Fairground (Map Ref 18-A3) holds a number of exhibitions throughout the year. For details of all planned exhibitions visit their website at www.kif.net

Raft Race

The annual raft race usually takes place at the Messila Beach Hotel, but has temporarily moved to the Aqua Park in front of the Kuwait Towers while a new hotel is built on the Messila site. Although a fun spectacle, the racing is taken very seriously indeed, with significant prize money at stake. It has even been known for some companies to hire or fire employees based on their performance! There are a number of different classes of rafts, and a series of heats are held before the final championship races take place at the end of the day. This is definitely not an event to be missed, and the day is rounded off with live entertainment and a BBQ. Held in April or May, you should keep an eye on the local media for the exact dates.

Main Annual Events – 2006/2007

January 2006

Feburary 2006

4 - 10	Info & Connect 2006
18 - 3	2nd International Consumer Festival
22 - 3	Kuwait Industries Exhibition
25	National Day
26	Liberation Day
tbc	Hala February Shopping Festival

March 2006

13 - 16	Education & Career Development Exhibition
20 - 31	Electro' 2006
22 - 31	Kuwait International Perfumes & Cosmetics Exhibition

April 2006

10	Prophet Mohammed's Birthday (1)*
19 - 28	Kuwait International Modern House Exhibition
19 - 28	MTC Carnival
24	Regional Environment Day
26 - 5	Kuwait International Trade Fair

May 2006

| 7 - 10 | Kuwait International Travel & Tourism Exhibition |
| 22 - 28 | Gold & Jewellery Exhibition |

June 2006

| 24 - 7 | Summer Carnival |

August 2006

| 22 | Ascension Day (1)* |
| 23 - 9 | School Stationery & Clothing Exhibition |

September 2006

| 13 - 22 | Kuwait Household Exhibition |
| 13 - 22 | Kuwait International Food Exhibition |

October 2006

| 11 - 21 | Ramadan & Eid Exhibition |
| 26 | Eid Al Fitr (3)* |

November 2006

| 8 - 17 | Green Gardens Exhibition |
| 22 - 1 | Gifts Exhibition |

December 2006

4 - 6	Info Biz - Business IT & Telecommunication Conference
16 - 22	Building & Reconstruction Exhibition
20 - 29	Autumn Perfumes Exhibition
20 - 29	Specialized Watches Exhibition
31	Eid Al Adha (4)*
tbc	Kuwait International 31st Arabic Books Exhibition

January 2007

tbc	New Year's Day (1)*
tbc	Eid Al Adha (4)*
tbc	Islamic New Year (1)*

Feburary 2007

25	National Day
26	Liberation Day
tbc	Hala February Shopping Festival

tbc – to be confirmed

Denotes public holidays

For more information on these events, see [p.42].

* Holidays dependant on the moon

General Info

Annual Events

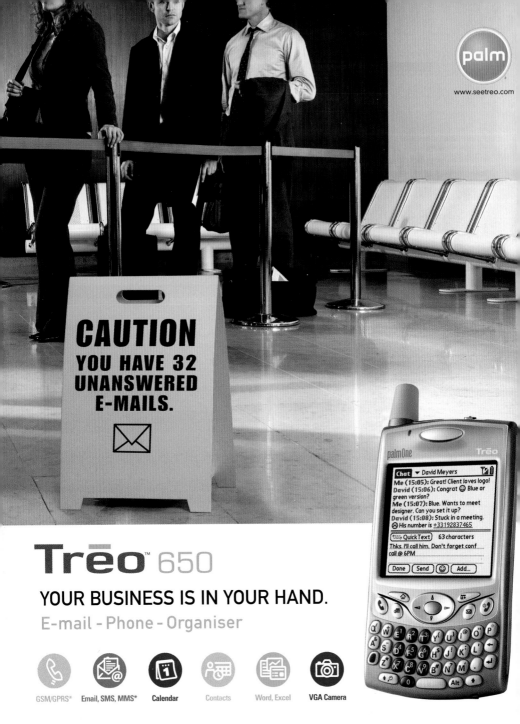

CAUTION
YOU HAVE 32
UNANSWERED
E-MAILS.

Trēo™ 650

YOUR BUSINESS IS IN YOUR HAND.

E-mail - Phone - Organiser

GSM/GPRS*   Email, SMS, MMS*   Calendar   Contacts   Word, Excel   VGA Camera

palm
www.seetreo.com

Available in Kuwait at branches of Yusuf Al Ghanim, Fono, Best Buy, Jarir Bookstore and AL Andalus.

Residents

EXPLORER

Highlights...

New to the GCC

[p.57]

If you're a new resident to Kuwait and want to familiarise yourself with your GCC neighbours or have done your Q8 time and are moving onto to pastures new, but not far, then the Explorer GCC *Complete Residents' Guide* series is a valuable source of information. Apart from the *Kuwait Explorer* you will find guides to living in Dubai, Abu Dhabi, Oman, Bahrain and Qatar. All of these guides are full of essential information, tips and tricks for living life to the full here in the Gulf.

Overview

Kuwait has progressed dramatically over the past forty years, especially over the last five. It is a country in which the most constant thing, apart from the sunshine, is change.

Policies change frequently and you will be shifted from pillar to post when dealing with the government ministries, whether you are getting your residence visa sorted out or arranging your medical tests. You should never assume that because you have read about a policy change in the media, it has actually taken place. With this in mind, the best piece of advice any newcomer should take is that you are a guest in the country; be patient!

A number of bureaucratic procedures still require the presence of the applicant, although in some circumstances the company 'mandoub' will be able to arrange all formalities without you tagging along. If you find that the going is getting tough and a little frustrating, a simple smile will help to move things along; voicing a negative opinion will result in further delays. When in the throes of processing your residence and/or work permit, it is sensible to always carry around all the documentation that you could possibly be asked for, just in case.

The Man Who Does

All companies have a 'mandoub', an employee usually of Arab or Indian descent, who has been with the company for a number of years, is usually registered with the Ministry of Interior and knows how the local bureaucracy works, including those all-important shortcuts. Make use of him and if his services aren't offered, ask him very politely for assistance.

More of the ministries are moving towards using the internet as a tool to provide a more efficient service. PACI (the Public Authority for Civil Information) has a website where you can renew your Civil ID card, in addition to checking the status of an application.

Remember that Kuwait is not Europe or America, and things are done differently and the bureaucracy is a small price to pay for the pleasure of living here.

In The Beginning...

The first step on the path to obtaining your residence permit if you are a non-GCC citizen, is to enter Kuwait on a valid visa, and be sponsored by a local company or a Kuwait citizen. Wives and children are usually sponsored by their husband or father.

There is no organisation in Kuwait dedicated to the processing of paperwork for new residents. The company mandoub or PRO (Public Relations Officer) will be responsible for processing most of the documentation and visiting the relevant ministerial offices.

A residence permit, which is issued in the form of a Civil ID card, is valid for an initial period of two years. It should be renewed prior to expiration and will require a visit to a PACI (Public Authority for Civil Information) office, or a visit to the PACI website at www.paci.gov.kw. It is also possible to call the PACI office on 889 988 between 14:00 – 22:00.

Once the renewal is carried out, the new Civil ID card will then have to be collected. On arrival at the PACI office, go straight to the Information desk and give them your Civil ID number. You will then be directed to one of the numbered dispensing machines into which you will need to insert KD 2 and your old Civil ID card and, hey presto, out will pop your new card!

It has always been common practice for expats to register with their embassy on arrival. Apart from the security aspect, embassy registration is a convenient way of establishing contacts when you first arrive, as you will usually be made aware of social groups and organisations of fellow expats meeting on regular occasions.

A labour card is not required, although a work visa is. Your Civil ID carries details of your sponsor, and must be kept up to date at all times.

Essential Documents

During the process of applying for your residence permit, make sure you have the following documents at all times. Procedures in Kuwait are such that you may need to produce an extra photograph or passport copy at short notice. The entire process will run far more efficiently if you have all the relevant documentation, and more, available at a moment's notice.

- Original Passport
- Passport copies showing the information page (including photograph) and the visa page
- Plenty of ID photographs in two sizes; 30 x 40mm and 35 x 45mm. The photographs must show the face clearly and without glasses

- Local currency in denominations of KD 1
- Birth certificate (for those born in Kuwait)

The company mandoub or PRO (Public Relations Officer) will have copies of all other documentation relating to the residence application, including medical certificates, blood certificates and the declaration signed by the company sponsor. Check with the PRO to establish whether you will be required to produce a security clearance certificate.

When signing a rent agreement you will be required to produce a copy of your Civil ID card. A basic savings account at a bank may be opened on presentation of your passport. Applications for loans and credit cards are to be accompanied by a copy of your Civil ID card and a salary certificate signed by your employer.

Documents

Entry Visa

Other options → Visas [p.20]

In order to begin the process of acquiring residence in Kuwait you are required to enter on either a residence visa or work permit.

You can also enter Kuwait on a temporary visa; these include visit, transit, business and multi-entry visas. Visitors entering Kuwait are required to have a passport valid for at least six months. Current visit visa regulations see the issue of a visa for a period of one month, with a maximum of two one-month extensions. However, this is likely to change to a visa being issued for an initial three-month period, with extensions possible to a maximum of one year.

All nationalities (except for GCC citizens) require a visa to enter Kuwait. For a list of the countries granted a visa on arrival, and a description of the different types of entry visas, refer to Entering Kuwait in General Information [p.20].

Entry Visa Regulations

- *Under current regulations a visit visa may be transferred to a work visa if the sponsor remains the same. A fee of KD 200 is payable.*
- *A commercial visit visa is for a maximum of one month; a private visit visa is valid for an initial period of three months.*

Lazy day at the dhow harbour

Health Card

Prior to a residence permit being issued or renewed, every expat is obliged to pay a government health insurance premium in return for a health card (the sponsoring company will usually complete this process). The cost of KD 50 (KD 40 for a spouse and KD 30 per child) is met by the sponsoring company, which is obliged to pay by law. Possession of this health card will ensure that you are able to receive medical treatment at any government hospital or clinic, on payment of KD 2 per visit, and be exempt from paying the daily in-patient charges. Free treatment includes x-rays, operations, laboratory tests and medicines; however, payment is required for specialised tests including MRI and CT scans. Nevertheless the costs are still heavily subsidised.

On receipt of a Civil ID card an expat must visit the governorate (municipality) building in their area, or an immigration office, to obtain a health card. These cards, which are issued on the spot, contain a person's medical history. Application requirements are:

- Two 30 x 40mm colour photographs
- Original Civil ID
- KD 1

Residence Visa

Other options → Visas [p.20]

All expats wishing to work and reside in Kuwait are obliged to obtain a residence permit ('iqama'). GCC citizens and expats who have been resident in Kuwait continually for a minimum period of 20 years may sponsor themselves if they can prove that they have the means to do so.

Work Permits

Work permits are either obtained under Article 17 (public sector) or 18 (private sector) of the Kuwait Labour Law (see Labour Law [p.55]). The process, which may be slightly amended at any time, tends to proceed as follows:

An offer of employment is made by an employer (sponsor), and accepted. The sponsor then has to apply to the Ministry of Social Affairs and Labour (MSA&L) to receive a work permit.

Employers in the private sector then present a copy of the employee's passport to the Criminal Investigation Department in order to obtain a No Objection Certificate (NOC). In certain circumstances some nationalities may also be required to obtain a certificate of good conduct from the relevant authorities in their home country.

When the sponsor receives a copy of the work permit from the MSA&L it is then sent to the employee in his home country who has to submit it to the local Kuwait embassy for endorsing, prior to an entry visa being applied for and issued. The employee has to obtain a medical certificate from a doctor or clinic, recognised by the Kuwait embassy, confirming that he is fit to work and does not suffer from tuberculosis or HIV/AIDS. If there is no Kuwait embassy representation in the employee's home country, the sponsor will obtain an entry permit from the Ministry of Interior in Kuwait and have it sent to the employee.

If an employee is in Kuwait on a visit visa when he signs his employment contract he will need to leave the country and obtain a medical certificate, as above, before returning on an entry visa. In this instance, if the employee cannot travel to his home country, his sponsor will more than likely send him to Bahrain to obtain the necessary certificate.

On arriving in Kuwait on an entry visa the employee will need to undergo further tests at the Ports and Borders Health Division in Shuwaikh, located in the Ministry of Health building in Gamul Abdul Nasser Street. This includes additional testing for tuberculosis and HIV/AIDS, as well as a chest x-ray, and tests for hepatitis, malaria and typhoid. Carriers of any of these diseases will not be issued with a work or residence permit and will be deported immediately. Make sure that you are taken through this process by your company mandoub or PRO; it is a little frustrating and stressful trying to work your way through the systems alone.

The next step in the process of getting your residency is to obtain security clearance and have your fingerprints taken at one of the four fingerprinting departments located in Ahmadi, Farwaniya, Jahra and Sharq.

On completion of these formalities the residence application can finally be submitted to the Immigration and Passport Department of the Ministry of Interior in Shuwaikh. A residence permit will be for a maximum period of five years, at a cost of KD 10 per year. Public sector employees are required to pay these costs, while employees in the private sector usually have the costs met by their employer, although this is not mandatory.

> **Gone too Long...**
>
> *Should a resident be out of Kuwait for a period of six continuous months or more, their residence visa will be cancelled without notification. Exceptions are made for those studying or receiving medical treatment abroad. However, permission will have to be obtained before you leave.*

Dependants' Visas

On receipt of his residence permit, a man earning a minimum monthly salary of KD 250 may sponsor his wife, parents and children. Daughters, wives and parents may be sponsored indefinitely, while sons may only be sponsored as dependants until they reach the age of 21. Dependants may not work unless they have a valid work permit. All dependants must undergo medical testing and fingerprinting, apart from babies born in Kuwait. Dependants' visas cost KD 10 per year, in addition to an initial charge of KD 100. An expatriate woman is not able to sponsor her husband, although she may sponsor her dependants if her husband is deceased or not resident in Kuwait.

The minimum monthly salary of KD 250 required in order to sponsor dependants does not apply to a wide number of professions, including lawyers, doctors, pharmacists, lecturers, teaching staff, engineers, clerics, librarians, nurses, reporters, graduate accountants, sports coaches, pilots, flight attendants, and those working in cemeteries.

Domestic Servants' Visas

An expat family resident in Kuwait may sponsor only one full-time domestic employee. Single men are not permitted to employ female servants. It is a requirement of the law that, in order for a man to sponsor a maid, he must have his wife and children living with him. Only maids between the ages of 20 and 50 may be sponsored and the documentation listed overleaf is required.

- Sponsor's original passport and Civil ID card and photocopies of both
- Sponsor's wife's original passport and Civil ID card and photocopies of both
- Sponsor's children's original passports and photocopies
- Sponsor's salary certificate
- Sponsor's rent agreement
- Domestic employee's original passport and photocopy, and eight photographs (max size 40 x 50mm; min size 35 x 45mm)
- Domestic employee's employment contract
- The residence permit costs KD 10 per year in addition to an initial charge of KD 200

Transfer of Residence to Another Sponsor

It is possible to transfer from one sponsor to another on the condition that an employee has been legally resident in Kuwait for a minimum of two years. However, a transfer requires that the current sponsor agrees to 'release' the employee. One regularly hears of employers refusing to allow employees to transfer, resulting in them either staying on in their current employment or having their residence visa cancelled and having to leave Kuwait. It is essential to maintain good relations with your current employer so that he/she agrees to the transfer. A signed release letter, and a copy of the current employer's commercial licence, will need to be submitted to the Immigration Department in Shuwaikh. A new work permit costs KD 2 and there is a KD 10 transfer fee. Laws governing the issue and transfer of residence and work permits do change from time to time, and you are strongly advised to have an understanding of all that is involved prior to resigning from your original job.

New Passports

Whether your passport expires, or you run out of space and need a new one, your residence permit will have to be transferred from the old passport to the new one. Once the new passport has been issued it will need to be submitted to the Passport Office in Shuwaikh with the following:

- Previous/expired passport
- Four photographs (max size 40 x 50mm; min size 35 x 45mm)
- Confirmation letter from your sponsor
- Copies of documentation required to process the original residence application

- KD 10

If everything is in order your residence permit will be transferred into your new passport immediately.

Civil ID Cards

You will have 30 days, from the issue date of your residence permit, in which to obtain the compulsory Civil ID card, which is valid for a period of two years and must be renewed prior to expiry. It includes your Civil ID number, visa type and sponsor's name, photograph, your name, date of birth, blood group and residential address. The information on the card must always be kept current. Keep a photocopy of your Civil ID somewhere safe. Should it be lost you will be required to produce a copy prior to collecting a new card. The number on your card is yours for life, irrespective of whether you change sponsors or leave Kuwait only to return a few years later.

Applications must be made in person to the Public Authority for Civil Information (PACI) office, which is located within the Ministries Complex in South Surra (off the 6th Ring Road and opposite the Ministry of Electricity & Water). To process the initial application the following documentation is required:

> **Old Passports**
>
> *When visiting your embassy to have a new passport issued make sure they don't cancel the page to which your residence is affixed. Should this happen your residence will more than likely be cancelled by the Department of Immigration.*

- Original passport and photocopy of information pages (including photo page) and residence stamp
- Four photographs, 30 x 40mm, clearly showing the face without glasses (for applicants over 11)
- Security Clearance form (for applicants over 16)
- Original birth certificate, if born in Kuwait
- Blood group certificate (for applicants over 5)
- Proof of residential address in Kuwait (rent agreement)
- Declaration signed by the sponsor
- KD 2 (payable when the card is collected)

Processing takes about ten days; call 889 988 between 14:00 and 22:00 or use the PACI website (www.paci.gov.kw) to check on the status of your application. As soon as the Civil ID card has been issued, you will need to return to PACI to collect it. On arrival, go to the information counter and ascertain which of the numbered vending machines holds your card. Pay your KD 2 into the machine and your card will appear in a couple of seconds.

Renewal of Civil ID Cards

An e-government project initiative now means that Civil ID cards may be renewed by telephone, although the new card will have to be physically collected. This is a big step forward for Kuwait and removes a substantial amount of paperwork. Civil ID cards must be renewed within 30 days of renewing your residency. A fine of KD 100 is payable for all late renewals, irrespective of the length of the delay. The procedure to renew is as follows:

1. Dial 88 99 88 between 14:00 and 22:00 from your mobile, land line or international line (including the country code) if you are out of the country.

2. Enter your Civil ID number.

3. Your card will be renewed automatically and you will have to collect your card from the PACI office. On arrival, proceed to the information desk and ask which of the electronic dispensing machines contains your card (they are numbered). You will then need to insert KD 2 into the relevant machine, as well as your old Civil ID, in order to have your renewed Civil ID released.

Replacement of a Lost Civil ID Card

To have a replacement card issued you will have to visit the PACI office in person, with a photocopy of the lost Civil ID and your original passport. The cost is KD 10.

Kuwait's Free Trade Zone

Free Zones

There is currently one Free Trade Zone (FTZ) in Kuwait, located adjacent to Shuwaikh Port. An additional FTZ has been planned at the Abdali border post on the Iraqi border.

Unlike some other regions in the Gulf (such as Dubai), regulations for working in the free zone are no different to those regarding working elsewhere in Kuwait.

Certificates & Licences

Driving Licence

Other options → Transportation [p.85]

The legal age for driving in Kuwait is 18. GCC Nationals must hold a valid GCC licence, while expatriates may drive on an International Driving Permit (IDP), but only for the duration of a visit visa, and only if local insurance has been arranged. Once a residence permit has been issued it becomes illegal to drive on an IDP and a Kuwait driving licence must be obtained. Temporary licences also exist for those who have arrived in Kuwait and are in the process of applying for their residence permit.

Expatriates from the UK, US and France may obtain a 10-year Kuwait driving licence on the strength of their national licence. All other nationalities will have to apply for a learner's test and then take a driving test and written examination. A maximum of three attempts at obtaining a driving licence is permitted. Please note that when your residence permit expires, your driving licence is immediately invalid.

The following documentation is required in order to get a Kuwait permanent driving licence:

- Original passport and copies of pages containing personal information (including photograph page)
- Original Civil ID card and copy
- Original driving licence (for those nationalities able to obtain a licence on the strength of their national licence) and a copy of the original licence certified by the respective embassy
- Letter from sponsor confirming your home address and your status ie. employee or dependant
- Proof of residential address eg. rent agreement or utility bill

Residents

Certificates & Licences

- Blood type certificate (use the paperwork issued when your medical tests were carried out)
- Eye test certificate (for drivers over 50 and those wearing glasses)
- Four colour photographs (20 x 30mm)
- KD 15

You will need to have your licence translated, if it is not in Arabic. The translation will require attestation at your embassy at a cost of approximately KD 15. The next step is to visit the Ministry of Foreign Affairs where the document will require further attestation; this time at a cost of KD 4. Once this is complete all of the documentation should be presented to the traffic department in the governorate (municipality) where you live. The application form at the traffic department needs to be completed in Arabic so make sure that you take an Arabic speaker with you. The blood type certificate and eye test certificate are required for the permanent driving licence. All eye tests are carried out at the Ministry of Health clinic in Qortuba (you will need to collect the form from your local traffic department).

Should you not be eligible to simply convert your licence you will need to pay a visit to the licence section of the main traffic department in Shuwaikh. The first step is to obtain approval for the learner's licence. For some, this requires that you have been legally resident in Kuwait for a period of two years and are earning a minimum monthly salary of KD 250. A number of people are exempt from these restrictions though, so please check with your local traffic department.

On receipt of the learners' licence approval you will then need to go to the traffic department in your local governorate with all of the above documentation. Purchase a KD 10 stamp, which needs to be submitted with the application form, make sure that you have had an eye test and have a blood type certificate, and pay the KD 10 booking fee for a driving test. An additional KD 10 is payable on the date of the test.

Licence Renewal

Renewal of the ten-year licence usually takes a day. Return to the issuing traffic department with the application form, your passport and Civil ID (and copies of both), the original expired driving licence and three colour photographs (20 x 30mm). The renewal process costs KD 10. All drivers over the age of 50 are obliged to undergo an eye test whenever a licence is renewed. A licence will be renewed for a further five years for those between

the ages of 50 and 55, three to five years for those aged 56 – 59, and drivers aged 60 or over are required to renew their licences every three years.

Driving Schools	
Al Hamdan Driving School	391 1921
Ali Naser Driving School	391 1669
Kuwait Motoring School	481 7176
Salmiya Driving School	575 0498

Birth Certificate & Registration

It is a criminal offence for a baby to be born in Kuwait to unwed parents. A copy of your marriage certificate is required prior to admission to a hospital.

It is a time-consuming process registering the birth of a baby. The process must be correctly followed to avoid complications and subsequent delays. Following the birth of a baby a hospital will issue a notification of birth, in Arabic. You will need to submit this notification, together with a completed birth certificate application form, copies of the parents' passports and Civil ID cards and an attested copy of the parents' marriage certificate to the governorate (municipal) office of the area in which the hospital is located. The birth is recorded in the register and an Arabic birth certificate will be issued after about a week. Prior to having the birth registered, ask an Arabic-speaking friend to write the translation of the child's name in order to ensure that it is correctly entered into the register.

To obtain Kuwait residence the child must be issued with a new passport, or added to the parents' passport. A translated copy of the birth certificate is to be submitted to your embassy. Please note that some embassies will require that the translated birth certificate is certified by the Kuwait Ministry of Foreign Affairs.

As soon as the passport is issued an application must be made for a residence permit. The process is the same as that for any other dependant, although infants born in Kuwait do not need to undergo medical tests and fingerprinting. The application for residence must be made within 60 days of the birth. Failure to do so will result in a KD 200 fine.

Children born in Kuwait automatically assume the citizenship of their father. Expatriate children have no claim to Kuwait citizenship and will not hold dual passports.

Marriage Certificate & Registration

Expats are able to get married in Kuwait. Prior to the ceremony being performed the Kuwait authorities require a Certificate of No Impediment (CNI) to confirm that you have not been previously married, or that your previous marriage has been legally terminated. These certificates are obtained in person from your embassy. You will be required to give notice to your embassy and show that you have been legally resident in Kuwait for a minimum of 21 days.

Civil weddings take place on Sundays and Wednesdays in the Ministry of Justice Building, which is located in the Ministries Complex in Soor Street, on the Ground Floor of Block 15. The couple should be accompanied by two adult male witnesses and should produce the following documentation at the information counter:

- CNIs for both bride and groom
- Civil ID cards of bride, groom and both witnesses
- Original passports and photocopies

The form will then be completed in Arabic, and you will be sent to the Typing Room to have the marriage contract typed in Arabic. On returning to the information counter the information will be verified and you are then required to wait your turn in front of the judge. On completion of the formalities, at a cost of under KD 5, you will now be legally married in Kuwait.

Registration of the marriage in your own country will require translation and attestation by the Ministry of Foreign Affairs prior to being accepted by your embassy.

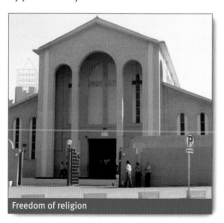
Freedom of religion

Church weddings are available in Kuwait with slightly differing legal formalities. Weddings conducted in both St Paul's and the Roman Catholic churches in Ahmadi may simply be recorded at the General Register's Office. A couple married in the Evangelical church will also be required to undergo a civil ceremony. In order for a Marriage Contract signed in a church to be recognised, it needs to be signed by a Notary at the Ministry of Justice. In addition to the above documents the Marriage Contract will have to be produced.

All Muslim weddings are held at the General Courts in the Palace of Justice in Fahad Al Salem Street, Kuwait City. Under Islamic Law a Muslim woman is obliged to marry a Muslim man. A Muslim man, on the other hand, may marry a non-Muslim.

Death Certificate & Registration

Should a death occur the police will need to be contacted immediately, followed by the respective embassy. Formal identification will have to take place and the body will then be transported to one of the mortuaries located in the major government hospitals. A coroner will examine the body to determine the cause of death prior to issuing the death certificate. Should a death have occurred at any place other than a hospital, police clearance will be required to confirm that the death was of natural causes. The coroner's report is then taken to the Central Registry for Births and Deaths in order to have a death certificate issued.

The body will be transported from the hospital to the cemetery by ambulance. There are two cemeteries in Kuwait in which a non-Muslim burial may be carried out – Sulaibikhat and Riqqa. Burials are conducted at no cost (cremation is prohibited under Islamic law). There are small offices located at the cemeteries; it is here that you will find out about burial details, including headstones.

Should the next of kin wish to have an expatriate's body repatriated, the death certificate will have to be attested by the Ministry of Health, Ministry of Foreign Affairs, and the police. A home country death certificate will be issued by the respective embassy on presentation of a translated, attested copy of the Kuwait death certificate. The passport of the deceased will be cancelled and the body can then be shipped home using one of a number of forwarding agents that your embassy can recommend.

Work

Working in Kuwait

Kuwait has a large population of expats working in both the public and private sector. Being able to speak Arabic is advantageous but not a prerequisite, as most industries make use of both Arabic and English in their day-to-day operations. There are no specific restrictions for working in Kuwait ie. you do not need to hold a degree to be issued with a work permit. Private sector companies rarely, if ever, offer share option schemes to expatriates. Working for an international company will sometimes mean that you are paid in a foreign currency, such as US dollars.

Accommodation allowances and annual airfares home, although generally included in employment contracts, are not mandatory.

Find out whether your employer offers any sort of medical insurance. If there is any chance of you being required to travel to Iraq, it is absolutely imperative that you are covered by fully comprehensive medical and life insurance.

Working Hours

From September 2007, the working week will be Saturday to Thursday. Currently, many firms work Sunday to Wednesday, with some insisting on a five and a half day week. Friday is always a day off. Working hours are either a single shift from 08:00/09:00 - 17:00/18:00, with a break for lunch, or a split shift, beginning in the morning from 08:00/09:00 and working until 12:00/13:00, then returning at 15:00/16:00 and finishing at 19:00/20:00.

Ministry hours are from 07:00 - 14:00. According to Kuwait Labour Law an employee is entitled to 14 days leave after completing a year of employment. Many employers are flexible on this in that you may be able to take leave prior to the completion of a year. Private international businesses generally give 30 days' leave per year. Before you sign your employment contract make sure that the leave period is understood. The 30 days' leave is usually calendar days and a vast majority of companies have a rather unscrupulous way of working out the dates, which often means that you are cheated out of a day or two. All public holidays are set by the government. Although religious holidays are set according to the phases of the moon, they may be adjusted by a day or two according to government regulations. If working for an American firm you will usually enjoy American public holidays as well as the Kuwait/Islamic holidays.

Finding Work

Employees in Kuwait are either recruited internationally or come to Kuwait looking for opportunities. The job market is buoyant so work is available. Make use of the recruitment agencies and newspaper adverts, but also tell everyone that you know, and meet, that you are looking for a job. Deliver CVs to prospective employers but remember that they possibly receive a multitude each month; yours will need to stand out to receive attention. If you have submitted your CV directly to a private firm follow it up with a phone call to ascertain whether you will have any chance of being offered a position. Not all firms will request the completion of an application form.

Minimum Wage

MaKuwait's Minister of Social Affairs recently announced plans to set a minimum wage for expat workers hired to work for government contracts. The KD50 minimum monthly wage will make a big differences for the hundreds of thousands of expat workers in the country who have struggled to make ends meet.

Whilst a number of jobs are advertised in the daily newspapers and on recruitment company websites, a large percentage of recruitment in Kuwait is based on word of mouth and personal recommendations.

Communicate with recruitment agencies to find out how they operate. Most of them prefer to receive e-mails or online applications, and may not see you if you appear at their office unannounced. The agent will collect a commission from the firm for whom they are filling vacant positions; they should not ask you for any payment whatsoever. You may be asked by more unscrupulous, unprofessional firms to pay a registration fee, but don't.

Kuwaitisation is a word that you will hear from time to time. It refers to a government initiative to get the younger citizens of Kuwait into the job market. All private sector companies are required

Keeping your Passport

Employers often insist on holding an employee's passport for 'safe-keeping'. You are advised against handing over this personal document. Doing so will mean that you are unable to travel in an emergency and you may face difficulties getting it back. If you are threatened in anyway seek the advice of your embassy. The residence permit will be affixed to your passport.

by law to employ Kuwait citizens. The percentage of Kuwait employees required differs from one industry to another.

Kuwait's expat communities are very close knit, and gossip circulates fast. You would be foolish to bad mouth anyone in a conversation, especially when talking to someone that you don't know very well.

Recruitment Agencies	
Bayt	461 0450
Heston	80 8182
Kuwait Recruitment Bureau	247 0850
Prolinks Kuwait	265 8036
SOS Recruitment	241 6107

Voluntary & Charity Work

There are opportunities to get involved in volunteer and/or charity work. Apart from the likes of the Red Crescent Society there are a number of ladies' groups in Kuwait who continue to carry out excellent charity work. These organisations are always looking for additional volunteers. No academic qualifications are required.

Organisations include the Kuwait Association for the Care of Children in Hospital (KACCH, 246 4723), the Kuwait Red Crescent Society (481 5478), the Society for the Handicapped (263 1510), Kuwait Blind Association (565 4105) and the animal welfare societies, PAWS (944 0089) and Animal Friends League (700 1622).

Business Groups & Contacts

Groups such as the British Business Forum and American Business Council are very useful for making business contacts and networking. Regular meetings are held, usually once a month at least.

Kuwait society is very close knit and personal connections play a very important role in carrying out business. A businessman arriving in Kuwait for the first time will invariably find things a little trying. Business appointments do not always take place on time and you will often find yourself waiting around while the person you are expecting to meet concludes other business. In addition, your visit may be continually interrupted as the person you are meeting receives additional visitors and consults with his staff. This is an unavoidable aspect of business and you should not show any negativity towards it. Never lose your temper or publicly make

a derogatory remark. Doing so will cause immense embarrassment and the person whom you have offended will have suffered a loss of face, the implications of which can be considerable.

You will regularly hear the word 'wasta' being used, the direct translation of which means 'influence'. Wasta is used every day and should not be associated with the term 'bribe'. As with other countries and nationalities, Kuwaitis will use their personal contacts and connections to their advantage.

Business Councils & Groups	
The American Business Council	564 3149
The British Business Forum	684 1114
Indian Business Council	253 0600

Employment Contracts

Always insist on a written employment contact. Most international companies issue your contract in English; however, it is possible that your copy will be in Arabic (the Arabic document is referred to in cases of dispute).

Do not be pressurised into signing an employment contract, and never sign it on the spot. If you are given an Arabic contract, don't sign it until someone you trust has given it the once-over.

A standard employee contract should include the following information as a minimum; job title and description, start date, salary and bonuses, period of employment (if the contract is for a specific term), notice period and leave entitlement. Negotiable items include an accommodation allowance, annual flight allowance, health insurance and school fees. Probation is for a maximum of three months.

Maternity leave is not always included in private sector contracts. As per the local labour law, a woman is entitled to maternity leave for a maximum period of 30 days prior to delivery and 40 days post delivery, on full pay. She may, for medical reasons and on submission of a medical certificate, be absent for a further 100 days with no pay.

Labour Law

The Ministry of Social Affairs & Labour (MSA&L) is the government body responsible for all aspects of the labour law and has three separate laws covering employment in Kuwait; one each for government employees, oil sector employees and private sector employees.

Those who are working in Kuwait on temporary contracts for a period of less than six months, as well as those employed as domestic servants, are not covered by the private sector labour laws.

All international firms are governed by the law of the country in which their head office is located, unless they have a branch office in Kuwait whereby Kuwait law will apply.

An employer is obliged to provide written notice of its intention to terminate an employment contract. A notice period is required. Should the employer not wish the employee to work the notice period they are required to pay the salary for that period. An employee wishing to leave a company is required to work a notice period. Failure to do so may jeopardise your rights. Any disputes between an employer and employee, if they cannot be resolved internally, may be submitted to the MSA&L through one of the six offices (located in each governorate). The MSA&L will determine whether the employee should pursue a claim and will bring the two parties together in an effort to settle the matter amicably. Should a settlement not be reached within two weeks of the matter originally being reported to the MSA&L, the matter will be directed to the labour court with all supporting documentation. A court (hearing) date will be fixed within three working days. Court fees for labour cases are not usually payable. However, in situations where the employee loses the case it may be required to pay a nominal fee to cover the costs of bringing the case to court. An employee must file a case with the MSA&L within one year of his employment being terminated.

You do have the option of acquiring the services of a lawyer to deal with your labour dispute. Although this will usually improve the outcome of your case, it is an expensive process for which you will be charged, unless of course you win your case and the judge rules that the employer is liable for all costs.

Labour unions do exist, although they are very tightly controlled. Employees are only permitted to be a member of one union at a time, they must be at least 18 years of age, and have been in Kuwait, and employed on a valid work permit, for a minimum of 5 consecutive years.

Copies of the Kuwait Labour Laws are available at all good bookshops, at a cost of KD 10.

'Banning'

If you are on a fixed employment contract which comes to an end, and there is no opportunity to have it extended, your residence permit and work permit will be cancelled. There are instances in which your employer may be willing to transfer your residence to another sponsor by signing a release; however, there will often be restrictions such as not being able to compete in the same industry for a period of six months to a year. The degree to which you will have a problem does sometimes depend on your nationality; unskilled labour and junior staff will often have no choice but to leave Kuwait. However, Senior management staff stand a very good chance of resolving such a situation amicably.

> ### Read the Small Print
> Check what you agree to in your employment contract, as this supersedes the local labour law. If you sign your contract agreeing to refrain from working in the same industry for a specified period after you leave the company, you will be obliged to honour your agreement even though the local labour law does not enable employers to ban employees from taking positions with competitors..

If an employer is not willing to transfer your residence and work permits to another sponsor, and you have been offered another position, your best course of action is to leave the country and come back in on new paperwork. Use the opportunity to go home for a break, or take advantage of the proximity of Bahrain and travel there and back in a day.

There are employers who will have no qualms about cancelling your paperwork and ensuring that you are on the next plane back home, but they are not in the majority. Leaving on good terms is essential for maintaining relations which will prove beneficial in the long term. Should you wish to stay on in Kuwait, it would be wise to look into the processes required to do so well in advance of your present employment contract expiring. Regulations do change frequently so it is essential to discuss the matter with someone who has inside knowledge of the workings of the Ministry of Immigration, whether it be the company mandoub or another contact.

An employer may not cancel an employee's residence and work permit prior to paying him all outstanding monies and indemnities.

Meetings

It is nearly impossible trying to get through to a point of contact at any of the Ministries, unless you have a direct or mobile phone number. Kuwaitis prefer to conduct business meetings in person.

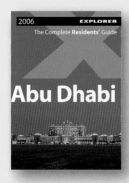
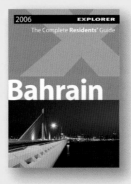

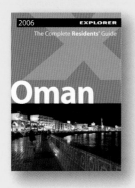
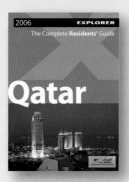

Hospitality is a key aspect of business and meetings will begin with pleasantries and the offer of refreshments. Always accept a glass of tea or a cup of coffee when offered; it would be impolite to refuse. Should the invitation to partake in refreshments not be forthcoming you can pretty much guarantee that the person you are meeting has no interest in your products or services.

Business in Kuwait is carried out in a gentle, unhurried manner. Kuwaitis will take their time to evaluate meetings and proposals, although when a decision has been made there will be no time wasted in concluding a deal. After an initial meeting, regular visits will need to be made in order to create a long-term relationship.

Always carry business cards with you. It would be beneficial to have an Arabic translation of the details printed on the reverse.

Never refuse an invitation to attend a 'diwaniya' as it is an excellent way in which to meet Kuwaiti businessmen. You should be aware that it is considered extremely impolite to ask a Kuwaiti man about his wife and family.

Business seminars and conferences do take place but not quite as frequently as they do in other GCC countries such as the UAE. The majority of international businessmen visit Kuwait from other Middle Eastern countries and the US, and Kuwait is used as the primary point of entry for entering Iraq.

Company Closure

There is an element of risk when accepting a job with a start-up company. Do your research before you sign an employment contract; find out if the firm has partnerships or agreements with other (larger) firms and establish whether they have won any contracts.

Having said that, it is quite a process to register a company in Kuwait, therefore the chances of the owners operating a fly-by-night operation are small. Should the company become insolvent while you are employed, your employer will have to pay you any outstanding money prior to paying creditors. If you are in any doubt as to your position, seek the assistance of a lawyer.

The Ministry of Social Affairs and Labour does make allowances for employees of companies that are closing down. You will be permitted to transfer your work permit and residence permit only on presentation of an attested certificate of closure of the company, which is issued by the local court.

Financial & Legal Affairs

Bank Accounts

The banking sector is currently dominated by local banks, although the government is in the process of issuing licences to international banks. A number of the local banks offer services akin to those found in most international banks worldwide, including savings and current accounts, credit cards, and loan facilities. Online banking is offered, although the quality of this service varies considerably from one bank to another.

> **No Bouncing**
>
> It is a criminal offence to issue a cheque when there are insufficient funds in the account. A bounced cheque is taken very seriously and will usually result in arrest.

Bank charges vary slightly from bank to bank but expect to pay 200 fils per withdrawal if you use a bank card in an ATM (cash machine) from another bank (use of your own bank's ATMs is free). A minimum deposit of KD 100 is required in order to open a savings account. Should the balance fall below KD 100 you will be charged KD 2 per month.

Credit cards are issued on approval and you will need to hold an account at the bank, into which your salary is transferred every month. Credit limits will depend on your salary and whether your company has been approved by the bank in question. Monthly repayments are approximately 8.33%.

> **Electronic Banking**
>
> A number of the commercial banks provide services including internet banking and SMS banking, where the bank will SMS you to advise of deposits and other balance changes.

Current accounts, although not common, are available. Approval will need to be obtained from the bank manager. The minimum balance is between KD 200 and KD 500, and accounts are available in either US dollars, pounds sterling, euros or Kuwait dinars. A 25 page chequebook costs KD 2.

Banks are open Saturday to Wednesday, although a few branches do open on Thursdays. Banking hours are generally from 08:00 – 13:00. Evening openings are generally from 17:00 – 19:00.

Financial Planning

Most expats come to work in Kuwait to save money. Having a financial planner may help you make the most of your earnings and maximise your savings.

Downtown Kuwait

Terminal Gratuity

The terminal gratuity (indemnity) is a payment made to an employee when employment is terminated. The amount is based on 15 days remuneration for every complete year worked (for the first five years), and 30 days for every additional year, up to a maximum indemnity of one and a half years' remuneration.

There are a number of financial advisers in Kuwait, most of whom will find you before you find them! There is no regulatory body for financial advisers operating in Kuwait so try to find a professional with a good reputation, or find out whether any of the big international firms have local representation. Expats have been stung by advisers offering advice which suits them, not the client, with the result that the client unnecessarily loses money. Take advice from expats who are long-term residents – they will hopefully know who to trust.

It is important to get yourself a good tax adviser who can advise you on the tax implications of any income in your home country, as well as give you advice on the repatriation of funds.

There are no expat pension schemes operating in Kuwait, although the labour law provides for an end-of-service gratuity, which is an agreeable substitute.

There are no offshore banking options. Most expats manage offshore accounts in tax havens around the world. Expats cannot invest in property directly.

Government discussions regarding the introduction of a personal income tax for expats regularly take place, although there are no immediate plans for this to come into effect .

Taxation

Neither personal income tax, municipal/government tax nor community tax are levied in Kuwait. Hotels add an additional 15% 'service charge' to all accommodation and food bills.

Legal Issues

Kuwait follows the civil law system. Islamic Sharia forms a major source of law, although it is not the exclusive source – laws do not have to conform to Sharia in order to become part of the constitution.

There are three tiers to the court system; the Court of First Instance is the first step in the process, followed by the Court of Appeal, and the Court of Cassation. Court proceedings are conducted in Arabic. Kuwait is a democracy and the constitution

Cost of Living

Beach club	KD 5+
Big Mac	KD 1.150
Bread (large loaf)	150 fils
Bus (Airport to Kuwait City)	250 fils
Cappuccino	KD 1
Car rental (compact)	KD 9/day
Catamaran hire	KD 7.5/hour
Chocolate bar	100 fils
Cigarettes (packet of 20)	400 fils
Cinema ticket	KD 2.500
Eggs (dozen)	850 fils
Falafel	250 fils
Film	KD 1
Film processing (colour, 36 exposures)	KD 4.800
Fishing (4 hours)	KD 100
Fresh meat	750 fils/kg+
Hair cut (female)	KD 5+
Hair cut (male)	KD 1+
Imported fresh fruit	950 fils/kg+
Laserquest hire	KD 5/hour
Milk 1 litre	480 fils
Museum	Free
Park	Free
Postcard	100 fils
Shwarma	250 fils
Sugar	KD 1/10kg
Taxi (Airport to Kuwait City)	KD 5
Taxi (Airport to Salmiya)	KD 5
Taxi (Kuwait City to Ahmadi)	KD 4.500
Tin of tuna	240 fils
Water 1.5 litres – hotel	750 fils
Water 1.5 litres – supermarket	150 fils

guarantees fundamental rights and freedoms, a number of which are governed by law.

It is unusual to hear of a violent crime being committed. Petty theft does exist but is not prolific. Kuwait has extremely strict laws regarding drugs and they are actively enforced. Anyone found importing narcotics will be liable to prosecution, and anyone caught and convicted of trafficking drugs will be subject to the death penalty. Severe punishments, including the death penalty, are dealt to those convicted of committing murder and rape.

Car accidents are very common in Kuwait. It is a criminal offence to flee the scene of an accident and doing so will result in a jail term, a fine, and ultimately, deportation. From time to time drivers

You Booze You Lose

The importation and consumption of alcohol is strictly prohibited. Should you be found in possession of large quantities of alcohol there is every chance that you will be penalised. Alcohol is confiscated at all ports of entry.

AL SARRAF & AL RUWAYEH

Attorneys & Legal Consultants
In Association With sh Stephenson Harwood

Gate 1, 3rd Floor, Salhiya Commercial Complex
P. O. Box 1448, Safat 13015, Kuwait
Tel: (965) 240 0061/2/3 Fax: (965) 240 0064
Email: asar@asarlegal.com
Web: www.asarlegal.com
Contact: Sam Habbas

The Firm:

Al-Sarraf & Al-Ruwayeh was established in 1977 and is the largest law firm in Kuwait and one of the largest in the Middle East with strong connections throughout the Gulf. It serves as counsel for many local and international public and private sector agencies and businesses, as well as for select families and individuals.

Stephenson Harwood, with whom Al-Sarraf & Al-Ruwayeh has had a relationship since 1991, is an international law firm based in London with around 70 partners and more than 500 staff worldwide.

The goal of the association is to ensure its clients receive only the highest quality of legal services in Kuwait or abroad.

Areas of Practice:

Agencies & Distributorships, Corporate and Commercial, International Banking, Finance and Capital Markets, Franchising, Construction, Government Contracts, Foreign Investment, Litigation and Advocacy, Real Estate, Insurance, Shipping, Securities, Taxation, International Arbitration, Intellectual Property, Oil and Gas Industry, Projects and Privatization, Capital Markets and Securities, General International Trade Law, Private Client Services, Regulatory Law and Iraq Reconstruction.

Members:

Hameed Al Sarraf, Ahmed Al Ruwayeh, Sam Habbas, Ahmed Barakat, Rob Little.

Associates:

Ahmed Zakaria, Paul Day, Hossam Abdullah, Kenton Gray, Hudhairam H. Rasheedi, Safwat Fahmi, Hisham Al-Qura'an, Edlyn Verzola, Arfan Tinawi, Mohamed Khodeir, Stephen Nelson, Paul Waltner, David Walker, Ibrahim Sattout.

Other Offices:
Bahrain.

Associated Offices:

London, Paris, Hong Kong, Shanghai, Guangzhou, Piraeus, Singapore.

Languages:

English, Arabic and French.

are caught driving under the influence of alcohol, resulting in a custodial sentence and deportation.

An area in which you may find yourself in need of a lawyer is in a labour dispute.

Ramadan Law

Anyone caught breaking the fast between dawn and dusk during the holy month of Ramadan, irrespective of their religion or nationality, will find themselves sitting in jail for the remainder of the month. The only exceptions are for pregnant women, young children, and those travelling. Hotels usually have one restaurant open for visitors to Kuwait and will provide room service for the duration of Ramadan. Most companies with expatriate staff do allow their staff to discreetly enjoy a quick lunch or tea break on the premise as long as they do so in a confined area, out of sight of their Muslim colleagues.

Divorce Law

Approximately 35% of all Kuwaiti marriages in 2003 ended in divorce. Reasons included jealousy, family interference and mistreatment. The government has subsequently set up a counselling office in an attempt to decrease the divorce rate.

Under Sharia law a husband is permitted to divorce his wife three times. The divorce is nullified if a husband takes back his wife within a 90-day period. Should the wife decide against going back

Law Firms

Abdul Razzaq Abdullah & Partners www.arazzaqlaw.com	244 9909
Abdullah K. Al-Ayoub & Associates www.al-ayoub.org	246 4321
Al Hekook www.alhekook.com	240 0700
Al Khebra Law Office www.alkhebra.com	244 4885
Al Markaz International Law Firm www.markazlaw.com	246 4640
Al Saleh & Partners www.alsalehandpartners.com	246 7670
Al Twaijri & Partners www.twaijri.com	240 2175
Al-Sarraf & Al-Ruwayeh P.61 ➔ www.asarlegal.com	240 0061
Ali & Partners www.mideastlaw.com	244 7415
Anwar Al-Bisher Law Firm www.albisherlaw.com	243 1122
The Law Firm of Labeed Abdal www.lalaw.com.kw	240 9476
The Law Offices of Mishali Al-Ghazali www.alghazali-law.com	243 9790

to her husband, the divorce is to be formalised in court. A divorce initiated by the wife is final, although it will take a considerable amount to time and energy to be processed.

Housing

Accommodation in Kuwait comes in a variety of forms. A wide range of apartments and villas is available, whether furnished or unfurnished, to suit all tastes and budgets. As expats are presently unable to purchase property in Kuwait, renting is still the only option. Most apartment complexes have a swimming pool, gym, 24 hour security and general maintenance included in the rental agreement.

Employment contracts sometimes include accommodation or an accommodation allowance. The oil companies, such as KOC and Chevron Texaco, and a number of the schools, have their own accommodation facilities. Should you not wish to live in company accommodation you may be able to negotiate an equivalent monthly payment prior to signing your contract.

A surburban street

Renting in Kuwait

Rents have increased dramatically since the war in Iraq, as more and more contracting firms, employing large numbers of staff, are now operating in Iraq with bases in Kuwait.

Low-rise or tower? Different styles of housing

It is possible to share accommodation to save money but bear in mind that unmarried men and women are not allowed to live together by law, unless they are members of the same family. Your best way of finding out about shared accommodation is by word of mouth.

The rent for an apartment will not necessarily include utility bills such as electricity and water. Maintenance services for air conditioning units should be covered by the landlord, and parking is usually provided for at least one vehicle.

Rental contracts are usually for a period of 12 months and payments are made monthly in advance, either by cash or cheques. After the first year the lease will either be renewed for a further year, or will continue on a monthly basis under the same terms and conditions, unless otherwise agreed in writing. Should your landlord sell the property during the lease period, the tenant will not be affected.

Using an agent is a convenient, albeit expensive, way of locating accommodation. They usually charge a fee of one month's rent, 50% of which may go to the landlord. In your initial meeting advise the agent of the maximum amount that you are prepared to pay and what you are after for your money. The agent will be able to advise as to whether your expectations are realistic or not, and will hopefully be able to offer suitable accommodation. It is possible to have the rental amount reduced on occasion; it pays to negotiate. Renting through an agent is convenient in that they will handle all of the paperwork and communicate with the landlord. Single women may find that they have to arrange accommodation rental through their company. Agents are not required to be accredited.

Should you not wish to use an agent, word of mouth and driving around are your two best options. Find out if your colleagues or friends know of any available accommodation, or jump in a car and drive around residential areas. Landlords often have signboards on their properties giving rental information. If you notice an apartment block that you like the look of, find the caretaker ('harris') and ask him if any of the apartments are available and leave your number with him.

Before signing the rent agreement make sure that the apartment/villa has a working telephone line. In some residential areas the local exchange is filled to capacity and there will be considerable delays before a telephone line can be installed.

Noise Control

Check the proximity of the rented property to the nearest mosque. Try not to have a bedroom window facing the minaret. Although the sound of the AC will tend to disguise the sound of the call to prayer during the summer, you will more than likely find that you are woken by the pre-dawn call to prayer on a regular basis. Find out who the neighbours are; many Kuwaitis keep poultry in their gardens. Not a problem if you don't own an alarm clock! Does you neighbour have dogs? Persistent barking is a nuisance which is not controlled by any municipal law.

Real Estate Agents

AAA Housing www.aaahousingq8.com	246 5888
Al Adwani Real Estate www.aladwanirealestate.com	240 4209
Better Homes P.75 www.bhomes.com	+971 4 3447714
Eastern Homes na	241 2697
Experts Real Estate Co. www.expertsq8.com	888 777
Form Arabia na	482 4572
Frost Real Estate www.frost-realestate.com	564 3149
Guide Real Estate na	574 0256
Lighthouse International www.lighthouseint.com	261 1342
Q8 Expats www.q8expats.com	574 4017
Salhia Real Estate na	299 6000
Tamdeen Real Estate Co. www.tamdeenrealestate.com	246 8881
United Real Estate Co. www.urconline.com	805 225
York Homes International na	261 3640

House for rent

Housing Abbreviations

A/C or AC	Air conditioned
Apts.	Apartments
B/R	Bedroom
Bldg	Building
C/AC or CAC	Central air conditioning
En suite	Bedroom has its own private bathroom
Fully furnished	Will have all basic furniture and the kitchen will be fitted
Shared pool	Pool is shared with other tenants
Unfurnished	No furniture although the kitchen may be fitted with fixed appliances (oven, refrigerator etc.)
W/robes	Fitted wardrobes (cupboards)
W/Tel	With telephone line
WC	Bathrooms / toilets

The Lease

Lease agreements are in Arabic, although a number of the estate agents with expatriate management will usually provide you with an English translation. Have an Arabic speaker that you trust check the wording of the lease before you sign it. The document will be signed by the landlord and the tenant, and you will be required to provide a copy of your Civil ID card.

Terms regarding lease agreements differ from one agent/landlord to the next. Negotiate the terms as much as you can to ensure that you are not over committing yourself, and always read the small print; landlords are very well protected in Kuwait. Notice periods are a minimum of one month, and can be as much as three months, depending on the duration of the lease. All notices must be given in writing. After the initial lease period of one year the lease may be extended for another year, at the discretion of the landlord. Standard practice is for the lease to continue on a month-to-month basis.

Main Accommodation Options

Apartment/Villa Sharing

If you have a limited budget you may want to consider shared accommodation. The only way to find this type of accommodation is through word of mouth. Do bear in mind that it is an offence in Kuwait for members of the opposite sex to live under the same roof if they are not family members, so be discreet.

Apartment

Apartments of various size and style are available in Kuwait. Whether you are after an unfurnished studio apartment or a furnished palace in the clouds, you will find it. Apartments to suit all budgets are available and will cost anywhere between KD 150 to KD 1,500+ monthly. The rent agreement will include the use of a pool and gym, if located on the premises, 24 hour security and parking. There is usually an option of a satellite TV service, and kitchens at the top end are fully fitted with refrigerator, oven and dishwasher. Most apartment buildings have either a central AC system or split AC units.

Villas

Reasonably priced villas are few and far between. Monthly rents start from about KD 1,000 and are in excess of KD 2,500 at the top end. The facilities on offer differ greatly from one villa to another. If you want a pool, garden and security you can expect to pay top dollar.

Hotel Apartments

Hotel Apartments vary considerably in terms of their condition, facilities and cost. Apartments may be rented daily, weekly, monthly or annually and are an ideal, albeit expensive, way of living if you require temporary accommodation. The monthly rent for a one-bedroom apartment averages KD 325, and KD 430 for a two-bedroom.

Residential Areas

Other options → Exploring [p.93]

Expat residents have historically lived in a few specific areas throughout Kuwait, including Ahmadi, Fintas, Jabriya, Mahboula, Salmiya, Salwa and Surra. This is now changing as development takes place and more accommodation is being built in previously undeveloped areas.

Read the property sections in the daily newspapers and check the various agents' websites to see what is on offer. Outlined here are a few of the primary

Finding the Perfect Home

Points to consider when looking for accommodation. Is the parking covered? Extreme summer temperatures cause vehicle interiors to get very hot. Where is your office located? Although Kuwait is a small country and the location of your accommodation can be pretty much anywhere, it would make sense to consider the morning traffic. Not all apartment blocks allow pets. Check in advance of signing your rent agreement.

residential areas. The annual rents indicated are meant to act as a guide only; you will find cheaper and more expensive accommodation in the same area. The primary factors in establishing the price of the rent are the age of a building, facilities and location.

Ahmadi   Map Ref → 2-D3

Ahmadi, Kuwait's oil town, is located approximately 35km south of Kuwait City and is home to Kuwait Oil Company (KOC). Almost all of the accommodation units are single storey buildings with gardens filled with trees. The area has its own hospital and sporting facilities and is home to oil company staff.

Fintas   Map Ref → 2-D3

The area of Fintas has come a long way in the last three years. It has always been a bit of a backwater, popular with expats because of the reasonable rents, and was previously a rather scruffy area, with old buildings and small apartment complexes surrounded by areas of desert used as car parks and soccer fields. There are a number of public beaches in the area and a launching area for boats next to the Coast Guard HQ and London Hospital (currently Kuwait's only private maternity hospital). For a three-bedroom apartment with basic amenities expect to pay KD 4,800 per year.

Jabriya   Map Ref → 12-C1

Jabriya is home to a number of embassies and schools, and is a convenient location for people working in Kuwait City. Bordered by the Fahaheel (Road 30) and Ahmadi (Road 40) Expressways to the east and west, and the 4th and 5th Ring Roads north and south, Jabriya is connected to the rest of Kuwait by major, albeit very busy, roads. A three-bedroom apartment will cost KD 7,200 per year.

Mahboula   Map Ref → 1-C3

This area has seen an extensive amount of development. Situated west of the Fahaheel Expressway (Road 30), the location is ideal for those who enjoy living in an apartment with a view and don't mind a 45 minute commute into Kuwait City in the rush hour. There are no expat schools in this area. For a three-bedroom apartment with all facilities expect to pay KD 7,800 per year.

Mishref   Map Ref → 18-C2

Mishref continues to undergo development and is home to Kuwait International Fair Ground, The Australian College of Kuwait, a number of embassies and one of the country's best co-ops, in addition to a couple of parks and a good walking/cycling track. Villas make up the majority of the accommodation and will set you back between KD 12,000 – KD 18,000 per year.

Salmiya   Map Ref → 8-C3

Salmiya, bordered by the Fahaheel Expressway (Road 30) to the west, the 5th Ring Road to the south and the Arabian Gulf to the east, is popular with expats of all nationalities. A good, central area, it is heavily populated and can sometimes be quite frustrating during peak traffic. Salmiya is Kuwait's main shopping area, and as such is full of restaurants, shopping malls, marinas, hospitals and a number of the good expat schools. A two–bedroom apartment with amenities will cost KD 11,400 and a large, new villa will cost KD 15,000.

High-rise housing

Salwa   Map Ref → 13-D3

Located between the Fahaheel Expressway (Road 30) and the Arabian Gulf and home to a number of beach hotels and good expat schools, the residential area of Salwa is very popular with expats. The commute to Kuwait City takes about 20 minutes during rush hour. A five-bedroom villa with pool will cost in the region of KD 12,000 per year.

Residents

Housing

Other Rental Costs

Prior to signing your rent agreement it is important to confirm exactly what costs are covered within the monthly payment. Landlords often require that tenants register with the Ministry of Electricity & Water (MEW), so that the tenant is liable for MEW charges. Telephone line rental costs KD 30 per year and must be paid in advance. Most agents and landlords insist on a minimum of one months' rent as a deposit. There are no hidden municipal taxes.

The estate agents will usually charge a commission fee equivalent to one months' rent. This amount is negotiable.

The upkeep of a garden is the responsibility of a tenant. Most maintenance will be arranged by the landlord, who will usually meet all costs.

Setting up Home

Moving Services

Well in advance of moving to Kuwait you will need to make arrangements to have your personal effects shipped out. Depending on what you want to bring, you have the option of shipping goods as air freight or sea freight. Air freight is considerably quicker although more expensive so it is suited to those who have limited belongings to move. Sea freight can take six weeks, sometimes longer, but is cheaper.

Choose a reputable international removals company to professionally package your belongings. All professional firms will have an agent representing them in Kuwait who will arrange all customs clearance. GAC Shipping offer a personalised service to cater to the various needs of both commercial and individual shipping requirements. Your presence is required at the port when your effects are being cleared and all shipments are subject to inspection to ensure that they do not contain any prohibited items. It is possible that videos and DVDs will be held by customs for checking. Make sure that you obtain a receipt for these and any other items. If they are found to be inoffensive they will be returned.

When it's time to leave the country, there are three primary shipping companies operating in Kuwait, all of whom can provide an international service in addition to a local service. They will pack all personal effects in Kuwait and ship them to any destination around the world, whether by air or by sea. Should you leave Kuwait and not have a forwarding address for your personal effects they will be held in storage, for a fee.

You will often see expat labourers, with their pickups and flat-bed trucks, hovering at major intersections all over Kuwait. Whether you have a few items to move or your are moving all personal effects from one building to another, and don't want to pay a professional firm, these are the people to ask. The going rate for a small flat-bed truck for an hour with two labourers is KD 10. They will usually quote about KD 15 to start. Negotiate them down but be reasonable.

> **Lists, Lists and More Lists!**
>
> *Make sure that you have an inventory, with values, of personal effects coming into Kuwait. The clearance agent will require a copy of the inventory in order to have your belongings cleared by customs. It's also worth taking out insurance.*

Relocation Companies

Alghanim Freight	474 5533
Crown Relocation P.viii	299 7850
Gulf Agency Company (GAC) P.IBC	483 6465
Inchcape Shipping Services	243 4752
Pack 'n Move	261 5144
The Relocation Specialists - Kuwait P.65	664 7634

Furnishing Accommodation

Other options → Home Furnishings & Accessories [p.171]
Second-Hand Items [p.175]

You will have the choice of renting either furnished or unfurnished accommodation. Unfurnished will generally not contain any furniture or kitchen appliances whatsoever; there are occasions however when the kitchen will contain an oven. Fully furnished accommodation will contain basic furniture and the kitchen is usually fully equipped with a refrigerator, oven and washing machine.

Some employment contracts do provide for a one-off furniture allowance; this furniture will either belong to you at the end of your employment (if you are with the firm for a set minimum period), or will become the property of the company. Make sure that the details are clearly stated in your employment contract to avoid confusion.

Furniture stores abound and you will be able to furnish your accommodation on any budget. A number of international chains operate in Kuwait, including IKEA, idDesign, Ethan Allen and The ONE. Local furniture stores cater for all budgets;

the top of the range items are usually rather elaborate. Check the supermarket notice boards to see if anyone is selling particular items that you need. Schools and embassies sometimes have clearance sales during which they auction off furniture; these are not made public so you'll have to keep your ears to the ground to find out about them.

Secondhand furniture dealers are found in Al-Rai, between the 4th and 5th Ring Roads, the Friday Market and the Ghazali Expressway (Road 60). Expats who are living are often keen to sell off their possessions, including electronics, and will advertise this through word of mouth and by placing flyers around their apartment buildings. Car boot sales occur from time to time; again this is all discovered through word of mouth although on rare occasions announcements will be made in the What's On section of the daily newspaper.

Custom-made furniture can be ordered but it is often expensive as all wood is imported. The best place to find a carpenter is along Street 16 in Shuwaikh Industrial Area 2, located parallel to Canada Dry Street and perpendicular to Banks Street (Street 14). Be very clear about what you are after, take along a drawing and dimensions if possible and remember to negotiate.

For electronic goods, Alghanim Electronics (p.161), with branches all over Kuwait, sells a wide range from different brands. The major supermarkets have substantial stocks of electronic items, from irons to DVD players to TVs.

Household Insurance

Burglary is not common but does occur. It is always sensible to obtain insurance if you are responsible for your company furniture, or if you have your own possessions in Kuwait with you.

Obtaining insurance is a straightforward process. You will be required to provide an inventory, with values of all possessions, and indicate specific items such as cameras or jewellery that are over a specified value (check this with your insurer). Check to see whether you will be required to pay excess in the event of a claim.

Household Insurance	
Bahrain Kuwait Insurance Co. (BKIC)	88 5511
Gulf Insurance Co.	242 3385
Kuwait Insurance Co.	242 0135
Warba Insurance Co.	80 8181

There are a number of brokers and insurance companies, many of which offer household insurance. In general, insurance is done face to face rather than over the phone or via the internet.

Laundry Services

Launderettes (as they are known in the west) are generally not available in Kuwait. An excellent alternative however is the local laundry, which for a small fee will wash, fold and iron the entire contents of your laundry basket. Prices range from 100 - 500 fils per item, depending on the laundry. The service provided is usually 24 hours from drop-off to collection, but an express service is also available for urgent items. There is a laundry and/or dry cleaning service located in every residential area, usually next to the corner shop (bakala) and/or the local co-op (supermarket). Most will also arrange collection from and delivery to your home. Prices are reasonable.

Laundry Services		
5 á Sec Dry Cleaning	Salmiya	574 0627
Al Rayyan Laundry	Salwa	564 3140
SAS Laundry Co.	Central Kuwait	372 3444

Domestic Help

Other options → Entry Visa [p.48]

It is very common for expatriates to employ domestic help. Most families have a maid, whether full-time or part-time, live-in or live-out. Although employment agencies do exist, they are primarily focused on bringing maids into Kuwait for the local community and therefore most maids are Muslim and speak more Arabic than English.

The best way to find a maid is through word of mouth. Expatriate families are regularly leaving Kuwait and will always want to assist their maid in finding new employment. Speak to friends and neighbours, or contact one of the many expatriate ladies' associations.

The hourly rate for a part-time maid is a maximum of KD 1. Full-time, live-in maids are paid anything from KD 45 to KD 125 per month.

Agencies involved with bringing maids into Kuwait often have a very poor reputation. You will often hear how maids are brought into Kuwait and are then held by the agency awaiting the arrival of a prospective employer. They are not allowed to go out, not allowed to phone home and have to surrender their passports. The agencies offer no protection from abusive employers, of which there are many. Further unscrupulous behaviour includes double-charging expatriates/maids; an expatriate will apply for a maid at a cost of about KD 200 (for a Christian maid; a Muslim made costs from KD 300!), which includes home-country embassy, medical and insurance costs of at least KD 50, a ticket of up to KD 100 and administrative charges. What the expatriates don't know is that the maid will also have had to pay the home-country charge of KD 50, and she will not get reimbursed.

An agency will have a three-month 'probation' period for a maid and, should you not be happy with the employee during this period, the agency has a responsibility to remove her from your employment and reimburse fees, less costs, or replace her with another maid who will be waiting in the wings at the agency.

A maid brought into Kuwait by an agency is on a two-year visa. At the end of this period one of three things will happen: the maid will have her residency cancelled and will return to her home-country; the maid will be released by her sponsor and given the opportunity to work elsewhere, or the maid will have her visa renewed and will stay on in her current employment. The most reputable agency is Adnan Al Ali (261 3075).

Babysitting & Childcare

There are a number of informal nursery schools. As not all of them are registered with the Ministry of Education they are discovered by word of mouth. They cater for children from the ages of 18 months to four years and are usually open from 07:30 – 13:00. Standards vary as not all have qualified teachers; they are often started by mothers with young children. For further information relating to Nurseries see the Education section, p.81.

Most parents hire a maid to assist with babysitting and childcare requirements. There are no agencies providing a babysitting service. Should you not have a maid and require someone to do a spot of babysitting your best bet is to speak to friends and ask whether their maid may be interested in helping out. Maids, most of whom are Sri Lankan, Indonesian, Indian, Bangladeshi and Filipino, do not usually have childcare qualifications. Some teenagers do babysitting; again, this is all found out through word of mouth.

Hotels provide babysitting services for their in-house guests. There are play areas located in IKEA (supervised) and the City Centre shopping centre in Souq Salmiya (not supervised). Gyms and shopping centres do not have crèches.

Domestic Services

Finding a plumber and electrician is the responsibility of your landlord. Advise the landlord or agent if you are having a plumbing or electrical problem and get them to arrange for a tradesman to visit. If you live in an apartment block the caretaker, who should be available 24 hours a day, is responsible for solving any plumbing/electrical problem, in conjunction with a tradesman approved by the building's owner. Should you arrange the services of a tradesman yourself, without the approval of the owner of the building, you may find yourself liable for the costs incurred.

Pets

Bringing your Pet to Kuwait

There are no restrictions regulating the type of pet that may be imported, and there are no quarantine requirements. All pets must be vaccinated against rabies and distemper. Owners are not able to bring pets into Kuwait until they have a residence permit. An import permit must then be obtained from the Public Authority for Agriculture Affairs and Fish Resources (476 1116), on presentation of the following documentation:

- Copies of the owner's passport and Civil ID
- Copy of the pet's export certificate
- Copy of the pet's health certificate
- Health booklet
- Vaccination certificates

The import permit can take up to a week to be approved, and is valid for a maximum of three months from the date of issue.

Importing pets into Kuwait during the hot summer months is not a good idea and could prove fatal due to the extreme temperatures that pets may be subjected to. Pets arriving by air are often offloaded from the cargo hold of an aircraft and left in their crates on the tarmac before being cleared by customs, which can take up to five hours. There is no holding facility for animals at the airport (pets are cleared through the cargo terminal) and they are subsequently not given much attention. It makes sense to engage the services of a shipping agent, such as Inchcape Shipping (243 4752 ext 203), Alghanim Freight (474 5533) or Gulf Agency (p.IBC, 483 6465 ext 37). With many years experience and excellent relations with the customs department, they should be able to process all paperwork and arrange for your pet to be cleared in the shortest possible time. The International Veterinary Clinic (326 1421) will also help with all import and export arrangements.

Should your pet be travelling with you, you will usually be reunited at the baggage carousel on production of the import permit; however, there are occasions when passengers are told to proceed to the cargo terminal.

Taking your Pet Home

All pets leaving Kuwait may only be exported after a health certificate has been issued by the Public Authority for Agriculture Affairs and Fish Resources (476 1116). In order to obtain this document you will be required to complete an application form and submit it together with a copy of your passport and the pet's vaccination certificate. The health certificate will be valid for a maximum of seven days from the date of issue. You will also need a current vaccination card showing all vaccinations received, and an import permit for your home destination. Prior to departing Kuwait it is prudent to visit your embassy and confirm that your paperwork is correct. Make sure that you book passage for your pet well in advance of the travel date to ensure that your pet can travel. Most airlines have restrictions on the number of live animals that can be carried at any one time.

Use a freight agent, as listed above, to handle the shipping of your pet. They are familiar with all procedures and will collect your pet from your home in Kuwait in preparation for the journey. As with passengers, all pets are required to be at the airport at least two hours before a flight departure to allow sufficient time to process all of the necessary paperwork.

Boarding facilities for pets are limited. The International Veterinary Clinic has kennel and cattery facilities which are manned 24 hours a day. All pets must receive vaccinations prior to being boarded, proof of which will need to be available. Vaccinations against kennel cough are also required and will need to be administered a minimum of seven days prior to boarding. The cost is KD 6. Daily boarding charges are KD 5 for dogs, and KD 4.500 for cats.

Keeping Domestic Pets in Kuwait

Attitudes concerning pets are mixed. Most Muslim people do not keep pets as they are considered unclean; dogs and cats are therefore not an important part of a household. There are, however, exceptions, and more Kuwaitis than ever before have pets. It is not a good idea to walk your dog in a public place, such as a park or on a running track, as some people can be hostile towards animals.

If you are going to move into an apartment building make sure that you are allowed to keep pets. There is no tagging system in Kuwait, although many people opt for chip implants, particularly if they have pedigree animals. There is a black market for pets, most of which are sold at the Friday Market. Pet shops are not regulated and keep animals in poor conditions.

Animal Souqs

The Friday Market, located on the southern side of the 4th Ring Road between the Airport Road (Road 55) and the Ghazali Expressway (Road 60), and behind the plant nurseries, is Kuwait's primary weekend market. A portion of the area is used solely for the selling of livestock and small animals. Although there are a number of vendors who do look after the creatures in their possession, most of them do not. Animals are kept in small cages and are not sufficiently nourished. Vendors smuggle wild animals into the country, with complete disregard for CITES regulations.

One of Kuwait's many stray cats

Veterinary Clinics

Al Dohamma Veterinary Clinic	472 2002
Fahaheel Veterinary Clinic	391 1247
International Veterinary Hospital	326 1421

Rescue Organisations

Two rescue organisations currently operate in Kuwait, both of which have commenced operations in the last year. Both Animal Friends League (700 1622) and PAWS (944 0089) are non-profit organisations run by volunteers from the expatriate community. PAWS is an associated member of WSPA.

If you would like to foster or adopt a pet, or would simply like to make a donation, the organisations can be contacted via their websites; www.paws-kuwait.org and www.animalfriendskuwait.org

Pet Services

Animal Friends League	700 1622	Pet Rescue
International Veterinary Hospital	326 1421	Grooming, Kennels, Cattery
PAWS	944 0089	Pet Rescue

Utilities & Services

Electricity & Water

Both water and electricity are provided by the Ministry of Electricity and Water (MEW), a government monopoly with offices located in every governorate. Water and electricity bills are paid annually and usually amount to about KD 45 for a small apartment and KD 150 for a small villa. Annual water bills for a large villa with a large garden that requires regular watering will be about KD 600. These costs will sometimes be included in your rent; check your rent agreement.

Electricity is 240v 50Hz. Sockets are primarily of the 3-pin square variety. Major appliances are sold with 2-pin or 3-pin sockets. You will find that a number of adapters are required which invariably results in your plug sockets looking a little over-laden.

Tap water is desalinated water mixed with about 10% of brackish water to provide extra taste and minerals. It is considered safe to drink. Although the majority of kitchens have water filters fitted, most people seem to prefer drinking bottled water.

The private water companies deliver water to every residential area on set days every week. You will be able to have water for your dispenser delivered to your door. It is a very cheap service and will save you lugging the bottles home from the supermarket. A book of 19 tokens costs KD 20 and will give you 19 five-gallon water bottles. The MEW website is www.mew.gov.kw, but it is in Arabic (apart from a few figures). The main emergency telephone number for electricity is 484 7329 and for water is 483 2933.

Water Suppliers

Al Rawdatain	245 7340
Aqua Cool	473 0943
Arwa Gulf Trading Co.	474 2500
Jawharat Al-Jumaira Est.	266 7790
Miraje Al-Kuwait Co.	474 9079

Sewerage

Most of the buildings in Kuwait are connected to an underground sewerage system which transports the raw sewage to treatment areas. The world's largest reverse osmosis-based sewerage treatment plant is being built in Sulaibiya, at an estimated cost of $380 million. The facility will recycle waste water, primarily for irrigation.

Gas

Mainline gas is only provided in parts of Ahmadi. All other requirements are met by the use of bottled gas, available from all co-ops, most of whom deliver for no extra charge. The initial outlay of the first bottle of gas and a regulator is less than KD 10 and refills cost 750 fils per bottle. It is a good idea to keep more than one cylinder; running out of gas whilst cooking the weekly roast is extremely annoying!

Rubbish Disposal and Recycling

Solid waste is regularly collected from residential areas and dumped in one of a number of landfills. Rubbish trucks visit on a daily basis emptying bins at individual houses. Some residential areas rely on skips, which are located on most streets, and emptied once or twice a week. There is no formal recycling system for household waste and no 'bottle bins' are in use.

Residents

Utilities & Services

Telephone

Landline Phones

Kuwait's landline telephone system is run by the Ministry of Communication (MoC) (481 9033). All local calls are free.

In order to have a telephone line connected you will need to go to the MoC building in your governorate to process an application. Take along copies of your Civil ID card and rent agreement. The cost of a standard line, without an international dialling facility, is KD 30 per year. The initial outlay will be KD 65 including stamp duty. International dialling facilities are available to expats on payment of a substantial deposit of KD 500. Standard lines are billed annually and international lines are billed monthly. Failure to pay the bill on time will result in the service being disconnected without notice. Payment of the outstanding monies and a reconnection fee will have to be made before the service can be reconnected. To check what is owed on your telephone line you can simply dial 123. Additional services offered by the MoC include an electronic answering service, caller ID, conference calling and call barring, although most of these services are offered on specific handsets only. Directory enquiries is available on 101.

Mobile Phones

There are two service providers in Kuwait, MTC Vodafone (www.mtc-vodafone.com, 107) and Wataniya Telecom (www.wataniya.com, 243 5500), both of whom operate on the GSM network. Visit any of the service providers' branches or your local telecommunications shop, all of whom will be able to sell you both a handset and a connection. In order to obtain a SIM card for KD 5 you will be required to produce your Civil ID card, or a copy of your passport and visa if you are not a resident. A deposit of KD 100 is required for a post-paid line, with an international dialling facility. Various packages are available and pre-paid lines allow for automatic access to international dialling. Pre-paid lines can be topped up online, or by purchasing a top-up card. Post-paid bills can be paid online.

Telephone & Internet Suppliers		
Fastelco	88 6666	www.fasttelco.net
Qualitynet	80 4444	www.qualitynet.net
ShowNet & Global Direct	434 7200	www.show-net.net
Zajil KEMS	82 0820	www.zajil.com

Internet

Other options → Websites [p.40]
Internet Cafés [p.223]

A small number of private companies provide a wide range of internet services, including dial-up, DSL and ISDN. Registration fees are not payable; you will simply be required to pay the subscription fee for the chosen service and period.

Prepaid internet cards are available in a number of denominations and are perfect for users who do not wish to be tied to a subscription. Qualitynet offers cards from KD 1 (12 hours) to KD 30 (90 days) and Fasttelco offers KD 1 for 15 hours to KD 5 for 30 days. All you have to do is dial a number from your computer, enter the user ID and password as provided on the card, and commence your surfing session!

Dial-up access will cost KD 8 – 10 for one month, KD 39 – 54 for six months and KD 60 – 102 for one year. A 64kbps DSL connection will cost KD 17 – 18 for one month, KD 95 for six month and KD 184 – 188 annually. A 1Mbps service will cost KD 110 – 120, KD 580 – 620 and KD 1,140 – 1,188 respectively. To obtain dial-up access simply visit your chosen service provider with a copy of your Civil ID card.

To subscribe for a DSL service you will need to have the telephone number registered in your name at the Ministry of Commerce (MoC), and a document from the MoC confirming that no monies are owed on the line. This document, together with a copy of your Civil ID card will need to be submitted to the service provider, along with a completed application form.

A DSL and Wi-Fi package from Qualitynet will cost from KD 18 per month. It is also possible to include the use of a laptop or desktop PC in your contract at a cost of KD 27 and KD 25 respectively.

Blocked Sites

The service providers in Kuwait block a number of sites due to their content. If you feel that a site has been blocked in error, let your service provider know. They will check it and, if appropriate, allow access.

Qualitynet provides a high-speed Wi-Fi service at a number of locations, including Starbucks, Costa Coffee, Pizza Hut, McDonalds and the departure lounges at the airport.

Internet cafes abound although their locations are not always noticeable. Internet access costs between 500 fils to KD 1 per hour.

Residents

Utilities & Services

Bill Payment

As a basic landline will only allow you to make local calls, all of which are free, you will not be billed. You will, however, need to make sure that you remember to pay the line rental of KD 30 per year. Reminders are not sent out and you could find that the phone is disconnected. Making a note in your diary!

International phone lines are billed monthly and must be paid immediately at any Ministry of Communication (MoC) office. Failure to pay the bill on time will result in the service being disconnected and the KD 500 deposit will be forfeited. To reactivate the line you will have to pay all outstanding monies, a disconnection fee and sometimes a penalty fee. Simply put; pay on time! Payment for landline bills can only be made at MoC offices.

Call the MoC billing department on 123 to check what is owed on your line.

Mobile phone subscribers receive monthly statements. Due payments must be paid by the date indicated on the statement or the subscriber will face disconnection. Both MTC-Vodafone (107) and Wataniya Telecom (121) bills can be paid online, at any of their dealers, or at any of their branches.

Postal Services

Other options → Post & Courier Services [p.39]

Delivery to residential addresses is not reliable and expats are advised to obtain a post office box if they are unable to use their company address. On production of your Civil ID a post box can be rented at your local post office for KD 4 per annum, payable in advance. An initial additional payment of KD 3 is charged for a key.

All posted items are sent by air. It is best to have items registered to ensure delivery, although express letters and packages are not able to be registered. Parcels may be sent from the main post office in Fahad Al-Salem street in Kuwait City and other major post offices throughout the country.

Mail sent by Mumtaz Post has priority in Kuwait and the country of delivery. Incoming parcels are held for collection and you will be notified by a green card left in the post box. You will need to present the green card, together with your Civil ID, at the parcel office in Keifan before you will receive your parcel. All incoming post is subject to customs inspections. The major problem with the postal service is that items are held up in the post offices for extended periods. The local post is diabolical; it can take weeks for a letter to be sent from one location to another.

Letters (up to 20g) cost 25 fils to Kuwaiti addresses, 50 fils to GCC countries, and 150 fils tinternationally.

Television

Kuwait has 5 channels, all of which are run by the state. KTV2 is the only English language channel and broadcasts a selection of programmes for a limited period, from early afternoon to midnight. The news is broadcast in English. As the local English television service is limited, and satellite television is fairly cheap, most households will make use of an additional television service.

Satellite TV & Radio

Orbit, Showtime, and Firstnet are the most popular satellite networks. The varied selection of programmes includes sport, entertainment, cartoons, movies, documentaries and news channels. On top of the cost of the decoder and satellite dish, the service costs from KD 5 per month, depending on the selection of channels. You'll be given a decoder on signing up and possibly a satellite dish; most apartment buildings have satellite dishes already installed on the roof. There are two types of channels:

Pay TV Satellite Channels

These channels require a subscription and the necessary decoder. Subscriptions are payable monthly, quarterly or annually. Compare the packages on offer to determine which service will suit you best.

Dishy neighbourhood

Free to Air Satellite Channels

These channels, of which there are in excess of 200, require a decoder. There is no subscription charge.

Digital Radio

Most radio channels are transmitted through the satellite television decoder.

Local Radio Stations

There are a number of radio stations broadcasting in Kuwait. Marina FM operates on 88.8FM and is primarily an Arabic channel, although they do play Western music. 90.1FM is the BBC service in Arabic. 99.7FM 'Super Station' is the primary English radio service playing a wide range of music with regular news reports, and 92.5FM is an 'easy listening' station. 107.9FM is the US Forces station 'AFN' and on 104.3FM is another US station 'NPR'.

Satellite/Cable Providers		
ART	574 4297	www.gd-tv.com
Orbit	80 2999	www.orbit.net
Pehla	88 0088	www.gd-tv.com
Showtime Arabia	80 7007	www.showtimearabia.com
Star	574 4297	www.gd-tv.com

Health

General Medical Care

Kuwait has a high standard of healthcare, and both private and public facilities are regulated by the Ministry of (Public) Health.

Public healthcare is provided through a number of clinics and hospitals. The clinics are located throughout Kuwait and can usually be found next to the local supermarket or co-operative. Clinics offer preliminary examinations and routine check-ups and services, and will refer a patient to a specialist where necessary. All public facilities are open to expatriate residents. There are currently five major (general) government hospitals throughout the country, all of which provide an outpatients service. These hospitals are recommended for emergency treatment although not all facilities have obvious emergency entrances. It is advisable to pass by when you are in the area to establish exactly where the entrance is. It will make life a lot less stressful if you ever need to find it in a hurry.

Your Civil ID card will need to be produced when visiting the government hospitals for treatment and a payment of KD 2 is required (KD 1 for government clinics). Should you have private medical insurance you will be obliged to pay KD 10. Each expatriate, when applying for or renewing a residence permit, is obliged to pay KD 50 (KD 40 for a spouse and KD 30 per child) for government medical insurance upon which they will receive a credit-card sized health card. This cost is usually met by the sponsoring company. The payment ensures that all expatriates are exempt from paying the daily inpatient charges at a government hospital. In addition, no charges are payable for x-rays, operations, laboratory tests and medicines. Payments are required for specialized tests including MRI and CT scans, although the costs are heavily subsidised.

Private healthcare is of a high standard, although it does come at a price. There is an ever-increasing number of private hospitals and clinics in Kuwait, all of which require a patient to register prior to treatment. Your Civil ID card is required (passports are accepted for visitors to Kuwait and new residents yet to receive their Civil ID card) and the procedure takes a couple of minutes and will usually cost KD 2. A registration card is issued and should be produced at every visit, although if you forget it your records can be checked electronically. Most private hospitals and clinics do not allow appointments to be made over the telephone. A visit to the respective facility will be required in order to book the appointment and pay the consultation fee which is a minimum of KD 10. There are occasions when a private hospital, with limited facilities, will refer a patient to a government hospital.

Private medical insurance is not absolutely necessary in Kuwait. However, expatriates generally prefer to be covered by private insurance allowing for the use of private hospitals and clinics where there are more comfortable facilities and shorter waiting periods. English is spoken at both government and private hospitals. Most employers provide medical insurance as part of the employee's package but this is not mandatory. One point to bear in mind is that a number of insurers will expect the policy holder to pay for treatment up front and then be reimbursed. It can prove quite stressful if you are required to cover the costs of a major operation out of you own pocket.

Pharmacies are located next to hospitals and clinics and at most co-operatives. A number of night pharmacies are listed in the newspaper on a daily basis, alongside the weather report and prayer timings. These night pharmacies tend to open from 08:00 – 23:00 with some closing at midnight. 24 hour pharmacies include Ahlam in Kuwait City (243 6184), Hawalli Pharmacy in Hawalli (261 2572) and Al Boudour in Abu Halifa (371 3077). All provide the usual services although they are not able to issue prescriptive medication without a prescription.

The current ambulance service in Kuwait is not on a par with western standards. Paramedics are often not properly trained and work from ill-equipped vehicles. They have been known to stop to refuel on the way to the hospital causing a great deal of concern and stress to the passenger being transported. It is recommended, if at all possible, that a person requiring emergency medical treatment make their own way to any of the five government hospitals with emergency medical facilities.

Government Hospitals

Adan General Hospital	394 0600
Al Sabah Chest Hospital	481 5000
Al Sabah Maternity Hospital	484 8067
Amiri General Hospital	245 0080
As'ad Al-Hamad Dermatology Centre	483 2067
Farwaniya General Hospital	488 3000
Ibn Sina Hospital	484 0300
Jahra General Hospital	457 5300
Mubarak Al Kabeer General Hospital	531 2700
Sabhan Renal Hospital	484 0027
Sulaibikhat Orthopaedic Hospital	487 4240

Private Hospitals

Al Rashid Hospital	562 4000
Dar Al Shifa Hospital	80 2555
Hadi Clinic	82 8282
London Hospital	88 3883
New Mowasat Hospital	572 6666
Salam Hospital	253 3177

Government Health Centres/Clinics

Dasman Clinic	244 7602
Faiha Polyclinic	254 5188
Farwaniya Polyclinic	472 6033
Hawalli Polyclinic	261 1645
Sabah Al Salem Clinic	552 4821
Salmiya Polyclinic	572 3500
Shamiya Clinic	561 0660
Shuwaikh Clinic	484 8913
Yarmuk Clinic	533 6482

Private Health Centres/Clinics

Boushahri Clinic	88 5544
British Medical Centre	371 3100
Care Clinic	261 0666
International Clinic	574 5111

Dermatologists

Al Salam Hospital	253 3177
As'ad Al-Hamad Dermatology Centre	483 2067
New Mowasat Hospital	572 6666

Maternity

Other options → Maternity Clothes [p.173]

The availability of excellent maternity and delivery facilities means that an ever-increasing number of expats choose to have their babies in Kuwait. All pregnant women can register with an obstetrician/gynaecologist of their choice at one of the clinics or hospitals. The London Hospital in Fintas is the only specialised private hospital. Al Sabah Maternity Hospital in Shuwaikh is the only government maternity hospital. The in-patient cost of having a baby is a mere KD 2 per day. There are no hidden charges and, if you have your baby during the holy month of Ramadan, you may well find that the KD 2 per day is waived! Women delivering in the government hospitals are not allowed to have any family or friends supporting them in the private labour wards. Visitors are only allowed once the new mother has been transferred to a general ward and even then there are restrictions.

Private hospitals tend to offer a complete delivery package whereby you pay a fixed fee for a normal or caesarean delivery. This fee usually covers the costs of the delivery room, post-delivery room and board, mothers' lab work, doctors and nursing staff, baby's basic tests, basic medicines, and the nursery. One home visit is also usually covered. There are additional fees for epidurals etc. Pain relief in Kuwait is a personal choice. Whether you wish to have an epidural, pethidine or use a TENS machine is up to you. Home and water births are not possible. A great advantage of having a baby in a private hospital in Kuwait is that you are allowed to have someone with you in the labour room, whether it is a female relative or friend, or your husband. This person will also be able to stay with you in your room post delivery.

Residents

Health

Most maternity costs are not covered by your insurance company. If offered, the private hospitals and clinics charge about KD 30 for a course of four ante-natal classes. As part of the package in a private hospital, one post natal home visit will be covered. This visit takes place within a week of the baby's birth. You will then need to return to the hospital to see a paediatrician who will carry out routine monthly checks.

Immediately after the baby is born the birth will have to be registered and a passport issued prior to a residence permit being issued. Failure to apply for residence within 60 days of the birth will result in a KD 200 fine.

It is a very good idea to visit your embassy well before the birth of a child to discuss the matter of citizenship, see birth registration, p.52..

Married With Children

As it is a criminal offence for an unwed couple to have a baby in Kuwait, you will be required to produce a copy of your marriage certificate prior to admission to hospital.

The maternity fees for giving birth in Kuwait differ hugely between government and private hospitals. On average a normal delivery package in a private hospital costs around KD350 (two-day stay) in comparison to KD600 (four-day stay) for a caesarean delivery. All in-patient care in government hospitals costs KD2 a day.

Private clinic

Paediatrics

Paediatricians are available at the government clinics as well as at the private hospitals and clinics. If you have private medical insurance, visits to paediatricians are usually covered. Most expat parents find a doctor for their children through word of mouth, so ask other expats who they would recommend.

Dentists/Orthodontists

Dental services are provided by both public and private practitioners. All the large hospitals have their own dental departments and there are a number of private clinics dedicated to the provision of dental treatment. A basic check-up at a private facility will cost up to KD 15, and a visit to a government clinic will set you back a nominal KD 2.

Maternity Hospitals & Clinics

Adan General Hospital General	394 0600
Al Rashid Hospital Private	562 4000
Amiri General Hospital General	245 0080
Dar Al Shifa Hospital Private	80 2555
Farwaniya General Hospital General	488 3000
Hadi Hospital Private	531 2555
Jahra General Hospital General	457 5300
London Hospital Private	88 3883
New Mowasat Hospital Private	572 6666
Salam Hospital Private	253 3177

Gynaecology & Obstetrics

Al Sabah Maternity Hospital	484 8067
Dr. Adel Al Zuhaur	253 3177
Dr. Imad Ghazzawi	572 6666
Dr. Layla Abou El-Leil	574 5111
Dr. Rachel Kurian	253 3177
Dr. Shadia Othman	572 6666
Dr. Yuliana Petrova	562 4000
Dr. Zoltan Lengyel	572 6666
London Hospital	88 3883

Dentists/Orthodontists

Al Forzan Dental Centre	265 7050
Al Salam Hospital	253 3177
Amiri Hospital Dental Clinic	244 5218
Bab Hani Clinic	573 0000
Balsam Clinic	575 5737
Bayan Dental Centre	573 0050
Bneid Al Gar Dental Clinic	257 1516
Dental Care Clinic	562 0111
International Clinic	574 5111
KOC Ahmadi Hospital	388 2564
Kuwait Medical Centre (KMC)	571 8990
Maidan Clinic	391 1026
Medical Centre of Qadisiya	251 5088
New Mowasat Hospital	572 6666
Shaab Medical Centre	262 9091

Government dental clinics offer a good general dental service including cleaning, filling, extraction and root canal. Some specialised services, including the fitting of crowns, are not provided for expatriates and therefore a visit to a private dental clinic will be required.

Cosmetic dentistry is available and services range from teeth whitening to veneers, contouring and reshaping.

Opticians

Opticians are found in shopping malls and co-ops, and a number have their own stand-alone premises. The major companies have various locations throughout the country. All opticians carry out eye tests, for which there is generally no charge.

An eye test is required in order to obtain a driving licence. This test can only be carried out at the Ministry of Health clinic in Qortuba.

Contact lenses are readily available, as are prescription lenses. Laser surgery is available through the major private hospitals, most of which have dedicated ophthalmic departments, including New Mowasat Hospital (572 6666), Al Salam Hospital (253 3177) and Hawalli Medical Centre (565 0555).

Opticians	
Al Jamil Optical	573 8181
Al Noor Optical Co.	572 0202
Dr. Abdulla Al Mansour	562 2444
Dr. Sabreyah Saleh	566 3000
English Optics	264 0411
Hassan's Optician Co.	571 3119
International Optique	571 4007

Hairdressers

Kuwait has a wide range of hair salons offering services ranging from KD 1 for a basic cut and head massage in a gents barber shop, to KD 20 for a restyle in an upmarket salon. The barber shops are located throughout Kuwait and offer an efficient service without the need for an appointment. A shave with a cut-throat razor is an optional KD 1, and a nose waxing will be thrown in for nothing! A number of ladies' salons offer the latest styles and treatments. A basic cut and blow-dry will cost anything up to KD 18 and a full head of highlights can cost anything up to KD 45.

Arnubah & Dabdoob is a fantastic children's 'barber' where young children from the age of one can have a very quick haircut for KD 1. They are located within the main co-op buildings in Rawda (257 2700), Mishref (538 4333), Rumaithiya (563 8880), Qurain (544 0028) and Qadsiya (254 8713). Appointments are not necessary.

There are a number of private stylists who are able to visit you at home but they prefer not to advertise, and are discovered through word of mouth. A small number of the major hotels have hairdressers.

Hairdressers	
Al Surra Co-op Salon	534 9358
Classic La Fem Hair and Beauty Salon	561 3675
Cutting Edge	571 8001
Elegance	572 7528
Hilton Barber Shop	372 5500
Images Salon & Day Spa	563 9388
Sheraton Kuwait Salon	244 9143
Strands Hear & Beauty Co	571 1237

Cosmetic Treatment & Surgery

In the past the local population had to travel abroad to receive cosmetic surgery. However, people are now opting to stay in Kuwait to receive treatments including breast reduction and augmentation, facelifts, liposuction and body contouring.

Non-surgical procedures available in Kuwait include hair removal and microdermabrasion.

Cosmetic Treatment & Surgery	
Al Salam Hospital	253 3177
As'ad Al-Hamad Dermatology Centre	483 2067

Alternative Therapies

There is a gap in the market for professional complementary (alternative) therapists. A number of expats have tried without success to set up practices offering a wide range of treatments. Regulations are prohibitive and it is very difficult, if not impossible, to provide such treatment without the backing of a prominent member of the local community. At the moment most treatments, if not offered by the major hotels, are discovered through word of mouth. Both The Orchid Spa at The Palms Hotel (824 060) and the Spa at the Hilton Kuwait Resort (372 5500) offer aromatherapy, reflexology and massage. In addition, The Chinese Health Centre (571 6599) offers Acupressure and Acupuncture.

Residents

Health

Public Hospital

Ayurveda

The Kempinski Hotel & Resort (844 444) in Julai'a offers a wide range of treatments in their Softouch Ayuverdic Centre. A 30 minute head massage will cost KD 10.

Back Treatment

There is only one independent osteopath (Dr Karam at Limelight Organic) practising in Kuwait, and he flies in from Beirut twice a month for a day each time! There is one dedicated orthopaedic hospital, and most major government and private hospitals have orthopaedic departments.

Back Treatment	
Adan General Hospital	394 0600
Al Salam Hospital	253 3177
Amiri General Hospital	245 0080
Farwaniya General Hospital	488 3000
Jahra General Hospital	457 5300
Mubarak Al Kabir General Hospital	531 2700
New Mowasat Hospital	572 6666
Osteopath at Limelight Organic	571 8551
Sulaibikhat Orthopaedic Hospital	487 4240

Rehabilitation & Physiotherapy

Whether you find yourself injured after a session on the rugby pitch or a stint on your jetski, you will be in good hands in Kuwait. Sports medicine and physiotherapy is available from any of the five general hospitals runs by the government, as well as the Orthopaedic Hospital in Shuwaikh. Al Salam Hospital has a dedicated physiotherapy

department. Both hospitals specialise in orthopaedic surgery and general physiotherapy.

Rehabilitation & Physiotherapy	
Adan General Hospital	394 0600
Al Salam Hospital	253 3177
Amiri General Hospital	245 0080
Farwaniya General Hospital	488 3000
Jahra General Hospital	457 5300
Mubarak Al Kabir General Hospital	531 2700
Sulaibikhat Orthopaedic Hospital	487 4240

Mental Health

Facilities do exist for people suffering from a range of mental health problems. The Iraqi occupation in the early nineties created a new set of needs in terms of psychological health care, as a large portion of the population was affected by post-traumatic stress. The Psychiatric Hospital (484 3900) has over 450 beds and caters for all patients; from those with addictions, short-term and long-term conditions, plus geriatric and forensic patients.

Outpatients clinics are located at all five of the government general hospitals, and psychiatric care is also provided at prisons and special needs schools, as required.

The Shuaiba Industrial Medical Centre (326 2040) offers family & marriage, youth, health and job related counselling.

Al Rashed Centre (266 6206) has experienced counsellors, offering assistance to children and teenagers, families, and those suffering from a range of conditions including eating disorders, phobias, obsessions, compulsive behaviour and depression. They also have counsellors who deal with physical and sexual abuse, trauma and psychological sexual dysfunction.

Counsellors/Psychologists	
Al Rashed Centre	266 6206
Psychiatric Hospital	484 3900
Shuaiba Industrial Medical Centre	326 2040

Support Groups

Many expatriates, particularly stay-at-home wives/mothers, do tend to suffer from culture shock, some far more than others. A number of husbands have been forced to give up their jobs in order to return to their home country, for the sake of their marital relationship. However, there are so many ways in which to get involved with the community, albeit the expatriate one, and create a wonderful life for yourself in Kuwait. This really is a country unlike any other and many people, once established, regret having to leave. The lifestyle that you can have here is quite unique.

Various support groups exist. Whether you are an expatriate wife here with your husband, or a stay-at-home mother with a brood of young children, there will be fellow, like-minded residents the length and breadth of the country, all of whom were new and felt alone at some point.

Alcoholics Anonymous (AA) (964 1389). Information on weekly meetings can be found at www.aainarabia.com.

The Autistic Children Parents Support Group (254 0351) meets at the Kuwait Centre for Autism on a regular basis. (www.q8autism.com)

The British Ladies Society (687 9836) is open to all British citizens and those married to British citizens, as well as citizens of countries whose affairs are represented by the British Embassy in Kuwait. The society holds regular coffee mornings and evening meetings. (bls_q8@msn.com).

The American Women's League (539 0356) has regular meetings for American citizens and those married to Americans. (awlkuwait@yahoo.com).

Education

Kuwait has a good education system catering for both local and expatriate children. Government-funded public education is available for Kuwait citizens only. All children between the ages of six and 14 are required by law to go to school.

Both government and private schools are regulated by the Ministry of Education. The private schools catering for the large expatriate population (and a number of the more westernised Kuwaiti youngsters) are obliged to include Arabic and Islamic studies in their curriculum. These schools tend to follow the British and American curriculum, both of which are recognised worldwide. There are a number of other international schools, including Indian, Pakistani and Filipino, which follow their respective curriculum. The examinations taken depend on the school's curriculum.

The good schools in Kuwait always have a waiting list so it is advisable to register a child as soon as you know that you may be relocating. A non-refundable admission fee is required by most of the schools and acceptance is at the school's discretion. A child will usually undergo a placement test to ensure that they are placed in the correct academic year/class. Those arriving from the southern hemisphere will need to keep in mind that the academic year differs by six months and that the child may have to repeat or jump six months. Children who arrive in the middle of a school year will be placed into the year that the school feels is appropriate.

The school year runs from September to June but actual term dates vary from school to school. Schools are open from Saturday to Wednesday and hours are usually 07:30 – 14:00. Where you live has no bearing on what school your children have to go to, it is entirely up to you and how long you want to spend doing the morning 'school run'!

You should try to negotiate your employment contract to include a separate payment for school fees. Private education is not cheap and the schools require advance payment, whether by term or annually, prior to admission. Refunds are not possible. Should you have more than one child at the same school ask about reduced fees; they are usually available. Advanced written notice of a minimum of one term is required when removing a child from a school.

Most of the schools only employ teachers with international qualifications. However, a number of the schools have a high staff turnover and do find that they have to employ non-teaching staff to cover the classes when looking for replacements. Prior to enrolling your child at a school try to talk to other parents to get an idea of what that particular school is like. Find out about staff turnover, class sizes, facilities, management attitude and anything else that is important to you as a parent. A number of the schools provide transport at an additional fee.

Required Documentation

The Ministry of Education requires that every school holds the following information for every pupil. It is up to the parent to ensure that the information is kept up-to-date.

- Application form for a foreign school (English copy)
- Application form for a foreign school (Arabic copy)

- Signed declaration letter
- Photocopy of the child's birth certificate
- Two passport photographs of the child
- Copies of the child's passport, including photograph page, residence stamp and date of entry into Kuwait
- Photocopy of the child's Civil ID card
- Photocopy of father's Civil ID card
- Medical card (as issued by the Ministry of Health – School Health Clinic)
- BCG vaccination card (as issued by the Ministry of Health – School Health Clinic)
- Transfer certificate if moving schools within Kuwait
- Copy of report from the previous school

In preparation for a child's application to a school it is worth maintaining a child's academic history. Indicate the attendance period at each school, school curriculum, samples of work and include contact information; obtain a letter from the teacher(s) outlining the child's abilities including strengths, weaknesses and social behaviour.

Nurseries & Pre-Schools

Free nursery education is provided by the MoE for all Kuwait citizens. Expatriate children will attend one of the private nurseries or informal playgroups, not all of which are officially registered. The age range is generally from two to five years, although there are nurseries accepting children from the age of 18 months. A number of the schools do have waiting lists so it is advisable to plan ahead and make enquiries well in advance. Annual fees range from KD 300 to KD 1,500 depending on the school and the number of days for which a child is enrolled; most payments are required in advance, whether for the term or annually. The school week is from Saturday to Wednesday and timings are usually 08:00 – 12:00/13:00. The nurseries listed in the table follow either the Montessori method or the British curriculum. Most teachers have international qualifications although classroom assistants are not always trained. The majority of

nurseries in Kuwait have structure to their days and a few require the wearing of uniforms.

Primary & Secondary Schools

Entrance exams are required prior to admission to most of the private schools in Kuwait, primarily as a means of establishing exactly which academic year/class a child will be placed into. There are waiting lists at the top schools, most of which have an excellent standard of teaching. All of the schools listed below follow the British or American curriculum. Other schools follow the Indian, Pakistani and Filipino curriculum.

Facilities vary from school to school. Classrooms are generally spacious and well-equipped. As not all schools have ample outside space they make use of sports facilities throughout Kuwait.

Most schools have their own nurse who will carry out first aid, be responsible for emergency medical assistance, administer prescription medication (submitted by the parents and ensure that all vaccination requirements are met.

The academic year runs from September to June and is broken into two, three, or four terms, depending on the school. The school week runs from Saturday to Wednesday, with timings varying slightly from one school to another. Expect the day to begin at about 07:30 and end at about 14:00. There are no regulations in terms of catchment areas.

Annual fees range from KD 1,500 to KD 2,500 and do not cover the costs of registration, text books, medical fees, extramural activities and transport. Transport to and from school will cost approximately KD 200 per annum.

One of Kuwait's most popular schools

Nurseries & Pre-Schools

The British School of Kuwait P.83	562 1701	Salwa
English Playgroup, The	566 8145	Salmiya
Gulf Montessori School	565 0125	Salwa
Happy Chappies	700 4777	Central Kuwait
HappyLand FunSkool	532 8005	Central Kuwait
Kuwait Montessori Nursery	532 0969	Central Kuwait

Box 26922, Safat 13130, State of Kuwait ◆ Salwa Area 1, Street 1, Block 214
562 1701 ◆ Fax: 562 4903 ◆ www.bsk.edu.kw ◆ excellence@bsk.edu.kw

THE BRITISH SCHOOL OF KUWAIT

BSK

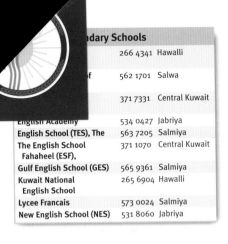

dary Schools

	266 4341	Hawalli
f	562 1701	Salwa
	371 7331	Central Kuwait

English Academy	534 0427	Jabriya
English School (TES), The	563 7205	Salmiya
The English School Fahaheel (ESF),	371 1070	Central Kuwait
Gulf English School (GES)	565 9361	Salmiya
Kuwait National English School	265 6904	Hawalli
Lycee Francais	573 0024	Salmiya
New English School (NES)	531 8060	Jabriya

University & Higher Education

Higher education in Kuwait continues to improve. Traditionally, many students travelled abroad to further their education; however, a number of private colleges and universities have recently opened in the country, some of which are affiliated to American and Australian universities. Entrance requirements differ from one institution to another. Female students are permitted to remain on a father's sponsorship whilst they are dependants and do not require a student visa; male students are obliged to obtain a student visa on turning 18.

Kuwait University offers a wide range of courses, including Islamic Studies, and has restricted access for expatriate students.

The American University of Kuwait (AUK) offers degrees in liberal arts, sciences and management.

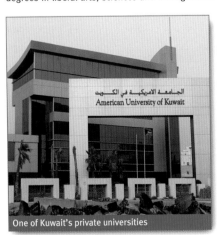

American University of Kuwait

One of Kuwait's private universities

The Australian College of Kuwait (ACK) offers engineering, maritime, and management diplomas, and all diploma holders will obtain credits for universities in Australia. Gulf University for Science & Technology (GUST) offers degree courses in arts, sciences, and business administration.

Universities

American University of Kuwait (AUK)	80 2040	Salmiya
Arab Open University	532 9013	Central Kuwait
Australian College of Kuwait (ACK)	537 6111	Mishref
Gulf University of Science & Technology (GUST)	88 6644	Hawally
Kuwait Maastricht Business School	263 6596	Central Kuwait
Kuwait University	481 1188	Shuwaikh

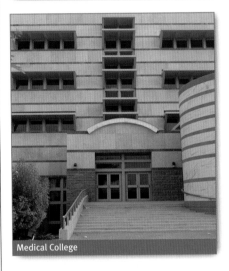

Medical College

Special Needs Education

The Kuwait government extends financial support to Kuwaiti children requiring special needs education. There are centres and schools for children with physical and learning difficulties, and most are open to expatriate children. Home schooling programmes are not easily available. There are a number of organisations catering for children with disabilities, and some of the mainstream schools have dedicated special needs units.

- Bayan Bilingual School (531 5125, www.bbs.edu.kw) has limited facilities for children with special needs.

Residents

Education

- The Centre for Child Evaluation & Teaching (484 5221) carries out assessments of all children with learning difficulties.
- The Conductive Education School Kuwait (CESK) (473 4370, www.kees.org) provides different levels of education and support to children with conditions including cerebral palsy, dyslexia, spina bifida, Asperger's Syndrome, Multiple Sclerosis and Parkinson's Disease.
- Dasman Model School (243 0607) has a special needs department providing extensive facilities for a wide range of support requirements, including ADHD.
- Ideal Education School (240 3668, www.idealeducationschool.com) prepares individual programmes for children with autism, Down Syndrome, Cerebral Palsy, ADHD, ADD, speech and behaviour disorders and hearing impairments.
- The Khalifa School (256 1839) caters for children with a wide range of conditions including autism, cerebral palsy and Down Syndrome.
- Kuwait Centre for Autism (254 0351, www.q8autism.com) offers a number of programmes for autistic children as well as support to the parents of an autistic child – the Autistic Children Parents Support Group meets here.
- Kuwait English School (KES) (561 4470, www.kes-kw.com) has a Green Unit which provides individual programmes for 50 children ranging from 3½ to 18 years of age. Green Unit children need to have a minimum IQ of 70 and have mobility; the unit is not geared up for severely physically disabled children.
- Kuwait National English School (KNES) (265 6904, www.knes.edu.kw) has a special needs department offering assistance to children with learning difficulties. Each child in the unit has a programme tailor-made to their specific requirements.

Additional clubs and schools include Kuwait Club for the Deaf (256 3204), Kuwait Association for the Blind (565 4105) and Kuwait Dyslexia Association (487 7394 ext.116).

Learning Arabic

Other options → Language Schools [p.152]

If you are intending to live in Kuwait or the Middle East for a considerable length of time it is worth learning spoken Arabic. Although not an easy language to pick up, any amount of effort that you make will be rewarded by smiles and encouragement when you converse with Arab-speakers. Arabic is taught at a number of centres offering day and night courses. All expat schools are obliged to teach Arabic to pupils in the lower years.

Learning Arabic

AWARE Centre	533 5260	Surra
Berlitz	254 2212	Bneid al-Gir
BITE	263 6596	Central Kuwait
The British Council	251 5512	Mansouria
British School of Languages	562 1701	Salwa

Transportation

Other options → Getting Around [p.30]
Car [p.34]

The primary mode of transport in Kuwait is the car; there are currently 2.25 cars in Kuwait for every person. The two bus companies do provide an adequate alternative service. The road system is of a high standard and is continually maintained.

In order to purchase a car you will have to have received your residence status and be in possession of a valid Civil ID card. Visitors to Kuwait may only drive on an International Driving Permit (IDP); they are not permitted to drive on their home country licence. There are a number of well known international rental firms who are able to offer short and long term leasing.

The traffic police must be called in the event of an accident, and are contacted by dialing 777, the emergency services number.

Parking facilities vary from one area to another. Trying to find somewhere to park in a built-up area usually proves to be a challenge. Dedicated parking garages and areas are found in downtown Kuwait; payment is usually 100 fils per hour but this does vary. Payment is currently made to the man in the booth at the exit. Shopping centres, supermarkets and beach clubs have parking facilities, not all of which are free. All over Kuwait you will find open areas of 'desert' where you are permitted to park at no charge. Do not park on any pavement that is painted black and yellow – you may get a ticket or have your vehicle clamped.

Parking spaces for the disabled are found in most public areas although don't always expect to find one; they'll invariably be taken by ignorant able-bodied drivers who don't like to walk too far!

...asing

...er of international leasing companies
...e in Kuwait. Vehicle leasing is the only option
for obtaining a car prior
to getting your
residence visa, although
some companies may
allow their staff the use
of a company vehicle, if
included in the
employment contract. It
makes more sense to rent a car if you are going to
be in Kuwait for a limited period; you will not have
to worry about trying to sell a car prior to departure,
and maintenance and insurance will be covered.

> **...c Warning**
>
> *A common sight in Kuwait is a pile of bricks or rocks at the rear of a vehicle that has broken down. This is the local version of a warning triangle!*

Visitors to Kuwait are permitted to lease a car on
the strength of an International Driving Permit.
Residents of Kuwait are required to produce their
Kuwait driving licence.

The cost of renting depends on the vehicle required
and the duration. It is possible to rent by the day,
week and month and, if you are not particular
about what you drive, you can hire a car short-term
for as little as KD 5 per day. At the top end, the
monthly rate may be anything up to KD 750, but
remember you can negotiate. Prior to signing a
lease agreement check to see whether you have 24
hour assistance and comprehensive insurance.

Vehicle Leasing Agents	
Al Babtain Car Rental	476 9353
Al Mulla Rental & Leasing of Vehicles	
& Equipment Co. W.L.L P.ix	482 3731
Al Sayer Car Rental & Leasing	244 1425
Avis Rent a Car	246 5082
Budget Rent a Car	431 0064
Europcar Alghanim Rent a Car	473 5626
Hertz Rent a Car	431 9326
Limousine Service	472 3932
National Car Rental	434 3139
Sixt Rent A Car P.87	84 3843

If you intend to use a rented vehicle to cross the
border you will need to advise the rental company
in advance to ensure that your insurance is valid.

Buying a Vehicle

A Civil ID card is required in order to purchase a
vehicle in your own name. Cars are affordable and
available new and second-hand. The most popular
brands seem to be Toyota, Nissan and Mitsubishi
although practically every make of car is available.
The Kuwaiti population loves to drive!

The preferred way of purchasing a second hand
vehicle is from a friend. Another option is to check
the notice board of your local supermarket and
the classified sections in the newspapers. If you
are interested in purchasing a vehicle, and have
any doubt as to whether it has been in an
accident, go to your nearest traffic department
and try to have the records checked. It is also a
good idea to have the car checked by a
professional garage. Don't automatically believe
what you are told by the seller.

Almost all of the new car dealerships also sell
second-hand vehicles, and usually with some sort
of guarantee. For an additional fee they will assist
with the arrangements for finance, registration
and insurance.

Catching the bus

Other second-hand dealers are dotted throughout
Kuwait and there is a car souq, Souq Al-Harraj, in
Ardiya. Auctions take place regularly although
there is an element of risk involved with every
purchase. The cars cannot be thoroughly checked
prior to sale and as soon as a bid is accepted you
will be bound by an Arabic contract and a cash
deposit. The final payment is expected once the
vehicle papers are transferred. There are many
second-hand car dealers in Al Rai, Block 2, Streets
9, off Mohammed Bin Al-Qassim Street (Road 601),
and 22, off the Ghazali Expressway (Road 60).
Don't buy a car that was manufactured in or before
1985 – you won't be allowed to drive it!

When you purchase a new car the registration will
be arranged by the dealer. Initial registration is for
a period of three years, and is renewed annually
thereafter. Prior to a vehicle being re-registered
after the initial three-year period, the insurance will
have to be paid and the receipt produced at the
traffic department. All vehicles undergo mandatory

50 Years of Leadership

Behbehani Motors Company

843843

50 Years
in Automotives

PORSCHE

Smart repair
Automotive cosmetic surgery

SiXT
rent a car

////ALPINE
Mobile Media Solutions

testing prior to the insurance being stamped by the traffic department. The receipt and the expired registration document will then be exchanged for a new registration document ('diftar').

Ownership Transfer

To transfer a vehicle from one owner to another will require the presence of both parties at the traffic department in the governorate in which the vehicle is registered. In addition to the vehicle's documents, including registration and insurance, you will need to produce your Civil ID card.

Vehicle Import

Only vehicles no older than five years are allowed to be imported into Kuwait on an import licence,

and this is only available to members of the Kuwait Chamber of Commerce. In special circumstances permits are available for the importation of classic cars. Vehicles may be imported by expatriates on a temporary basis for a maximum of three months.

Vehicle Export

Owners wishing to export their vehicles are required to visit their nearest traffic department. Outstanding fines have to be paid prior to the issue of an export number and all relevant paperwork. This documentation will then need to be taken to the customs department for approval, and the issue of an export permit. Vehicles may be driven out of Kuwait or shipped by sea.

New Car Dealers

Alpha Romeo	Al Qurain Automotive Co.	80 5008
Aston Martin	Al Khalid Automotive Co.	88 8111
Audi P.89	Fouad Alghanim & Sons	81 1118
Bentley	Al Zayani Trading	473 5199
BMW	Ali Alghanim & Sons	80 4200
Cadillac	Alghanim Automotive	88 1111
Chrysler	Al Mulla Group	242 3250
Daewoo	Ali Alghanim & Sons	80 4200
Ferrari	Al Zayani Trading	80 8010
Ford	Arabian Motors Group	82 8828
Honda	Mutawa Al Kazi Co.	83 3334
Hyundai	Northern Gulf Trading Co.	80 8444
Infiniti	Al Babtain	80 4888
Jaguar	Al Zayani Trading	80 8010
Jeep	Bebbehani	476 4587
Kia	Al Qurain Automotive Co.	80 5008
Lamborghini P.89	Fouad Alghanim & Sons	81 1118
Land Rover	Ali Alghanim & Sons	80 4200
Lexus	Al Sayer Group	80 2008
Lincoln	Arabian Motors Group	82 8828
Maserati	Al Zayani Trading	80 8010
Mazda	Kuwait Automotive Imports Co.	473 3334
Mercedes	Al Bisher & Al Kazemi	481 0277
Mercury	Arabian Motors Group	82 8828
MG Rover	Ali Alghanim & Sons	80 4200
Mini	Ali Alghanim & Sons	80 4200
Mitsubishi	Al Mulla Group	474 1822
Nissan	Al Babtain	80 4888
Peugeot	Kuwait Automotive Imports Co.	473 3334
Porsche P.87	Behbehahi Motors Co.	88 8911
Renault	Al Babtain	80 4888
Rolls Royce	Al Zayani Trading	80 8010
Skoda P.89	Fouad Alghanim & Sons	81 1118
Suzuki	Mustafa Karam & Sons	80 3003
Toyota	Al Sayer Group	80 2008
Volkswagen P.89	Fouad Alghanim & Sons	81 1118
Volvo	Al Qurain Automotive Co.	80 5008

Used Car Dealers

Al Mulla Used Cars P.ix	243 5495
California Auto Sales	566 2063
Hala Motors Est.	246 2471
Junior Car Centre	575 5955
My Car Centre	266 5801
Shereen Motor Co.	482 8612
Wara Cars Co.	244 4500

Vehicle Insurance

Third party insurance, which costs approximately KD 20 per year, is compulsory and a pre-requisite to registering a vehicle. This insurance provides cover for circumstances including death or injury, and property damage. Comprehensive insurance may also be purchased to cover accidents, theft, fire, etc., the cost of which will vary from vehicle to vehicle. Again, the dealer will usually arrange insurance. Comprehensive insurance is calculated based on the make and model of the vehicle, and your driving history. Following an accident some insurance companies will provide a recovery service and a replacement vehicle for a maximum of five working days. Check to see what your contract covers. If you intend to take your vehicle across the border you will need to advise your insurance company in advance. You will be issued an orange insurance card to travel through Arab countries, and a green insurance card to travel through European countries. A Kuwaiti guarantor is required.

Vehicle Insurance

Al Ahlia Insurance Co.	244 8870
Al Khaleej Insurance Co.	80 2080
First Takaful Insurance	88 0055
Gulf Insurance Co.	242 2285
Kuwait Bahrain Insurance Co.	246 6837
Kuwait Insurance Co.	242 0135

Registering a Vehicle

When purchasing a new car the dealer will arrange your registration. In all other instances you will be required to register your vehicle at the traffic department at the governorate in which you reside. You will need to have a valid Civil ID card and driving licence, both of which will have to be presented with your application.

The vehicle registration period, after the initial three-year period for a new car, is 12 months. Prior to re-registering a vehicle a roadworthiness test is conducted, and the insurance and all outstanding fines will have to be paid. On completion of the test, and payment of the premium (third party insurance of approximately KD 20 is mandatory), the insurance company will issue a receipt. Take the receipt back to the traffic department and purchase a KD 5 revenue stamp, which needs to be affixed to the receipt. If any traffic fines are due they will have to be paid before the insurance receipt can be stamped. The old vehicle registration ('diftar') is then exchanged for the new one.

There are no companies authorised to process registration documentation on behalf of vehicle owners.

Traffic Fines & Offences

Traffic violations are a common occurrence in Kuwait. Although there is a comprehensive list of violations and their respective fines/jail time, one wonders how rigorously the traffic laws are actually policed. It seems as though drivers of every nationality are permitted to break speed limits and drive recklessly, use the emergency lanes on motorways, and park illegally.

The current listed fines are KD 5 for illegal parking, KD 20 – 50 for exceeding the speed limit, KD 10 for driving without a licence and KD 10 for not wearing a seat belt. Jumping a red light will cost you KD 50 and driving with tinted windows will cost KD 10. Tinting of windows to any degree is now completely banned, even for citizens.

If you are caught driving under the influence of alcohol the consequences can be severe and expatriates face a fine, custodial sentence and/or deportation. It simply is not worth drinking and driving. You will not be given any support by your company and you will lose your job.

Traffic fines are not sent to your address. They accumulate at the traffic department and are payable prior to re-registration of a vehicle. It is possible to pay traffic fines at a police station prior to re-registering a vehicle. You can also check for traffic fines online via the Ministry of Interior website. Non-Arabic speakers will find it impossible to navigate from the homepage though, so try entering the (very long) web address exactly as it appears here, (http://213.132.241.12/moieservices.nsf/MOIViolIndividual), then type your Civil ID number in the box to see a list of all the fines due.

Should you have your residence permit cancelled and attempt to leave Kuwait without paying traffic fines, you will be stopped at the airport and not allowed to travel until payments are made. It's not possible to pay fines at the airport; you will have to go to the traffic department and do so in person.

Parking not fine!

There are two types of speed camera in operation. Static cameras are mounted on central reservations on the expressways and other major roads, and at a number of major intersections. They very rarely flash, even if you are doing 140km/h. However, don't be too complacent; you'll only get caught out! Mobile cameras are mounted in the rear window of small jeeps and are moved around Kuwait. They are usually located at underpasses on expressways and are always manned.

Breakdowns

If you should breakdown try to move your car off the road. If you breakdown on a motorway, move your vehicle as far off the carriageway as possible and then stand well out of the way until help arrives. The standard of driving in Kuwait is poor and many accidents have been caused by someone hitting a vehicle that has not been removed from the motorway after breaking down.

You will invariably find that someone will stop to offer assistance. Accept the assistance, however, if you are a woman on your own it is common sense to be wary of the good Samaritan.

It would be foolish to travel off-road in Kuwait without an ample supply of drinking water. Having a breakdown in the middle of summer and not being able to sit in an air-conditioned vehicle while you wait for help could prove disastrous. Carry a mobile phone with you if you are driving in the desert, although be aware that the coverage in Kuwait is poor in some areas and you may not be able to pick up a signal. Kuwait is a small country and it makes it all the more frustrating if you break down in a remote area and cannot get help.

Traffic Accidents

Other options → Car [p.34]

Traffic accidents are a common occurrence in Kuwait. For a population of almost 2.5 million, there were in excess of 45,878 traffic accidents in 2004. Hotspots include the Fahaheel Expressway (Road 30) and the Ahmadi Expressway (Road 40) south of the 4th Ring Road, and the 4th, 5th and 6th Ring Roads. Essentially, any fairly long stretch of road where motorists can reach high speeds is a hotspot. The best advice is to always be vigilant, expect the unexpected and be aware of vehicles around you. Just because a motorist is indicating left, don't be surprised if he turns right!

All traffic accidents must be reported to the police. Call 777 to speak to the emergency services. A police car will be dispatched, along with an ambulance/fire crew if required. A severely injured person should be immediately evacuated from the scene to a hospital, but it is important that, if at all possible, you do not leave the scene prior to the police arriving. This may result in you getting the blame, even if the accident was not your fault, or you may be charged with fleeing the scene. The police will want to see your Civil ID card, Kuwait driving licence and vehicle registration papers. All parties involved in a traffic accident will usually be required to go to the nearest police station. There is every likelihood, if an accident is very serious and has resulted in severe injuries or death, that the drivers may be taken into custody pending a court appearance. Contact your embassy immediately. They will visit you, send messages to your relatives and/or friends, and put you in touch with local lawyers who will provide legal assistance.

If necessary, drivers will have to go to court for a ruling on the cause of an accident. All evidence will be presented to the judge, who will ask questions before making a judgement. Minor accidents are usually dealt with in a day; major/serious accidents will often see the judge retiring to consider the facts prior to passing judgement. Court proceedings are usually in Arabic. Make sure that you have someone that you trust representing you.

Repairs (Vehicle)

Professional garages include those run by Al Mulla, Bosch and AC Delco. There are hundreds of small garages located throughout Kuwait, a large number of which are found in Shuwaikh. Behbehani Motors also have an excellent car repair service (Smart Repair, p.86, 843 843).

An accident report must accompany all vehicles taken in for repairs. Changes to the law now make it illegal for a garage to carry out major repairs to a vehicle without this paperwork. Not having an accident report from the police will render the insurance valid.

Local insurance companies tend to have lists of specific garages authorised to carry out repairs. A deductible ('excess') is payable to the insurance company. This amount varies slightly from one company to another and depends on the make and model of vehicle.

Vehicles under warranty will be repaired by the dealer only if the mechanical defect is covered in the warranty. Vehicles under warranty that are involved in traffic accidents will be repaired by a garage authorised by the insurance company.

Simple, Effective, Appealing – three qualities essential to great design.

The **Explorer Designlab** team approaches every project with this in mind, creating perfect solutions to everyday design problems while challenging trends and exploring the boundaries of creative design.

Design is central to your company's image, and has a direct effect on how you are perceived by your customers. Contact us to learn how you can benefit from our services.

CORPORATE IDENTITY • BROCHURES & REPORTS • PACKAGING • ADVERTISING • PRINT • WEB

PO Box 34275 Dubai, UAE
Phone (+971 4) 335 3520 **Fax** (+971 4) 335 3529
Email Info@Explorer-Publishing.com

Exploring

EXPLORER

Exploring

Exploring

Table of Contents

Highlights...

Somewhere For the Weekend...   p.122

They say that location is everything and Kuwait is blessed with many neighbours worth a visit or two. If you fancy a weekend break but don't want to break the bank then you can make the short hop to one of Kuwait's fellow GCC countries. Whether you fancy some shopping in Dubai, a luxury hotel in Abu Dhabi, a trek in Oman, a spot of sport in Bahrain or rest and relaxation in Qatar, you can get the heads up in one of the Explorer Residents' Guides.

Check Out the Checklist   p.96

Whether you're in Kuwait for the weekend or for the working week it is worth checking out some of the local attractions. From souks to shopping malls, the Maritime Museum to the Friday Market, Kuwait has a surprising number of sights and sites worth a look. You will also find a subtle reminder of the Gulf war at the Al Qurain Museum and the infamous Mutla Ridge.

Kuwait's New Hotspot - Fahaheel   p.122

Kuwait is, like its GCC counterparts, currently undergoing some impressive expansion with projects in and out of the city. One up and coming area definitely worth keeping an eye out for is Fahaheel, where real estate giants Tamdeen have set up shop - literally. Tamdeen's Madinat Fahaheel is home to the impressive Al Kout Mall as well as the Al Manshar complex where there will be residential towers and a five star hotel.

Exploring

Kuwait may be one of the smallest countries in the world but its 500km coastline has endless beaches that not only attract visitors from the GCC but also international interest is constantly increasing. Just over 17,000 square kilometres the country is slightly smaller than New Jersey and is still one of the fastest growing countries in the world. It is a country rich in natural resources - oil was discovered in 1938 and exports began in 1946 after the Second World War. Today 90% of Kuwait's oil reserve is exported, a relatively easy task considering the country has one of the best natural harbours in the Middle East and is regarded as a gateway to the Arabian Gulf.

Before the discovery of oil Kuwait was home to tradesmen who made their living from selling camel fleeces and craftsmen who built the renowned Dhow merchant ships. As a result a 'Koute' (fort close to the water) was built on the 'Qurain' (high hill) which in turn became the beginnings of the State of Kuwait.

Although most of the visitors coming to Kuwait from neighbouring GCC countries are for business purposes, there are a number of visitors coming to discover the country's cultural and luxury appeal, be they locals or expats from various Middle East countries or adventurous international visitors. There are also a lot of people from all corners of the world visiting friends and relatives who live in Kuwait. The best season to visit is either October to December or March to May. From June to August temperatures can rise to 60 degrees, although it's a dry heat and the humidity is generally bearable.

With a greater number of visitors coming to Kuwait there are many hotels under construction now with a staggering 21 more expected in the next 3 years, primarily catering to the business traffic and the movement of people to/from Iraq. The hotels are spread out over the city and all along the coastline of the Arabian Gulf almost down to the Saudi Border. If you are after a quiet relaxing beach holiday then the resorts are the best option, otherwise you will be able to find plenty of hotels in the city.

Today, Kuwait is a flat desert country where low and old houses still populate the horizon. However, with the Iraq invasion behind them and the high oil prices, Kuwait is starting to take a new shape. Modern high rises designed by international architects have begun to emerge and more and more tourists are coming for a leisurely holiday.

Kuwait borders with Saudi Arabia to the south and Iraq to the north and it takes only around two and a half hours to drive from border to border. The infrastructure is well developed with three-lane ring roads throughout the country and well-established road networks in most developed areas. The speed limit is 120km per hour, but is often not adhered to. Do not be surprised if you get overtaken from the slow lane by buses or trucks, even though you are in the fast lane.

Outside the bustling city, areas such as Wafra, Sulaibiya and Abdali provide some peace and quite. These areas are home to many modern farms where vegetables are harvested and many animals such as cattle, camels and chickens are reared. Many of the locals and expats will take a drive to the markets in these areas to bargain for the vegetables.

In the City, Sharq offers you some decent shopping and restaurants, and a large fish market. Salmiya is a good place to catch up with friends in one of the modern coffee shops or go shopping for designer brands in the modern shopping malls. For those looking for computers or jewellery, Hawalli is the best bet. For a more authentic area with markets and bustling streets, head down to Kuwait City and visit the old souk area, or to Shuwaikh where you can find everything - including a kitchen sink. Shuwaikh is divided into different areas such as the 'Lights and Electrical Area', 'Car Area', 'Paint Area' and the 'Mechanic Area'.

Explore the GCC

If you want to drop in on your neighbours then go prepared with one of the Explorer Insider Guide series. Be it for a shopping spree in Dubai, a luxury holiday in Abu Dhabi, a get-back-to-nature trip to Oman, a long weekend to Qatar or a sporting event in Bahrain, don't leave Kuwait without an Explorer!

Gulf War: Over but not forgotten

Although no one wants to talk about it, Kuwait still has a few reminders of the Gulf War. Some of the houses opposite the British Embassy have traces from the war and the Al Quarain Museum is a living example of the past. Most of the buildings have been pulled down or redeveloped in an effort to erase Kuwait's many Gulf War scars.

Kuwait Visitors' Checklist

Other options ➜ Key Kuwait Projects [p.6]

Despite its relatively small size, just over 17,000 square kilometres, Kuwait has a surprising number of interesting aspects worth exploring. Whether it is traces of a war-torn past which is dead but not buried, or the committment to culture and traditions that remains steadfast, there is something for every type of intrepid explorer. Check out the list below which highlights the many historical, shopping and exploring activities that will open up a whole new world to any Kuwait resident or visitor.

The Grand Mosque [p.117]

Kuwait's largest mosque, which accommodates approximately ten thousand men at prayer time on Fridays, is not to be missed. Experienced guides will take you around the Mosque and provide an insight into the Muslim faith.

Heritage Souk [p.107]

Partly destroyed in 1990, the Heritage Souk (Souk Al Hareen) is now being restored. Women have been trading in the souk for centuries and all the traders are still women today. Each part of the souk specialises in different products such as clothes, hardware or spices.

Kuwait Towers [p.118]

Don't miss the stunning view from the revolving restaurant atop the Kuwait Towers where you can enjoy a delicious buffet. Apart from being a distinguished landmark for Kuwait, the tall tower also stores the country's largest water reservoir.

Textile Souk [p.178]

The Textile Souk, or Fabric Souk has endless metres of fabric, colours and buttons as well as souvenirs, clothes and shoes at bargain prices. The choice of fabric and materials caters to various fashion styles from the traditional to the modern.

Liberation Tower [p.98]

Open only once a year the Liberation Tower is Kuwait's most famous landmark. It opened in 1996 and is the fifth tallest communication tower in the world. It marked a new era for Kuwait after the Gulf War. A restaurant was initially planned but never opened.

Dhow Building [p.118]

The Dhow Harbour and shipbuilding yards provide a glimpse of a traditional Arabian craft. Arrive early morning to the Dhow Harbour between the Seif Palace and the Fish Market for a taste (and a smell) of the local fishing tradition in Kuwait.

History Lesson [p.109]

The National Museum is a compound that houses a number of buildings. Some parts are in disrepair, however, the excellent Cultural Museum gives you a fascinating insight into Kuwait's traditions and heritage, and Sadu House is a centre for Bedouin art.

Failaka Island [p.109]

The history of Kuwait can be traced back to the 4th century BC when one of Alexander the Great's admirals visited and discovered Failaka Island, now regarded as Kuwait's main archaeological site. It is 18km to the east of Kuwait City and is a one-hour ferry ride away.

The Five Gates [p.108]

The wall around the Old City was demolished in 1957 but the five gates (Maqsab Gate, Jahra Gate, Shamiya Gate, Beraisi Gate and Bneid Al-Qar Gate) still stand. The gates were damaged during the Gulf War but have since been restored.

Record-Breaking Dhow [p.118]

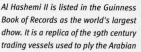

Al Hashemi II is listed in the Guinness Book of Records as the world's largest dhow. It is a replica of the 19th century trading vessels used to ply the Arabian Gulf and subcontinent sea routes. It has two storeys, one housing an impressive ballroom.

Exploring

Kuwait Visitors' Checklist

Animal Magic [p.122]

The Zoological Park in Kuwait has been rebuilt since the Iraq invasion and as well as lions, zebras and giraffes, 60 other species of animals and 129 species of birds make themselves at home in this park. There is also five species of reptile.

Al Qurain House [p.111]

One of Kuwait's Liberation monuments, also known as the War Museum, is Al Qurain House. Riddled with bullet holes, it shows the reality of the bloody battle between the Messilah Resistance Group and Iraqi Occupiers during the Iraqi invasion.

Amusing Thrills [p.120]

The City of Entertainment (Al Madina Al Tarfihiya) is the Arab version of Disneyland. With more than 40 rides, and different themes, this Doha Entertainment complex is a good family day out, and a tower offers good views over Kuwait City and out to sea.

Marina Stroll [p.186]

Marina Mall and Crescent is a new development on the waterfront in Salmiya. It houses restaurants and retail outlets, including a large Virgin Megastore. Marina Crescent has outdoor coffee shops and restaurants overlooking the marina.

Democratic Choice [p.98]

Being the first country in the GCC to have a democracy, Kuwait's National Assembly building is an imposing building in the downtown Sharq area. It is a must-see building with a 3,000 square metre concrete canopy based on the design of a traditional Bedouin tent.

Green Island [p.114]

Linked by a short bridge this artificial island houses an amphitheatre, restaurants, viewing tower, children's castle and an alternative view of Kuwait's shoreline. Easily accessible from the Gulf Road, the Green Island makes for a good day out.

Wafra [p.102]

Drive to Wafra for the freshest vegetables you can find in Kuwait. The 45 minute drive is also interesting, with camel herds crossing the road. It's the greenest area in Kuwait and makes a refreshing contrast to the city skyline.

Scientific Center [p.110]

The Scientific Center houses the largest Aquarium in the Middle East. It offers environmental education and a 3D IMAX movie theatre. You can watch and learn about the sharks and other marine inhabitants of the Arabian Gulf.

Cultural Dining [p.106]

Located close to the Sheraton Hotel in some old houses are a number of restaurants worth a lazy lunch or decadent dinner in traditional surroundings. You'll also find Dar Al Funoon, a hidden gem of an art gallery with a funky shop attached.

Friday Market [p.192]

Bargains can be had at the outdoor Friday market (Souk Al Jum'a) and despite the name it actually starts from Thursday afternoon. Everything is on offer and bargaining is expected. It is seriously busy but the hustle and bustle is all part of the experience!

Gold Digging [p.192]

The central gold market (Souk Al Dahab Al Markazi) contains a government office where gold can be checked for its purity and hallmark. Jewellery designs cater to all tastes and various international styles can be found.

Ahmadi [p.99]

Ahmadi was built in the 1940s and 50s for Kuwait's oil industry, and is a well-planned township outside Kuwait City. It is home to a cricket ground, golf course, the Kuwait Little Theatre and much more. It is a full community in itself and very popular with expats.

Kuwait City - Main Areas

The Kuwait skyline is generally low-rise due to restrictions on building heights imposed by the government. In 2003 this restriction was eased allowing for the construction of buildings exceeding 10 storeys. The limit was initially raised to 40 storeys then to 70 storeys in 2004, so there is likely to be a significant change to the skyline in the imminent future. Today, Kuwait City is in a transformation stage where new modern high-rises emerge every week. However, in many ways Kuwait City has not lost its personal touch. The diverse city still cleverly blends local architecture with new modern designs, together with old cars parked beside the latest Ferrari or Rolls Royce. Although there are mostly only commercial buildings within the city area, there are still some residential houses along the Arabian Gulf Street. Walking, jogging or biking along Arabian Gulf Street is a common practice and many people either come down for their daily walk or take the whole family for a day out especially on Fridays. Arabian Gulf Street offers many restaurants and food outlets along the seafront. On Friday afternoons and evenings many local Kuwaiti families take a picnic and find a pleasant spot somewhere on the grassed areas along the Gulf Street. When the temperature drops in the winter months the crowds stay until the early hours, relaxing and catching up.

It is possible to walk around Kuwait City, however most people still use their cars. If you do decide to walk it is important to be careful and look down as there can be potholes in the pavement and not all streets have footpaths to walk on.

The main area of the Kuwait City Governate is the Downtown area, which itself is divided into five distinct areas – Dasman, Mirqab, Safat, Sharq and Qibla. Many of the main attractions are located in the downtown city area. These include the Heritage Souk, Grand Mosque, Green Island, Liberation Tower, Jahra Gate and the main entertainment, shopping and restaurant areas. The downtown area has a number of separate suburbs. This area is not that big and is a good place to walk around the streets of the old souk and get an impression of the traditional way of life in Kuwait. The ambience is that of an old Arab market place and the atmosphere is quite vibrant. There are many bargains to be had and visitors never seem to leave empty handed.

Dasman   Map Ref 4-A1

Between the 1st and 2nd Ring Roads on the Arabian Gulf Street lies the Dasman area, which is the most visually interesting area in Kuwait. Here you will find some of Kuwait's most distinguished landmarks, including The Kuwait Towers. The towers are open to visitors every day and are located on the edge of a small peninsula. The largest of the three towers is 187m high and has an revolving observation area at the top (it makes one full turn every half hour). The restaurant and cafeteria are accessible via a high speed lift. The entrance fee for the observation tower is KD 1 and the views are simply stunning. There is no charge to visit the restaurant or cafeteria.

Mirqab   Map Ref 3-D4

Mirqab is the area of downtown Kuwait City in which you will find a number of government buildings, including the Ministry of Interior and Ministry of Public Works. The Ministries Complex off Abdullah Al-Salem Street houses the Ministries of Finance, Justice, Housing, Commerce & Industry, Social Affairs & Labour, Islamic Affairs and Awqaf. The main bus terminal is located off Al-Shuhada Street and the ice-skating rink and musical fountains are found sandwiched between the 1st Ring Road and Soor Street. The Courtyard Marriott Hotel, Arraya Convention Centre and Arraya Centre are all found in Mirqab.

Safat   Map Ref 3-C3

The area of Safat is the heart of Kuwait's commercial (downtown) district, is the origin of most of Kuwait's major roads (all distances in Kuwait are measured from Safat Square), and is home to the country's main post office. Safat Square is surrounded by souks selling wares of every shape and description. The municipal gardens provide refuge during the heat of the day.

Sharq   Map Ref 3-D2

Sharq is adjacent to Dasman, and houses the traditional Heritage Souk, the Dhow Harbour, as well as the Grand Mosque and National Assembly Building. An impressive new shopping and retail area, Souk Sharq, was built in 2001 and is a popular meeting area for locals and expatriates. Sharq is an interesting combination of old residential and commercial areas. It is probably one of the few areas that hasn't changed too much in the last couple of years with low-rise buildings and narrow streets without footpaths remaining. The Fish, Meat and Vegetable market in Sharq is an interesting experience and the building itself makes for a good photo opportunity. The Dhow Harbour is close by as well as the popular Souk Sharq, the perfect place to catch up with friends.

Qibla   Map Ref 3-B3

Qibla is where you'll find numerous souks and all banking headquarters. The National Museum, Planetarium, Sadu House and Bader House are all located on the Gulf Road, as is the National Assembly building. The Chamber of Commerce building, with its distinctive orange saucer top, is located on the corner of Al-Shuhada Street and Mubarak Al-Kabeer Street. The JW Marriott, Sheraton Hotel, Four Points, Le Meridien Tower, Swiss Inn Plaza and Carlton Tower Hotel are all located off Fahad Al-Salem Street. Salhiya Complex, home to a number of Kuwait's exclusive retail outlets, is at the back of the JW Marriott.

Kuwait City - Other Areas

As with Kuwait City, the outer suburbs tend to still be relatively low-rise with apartment buildings up to 10 storeys and three to four level villas. The main residential areas are relatively green with narrow streets and pleasant gardens. The outer suburbs are divided into a number of distinct areas that are either mainly industrial or residential.

Bneid Al-Gar   Map Ref 4-A3

Bneid Al-Gar is situated between the Gulf Road and Istiqlal (Fahaheel) Expressway. A number of hotels including the Safir International, Le Meridien, Continental, Second Home and Imperial are found here, as is the Vatican Embassy. Al Salam Hospital is located on Bour Said Street. There are numerous apartment complexes with great views over the Gulf, and a number of restaurants including Fuddruckers and Le Nôtre situated on the Gulf Road.

Qurtoba and Surra   Map Ref 12-A1

These two areas are more upmarket residential areas with various interesting and traditional architectural styles. Modern and traditional architecture can be seen side by side and the attention to detail on many of the buildings adds interesting features and keeps the area unique. The villas tend to be very large and it is not unusual for expatriates to rent floors of villas, some of which are much larger than a three bedroom apartment. The areas are a mixture of local and

expatriate residents and are also home to many embassies which are based inside some of the larger villas.

Shuwaikh   Map Ref 5-D3

The main industrial areas are located further away from the city. The closest is Shuwaikh which has evolved around the Shuwaikh Port and is located between the 3rd and 5th Ring Roads and is an interesting mixture of old and new. Al Rai, alongside Shuwaikh, is made up of many small industries, as well as a new shopping area, 'The Avenue', which is scheduled to open in 2006. It is rumoured to be one of the largest shopping malls in the Middle East. It present it may be bustling, noisy and very busy but Shuwaikh makes for an interesting experience. You can find all sorts of household items from the modern to the antique.

The Shuwaikh area is divided into sections such as the light area, car mechanical area, paint area and so forth. You can tell the different areas by the changing names of the small shops as well as the produce that overspills from their doors, be it lamps and lightbulbs in their millions, or endless rows of small mechanical shops. Shuwaikh gets very busy during the evening and it can be a bit of an adventure to drive down Canada Dry Street around 20:00 when the whole of Kuwait and his wife seem to be out. The street was named after the old Canada Dry factory that was once located there. The traffic is pretty horrendous, road rage is prevalent, manifesting in consistent horn beeping and selfish driving so be calm and enjoy the ride!

> **Lost and Found**
>
> *A lot of Kuwaitis and taxi drivers do not know their way around by road numbers. Every road has a name, be it a pseudonym like Canada Dry Street or University Roundabout, or a local name, like Ghazali Street, so if you need directions use the name that is known by the locals.*

Kuwait - Other Areas

Ahmadi   Map Ref 1-C4

Ahmadi was named after the late Amir Sheikh Ahmad Al-Jaber Al-Sabah. Compared to the rest of Kuwait, it is a quaint little town with around 30,000 inhabitants who live in small houses with big gardens situated along bushy roads and avenues. Located 40 minutes from Kuwait City on Road 40

Exploring

Kuwait City - Other Areas

(exit 212), Ahmadi (or Al Ahmadi as it is sometimes called) was originally built in 1948 for the pioneering oil workers. The area is home to many of the local sporting teams and expats enjoy activities including baseball, rugby and cricket at the large sports centre, as well as spectator sports at the stadium close by.

The town's museum (see p.109), which displays the history of oil exploration in the area, was destroyed by the Iraqi invasion in 1990 but was rebuilt after the war with a new exhibition displaying the geological formation through oil exploration, drilling and recovery. If you want to find out more about the oil industry you can call the museum (398 9111) or contact the Kuwait Oil Company (KOC) information office (398 1678) who organise guided tours for groups that want to explore the oilfield. As well as the museum, a visit to the large public garden is recommended as it has mature trees and grassed areas ideal for a family picnic. Many employees of KOC, expats and locals live in Ahmadi. The Ahmadi Golf Club, an 18 hole sand golf course, is popular and has a small clubhouse serving basic snacks and refreshments. Ahmadi is also home to the Kuwait Little Theatre that runs five or six amateur plays each year (see p.224).

Fahaheel   Map Ref 1-D3

The main development outside of the city has been to the south, in Fahaheel. Connected by the relatively new Fahaheel Expressway (Road 30), the drive takes around 30-40 minutes in comparison to the half a day's drive when there was just one bumpy lane between the two cities. Offering similar facilities to Kuwait City, Fahaheel has a more of a relaxed way of life with a Bedouin influence. The majority of females walking or driving around are still covered in their local black abaya.

Al Kout Mall in Fahaheel

Although some areas of Fahaheel are going through a makeover, the new houses and shopping malls that are being built still retain the character of old Arab architecture. Fahaheel is a good place to bargain for gold, clothes or shoes in the many souks and small shops dotted around. It is a lot easier to walk around Fahaheel compared to Kuwait City and almost each block has a souk of some sorts, selling an interesting mix of household items and Arabian souvenirs with the old central souk alongside the very latest modern electronics stores. While many people stockpile on trips abroad you can find virtually everything you need in Fahaheel. You can even get the latest interior magazines from Europe and America.

The Fahaheel fish market is worth a trip if you want to stock up on seafood for a bbq. The latest commercial development in this up-and-coming area is the Madinat Al Fahaheel (see p.190), a huge complex that is set to become the new Fahaheel city centre. Al Kout Mall is already open and has become a popular shopping location thanks to its many fashion stores, including high street favourites such as Next and Zara. There are also a few outdoor cafes where you can enjoy a leisurely lunch overlooking the sea and fountains. Also part of the development will be the Al Manshar commercial complex, which will also feature a shopping arcade and family entertainment centre as well as residential towers, office blocks and a five-star hotel, all to be completed sometime in 2006.

Currently the main residential area is on the outskirts of Fahaheel. There are mostly blocks of flats of varying quality in this area. Most western expats who are attracted to Fahaheel and its facilities have settled down in either Mahaboula or Fintas, which is closer to Kuwait City.

Even though Fahaheel was not damaged by the Gulf War and is one of the oldest suburbs of Kuwait City, it is mainly a residential and shopping location with no real heritage sites and landmarks. The only real sights to see are the oil refineries nearby, that when driven past at night look somewhat like a futuristic landscape.

Farwaniya   Map Ref 16-B2

Farwaniya is located between Airport Road (55) and Ghazali Road (60) along the 6th Ring Road. The best landmark is the Crowne Plaza Hotel on Airport Road. The Crowne Plaza has a number of popular restaurants and many expats go there for an evening out. Check with the hotel or local press for special deals at the restaurants. Farwaniya has a

Exploring

Kuwait - Other Areas

few independent shops selling clothes and electrical items, but its mostly a residential suburb with villas and flats. Away from the chaos of the main roads this small area is still popular with Bedouin women looking for their supplies and is worth a quick stroll for the cultural insight.

Hawalli — Map Ref 7-B3

Hawalli is a bustling residential and shopping area located inland and slightly north of Salmiya. The area is quite built up and is home to a large section of the Indian community. Shopping varies from modern malls like the Mohalleb Complex, which is shaped like the transom of a boat and houses a cinema, as well as many small low cost shops where you can pick up counterfeit copies of the latest DVDs and computer software.

Jabriya — Map Ref 1-C2

Another residential area is Jabriya located just off 4th Ring Road from Fahaheel Expressway. There are a few independent shops and most of the villas are very big and tend to be shared by families occupying separate floors. There are also a number of embassies in this area and a large hospital.

Jahra — Map Ref 1-A2

Today Jahra is a residential area but it was once of strategic importance as a verdant garden settlement, as it marks the intersection of several old caravan routes. Some archaeological sites provide evidence of pre-Islamic times but unfortunately these are not open to the public. Jahra is located 24km north-west of Kuwait City. In 1920 troops from Saudi Arabia (the Ikhwan) invaded Jahra but were eventually defeated by the Kuwaitis with British help. Some of the Kuwaitis took cover in the Red Fort and outlasted the siege. The Fort, named after the red clay that was made to construct the walls, was partially restored but only the shell of the building remains, which can be seen on the way into Jahra from road number 80.

On Fridays Jahra has an outdoor market where you can bargain for many items, including clothes and old electronic items. Fresh vegetables from Abdally are also available.

> **Explore the GCC**
>
> *If you want to drop in on your neighbours then go prepared with one of the Explorer Residents' Guides. Be it for a shopping spree in Dubai, a luxury holiday in Abu Dhabi, a get-back-to-nature trip to Oman, a long weekend to Qatar or a sporting event in Bahrain, don't leave Kuwait without an Explorer!*

Jahra is also the location of the famous 'turkey shoot', where coalition allies destroyed a stalled Iraqi convoy that was heading up the 'Mutla Ridge' on its way back to Iraq. The road was cleared of any evidence of the incident by dealers and other souvenir hunters and a tank graveyard is the only physical reminder.

Jahra Red Fort

Mutlaa Ridge — Map Ref 2-C2

Mutlaa Ridge is an area west of the city made infamous by the Desert Storm operation. The series of sandstone ridges rising up to 60m high are a stark contrast to the vast flat desert landscape. No permit is required to camp, making it a popular weekend retreat for campers and day-trippers. There are a number of camp resorts and farms with facilities, and you are sure to see plenty of camels, sheep, goats and horses. Many of the camps are run by private companies for their employees but several are open for the general public and are popular with both Kuwaitis and expats (see p.30). The area was heavily mined during the war, but most areas have been declared safe, however it is better to stick to the camps and farms.

Desert

In addition to Mutla, Kuwait is blessed with a large expanse of desert that is worth exploring, if for nothing else for the arresting tranquility. The gas flares from the oil wells light up the night sky and star gazers won't be disappointed. Remember to take your compass and plenty of water, and a GPS can also be handy, especially if you're unlucky enough to get caught in a sandstorm (relatively frequent in the late winter months). Although flat

Exploring

Kuwait - Other Areas

Camping

Most Kuwaitis have a farm or access to a camp in the desert and frequently in winter there are evening parties with dancing and traditional food cooked on the campfire. Temporary toilets are generally available, and some even have air conditioning in the tents. Flies can be a bit of a nuisance so a small hand fan is a useful accessory. If you're lucky you may see a desert wolf which was almost hunted to extinction, as well as some desert foxes and cats.

and relatively inhospitable, the desert is home to more than 400 species of plants and numerous exotic birds and animals. After the winter rains the spring sees the desert becoming a small oasis with many beautiful wild flowers, including the desert truffle which is sold as a delicacy. Although there are some snakes they are generally not poisonous. While the possibility of mines is remote, it is still best to stick to the established trails. Unfortunately, Kuwait doesn't have any large dunes or wadis and the terrain is generally flat, so extreme off-road driving is not really an option.

Salwa   Map Ref 13-C4

Alongside the Arabian Gulf Street, between the 4th and 5th Ring Roads, is a popular residential area for expats in Kuwait and is also home to many of country's western schools. However, the majority of the accommodation options are apartments and parking can be a major problem. The Radisson SAS hotel and Palm Beach Resort are also located in Salwa.

Wafra   Map Ref 2-C4

South of Kuwait City, Wafra is a small market town populated with around 200 farms and many large trees making it one of the greenest areas in the country. It is also home to an experimental farm funded by the Kuwait Government that assesses the commercial feasibility of growing crops and vegetables in the harsh desert climate, and develops new products that can survive on less water. The farms rear dairy cattle and poultry and harvest grains, vegetables and fruit. Many Kuwaitis make their way to Wafra on Fridays when the open market sells locally produced vegetables and fruit. Although it is around 40 minutes drive from the city, it is still well worth a visit if just to get a feel for a different side of Kuwait. Drive south out of the city either on Road 30 or 40 past Ahmadi and follow the signs for Wafra. From the exit you need to drive for another 20 kilometres until you reach the farms.

Museums, Heritage & Culture

With its rather colourful history Kuwait has some interesting cultural and heritage sites, be they a tribute to a bygone era or a reminder of past struggles. Unfortunately a lot of the country's historical treasures in The National Museum were either transported to Baghdad or destroyed during the Gulf War, and the museum itself still carries the burn scars in the main hall entrance. The museum contains four buildings, each focusing on a specific aspect of Kuwait's history and heritage. There is also the new Cultural Museum which educates its visitors on life in Kuwait before its modern developments, and includes displays on the interior of a traditional house. The National Museum also hosts the Dar al-Athar-al-Islamiyya, a 30 year collection of art from around the world by Sheikh Nasser al Sabah and his wife Sheikha Hussah.

The Iraqi invasion of Kuwait during the Gulf War is very much part of Kuwait's history and despite the country being committed to eradicating the scars of the war, the wounds remain relatively fresh. The Kuwait House of National Works (484 5335), located in north Shuwaikh, has photo, video and artwork displays of the horrific memories that occurred during the invasion. Located in Qurain, the Bayt Al-Qurain House (543 0343) is another reminder of the war as it was nearly destroyed in the invasion. Today the house tells you the story of the martyr Bader Al Eidan, who was killed here together with 11 of his friends (seven were rescued).

Sadu House

Cultural Museum

While the Gulf War is a distinct part of Kuwait's history, the country also has strong memories of a more relaxed heritage when pearl diving and dhow building were the country's main source of income. The Al-Hashemi Marine Museum (575 6000) is testament to this era. Traditional arts and crafts are also very much a part of Kuwait's cultural heritage and Al Sadu House, close to the National Museum, promotes Bedouin art while the Tariq Rajab Museum in Jabriya is a private museum but has an open display of Arabic manuscripts, calligraphy, ceramics and pottery. Dickson House, the residential headquarters for the first British political agent in Kuwait in 1870, features traditional Arabic architecture and although it is undergoing restoration it still makes for an interesting visit.

Archaeological Sites

The oldest known settlement in Kuwait is at Failaka Island, which can be reached only by public ferry. It is really the only archaelogical site in Kuwait worth visiting (see p.109 for more information). While other known archaelogical sites are scarce a recent joint British and Kuwait study did discover evidence of seafaring in Kuwait some 7,000 years ago. It is believed that sophisticated boats travelled between the Arabian Peninsula and Southern Mesopotamia trading in exotic stone and painted ceramics. A stretch of the coastline supported a cosmopolitan and industrious community at this time, and some of the remains left by these ancient inhabitants are being investigated by the British Archaeological Expedition to Kuwait (BAEK) at a site known as H3, Al-Sabiyah. Unfortunately the site is not yet open to the public.

Art Galleries

Other options → Art [p.162]
Art Supplies [p.164]

Kuwait is definitely not a cultural desert and actually has a rich tradition and heritage in contemporary Islamic art and calligraphy. There is an Art Council and several art galleries displaying both Arabic and modern art, and exhibitions are held throughout the year. Kuwait is also fortunate to have a number of internationally recognised Kuwaiti artists that have displayed their work both here and internationally.

In addition to the established galleries, there are many private collections that survived the Iraqi invasion, and are definitely worth seeing if you get the opportunity.

Beit Lothan

Location → Arabian Gulf Street · Salmiya
Hours → 09:00 - 13:00 16:30 - 21:00 Thu & Fri closed
Web/email → na   Map Ref → 8-C2
| 575 5866

Beit Lothan is dedicated to the promotion of arts and crafts and is host to various exhibitions and diplays throughout the year. It covers an area of 4,000 square metres on the Arabian Gulf Street and caters to all tastes and themes, including sculpture, ceramic arts, jewellery and photography, as well as contemporary art and calligraphy. Watch out in the local press for details of current and forthcoming exhibitions or seminars. There is also a small coffee shop for basic refreshments and for theatre luvvies they also hold drama classes throughout the year culminating in an annual concert in March/April.

Boushahri Art Gallery

Location → Beh Arabian Gulf Street · Salmiya
Hours → 09:00 - 13:00 16:00 - 19:00
Web/email → na   Map Ref → 8-C2
| 571 4883

Established in 1968, this is the oldest and largest gallery in Kuwait. Temporary exhibitions are regularly held showcasing works from both regional and international artists, as well as local Kuwaiti artists, and it's a great place to discover authentic Arabic art.

British Council in Kuwait

Location → Al Arabi Street, Mansouriya · Safat
Hours → 08:00 - 15:00 Thu & Fri closed
Web/email → www.britishcouncil.org/kuwait   Map Ref → 3-E2
| 251 5512

At their centre in Mansouriya, the British Council offers you a place to learn, study and take exams, access the internet for online information, attend events and exhibitions, and receive advice on UK culture and education. It can also advise on the cultural events and heritage of Kuwait and is also a valuable source of information on arts and crafts, both in this region and internationally.

British Studio Arts

Location → Off Street 208, Funaitees
Hours → By Appointment
Web/email → na   Map Ref → 1-D3
| 390 5263

This small but interesting collection is housed in a private villa and can only be viewed by making an appointment. Located about 20km south of the city

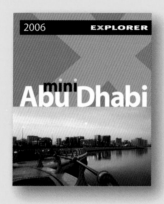

Made with hand luggage in mind

Don't be fooled by their diminutive size, these perfectly pocket proportioned visitor's guides are packed with insider info on travel essentials, shopping, sports and spas, exploring, dining and nightlife.

Phone (971 4) 335 3520 • **Fax** (971 4) 335 3529
Info@Explorer-Publishing.com • www.Explorer-Publishing.com
Residents' Guides • Visitors' Guides • Photography Books • Activity Guidebooks • Maps

EXPLORER

Passionately Publishing...

it was established in 1998, and displays arts and crafts by leading British artists. More than 300 pieces of art are on permanent display and commissions can be arranged should you have the desire (and the wealth) to own a unique piece of art.

Dar Al Funoon

Location → Beh churches, nr Sheraton Htl · Salhiya   243 3138
Hours → See below
Web/email → www.daralfunoon.com   Map Ref → 3-B3

Established in 1993, the gallery focuses on contemporary Arab art as well as Arabic calligraphy. Exhibitions are held monthly from October to May, and a special silk exhibition of arts and crafts is held in December. Between temporary exhibitions, items from the private collection are on display, which can be bought. The gallery is located behind the church area, between the Sheraton Hotel and the Arabian Gulf Street. The area itself is interesting thanks to its old Kuwaiti-style houses and a large courtyard which includes a number of excellent restaurants. Not only is the gallery renowned for furnishing many of the hotels in Kuwait, but many visitors or departing expats go there to buy their very own piece of local art.

Timings: *10:00 - 13:00, 16:00 - 20:00, Thu 10:00 - 13:00, Fri closed.*

Dar Al Funoon

Free Atelier

Location → Nr British Embassy · Dasman   243 6023
Hours → 09:00 - 13:00   Thu & Fri closed
Web/email → na   Map Ref → 3-C2

The Free Atelier on Arabian Gulf Street opened in 1960 to provide a government-funded studio space for budding artists. Art courses are offered, with tutoring from professional artists. There is a gallery that stages exhibitions of artists' work. The Free Atelier model has since been adopted by other GCC states.

Forts

Kuwait doesn't have many forts, mainly because centuries ago this relatively small country was a stable community only really threatened by Bedouin tribes from the desert. The only fort in existence is located in Jahra, about 20km west of Kuwait City, and is called the Red Fort. It is a shell of a building that was recently restored but is a reminder of the heritage of the area.

Red Fort

Location → Al Qasr al Ahmar   na
Hours → 08:00 - 13:00   16:00 - 18:00   Holidays closed
Web/email → na   Map Ref → 1-C2

Designed to keep the local tribes at a distance, the Red Fort was built to protect the natural wells around Jahra. In 1920, when the Kuwaitis and the Ikhwan (troops from Saudi Arabia) went to battle many Kuwaitis took shelter in the Red Fort. The fort is made out of thick red mud walls and towers, and has a large courtyard. It was recently renovated but there is little to see apart from the shell of the fort, however it is one of the few memories of a past civilisation and the troubles they encountered. Admission is free (and the place is rarely busy), but often a security guard or 'tour guide' will accompany you around the fort and expect payment for his troubles. The security guards generally don't speak any English so remember to take that phrase book with you! To reach the fort from Kuwait City take the main Al-Jahra Road, off road number 80, and exit onto Marzouk Al Mat'aab Street.

Heritage Sites - City

Other options → Art [p.162]
Mosque Tours [p.117]
Museums - City [p.109]

Kuwait is an intriguing mix of old and new, with traditional beliefs and a strong desert culture. The main heritage sites and museums are located in the downtown area of Kuwait City. Initially Kuwait was a very small city surrounded by a large wall to protect it from roaming Bedouin tribes, but as the wall was demolished the city grew and it now stretches over a large area. The houses in the city and surrounding areas are relatively new, with few having the typical Arab windtower. However, some windtowers can be seen in the downtown Quibla area behind the churches, and visits can be arranged to the Kuwait Water Towers (244 4021) on Arabian Gulf Street. The old souk area is interesting, as it rekindles the old traditional feel of Arabia and its architecture, and downtown you will also find Sadu House and Beit al Badr, which are some of the older heritage buildings in the city.

Other sites worth visiting include the Mubarika School for boys which opened in 1911, making it the first middle school in Kuwait. The school is a good example of traditional architecture of that time. The Museum of Modern Art is located in the Eastern School for Girls, which opened in 1938. The museum holds a collection of works and pictures from the 1950s, and can be visited from 09:00-13:00, and 17:00-21:00 daily - entrance is free.

There has always been a desire to maintain a traditional feel within Kuwait, certainly compared to other developing countries in the Middle East, and this is clearly demonstrated in the Arab Organisations Headquarters Building which opened in 1994. The interior of this modern building echoes various architectural styles from across the Arab world.

Al Khalifa Mosque

Location ➜ Arabian Gulf St · Central Kuwait	na
Hours ➜ By arrangement only	
Web/email ➜ na	Map Ref ➜ 3-C2

This 18th century mosque is the oldest in Kuwait and is located opposite the Ministry of Foreign Affairs. It is still used today. It was built by Sheikh Khalifa Bin Mohamed, the great grandfather of the Khalifa family, and was funded from the sale of date palms grown in Al Hasa. Access can be arranged, preferably through a travel agent, although you can visit the site to arrange a suitable time.

Al Sadu House

Location ➜ Arabian Gulf St · Qibla	243 2395
Hours ➜ 08:00 - 13:00 16:00 - 19:30 Fri closed	
Web/email ➜ www.sadu-house.com	Map Ref ➜ 3-C3

Al Sadu House is alongside Bayt Al Bader on the Arabian Gulf Street, and is next to the National Museum. It is a centre for Bedouin art and handicrafts. Bedoiun women can be seen working

at their looms weaving carpets, bags and tent screens, which along with other handicrafts are available at very reasonable prices. Special exhibitions are often held with accompanying seminars on traditional Bedouin life, so if you're interested keep an eye on the 'To-Do' pages of the *Arab Times*.

Bayt Al Bader

Location ➜ Nr National Museum · Qibla	243 2395
Hours ➜ 08:00 - 13:00 16:00 - 19:00 Thu & Fri closed	
Web/email ➜ na	Map Ref ➜ 3-C3

Bayt Al Bader (or Beit Al Badr) is a reminder of life in Kuwait before the discovery of oil. Situated close to the National Museum, the house dates back to the mid 19th century. Set in 2,825 square metres, it is a typical desert style mud-brick house with a private courtyard and is a very rare sight in modern Kuwait. The arched entrance and main doors are certainly impressive, and the house often hosts exhibitions of local arts and crafts.

Dickson House

Location ➜ Off Arabian Gulf St · Central Kuwait	na
Hours ➜ Call to check	
Web/email ➜ na	Map Ref ➜ 3-D2

Located opposite the Dhow Harbour in Sharq, and east of Seif Palace, is Dickson House, a classic example of early 19th century Kuwaiti architecture. Recently restored by the National Council for Arts, the house was the original residence of the first British political agent Colonel Dickson. His wife actually resided there until her death in 1990. Initially built in 1870, the compound was extended several times over the years, and is a good example of life in early Kuwait.

Heritage Souk

Location ➜ Old Souk · Central Kuwait	na
Hours ➜ 09:30 - 12:30 16:30 - 21:00 Friday 16:00 - 21:00	
Web/email ➜ na	Map Ref ➜ 3-C3

The Heritage Souk (or Old Souk) has undergone some restorations but its authentic atmosphere remains. A mixture of traditional culture and old markets, the souk is divided into several areas where you can buy everything from electrical equipment and household items to clothes and the latest watches. The Fish and Spice Market is indoors and some other areas of the souk are partly covered – the entire souk area spans more

Exploring

Museums, Heritage & Culture

than a whole block. On one of the streets just off the square you will find restaurants, toilets and a children's playground area. Nearby is the women's market, called the 'Hareem Souk'. Take a walk down this narrow street and you'll find that all stalls are attended by Bedouin women in traditional dress.

It is best to visit the Heritage Souk during the evenings to make the most of the traditional atmoshphere. Go when you can spend plenty of time, as the labyrinth of narrow streets and the eclectic mix of goods for sale can keep you occupied for hours.

Old City Wall Gates

Location ➜ Various locations · Safat	na
Hours ➜ Visit anytime	
Web/email ➜ na	Map Ref ➜ na

It may not have exactly been the Great Wall of China, but until relatively recently old Kuwait City was surrounded by an impressive wall. The first part was built in 1760, the second in 1814 and final part in 1920. The walls were then demolished in 1957, but the gates remain. The gates stand along the 1st Ring Road at Bneid Al Qar, at the end of Mubarak Al Kabeer Street, end of Riyadh Street and the last gate is located at the roundabout opposite the Sheraton Hotel. (Jahra Gate map ref 3-B4, Shamiyah Gate map ref 3-C4, Shaab Gate map ref 3-E3, Al Haqsab Gate map ref 3-B3, Dasman Gate map ref 4-A2).

Old Kuwaiti Town

Old Kuwaiti Town

Location ➜ Nr National Assembly Building · Qibla	na
Hours ➜ 00:00 - 24:00	
Web/email ➜ na	Map Ref ➜ 3-C3

Located just west of the dhow harbour on Arabian Gulf Street, the Old Kuwaiti Town is a replica of a 19th century town. It is made up of a number of small houses and streets. The houses are made of sun-baked mud, coral and seashells, and are an interesting contrast to their modern architectural neighbours. Admission is free, and the area makes quite a good play area for children.

Yaum Al Bahhar Village

Location ➜ Nxt to Dhow Harbour · Shuwaikh	na
Hours ➜ Various timings	
Web/email ➜ na	Map Ref ➜ 3-C3

A popular destination with visitors, this traditional development along the Shuwaikh coast is designed to maintain a traditional Kuwaiti feel and covers an area of 5,000 sq m. The area houses 20 traditional handicraft shops, and during the day craftsmen can be seen demonstrating their trades from a bygone era. The development is currently being extended further down the coast, and will later include fountains and a walking area

Heritage Sites - Out of City

Other options ➜ Tours & Sightseeing [p.114]
Museums - Out of City [p.111]

The best site to find out about the lives of early settlers is Failaka Island, which is a short ferry ride from Ras Al-Ardh in Salmiya.

A recent study, undertaken by the British Archaeological Expedition to Kuwait and the Kuwait Department of Antiques and Museums, uncovered some fascinating insights into the history of seafaring in the region. A number of digs at the H3 site on the Jazairat Dubaij in Al Sabiyah have yielded evidence that a sophisticated shipping and trading population inhabited this area 7,000 years ago. Members of the public are not currently allowed to visit the H3 site.

Hidden Gems

Explorer takes pride in its research and enlists the skills of residents to get the inside scoop on a country. However, even we admit no-one's perfect, so if we have missed out a hidden cultural gem then please let us know (info@Explorer-Publishing.com) and so we can makes sure it is included in our 2nd edition.

Salmiya

Failaka Island

Location → Failaka Island	na
Hours → na	
Web/email → na	Map Ref → 1-D2

The beautiful Failaka Island lies 20km off the coast of Kuwait. Its history can be traced back to the Bronze Age and many of the artefacts and old pottery which have been discovered in archaeological digs date back more than 4,000 years. It is believed that admirals of Alexander the Great stayed on the island at one time.

It has always been one of the most significant archaeological sites in Kuwait, and was inhabited right up until the 1990 Iraq invasion. In 1958, archaeological excavations started to reveal the wealth and historical influence of Failaka. Archaeologists have uncovered evidence of an island settlement believed to have lived on the island between the third and first century BC. This rich history is represented today by a large collection of dwellings, fortifications and temples, as well as coins, figurines and molds.

The only way to reach Failaka Island is by public ferry from Ras Al-Ardh (also known as Ras Salmiya). Ras Al-Ardh is located behind the Pearl Marzouk Building in Salmiya, and the journey from there to Failaka Island takes just over an hour. The ferry departs every morning at 08:15 (except for Saturdays and Mondays), and returns at 12:30. However, before you plan your trip it is advisable to check the timings with the KPTC (571 3544).

On the island is the Safir Heritage Village, a hotel with a shawarma bar, shisha cafe and restaurant as well as a swimming pool (for families only) and children's play area. Visitors can walk around the ruins on the island but the best way to explore is by bike. Either take your own or hire from the Safir Heritage Village for KD 2.50 a day.

Many Kuwait residents take a picnic basket with them on Fridays to enjoy a leisurely brunch among the ruins.

Museums - City

Other options → Heritage Sites - City [p.106]
Mosque Tours [p.117]
Art [p.162]

Considering its relatively small size, Kuwait has its fair share of interesting museums charting both the region's ancient past and its more recent history such as the events of the 1991 Gulf War. A visit to one of these museums is a great way to learn about the culture and history of Kuwait.

The National Museum

Location → Dasman	245 1195
Hours → 08:30 - 12:00 16:00 - 19:00 Sat 16:00-19:00	
Web/email → na	Map Ref → 3-B3

The National Museum was once home to many treasures, but sadly it was looted and badly damaged during the Iraqi invasion. Many of the prized possessions, accumulated over many years were taken to Baghdad and the building torched; however, Iraq has begun the process of returning some of the items. The museum is now regaining some of its former magnificence and over 2,000 items are on display, tracing various aspects of Kuwait's history and heritage. The range covers the ancient past, the development of the Islamic nations, and the impact of the discovery of oil. Part

National Museum

Exploring

Museums, Heritage & Culture

of the Dar Al Athar Al Islamiyah collection is also on display, and the replica of the Muhallab II gracing the entrance has also recently been restored as a reminder of Kuwait's seafaring past. Admission to the museum is 250 fils and access is on the western side next to Sadu House. On approach the museum looks a little unwelcoming and the layout is somewhat confusing – Sadu House is a little barren, as is the building which appears to be the National Museum, however, across the central plaza is the 'Cultural Museum' – an adjoining building that traces Kuwait's history and has excellent displays warranting at least an hour or so to peruse.

There is also a modern Planetarium (built by Carl Zeiss) which is a pleasant educational experience for both adults and children.

Science and Natural History Museum

Location → Abdullah Al Mubarak St · Safat | 242 1268
Hours → 09:00 - 13:30 16:30 - 19:30 Thu & Fri closed
Web/email → na   Map Ref → 3-C3

This interesting museum contains displays of scientific discoveries across various sectors, including electronics, machinery, space, aviation, zoology and petroleum. Each gallery houses a particular theme, and there are some fascinating items on display, such as fossils, skeletons, dried flowers and stuffed animals.

Inside there is also a health hall and a planetarium showing a daily Galaxy Skyshow at 18:00.

The entry fee is just 150 fils for adults and 100 fils for children. Refreshments and toilets are available on site, and there is adequate wheelchair access.

The Scientific Center

Location → Ras Al-Ardh · Salmiya | 84 8888
Hours →   See below
Web/email → www.tsck.org.kw   Map Ref → na

Housing a range of facilities to keep young and old entertained for hours, this unique, sail-shaped building is a landmark on Arabian Gulf Street. Apart from having the largest aquarium in the Middle East and 'Discovery Place' for children, it also has an IMAX theatre that shows several presentations each day (changed on a regular basis). The presentations cover space, technology and educational themes, as well as the 'Fires of Kuwait' presentation, based on the Iraq invasion. The museum is dedicated to the cultural heritage of Kuwait, as well as to preserving the natural history

of the earth and its environment. A restaurant and coffee shop are located inside, and the facility is wheelchair friendly. Entrance fee to the aquarium or IMAX is KD 3 for adults and KD 2 for children under 13. Entrance to Discovery Place is KD 2 for adults and KD 1.500 for children. Combination tickets are available.

Timings: 09:00 - 12:30, 17:00 - 21:30, Thu 09:00 - 21:30, Fri 14:00 - 21:30

Scientific Center

Tareq Rajab Museum

Location → Nr New English School, Jct 5 · Jabriya | 531 7358
Hours → 09:00 - 12:00 16:00 - 19:00 Fri pm closed
Web/email → www.trmkt.com   Map Ref → 12-E1

Tareq Rajab was Kuwait's first Minister of Agriculture and he opened his extensive collection of Islamic art and crafts to the general public in 1980. The collection includes a large collection of ethnic and Islamic jewellery, costumes, ceramics and metalworks. Tapestries and manuscripts round off this very interesting collection along with some unique musical instruments. All articles on display are of Arab or Muslim origin and are clearly marked in English. Entrance is free.

The collection is housed in a private villa located in Jabriya (Block 12, Street 5, House no 16), near the 5th Interchange of the Fahaheel Expressway and the New English School. The museum's name is above the elaborate gilt-metal doorway and all the artefacts are displayed within glass cabinets within the house's basement.

Museums - Out of City

Other options → Tours & Sightseeing [p.114]
Heritage Sites - Out of City [p.108]

As Kuwait is relatively small, most of its museums are located within the city. Those interested in fossil fuels will find the interesting Petroleum and Oil Museum (at KOC Headquarters in Ahmadi) worth a visit. The museum traces the history of oil in Kuwait, and has some very interesting pictures dating back to the 1930s. Also on display is some of the old equipment used for drilling, and an interesting geological section explaining how oil is produced and replenished.

The small War Museum in Qurain is an interesting and poignant reminder of the many Kuwaitis who lost their lives trying to defend their country during the Iraqi Invasion. There is also a tank graveyard in Jahra – however, access is restricted and the area is not considered safe. It is routinely guarded by police, so it is best to stay away.

Qurain War Museum

Location → Follow signs off Rd 208, Qurain | na
Hours → 08:00 - 14:00   Fri closed
Web/email → na   Map Ref → 1-C3

You'll find this war museum 20km south of Kuwait City – it marks the spot of the last stand of the Messila resistance fighters against the Iraqi invaders, and has been preserved as a memorial to those that lost their lives. It is located in a residential area off Road 208, and is easily identified by the mounted tank outside and the bullet marks and rocket holes in the building walls, which have been left untouched. The cars belonging to the Kuwaitis that died also remain outside the building to this day. The interior of the house has been converted to a war museum, detailing their valiant fight to the death.

Parks & Beaches

Family life and leisure time play an important part in the lives of both Kuwaitis and expatriates, and apart from during the cool winter months, much time is spent near the water. There are a number of parks situated on the beach that are open to the public for a very low fee – normally 500 fils to KD 1.

Beach Parks

Other options → Parks [p.112]

Because of the hot, sunny climate and the focus on family activities, there are plenty of water-based activities for residents of Kuwait. You can swim almost year-round here on beaches that are safe and clean. Not many beaches have lifeguards though, so bear that in mind before you charge off into the waves. Currents can be very strong, especially in the spring tides. There are some sea urchins and stone fish, but they are few in number and should generally not bother you as long as you don't bother them. Sharks are virtually non-existent in the shallow waters off the coast.

Your possessions are generally safe if left on the beach while you are swimming, although you should err on the side of caution and not leave any valuables unattended for long periods.

Most beaches have refreshment facilities or fast food outlets nearby.

Most of the coastal resorts offer annual membership, which will give you access to a private beach and their health club.

Egaila Beach Park

Location → Street 209 · Fintas | 390 6420
Hours → 10:00 - 22:00
Web/email → na   Map Ref → 1-D3

This beach park is located in Fintas, 20km south of Kuwait City. It is a popular picnic spot for families and gets especially busy at weekends, so get there early to claim your spot (and your parking space!). It has lovely gardens and a nice beach area that is suitable for swimming and quite safe, thanks to the presence of a lifeguard. There are barbecue facilities, changing rooms and plenty of activities to keep the kids amused. Refreshments are also available.

To get there, drive towards Fahaheel on Road 30 (the Fahaheel Expressway), and take Exit 209. Turn left at the traffic lights and follow the road – the Egaila Park is just after the first bend in the road.

Messila Family Beach Park

Location → Arabian Gulf St / 6th Ring Rd · Messilah | 565 0642
Hours → 08:00 - 23:00
Web/email → www.tec.com.kw   Map Ref → 18-E3

Messila Beach Park is the closest beach park to the city and is located at the intersection of Arabian

Exploring

Parks & Beaches

Gulf Street and the 6th Ring Road, running alongside the Fahaheel Expressway. It covers an area of almost 75,000 square metres. Changing rooms are available, along with shaded areas, and there are food and drink kiosks situated around the park. There are plenty of parking bays and a Burger King is handily located nearby.

The beach is clean and safe, with access restricted to ladies only on Saturdays, Mondays and Wednesdays. The entrance fee is 500 fils, except for Fridays when it is KD 1.

Beaches

Other options → Beach Clubs [p.148]
Swimming [p.142]
Parasailing [p.139]
Parks [p.112]

Apart from the beach parks there are also a number of public beaches. The main public beaches are in Salmiya (just 6km from the city centre) and Dasman. There is also a good public beach just south of the Hilton Resort in Fahaheel (25km south of Kuwait City).

Along the southern coastline, chalets and other weekend accommodation options can be rented – Khiran Resort (395 1122) is one of the more well-known. It has several hundred chalets and studio apartments. The government started developing Khiran in 2004 with a view to it becoming a major tourist and residential area, and most of the infrastructure is expected to be in place by 2006.

Clean Beaches

Environmental damage caused by the war and relaxed attitudes to the dumping of waste and oil in the Arabian Gulf have led to concerns about harmful levels of pollution in the waters off the coast of Kuwait. In 2001, large quantities of dead fish (as much as 2,000 tons, according to one report) washed up on Kuwait's beaches, crippling the country's fishing industry. No official explanation has been agreed upon, with theories ranging from extreme temperatures to bacterial infections. However, the possibility that these fish died as a result of high pollution levels in Kuwait's waters remains open.

As Kuwait rebuilds itself after a difficult, war-torn decade, one can only hope that environmental issues, such as the dumping of waste into the Arabian Gulf, are pushed closer to the top of the country's political agenda.

Parks

Other options → Beaches [p.112]

In recent years the government has placed emphasis on developing Kuwait's desert environment, and public parks have been built in most residential areas. The parks have amusement centres and children's play facilities, and some have specific walking and cycling tracks. Timings and regulations change according to season, and sometimes access is restricted to women or families only, so it's best to check beforehand.

Green Island

Closer to the City is Green Island that is linked to the mainland by a causeway. The artificial island houses entertainment facilities, a 700 seat amphitheatre, a restaurant and a swimming pool.

The Kuwait Touristic Enterprises Company (TEC) manages a number of recreational parks and three of the more popular ones are located in Shaab, Sabahiya and Jleeb Al-Shyoukh. Each park features rides and amusement activities. The Shaab Leisure Park can be clearly seen from Arabian Gulf Street.

Each year during 'Hala February' many of the parks have special activities and entertainment for the public.

Al Shaab Leisure Park

Location → Off Arabian Gulf St · Salmiya | 561 3777
Hours → See below
Web/email → www.shaabpark.com   Map Ref → 7-E2

Al Shaab Leisure Park is close to the city and can be seen clearly from Arabian Gulf Street. It has a variety of rides, games and activities for all ages, including bungee jumping. It also has snooker

and tennis facilities and is situated in a park with interconnecting pathways. This fun-packed site also houses a cinema and theatre. The park is located just 3km south of the Kuwait Towers, and the entry fee is just 500 fils. Many of the rides cost extra (anything from 250 - 750 fils per ride). There are a number of outlets within the park that sell refreshments.

Underwater Explorer

If you're a keen diver and are looking from some new waters to explore then why not pick up a copy of the Underwater Explorer. Full of helpful advice and guidance on diving as well as information on some of the UAE's most popular dive sites, it is the perfect reason for a Dubai mini break!

Green Island

Location ➜ Arabian Gulf Street · Dasman		252 6153
Hours ➜ 09:00 - 24:00		
Web/email ➜ na		Map Ref ➜ 4-C4

This man-made island is set on 16 acres of reclaimed land, east of Kuwait Towers. It is accessed on foot via a 250m causeway, and is ideal for a relaxing walk in beautiful surroundings. There are plans to develop the island into a larger tourist resort. Current amusements include an amphitheatre (frequently used by musicians for impromptu concerts), two restaurants and a game park for children. During the day, you can take a train ride around the island, and there is also an observation deck offering spectacular views over the gulf.

The park is open from 08:00 - 23:00 daily, and entrance is just 500 fils for adults and 250 fils for children.

Sabahiya Garden

Location ➜ Ahmadi Governorate		361 0472
Hours ➜ 15:00 - 22:30		
Web/email ➜ na		Map Ref ➜ 1-C3

This public park is run by Touristic Enterprises and is located in central Ahmadi, about 40km south of Kuwait City.

It has amusements, games and rides for children, as well as snack bars and other refreshments outlets. There are several stalls selling toys and games for children. Entrance to the park is 500 fils.

The park is pleasant but is probably not worth a specific visit unless you are in the area.

Touristic Garden Park

Location ➜ Jleeb Al Shyoukh		242 8394
Hours ➜ 15:00 - 22:30 Summer 16:00-24:00		
Web/email ➜ www.kuwaittourism.com		Map Ref ➜ 1-C3

This green oasis in Jleeb Al Shyoukh is managed by Touristic Enterprises. Covering 87,000 square metres, the park has plenty of activities for children, as well as snack bars and other refreshments outlets. An amphitheatre with seating for up to 2,000 people is often used for plays or shows - entrance to the park is usually free except for Fridays or days when there is a show on, when it goes up to KD 1.

Tours & Sightseeing

Other options ➜ Weekend Breaks [p.122]
Activity Tours [p.114]

Kuwait does not cater that well to the needs of tourists as the number of visitors is relatively small, most being either business visitors or people visiting friends and relatives. The reception desk and the concierge at the main hotels can provide information on tours available and may even be able to assist with a driver.

Alternatively, most of the larger and reputable travel agencies can arrange day and half-day tours if you give them one or two days' notice, and tours can be tailored to match the needs of the individual.

Activity Tours

Other options ➜ Tours & Sightseeing [p.114]

Kuwait does not have many activity tours as such. Apart from trips into the desert, the majority of organised activity tours revolve around the sea with diving and fishing trips. In line with its unique position in the Gulf, Kuwait has many established and professional dive tour operators. All aspects of training are available, and courses range from beginner level to dive master and instructor. The best sites are offshore at Umm Al Maradam and Qaruh Islands. Costs vary but can range from KD 15-20 per day, and up to KD 150 for a full beginner's course. The courses are based on PADI certifications. Dive trips are available most weekends.

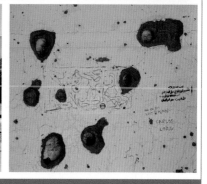

Al Qurain House

Reef diving is available south of the city, and there are some wrecks that attract a good variety of marine life. Dolphin and manta ray sightings are not unusual. Some good places to start with enquiries about technical or recreational diving are:

- Dive Caroline - located at Fahaheel Sea Club (371 9289). www.divecaroline.com
- British Sub Aqua Club (536 4937). www.kuwaitmantas.com
- Palm Dive Centre Palm Hotel, Salmiya. (563 7503) www.bbrdive.com
- Happy Diver (566 1751)
- Nuzha Touristic Enterprises (575 5825, www.nuzha.com.kw) offer horse and camel riding, desert safaris, climbing tours and more.

For other activities, there is a group called Aware that organises many cultural and activity tours each month. Contact them on 532 2555 or check their website (www.aware.com.kw).

Bicycle Tours

A group of enthusiasts heads out into the desert most weekends and it's a great opportunity to see some of the normally unexplored parts of Kuwait. For visitors, bicycles can be hired but you need to call in advance to check availability. Depending on the season the rides are normally planned for the mornings or late afternoons, and many are arranged to start and finish in the desert away from the city. Mutla Ridge in northern Kuwait is a popular area. Take plenty of water and puncture repair kits, and of course dont forget you bicycle pump.
Bicycle Tours (482 4741/952 9567)

Boat Tours

Nuzha Touristic Enterprises (575 5825/35, www.nuzhatours.com) offes full and half-day boat trips, as well as trips to Bahrain and Qatar, and boat trips for special occasions. There is also a daily ferry to Failaka Island from Ras Al Ardh. Recently MV Umm Al Khair started a trip to Failaka each Saturday costing KD 15 (KD 10 for children) including lunch. The boat leaves from berth G6 at Marina Crescent, Salmiya. To book call 224 4988 or 484 8161.

Small water taxis run throughout the day from the tourist enterprise office in Shaab, across the bay to the towers. The cost is 500 fils. Boats can also be taken for bay trips from a small jetty on the south side of Marina Crescent. The trip lasts for about 20 minutes, costs KD 1, and enables you to enjoy spectacular views of Kuwait City and the towers

A number of dhows are also available for hire through local travel agents or the hotels. These can be chartered for social and business functions, and for day trips to Kubbar Island. Catering can be provided if required. Radisson SAS organises tours out into the Arabian Gulf for a few hours during the day. Booking is essential.

Bus Tours

There are no specific daily city tours that run on a scheduled basis. Before the Gulf War there were technicolour London buses providing tours, but these were damaged and never resumed service after the liberation. It is understood there are plans to reintroduce a tourist bus, possibly sometime in 2006. Check with one of the main travel agents to be sure. Private bus tours can be arranged through the hotels and agents. Two of the old London buses can still be seen on the seaward side of the fahaheel expressway (road no 30) – looking somewhat unloved, so if you fancy a restoration project....!

Kuwait City Tours

A number of the larger travel agents can arrange city tours if given enough notice. The main tourist and business hotels will also be able to make arrangements and tours can be tailored to meet the specific needs of the visitor. Most of the tours will take you round the main sights including the Kuwait Towers, old Souk and Grand Mosque, as well as take in the more well known shopping malls like Marina Mall and Souq Sharq. The tour is normally in a small bus or private taxi and the guides speak good English.

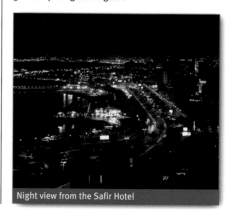
Night view from the Safir Hotel

There are no specific tours organised outside of the city apart from boat and dhow trips that are covered elsewhere in this chapter. The larger travel agents such as Dnata, Al Ghanim, Al Mulla and Nuzha Touristic Enterprises can organise desert tours or tours to Failaka Island.

The Aware group (532 2555), or 'Advocates for Western Arab Relations and Exchanges', is worth contacting to see if they have any trips organised. They often plan a different tour each month.

Helicopter & Plane Tours

These are not currently available in Kuwait, although with the development of Failaka Island and a separate private air charter terminal, they could start in 2006. Charter aircraft are available from a number of private operators and need to be arranged through the travel agencies.

The new private air terminal will be located adjacent to the main international airport and contruction is expected to start late in 2005. It will cater for non-commercial traffic and include all private aircraft. There are no other commercial airstrips in Kuwait, and none is planned for Failaka. Flying lessons are currently not available for those that are so inclined, the nearest location is probably the UAE. However, you can check with the Kuwait Air Pilots Association on 256 1638 for up-to-date information, as this is planned for the future.

Mosque Tours

Other options → Museums - City [p.109]

Although there are more than 800 mosques in the state of Kuwait, the Grand Mosque is by far the most impressive, and is a distinguished landmark in Kuwait. Not all mosques in Kuwait will allow tourists in, so this is a good opportunity to experience the Muslim religion. Guided tours lasting around one hour can be arranged by calling in advance (tours are for two or more people) and include an experienced guide that will tell you about the history of Islam and the mosque. Questions are welcomed and the guides try to be as accommodating as possible. The tours are in English and are open to males and females. The mosque will provide a hijab (headscarf) for the women if you have forgotten yours. You are not obliged to wear long sleeves or long trousers, but as a courtesy to the religion it is recommended. When entering the mosque you need to remove your shoes and they will be safely placed outside in

a shoe rack. The courtyard can hold 10,000 people (men only), while on the first floor (no men allowed) is the women's section that can accommodate around 400 people. There is also a 350 square metre library within the grounds of the mosque. This is definitely worth a visit if you have never been inside a mosque before. Grand Mosque (241 8447/8, www.freekuwait.com/mosque)

Safari Tours

Very few desert safari tours are available in Kuwait as the terrain is generally very flat and not particularly interesting – dunes are pretty well non-existent. However, tours can be arranged through some of the larger travel agents. Desert camps are privately run and often you do not need a 4WD to get there. Catering can be provided, and although most tend to be a daytime activity, overnight stays can be arranged. The season is from around October to March when the weather is more bearable, although be warned, the temperature can fall to zero in the winter. Most camps have camels, as well as quad bikes to keep the children occupied. Nuzha Touristic Enterprises (575 5825, www.nuzha.com.kw) offer some seasonal desert tours, with tents and transportation provided. For those who prefer to experience the peace and tranquility of the desert at their own pace, see Camping in the Activities section on p.132.

Tour Operators

Tour companies offer a variety of trips enabling you to experience the best that Kuwait has to offer, and most will be able to provide tailor-made itineraries to suit the needs of the visitor. An organised tour is the ideal way to discover Kuwait's historic buildings and areas, the old souks and modern malls, the heritage and culture of the region, and all the city's well-known landmarks. The companies listed

Tour Operators	
Al Mulla Travel Bureau	243 7333
Al Waseet Travel	245 6880
Alghanim Travel	80 2112
American Women's League (AWL)	925 9878
Boodai Aviation Group	88 7887
DNATA	249 1000
Kuwait Tourism Services	245 1734
Nooran Travel & Tourism	240 9900
Nuzha Touristic Enterprises	575 5825
Sanbouk Travel	245 7267
Touristic Information Centre	572 7183

Exploring

Tours & Sightseeing

should be given a couple of days notice if possible to ensure availability, and hotels should also be able to help guests to organise excursions.

Other Attractions

The Al Hashemi II

Location ➜ Beh Radisson SAS Hotel · Salwa	565 7000
Hours ➜ On request	
Web/email ➜ na	Map Ref ➜ 13-D2

At nearly 85 metres long the Al Hashemi II is recognised as the biggest dhow in the world, earning it a place in the Guinness Book of Records. The dhow is located just behind the Radisson SAS Hotel and you cannot miss it at its permanent beachside location. Set in concrete, and with a car park underneath, it dwarfs the small but popular restaurant behind it. The large and impressive main banquet hall is a popular venue for weddings, conferences, state dinners and other major corporate events. The certificate at the entrance gives details of the quantity of iron nails and wood that was used during the three-year construction period. Based on the ground floor is also a Marine Museum containing models of dhows. This is accessible during the day between 09:00 and 17:00.

Dhow Building Yard

Location ➜ Along the Arabian Gulf St · Salmiya	na
Hours ➜ Open all day	
Web/email ➜ na	Map Ref ➜ 3-C3

In line with its seafaring past and unique location at the top of the Arabian Gulf, Kuwait has a long tradition as a builder of quality trading vessels – more commonly known as dhows. The dhow harbour located opposite the National Assembly has a dhow building yard, although the number produced today is a fraction of what it was in years gone by.

Kuwait Towers

Location ➜ Ras Dasman · Dasman	244 4021
Hours ➜ 08:00 - 23:30	
Web/email ➜ na	Map Ref ➜ 11-B3

The Kuwait Towers are the most visual landmark in the country and are recognised all over the world. They are not to be missed. The unique towers have a dual function as both entertainment facilities and

water reservoirs. The upper sphere of the main tower has a revolving deck housing the restaurant that provides a full panoramic view of the City and the Arabian Gulf every half hour. The top half of the lower sphere houses the Al Ufuq restaurant with a daily buffet, while below is the more downmarket Le Café. The observation deck at the top is worth a visit - the views are spectacular so dont forget your camera. The bottom section of the larger tower houses a one million gallon water reservoir.

The globe on the middle tower is used only as a water reservoir, also with a one million gallon capacity. The long, thin tower illuminates the other two towers and the surrounding grounds with 96 concealed spotlights, making this a definite photo opportunity day or night.

Entry is a bargain at only KD 1, and free for children under four.

Kuwait Towers

Amusement Centres

Other options ➜ Amusement Parks [p.119]

In the absence of some of the other more familiar after-hours activities, Kuwait has a large number of amusement centres catering for all ages. Many of

Exploring

Other Attractions

these are located in Kuwait City, but most suburbs will have at least one dedicated amusement area or an area set aside in the larger shopping malls. Most facilities are suitable for small children, although some are taken over by the teenage crowd who tend to hog the games for hours on end. The centres often stay open beyond midnight on non-school nights.

The centres in the malls often have dedicated areas for smaller children, which tend to be located in close proximity to the food courts. It is not unusual to see maids looking after young children while parents are sampling the many delights of the fast-food outlets.

One of the largest amusement centres outside of the city is in Fintas in the Kuwait Magic Mall on Road 209.

The country has several outdoor amusement facilities. In the hot summer months many of these operate with different timings and extended evening hours to take advantage of the cooler temperatures. Doha Entertainment City is one of the largest entertainment centres in the Middle East, offering both indoor and outdoor attractions and rides. The water parks are popular in the spring and through summer and early winter.

Cozmo Entertainment

Location ➜ Nr New Souk · Salmiya | 574 4975
Hours ➜ 11:00 - 01:00   Thu & Fri 10:00 - 01:00
Web/email ➜ www.cozmobowling.com   Map Ref ➜ na

Located on the top floor of Souq Salmiya, Cozmo has everything from indoor amusement games to a full-blown bowling alley and pool hall with electronic games. Tokens normally need to be purchased in advance, and bookings are needed for the bowling. It can get very busy at weekends and later on in the evenings. Refreshment facilities are available in the amusement area, or downstairs in the foodcourt.

Gameworks

Location ➜ Arabian Gulf Street · Salmiya | 224 4873
Hours ➜ 11:00 - 23:00
Web/email ➜ www.gameworks.com   Map Ref ➜ 8-C3

Part of an American franchise, Gameworks hit Kuwait in 2003 and has proven to be very popular with both adults and children alike. It's a children's paradise with hundreds of different activities, and almost every type of electronic game available. A fully equipped restaurant that can be reserved for private or corporate functions ensures that you will not go hungry. Located in the Marina Mall, you can be sure that the kids will be occupied while you do some shopping or take a coffee break. To play you need to buy 'playcards' costing KD 3.500 (160 credits) or KD 5 (240 credits - with KD 1 free).

Giggles

Location ➜ Nr Kazma Sports Stadium · Adailiya | 254 8513
Hours ➜ 10:00 - 22:00   Fri 14:00 - 22:00
Web/email ➜ www.kuwaittourism.com   Map Ref ➜ na

This bright and colourful children's centre is great for toddlers and young infants. They also cater for birthday parties and their soft play area is one of the best in Kuwait.

Kuwait Magic

Location ➜ Abu Halifa | 371 0866
Hours ➜ 10:00 - 13:30 17:00 - 22:00 Fri 15:00 - 22:00
Web/email ➜ www.kuwait-magic.com   Map Ref ➜ 1-C3

Located in Abu Halifa, 25km south of Kuwait City, the imposing Kuwait Magic shopping mall rises out of the sea like a large Arabian majlis. Apart from the boutique shops, the mall has an extensive amusement centre with funfair rides upstairs, and electronic games downstairs for the bigger kids. Tokens for the rides and games must be purchased from the booths, and rewards tend to be in tickets that can be traded in for gifts. The area is next to a large foodcourt so the kids won't go hungry, and there is a coffee shop and outdoor terrace for the parents when the noise gets too much.

Showbiz

Location ➜ Salmiya | 571 4094
Hours ➜ 16:00 - 23:00
Web/email ➜ na   Map Ref ➜ 8-E2

Open every day, Showbiz is a mini funfair located on Arabian Gulf Street in Ras Al Ardh. It is best suited to children as opposed to adults, with carousels, bumper cars and various stalls to keep the children amused for a while. There is also a big wheel. Entry fee is 500 fils every day apart from Friday when it is KD 1.

Exploring

Other Attractions

Amusement Parks

Other options ➜ Water Parks [p.121]
Amusement Centres [p.118]

There are several small entertainment centres in or near the city, the main ones being Al Shaab and Showbiz. Entertainment City has three separate themed areas and many restaurants - definitely a full day out. The view from the observation deck is also worth seeing so take your camera.

Al Shaab Leisure Park

Location ➜ Off Arabian Gulf St · Salmiya
Hours ➜   See below | 561 3777
Web/email ➜ www.shaabpark.com   Map Ref ➜ 7-E2

Al Shaab Leisure Park is located 3km south of the Kuwait Towers and can be seen clearly from Arabian Gulf Street. It has a variety of rides, games and activities for all ages, including bungee jumping. It also has snooker and tennis facilities, a number of refreshment outlets, and is situated in a park with interconnecting pathways. A cinema and theatre are also on site. Entry fee is only 500 fils, with the rides costing anything from 250 - 750 fils per go. Open every day of the year, the park is open weekdays from 16:00 - 24:00 (November to April) and 17:00 - 01:00 (Mat to October). Weekends (Thurs/Fri) and public holidays the hours are 10:00 - 24:00, although the park does close for one hour for Friday prayers.

Entertainment City

Location ➜ 20km from Kuwait City · Doha
Hours ➜ 15:30 - 22:00   Fri 10:00-22:00 Sat closed | 487 9545
Web/email ➜ na   Map Ref ➜ 1-C2

The largest amusement park in Kuwait, located in Doha 20km from the city along Road 80. The park is open every day and has three themed areas: Arab World, Future World and International World. It is very popular on weekends and public holidays. The complex includes a complete range of amusements and rides to suit all tastes, although some rides do have height or age restrictions. There are several restaurants and fast food outlets on site.

Entry fee is KD 3.500, which covers access to the majority of rides, although tickets need to be purchased for some of the more elaborate and exciting ones.

Hawalli Park

Location ➜ Tunis Street · Hawalli
Hours ➜ 10:00 - 22:00 | na
Web/email ➜ na   Map Ref ➜ 8-C2

Located in Tunis street, this park offers a range of attractions and rides. Definitely a place worth visiting if you want to keep the kids happy, but get there early as it can get busy later in the evening. The rides are probably better suited for small children. Refreshment facilities are available on site.

Marah Land Leisure Park

Location ➜ Along Highway No 40/212
Hours ➜ 16:00 - 24:00 | 535 8100
Web/email ➜ na   Map Ref ➜ 1-D3

Located south of the city in South Sabahiya close to Ahmadi, Marah Land Leisure Park opened in 2004. This new park has many games, rides, facilities and lots of green space for the kids to romp in. It is a real green oasis in the desert with fountains and a lake. Due to its location it is a popular venue for corporate days out and for residents living south of the city. Several food outlets are available. Entry fee is only KD 1.

Camel Racing

Camel racing has a long history in Kuwait and is very popular with the Bedouin tribes. The racing appeals to all ages and a day at the races is a big occasion. The majority of spectators tend to be Kuwaitis or other GCC residents, and it's a good excuse for the locals and their extended families to enjoy some time together.

The races tend to take place early in the morning around 07:00 or 08:00, and can involve up to 60 camels. It's quite a memorable event for first time visitors. Races can be over 5km, and are held on Thursdays and Fridays. The main races are held at the Al-Atraf Camel Racing Club (539 4014) on Salmi Road (Road 604) west of Jahra. Refreshments are available at the couse. Laws were recently passed to restrict the use of under-age camel jockeys.

Horse Racing

Other options ➜ Horse Riding [p.136]

Although horse racing was popular in Kuwait in the 1970s (it was one of the first GCC countries to have a dedicated horse-racing track), interest has dwindled in recent years. Kuwait does still have the horse-racing track at the Hunting & Equestrian Club (473 9199), with racing held on Monday evenings during the cooler winter season. The club is undergoing redevelopment, with a new clubhouse and 18 hole grass golf course. The course inside the track has been sunk to aid spectator visibility, and the clubhouse will have a separate entertainment centre with a small artificial ski slope and several restaurant outlets.

The season was suspended during the reconstruction, but was set to resume with several large race meetings planned for winter 2006.

Nature Reserves

The largest environmental nature reserve in Kuwait is situated on Bubiyan Island at the top of the Arabian Gulf, just south of the Iraq border. At 863 sq km, Bubiyan is larger than the State of Bahrain, and the top third has been designated as a nature reserve, which is home to many species of birds and animals, some of which are unique to the island. The northern part is made up of marshland and many small rivers, making it a haven for wading birds. Access to the island is currently restricted. A causeway linking the island to the mainland was bombed during the Gulf War, and the island was heavily mined. In April 2005 a tender process was started to build a new 1.4 km three-lane causeway. This is the first phase of the redevelopment of Bubiyan Island which will include a port and residential/commercial complex on the southern coastline. Thankfully, the north will remain as a nature reserve.

Smaller nature reserves are located along Mutla Ridge in northern Kuwait, and the mudflats in Sulaibikhat Bay before Jahra support many species of marine and bird life. Try to spot a mudskipper if you can; a real life example of zoological evolution, they breathe like fish in the water but at low tide sit up in the mud and get their oxygen direct from the air.

Powerboat Racing

Powerboat racing was very popular in Kuwait up to the time of the Gulf War in 1990, resulting in a number of world champions from this very small nation, and to some extent putting Kuwait on the international sporting map. Although several of the boats remain and can be seen out at weekends,

many were destroyed or sunk during the war and the sport has never really recovered. However, the local boys with their toys can still be seen heading off to the islands at the weekends to enjoy the delights of Kuwait offshore and its islands. Kubbar Island in particular is a regular meeting place for weekend parties.

Water Parks

Other options → Amusement Parks [p.120]

Being a coastal country it's not surprising that Kuwait has a close affinity with water. There are several water parks but the two main ones are in Dasman and next to Messila Beach. They are run by Touristic Enterprises Company. The parks are safe for children of all ages and both have lifeguards on duty. Changing rooms with lockers are available, as are refreshments. Once you've paid the entrance fee there are no further costs inside.

Aqua Park

Location → Beh Kuwait Towers · Dasman   │243 1960
Hours → 10:00 - 22:00
Web/email → na   Map Ref → 4-A1

Aqua Park is situated in downtown Kuwait City, behind the Kuwait Towers. It is smaller than the Messila Beach water park but remains very popular due to its central location. Favourite features include the water slides of varying degrees of steepness, and the wave pool. A visit makes a good day out for the family as the park also has children's pools. The entry fee of KD 3.500 also includes meals.

Messila Water Village

Location → Nr Messila Beach Hotel · Messilah   │565 0505
Hours → 10:00 - 22:00
Web/email → www.kuwaittourism.com   Map Ref → 18-E3

This extensive complex of pools and slides is situated by the beach next to the site of the Messila Beach Hotel, which was pulled down in early 2005 to make way for a new hotel. The water park is well managed, with changing rooms and towels available. There is a good selection of slides and water floats to keep all ages entertained for hours, and the water is chilled in the hot summer months and heated in the winter. Entrance to the park is KD 3.

Exploring

Other Attractions

Zoo

The main Kuwait Zoo is located near the airport. It is not exactly London Zoo and is still recovering from the damage of the Gulf War, but it does have a reasonable selection of animals. A separate environmental nature reserve on Bubiyan Island houses many species of birds, but access is restricted. There is also a small private zoo is located in Funaitees, south of the city. For bird watchers there are some mudflats near Salaibikat with various species of birdlife, including Flamingos.

Kuwait Zoo

Location → Omariya on Airport Rd · Farwania   473 3389
Hours → 08:00 - 20:00   Sat closed
Web/email → na   Map Ref → 11-B3

Close to the airport, the zoo is open every day except Saturday and is extremely popular at weekends and on public holidays. The cost of entry is only 500 fils. There is a reasonable selection of animals but in all honesty it looks a little run down. Some endangered species are bred at the zoo, and it also houses a research centre. The zoo has around 65 species of animals (including lions, tigers, elephants, giraffes, and zebras), 129 species of birds and five species of reptiles. Funds have been set aside to build a new zoo in a different location. Summer timings are 08:00 - 12:00 and 16:00 - 24:00.

Kuwait Zoo

Little Jungle

Location → Off Fahaheel Expressway No. 30 · Bayan   390 2635
Hours →   On Request
Web/email → www.littlejungle.net   Map Ref → 1-C3

This small private zoo is located in Funaitees south of the city, just off the Fahaheel Expressway (Road 30). It has everything from giraffes to gazelles, and has many menbers of the cat family including jaguars, cheetahs and tigers. The entrance fee is a bargain at only 250 fils, and horse and camel rides are also available for the kids.

Weekend Breaks

Other options → Hotels [p.26]
Tours & Sightseeing [p.114]

Kuwait offers some interesting opportunities to chill out from city life and get away from it all for a weekend. The Khiran area, 75km south of Messila, (where the 6th Ring Road meets Road 30), offers a number of resorts where rooms and beach chalets can be booked for KD 60-150 per night. Slightly closer to Kuwait City (55km from Messila) is the Kempinski Hotel that offers a popular Friday brunch, and has rooms available for those that do not fancy the drive home. Just 25km south of the city is the Hilton Beach Resort in Mangaf that offers facilities for those special occasions – rooms cost around KD 70-80 per night and it's quite popular, and is often full of military personnel. Beachfront chalets that can host whole families are available, costing up to KD 300. The resorts further south are popular with inter-GCC traffic. Watch for the special summer rates normally available in July and August.

If you prefer the outdoor life, during spring and autumn a number of desert camps operate. Facilities are fairly basic but a few days of 'roughing it' can be quite refreshing, although the desert landscape is remarkably flat. There may be opportunities to spot a little wildlife, and many camps provide distractions such as quad bikes to keep children (and adults) amused.

The government is planning to develop Failaka Island as a major tourist attraction, catering to GCC citizens, residents and visitors alike.

Khiran   Map Ref 2-D4

Located 80km south of Kuwait City, Khiran is a popular weekend retreat for locals and expats. The area boasts golden beaches and the Khiran Resort (see p.124) was built by the Touristic Enterprise

Exploring

Weekend Breaks

Company, a government-funded organisation, in the early 1980s. The resort includes a marina, amusement complex, restaurants, and pleasant gardens that are a real rarity in Kuwait. The resort is frequently fully booked so it's better to phone in advance (562 8493 or 395 1122). To rival the resort a new development is under construction, The Pearl, which will be based around a series of man-made inland waterways.

Weekend Breaks Outside Kuwait

If you fancy getting away from Kuwait for a few days there are many interesting and varied opportunities just a short hop away in neighbouring GCC countries. The local operators, including Kuwait Airways, Qatar Airways, Oman Air, Gulf Air, Emirates, and Air Arabia, offer regular flights throughout the region, plus you may find a flight with one of the international carriers who often make stopovers. Depending on your nationality you may be eligible for a visa on arrival in certain GCC countries. Just remember, if you are in Kuwait on a visit visa and you leave, you will need another one to get back in. However, access is a little easier now the government allows 33 nationalities to obtain visas on arrival.

Bahrain

Bahrain is a popular jaunt for a quick break from Kuwait. There should be a little something for everyone, from the wide selection of fine dining (and drinking!) to a spot of shopping and sightseeing. You could visit a fort or two, take in a museum, have a spin around the new grand prix circuit or hop on a boat to one of Bahrain's many islands. If you have a Kuwait residency visa you may be able to get a transit visa for Saudi, allowing you to drive to Bahrain. The drive takes about four hours but some delays may be experienced at the border, and women, who should be covered, are not allowed to travel alone or with a man to whom they are not related. You may therefore prefer to fly. For more information and inspiration, check out the *Bahrain Explorer* from Explorer Publishing.

UAE

Often described as the city of gold, a shopper's paradise, and one of the best nights out in the Middle East, Dubai is by far the favourite destination in the Emirates. There's so much to see and do you're unlikely to fit everything into one weekend, but some visitor 'musts' include exploring the creek and the historic souks, enjoying the thrill of a desert safari, doing some serious shopping, and then treating yourself to some hard-earned pampering at one of Dubai's luxury spas. The range of eating, drinking, and dancing options is also worth the airfare alone! Don't forget the other emirates though, including Abu Dhabi, Sharjah and Fujairah. There's bags of culture and heritage to discover, no end of golden sandy beaches, and the east coast has some great snorkelling and diving sites. To help you make the most of any trip to the Emirates, don't miss the *Dubai Explorer*, the *Abu Dhabi Explorer*, the *UAE*

The famous Burj Al Arab in Dubai

Off-Road Explorer, and the **UAE Underwater Explorer** – all from Explorer Publishing.

Qatar

Qatar once had something of a sleepy reputation, but things are changing fast and the amount of development and investment in the country means it is becoming increasingly popular with visitors. With an attractive corniche, world-class museums and cultural centres, and plenty of hotels with leisure and entertainment facilities, the capital Doha makes a perfect weekend retreat from Kuwait. The inland sea, or Khor Al Udaid, in the south of the country also makes a great day trip, usually as part of an organised tour. The **Qatar Explorer** from Explorer Publishing has details of all these activities and many more.

Oman

There are countless reasons to visit Oman, and with frequent flights from Kuwait there's really no excuse not to. The Gulf of Oman's rich sea life, the historic buildings, the wildlife, and the variety of unspoilt landscapes including vast dramatic deserts, rugged mountains and lush green wadis and valleys, are all things that you will remember fondly. The fascinating sights and sounds of the capital Muscat will provide more than enough to keep any weekend visitor busy, but Oman has much more. You should also consider exploring the Mussandam Peninsula with its amazing dive sites, the historic mountain towns and villages with stunning scenery, the turtle beaches in the east, and the blissful summer rain in the southern Dhofar region. For more information on all these areas, and details of all there is to see and do, see the **Oman Explorer** and the **Oman Off-Road Explorer**, both from Explorer Publishing.

Travel Agencies

Other options → Tour Operators [p.117]

There are more than 40 registered travel agencies in Kuwait and many of the larger companies have multiple braches spread throughout the city and the main commercial areas. They offer a full range of facilities and cater to both tourists and business travellers. Recently Dnata and BTI launched in Kuwait offering an extended range of services, and 24 hour ticket desks are now available at the airport. All agents offer facilities for tickets to be delivered to clients and the service is generally very good. Its better to shop around or watch the local press to get the best deal. Some agencies are closed between 13:00 and 16:00.

Travel Agencies

Al Kazemi Travel Agencies	245 0655
Al Manea Travels	245 3580
Al Mishaal Tours & Travel	262 3510
Al Mulla Travel Bureau	241 1526
Al Mustaqbal Travel	245 6880
Al Rashed Int'l Travel	246 1538
Al Shamel International	297 6000
Al Waseet Travel	245 6880
Alghanim Travel	80 2112
Bahman Int'l Travel	242 6006
Boodai Aviation Group	88 7887
Ceaser Travel Co.	242 3054
Dnata	249 1000
Jumbo Travel	241 4655
Kuwait Int'l Travel & Tourism Center	240 5851
Nooran Travel	240 8800
Osama Travel & Tourism	264 7151
Sanbouk Travel	245 7267

Oman's Natural Beauty

Weekend Break Summary

Hotel	Phone	Email	City	Rate
Hilton Kuwait Resort	372 5500	www.hilton.com	Manqaf	KD 100
Kempinski Julai'a Resort	84 4844	www.kempinski-kuwait.com	Kuwait City	KD 200
Khiran Resort	562 9493	na	Kuwait City	KD 150
Watania Resort	245 7806	na	Kuwait City	KD 120

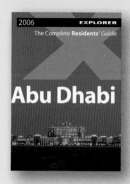
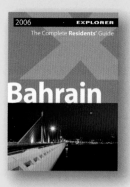

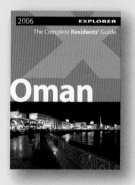

...We put the FUN in function.

Corporate Family Days
Theme Decoration • Birthday Parties

Activities

EXPLORER

Activities

Highlights...

Aaaah, This is the Life! [p.144]

Beauty Salons, luxurious spas, sunshine and swimming pools - Kuwait has its fair share of pampering pick-me-ups to help you forget your troubles. Whether it's a new hairdo or a full body massage at the opulent Elysium Spa [p.145]; or a day of lazing by the pool at the beach club at Palms Beach Hotel [p.148], you can easily escape the rat race and recharge your batteries.

Cool Kids [p.156]

The challenge of keeping a bevy of overactive kids occupied and boredom-free is a pretty tall order. Luckily, there are countless amazing activities for the younger generation in Kuwait. It's easy when the weather's good, but when it gets too hot to be outside, take them roller- or ice-skating at Al Sha'ab Leisure Park, unleash their creativity with a bit of ceramic painting at Colour Me Mine, or even let them have breakfast with a chimpanzee at Little Jungle!

We Want You... [p.154]

Do you run a sports club or a social group? Are you a member of the Kuwait Kite-Flying Association or the Bneid Al-Gir Barbecue Brothers? We have worked hard to uncover all the facts about activities in Kuwait, but we're not too proud to admit that we may have left someone out. So this is your chance to give your group a shout-out in our next edition - no catches, no hidden charges, all you have to do is email us at Info@Explorer-Publishing.com and tell us all the details.

Activities

Table of Contents

All work and no play makes you a very dull expat. There are plenty of clubs and associations catering especially for expats in Kuwait, all offering activities to keep you busy. Apart from doing activities that you already know and love, or discovering a totally new activity, you'll probably find that this is the quickest way to meet new friends.

Step Forward

The meek may inherit the Earth, but they won't make it into this chapter! Don't be shy... if you are the organiser or member of a club that isn't in here, we need to hear from you. Send us an email (Info@Explorer-Publishing.com) and see your name in print in our next edition.

If you are an organiser or even just a member of a social or sports club that we haven't mentioned in the following pages, then we'd love to hear from you! Send us an email (Info@Explorer-Publishing.com) and let us know what you do, when you do it and how much it costs, and we'll definitely include your details in our next edition, completely free of charge.

Aerobics

Other options → **Dance Classes [p.151]**
Sports & Leisure Facilities [p.148]

While it may not be the most widely available activity in Kuwait, if you look hard enough you'll find enough of a variety of Aerobics classes to keep your body moving. Class timetables can change without warning, so always call ahead to make sure that your scheduled class is still on.

Al Futouh Health and Fitness Centre

Location → Kuwait Regency Palace Hotel · Salmiya | 572 8000
Hours → 07:00 - 22:00
Web/email → na   Map Ref → 12-D1

This club has various classes, including Step, Total Body Workout, Abs, Hips and Thighs, and Abs Workout. Each class costs KD 3. You can get a three-month membership for KD 100 or a six-month membership for KD 200, and members are allowed to use all club facilities such as the swimming pool, jacuzzi, sauna, and the tennis and squash courts. You can also get a racquet sport membership (KD 65 for three months and KD 125 for six months) if you only want access to the tennis and squash facilities.

Flex Health Club for Women

Location → Bes Villa Fairoz Cafe, Istiqlal Rd · Dasma | 261 6661
Hours → 08:00 - 22:00   Fri 12:00 - 22:00
Web/email → www.flexq8.com   Map Ref → 5-D3

Flex has separate clubs for men and women, and the women's club offers several fitness classes including abdominal workouts and lower body workouts. Other facilities include a cardio room, gym, two aerobics studios (one small and one large), a sauna, jacuzzi, swimming pool, steam room and massage room. Various membership options are available, starting from a day pass (KD 15, which includes the class and access to all facilities) and going up to a year-long membership for KD 525.

For more information on the men's club membership and the fitness classes on offer, call 252 2006.

Nautilus Fitness Center

Location → Crowne Plaza · Farwania | 474 2000
Hours → 24 hrs
Web/email → www.kuwait.crowneplaza.com   Map Ref → 16-C3

This well-equipped fitness centre offers classes in Splash Aerobics, Tone & Stretch, Muscle Endurance & Training, Power Crunch, Aerosculpt, Aero Habits, Pump & Abs, Aerobics 'R' Fun, Body Blitz, Dynamic Step, Weights Unlimited, Cardio Kickbox, Basic Step and Dance Aerobics.

Nautilus is open 24 hours a day throughout the week and has all the latest fitness equipment, individual TV/audio monitors, five squash courts, and a temperature controlled swimming pool. Separate facilities for men and women include the gyms, saunas, steam rooms, jacuzzis and changing rooms. The fitness centre also has the only supervised children's gym in Kuwait.

Archery

Somewhat of an unusual sport, Archery is not only an excellent discipline for control and precision but also will improve your upper body strength and arm muscles. Local archery enthusiast Rashmi Gandhi offers lessons in this age-old sport for school students. For more information, contact him by phone (mobile 709 6248) or email (rashmi_archer@yahoo.co.in). Or take a look at his website: www.geocities.com/rashmi_archer/Kuwait_Archery.html.

Activities

Aerobics • Archery

Baseball

Kuwait Little League

Location → 6th Ring Road · South Surra
Hours → Timings on request
Web/email → www.q8ll.com
973 3853
Map Ref → na

This nonprofit project is run for children between the ages of 5-18. The children are placed into the various divisions by age. Regular competitions are held on Thursday and Friday mornings. Parents are actively involved and assist with coaching, umpiring and scorekeeping. For directions check the webpage.

Basketball

There are no official basketball clubs in Kuwait, but fortunately it is a sport that can be played just about anywhere. Many of Kuwait's schools and sports clubs have either an indoor or outdoor court, and the Ras Al-Ardh Club (574 7023) has a court that anybody can use after paying the entrance fee of KD 1 (KD 2 on Wednesdays, Thursdays and Fridays).

Boat & Yacht Charters

Other options → Dhow Charters [p.133]

There are several sailing clubs in Kuwait, many of which allow members to bring friends as day-guests. Good weather and calm waters makes sailing a popular activity and a number of sailing events take place throughout the year, in which boats of all shapes and sizes take part. Many Kuwait residents are proud boat-owners – if you are not one, you can always charter a boat to sail off into the sunset! The following companies offer charter services; alternatively you can go the independent route and call Mr Abdullah (977 9880) – he can arrange a yacht large enough for 25 - 45 people at a cost starting from KD 120.

Nuzha Touristic Enterprises

Location → Al Bustan Mall · Safat
Hours → Timings on request
Web/email → www.nuzhatours.com
575 5825
Map Ref → 8-C2

Boat trips with Nuzha can be arranged on a full-day or half-day basis on a yacht that is equipped with a bedroom, kitchen and TV. Prices range from KD 220 to KD 650 during the week – for information on prices over weekends or for special occasions (like weddings or birthdays), call Nuzha. Long distance trips to other GCC countries are also available.

The Yachts Club

Location → Nxt Shaab Sea Club · Salmiya
Hours → Timings on request
Web/email → www.tec.com.kw
565 6741
Map Ref → 7-E2

The Yachts Club has a 74 foot vessel that is available for rental at a daily rate of KD 250. It can hold up to 35 people. The club has a marina, operating on a membership basis, that is large enough to hold nearly 400 yachts and boats. Call the club for more information, either on the above number, or on 565 6741/9.

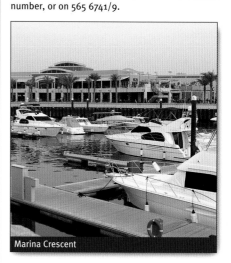

Marina Crescent

Bowling

300 Club Bowling and Billiard

Location → Opp Safir Int Htl · Bneid al-Gir
Hours → 10:00 - 03:00
Web/email → na
244 8000
Map Ref → 4-A2

300 Club has six bowling lanes and each game costs 750 fils (including the hire of a pair of bowling shoes). Every month there is a tournament, in which the cost per game is KD 1. The club is located in the Al Bisher Al Kazemi Towers, and also houses a cafeteria selling refreshments and snacks.

Cozmo Entertainment

Location → Souq Salmiya · Salmiya
Hours → 11:00 - 01:00   Thu & Fri 10:00 - 01:00
Web/email → www.cozmobowling.com | 574 4975   Map Ref → 8-D4

Cozmo has 16 state-of-the-art AMF bowling lanes and hosts regular tournaments. Bumper bowling for children and special facilities for the disabled. Every Wednesday and Thursday from 7.30pm - 10.30pm is Cozmo night, with glowing balls and pins, a laser light show and the latest sounds courtesy of the in-house DJ.

The Hunting & Equestrian Club

Location → Nr Military Hosp, Wista · Subhan
Hours → Timings on request
Web/email → www.tec.com.kw | 473 9199   Map Ref → 17-D4

This exclusive sports club has a bowling hall where you can have a game for 500 fils. Apart from bowling, other activities available include equestrian sports, billiards, swimming, basketball, volleyball, tennis, squash and a health club. To become a member you need to be a resident in Kuwait and fill in the application form supplied, to which four passport photos and a copy of your civil ID should be attached. When the application is approved you have to pay the membership fees – KD 220 for husband and wife, and KD 5 per child under 18 years. After the first year, membership renewal costs KD 100 for husband and wife and KD 5 per child.

Camping

Other options → **Outdoor Goods [p.174]**

There can be no better way to experience life in the Gulf as it must have been long before the days of oil and big business, than spending a night camping in the desert. The climate between October and March is ideal for sleeping out under the stars, with comfortable temperatures and relatively low chance of rain. You can generally camp wherever you happen to find a flat spot, although it is advisable not to wander too far off the beaten track – many landmines have been discovered since the end of the Gulf War, and although authorities have officially cleared most areas, it is better to err on the side of caution. If you're fairly new to camping and don't know where to start, the south coast is a popular spot and you'll find plenty of fellow tent-dwellers there.

Nuzha Touristic Enterprises

Location → Al Bustan Mall · Salmiya
Hours → Timings on request
Web/email → www.nuzhatours.com | 575 5825   Map Ref → 8-C2

Whether you want to camp overnight or just take an organised daytrip in the desert, Nuzha can arrange it for you. Camping takes place on the northern side of Kuwait, near the Sheikh Subah Al Ahmed Nature Reserve. For a weekend trip, departure is usually at 14:00 on a Thursday, and you return to Kuwait City at 18:00 on Friday. If required, Nuzha can make special arrangements for occasions like New Year, birthdays and corporate team building.

> **It's Your Shout**
>
> *Did we miss your tiddlywinks club or model railway society? If you are an organiser or member of an activity that deserves a mention, then drop us a line to Info@Explorer-Publishing.Com. We'll make sure your details appear in print for all to see next time around.*

Cricket

British School of Cricket

Location → The British School of Kuwait · Salwa
Hours → On request
Web/email → www.bsk.edu.kw | 562 1701   Map Ref → 13-B2

ECB certified coaches conduct courses throughout the academic year for boys and girls aged 6-16. Certficates on completion with medals and trophies awarded to outstanding players. Individual and team coaching.

Cycling

Desert Biking Club of Kuwait (DBCK)

Location → Various locations
Hours → On request
Web/email → na | 952 9567   Map Ref → na

DBCK is an informal, mixed group of cyclists who have a passion for recreational cycling. The group meets weekly between the months of October and May and cycles all over Kuwait, be it in the desert, along the seafront, through the souqs or on any of the number of cycle/walking tracks located throughout Kuwait.

Darts

Kuwait Darts League

Location → Various locations	600 8267
Hours → Timings on request	
Web/email → michaeldpreston@hotmail.com	Map Ref → na

There is an active darts league in Kuwait with several enthusiastic teams who get together for matches every Wednesday from September to May. The League upholds the principles of fair play and abiding by the rules, but if this all sounds like serious stuff then don't worry – the league is also committed to making darts night a fun way to meet new people in a festive environment. If you visit the League website you can get contact information for participating teams, which is a good starting point if you're new in town (http://kdl8.tripod.com).

Dhow Charters

Other options → Boat & Yacht Charters [p.130]

Kuwait is ideally situated for boat trips, with calm waters, wonderful weather and a number of islands within easy reach. You can hire a dhow, including crew, for around KD 200 a day. Just make enquiries at any dhow harbour, and you'll get pointed in the right direction. Mr Abdullah can arrange a dhow charter from Khiran Resort to one of the nearby islands, in a boat that can carry up to 25 people. It takes one and a half hours to reach Umm Al Maradim Island, and two and a half hours to reach Qaruh Island. Costs vary, but as a guideline it costs about KD 120 to get to Umm Al Maradim and KD 160 to get to Qaruh. Booking is essential; call Mr. Abdullah (977 9880) for more information.

Kuwait Public Transport Company

Location → Safat	574 2664
Hours → 08:00 - 12:30	
Web/email → na	Map Ref → 3-C3

KPTC (Kuwait Public Transport Company) runs a daily ferry (except Saturdays and Wednesdays) to the beautiful Failaka Island, 20km off Kuwait's coastline. The ferry leaves Ras Salmiya at 08:00, and the return trip departs from Failaka at 12:30. You can take your car with you, in which case the cost for the ferry for the car, a driver and a passenger is KD 20. Alternatively, you can board the ferry as a pedestrian and the cost is KD 2.500

(return). There is no need to book, but it's advisable to check with KPTC for any schedule changes.

Diving

Other options → Snorkelling [p.141]

Diving is a popular sport in Kuwait, which has survived even though the oil fires of the war caused untold pollution. Apart from clear seas and good coral reefs, Kuwait also has three nearby islands that are great dive sites. Fluctuations in water temperatures combined with high salinity should by rights limit the ability of coral reefs to flourish, but several species have survived against the odds. Many people who have dived in various GCC waters say that Kuwait offers some of the best diving in the region.

Al Hashemi II

The various dive centres in Kuwait offer trips and courses in line with some of the world's best diving organisations, including PADI and BSAC.

Al Boom Marine & Diving Center

Location → Beh City Centre · Shuwaikh	483 0474
Hours → Timings on request	
Web/email → www.alboommarine.com	Map Ref → 5-E2

The Al Boom Dive Center offers a full range of NAUI courses for all levels from beginner to instructor. A Junior Scuba Diver course costs KD 125, and prices range right up to KD 450 for the NAUI Instructor course. The centre provides personal attention both in the swimming pool and classroom environments. Open water dives take place from boats moored off islands near the Kuwait coastline. After successfully completing requirements, you will get a NAUI certificate which will enable you to dive anywhere in the world. Al Boom has a comprehensive website that you can consult for further information.

Dive Caroline

Location ➔ Fahaheel Sea Club · Fahaheel | 371 9289
Hours ➔   Timings on request
Web/email ➔ www.horn3.com   Map Ref ➔ 2-D3

Based in Fahaheel Sea Club, Dive Caroline is the only dive centre to offer night dives. They have two dive boats, based in Khiran and Messilah, with a capacity for 25 divers. Boats meet and exceed safety standards, and are fitted with equipment for emergency communications, first aid kits and oxygen.

Boats leave twice a day (08:00 and 14:00) for reef trips to Donkey Reef, Umm Al Muradum, Qaro, Taylors Rock, Five Mile Reef and others.

KIM Center

Location ➔ Hilton Kuwait Resort · Fahaheel | 371 6002
Hours ➔   Timings on request
Web/email ➔ www.kimcenter.com   Map Ref ➔ 1-D3

KIM is a 5 Star PADI dive centre, offering over 30 Scuba diving and related courses taught by qualified instructors. Whether you're a beginner or you want to take your instructor course, you can do it at KIM, as long as you meet the pre-requirements for your desired course. Apart from training, KIM also arranges regular diving and snorkelling trips to Kuwait's beautiful islands of Kubbar, Qarough and Umm Al Maradem.

Kuwait Mantas Diving Club

Location ➔ Various locations | 794 3783
Hours ➔   Timings on request
Web/email ➔ www.kuwaitmantas.com   Map Ref ➔ na

This diving club prides itself on keeping the costs of diving low and therefore accessible to as many people as possible. However, low costs are not a sign of cutting corners, but rather a deep commitment from members to raising funds and volunteering their own time to undertake tasks such as accounting, boat repairs and even filling cylinders.

Training is provided under the internationally recognised BSAC system, and involves both theory and practical sessions. Safety and rescue skills are seen as very important, and therefore they form an important topic of training, even in beginner courses.

Palms Dive Centre

Location ➔ Nr Palm Beach Hotel · Salwa | 563 7503
Hours ➔   Timing on request
Web/email ➔ www.bbrdive.com   Map Ref ➔ 13-D2

This PADI 5 Star dive centre, previously known as the BBR Dive Centre, is based at the Palms Hotel & Spa in Salwa. PADI dive courses on offer range from Discover Scuba, for beginners, to Assistant Instructor courses. It has fully equipped dive boats for trips to Kuwait's best dive spots, and weekend dive trips can be arranged. Other facilities include an indoor swimming pool and a retail shop stocking a wide range of dive gear (the shop is open from 12:00 – 19:00, Saturday to Wednesday; and 10:00 – 17:00 on Thursday).

Fishing

Other options ➔ Boat & Yacht Charters [p.130]

The waters off Kuwait are a rich hunting ground for many fish species, including some big-game fish like shark, tuna and barracuda. Some companies offer fishing trips (see below), but you can also book independent trips through word of mouth (eg. Mr Abdullah, 977 9880). Common fishing destinations are Kuwait's islands, in particular Umm Al Maradem and Qaruh.

Fishing

Dive Caroline

Location ➜ Fahaheel Sea Club · Fahaheel	371 9289
Hours ➜ Timings on request	
Web/email ➜ www.horn3.com	Map Ref ➜ 2-D3

Although it is predominantly a dive centre, Dive Caroline also arranges fishing trips for up to four people. A 4 - 6 hour trip costs KD 100, which includes all equipment. Prices vary according to length of trip and day of the week. Booking is essential, and 50% of the fee has to be paid at time of booking. For more information on fishing with Dive Caroline, contact Marc Horn at the centre.

KIM Center

Location ➜ Hilton Kuwait Resort · Fahaheel	371 6002
Hours ➜ Timings on request	
Web/email ➜ www.kimcenter.com	Map Ref ➜ 1-D3

Although KIM's main activity is diving, it is possible to book a fishing trip through them as well. They offer a fishing trip (minimum of six people) for KD 20 per person. The cost includes fishing equipment, bait and soft drinks. For more information about the centre, see their entry under Diving [p.130].

Football

The universal sport, football is not only popular in Kuwait as a spectator sport with various restaurants and cafes showing important international matches with a mixed audience of local Kuwaitis and expats, but also is played by many, whether serious, semi-serious or purely for a kick around. The Kuwait Academicals FC organise various friendly matches and always welcome new members, alternatively if you fancy organising a league or team of your own then drop Explorer an email (info@Explorer-Publishing.com) and we'll put you in the 2nd edition of the Kuwait Explorer.

Kuwait Academicals FC

Location ➜ British School of Kuwait ,The · Salwa	562 1701
Hours ➜ Timings on request	
Web/email ➜ na	Map Ref ➜13-B3

The Kuwait Academicals FC organises friendly expat five-a-side football games on Monday evenings at The British School of Kuwait in Salwa. Teams are formed weekly and all players are welcome, whatever age, skill and level of fitness.

Call Mike Finn on the above number, extention 139 or on his mobile 986 8287 for more details.

Golf

Dedicated golfers will be able to practise their game in Kuwait, although it will predominantly be on sand courses. The experience of playing on a sand course is different in many ways to grass: You tee off using a rubber mat or piece of artificial turf that you carry round with you, and instead of driving your ball onto the greens, you aim for the 'browns'! Browns are made of compacted sand that is sometimes mixed with other substances (even oil) to make it hard and smooth – they make a fairly true putting surface although may be slightly slower than grass.

Ahmadi Golf Club

Location ➜ Ahmadi	398 3650
Hours ➜ 07:00 - 21:00	
Web/email ➜ na	Map Ref ➜ 1-C4

This 18 hole sand course, run by the Kuwait Oil Company, used to be just for employees but is now open to the public. A single round costs KD 5, and annual membership to the course is KD 175. Booking is required, especially to confirm opening times, which can change in the summer to beat the heat; tee-offs at 04:00 are not uncommon!

Hunting & Equestrian Club

Location ➜ Nr Military Hosp, Wista · Subhan	473 9199
Hours ➜ Timings on request	
Web/email ➜ www.tec.com.kw	Map Ref ➜ 17-D4

Kuwait's first 5-star golf course has recently opened. The course is unique; 13 of the 18 holes are located within the horse racing track; the remaining 5 are outside the track. The clubhouse has not yet been completed.

Saudi Arabian Texaco Club

Location ➜ Al Zoor	395 0444
Hours ➜ 07:00 - 16:00	
Web/email ➜ na	Map Ref ➜ 2-D4

This 18 hole sand course is located 95km south of Kuwait near the border with Saudi Arabia. Annual membership is KD 180, and non-members are allowed to play (at a cost of KD 7) only if accompanied by a member. Booking is essential, and a tournament is played every Friday. Call for more information.

Hashing

Other options → **Running [p.140]**

Kuwait Hash House Harriers

Location → Various locations | 916 8851
Hours → Timings on request
Web/email → na | Map Ref → na

Hashing combines running with social activities, although with Kuwait being a dry country, some of the more traditional hasher pastimes have to take a backseat! The Kuwait Hash House Harriers meet every Thursday and Sunday, in various locations. Contact Paul Stock (916 8851) or Pier Luigi Brega (600 9590) for more information.

Horse Riding

Hunting & Equestrian Club

Location → Nr Military Hosp, Wista · Subhan | 473 9199
Hours → Timings on request
Web/email → www.tec.com.kw | Map Ref → 17-D4

The Hunting and Equestrian Club (located on the 6th Ring Road) offers a long list of activities including bowling, basketball, tennis and swimming; but equestrian sports are a definite focus. Riding lessons are available daily (except Mondays, when there is horse racing) and cost KD 3 per half-hour lesson. Members can stable their horses at the club for a monthly fee of KD 120 (including food, grooming and basic veterinary care). Annual membership for a couple costs KD 100 (KD 220 in the first year) plus KD 5 per child under 18. Only residents of Kuwait can become members. For further enquiries, call the above number or 471 7271 (ext. 181).

Lausanne Riding Centre

Location → Nr St 208 & 303, Mubarak Al Kabeer | 390 7070
Hours → Timings on request
Web/email → na | Map Ref → 1-C3

Basic and advanced training of trail riding, dressage, show jumping, endurance and cross-country riding. Suitable for all ages. Horses and ponies of various breeds.

Ice Skating

Al Sha'ab Leisure Park

Location → Off Arabian Gulf St · Salmiya | 561 3777
Hours → Timings on request
Web/email → www.shaabpark.com | Map Ref → 7-E2

In addition to an ice rink, Sha'ab Park has a rollerskating/blading rink, various fairground rides for both adults and children, a haunted house and ghost ride, a climbing wall and mini golf to name a few. It is a great day/night out for the family and worth a visit.

TEC Ice Skating Rink

Location → Off 1st Ring Rd at Shamiya Gate · Shamiya | 241 1151
Hours → 08:30 - 22:00
Web/email → na | Map Ref → 3-C4

This Olympic-size rink, located at Shamiya Gate, is one of the biggest in the Gulf. There is seating for 1,600 people, so even if you don't want to skate yourself, you can go down and watch some of Kuwait's top skaters in action. Entry to the rink is 500 fils; skating costs KD 1.500 including skate rental. There is also a smaller rink, which is often limited to women and children but can also be rented for special occasions. There are various onsite facilities such as restaurants, retail and equipment hire and coaching is available.

Kayaking

Other options → **Tours & Sightseeing [p.114]**

Dive Caroline

Location → Fahaheel Sea Club · Fahaheel | 371 9289
Hours → Timings on request
Web/email → www.horn3.com | Map Ref → 2-D3

Although it is predominantly a dive centre, Dive Caroline also offers a range of watersports for the enthusiasts including water skiing, kayaking and sailing. The cost to hire a kayak is KD 7.500 for four hours. Contact the centre for more information.

Fly Dive

*If you're a keen diver and fancy checking out the reefs of the UAE then pick up a copy of the **UAE Underwater Explorer** that not only gives you the lowdown on the country's dive sites but also includes safety info.*

Kuwait's many doors

KIM Center

Location → Hilton Kuwait Resort · Fahaheel | 371 6002
Hours → Timings on request
Web/email → www.kimcenter.com   Map Ref → 1-D3

KIM is a renowned dive centre, offering diving trips, training and equipment retail. But they also offer other water-based activities, such as kayaking, water skiing, windsurfing and parasailing. These take place in the Hilton Kuwait Resort in Mangaf, daily from 10:00 to 17:00.

Kuwait Surf-Ski Kayak Club

Location → Various locations | 970 6742
Hours → Timings on request
Web/email → na   Map Ref → na

For further information, please contact Alan Hall.

Kitesurfing

Other options → **Windsurfing [p.144]**
Beaches [p.112]

KIM Center

Location → Hilton Kuwait Resort · Fahaheel | 371 6002
Hours → Timings on request
Web/email → www.kimcenter.com   Map Ref → 1-D3

Apart from the many other watersports offered by KIM, such as diving, fishing, windsurfing and parasailing, they also offer kitesurfing for KD 10 per hour.

Wind Rider

Location → Al Muthana Club · Abdulla al-Salim | 247 4788
Hours → Timings on request
Web/email → www.windrider.com.kw   Map Ref → 3-B4

Wind Rider offers training in kitesurfing for beginners, intermediates and advanced kitesurfers. A course costs from KD 40 to KD 60, including insurance, and you can hire equipment for KD 40. Kitesurfing takes place at the McDonald Beach in Al Sha'ab, and the peak season is between March and October. If, at the end of your course, you purchase equipment from the Wind Rider shop, you get a special discount. The Wind Rider shop also sells power kites, kite boards, kite buggies, kite land boards, safety helmets, wind meters and other accessories. Wind Rider can also arrange kite buggying and land boarding at Janoob Al Surra, for KD 20 including all equipment.

Martial Arts

British School of Karate

Location → British School of Kuwait · Salwa | 951 4014
Hours → Timings on request
Web/email → www.bsk.edu.kw   Map Ref → 13-B3

Various Kyukoshinkai courses from the age of 4 to adult with special ladies classes. Sundays, Tuesday and Thursdays (adults only). For further information contact Captain Munir.

Kuwait Karate Federation

Location → Salmiya Sport Club · Salmiya | 575 6633
Hours → See below
Web/email → na   Map Ref → 8-D2

Courses for children between the ages of 6-16. Saturdays, Mondays and Wednesdays from 4pm-5pm. A KD20 fee covers an entire year's worth of classes!

Kuwait Kung Fu Centre

Location → Rawdah - Block No 1 · Rawdah | 682 6703
Hours → See below
Web/email → www.geocities.com/kuwaitkungfu   Map Ref → 6-D3

The aim of this centre is to promote the ancient martial art of kung fu in Kuwait. Both adults and children can partake in classes, taught by dedicated kung fu masters. The centre also organises various tournaments, selects the national team and prepares it for participation in international competitions and world championships. Beginner classes take place on Saturdays, Mondays and Wednesdays from 19:00 to 20:30; advanced classes are on Saturdays, Mondays and Wednesdays from 20:30 to 22:00; and there are tai chi classes for men on Saturdays, Mondays and Wednesdays from 08:30 - 10:00. The monthly fee is KD 20 for children and KD 30 for adults.

Nautilus Fitness Center

Location → Crowne Plaza · Farwania | 474 2000
Hours → 24 hrs
Web/email → www.kuwait.crowneplaza.com   Map Ref → 16-C3

Crowne Plaza holds karate lessons for children three times a week. Karate lessons are suitable for children aged 5 - 12 and are taught by Sensei Jesse. Call the Crowne Plaza for more information.

Motor Sports

As is the case with most Gulf countries, off-road driving is a popular motor sport in Kuwait. However, it is always wise to stick to existing tracks, not just to protect the environment but also to minimise the risk of driving over any unexploded landmines left behind from the Iraq invasion. The chances of this happening are very small, but due care should be taken just in case.

Aside from desert driving, the Amateur Car and Motorbike Association (located at the Science Club on the 6th Ring Road) organises a variety of motor sports including drag racing and motorbike rallies.

Amateur Car & Motorbike Association	
Location → Kuwait Science Club · Slmiya	539 5468
Hours → Timings on request	
Web/email → na	Map Ref → 8-E1

There are drag races held every Thursday at the Science Club on the 6th Ring Road, and various motorbike races and driving competitions are held throughout the year. Call the Amateur Car and Motorbike Association for more information.

Netball

British School of Netball	
Location → Various locations	562 2701
Hours → Timings on request	
Web/email → www.bsk.edu.kw	Map Ref → na

Practice is on Saturdays at 4.30pm. Call for further details.

Paintballing

Other options → Shooting [p.140]

Paintball Kuwait	
Location → Adjacent to Aqua Park · Dasman	243 1101
Hours → Timings on request	
Web/email → www.paintballkuwait.com	Map Ref → 4-A1

Since 2000, Paintball Kuwait has encouraged men, women and children of all ages to get involved in this fun, unique sport. If you are in a group of six or more, you can book the whole field

for parties or special events. Paintball Kuwait has up-to-date equipment and they are flexible in terms of arrangements, so give them a call to discuss your requirements.

Paintball Kuwait operates from a grass field adjacent to the Kuwait Towers in Dasman. The field consists of various obstacles including two castles, seventeen pro-ball, air-filled obstacles, four ditches and a number of grass platforms. Guns, ammo and safety equipment provided.

Parasailing

KIM Center	
Location → Hilton Kuwait Resort · Fahaheel	371 6002
Hours → Timings on request	
Web/email → www.kimcenter.com	Map Ref → 1-D3

Parasailing is just one of the many watersports offered by the KIM Center. It takes place at the Hilton Kuwait Resort in Mangaf from 10:00 to 17:00, and costs KD 10 for a 15 minute session. No booking required.

Rollerblading & Roller Skating

Other options → Parks [p.112]
Beaches [p.112]

Al Sha'ab Leisure Park	
Location → Off Arabian Gulf St · Salmiya	561 3777
Hours → Timings on request	
Web/email → www.shaabpark.com	Map Ref → 7-E2

This huge park has a variety of family activities, including a rollerskating rink. Entrance to the park is 500 fils, and access to the rollerskating rink is KD 1 per hour.

Rugby

Kuwait Nomads Rugby Team	
Location → Various locations	551 9357
Hours → Timings on request	
Web/email → www.kuwaitnomads.com	Map Ref → na

Apart from teams for men, women, children (5 - 18 years) and veterans (over 35s), Nomads also has a large number of social members and supporters. Regular matches take place in Kuwait and throughout the Gulf. Men's and women's teams

Motor Sports • Rugby

train on Tuesday evenings and play matches on Thursdays and Fridays between September and May. Youth teams have training and matches on Friday mornings from September to April. For more information on teams, contact the following:

Rugby Contacts

Nigel Tatham (youth rugby) tathams@qualitynet.net	759 5168
Simon Cottrell (men's rugby) simon@cottrells.org	784 5392
Kate Allen (women's rugby) kuwait8@yahoo.com	565 6162

Running

Other options → **Hashing [p.136]**

As long as you stay away from the busier roads where you're likely to experience crazy traffic, you should find plenty of running routes around Kuwait. The strip along the beachfront (from Kuwait Towers to Ras Al Salmiya) is a runners' hotspot.

Kuwait Hash House Harriers

Location → Various locations | 916 8851
Hours → Timings on request
Web/email → na   Map Ref → na

Runners of all fitness levels are welcome to join this social running club. They meet regularly on Thursday and Saturday evenings to run in various locations. To find out more, call Paul Stock (916 8851) or Pier Luigi Brega (600 9590).

Sailing

Other options → **Boat & Yacht Charters [p.130]**
 Dhow Charters [p.133]

Catamaran Club

Location → Fahaheel Sea Club · Fahaheel | 939 2484
Hours → Timings on request
Web/email → na   Map Ref → 2-D3

This group of enthusiasts usually meet on Friday afternoons. All boats are privately owned but newcomers are welcome to join as crew. The two boats available for hire are a Dart 18 and a Hobie 16, and are currently moored at the Shiik Flamingo Resort in Salwa. For further information contact Mr Simon Balsam.

Kuwait Offshore Sailing Association

Location → Various locations | 973 1859
Hours → Timings on request
Web/email → na   Map Ref → na

KOSA offers a sailing course – the KOSA Dayskipper. It usually takes place once a year (unless demand requires otherwise), starting in October. The course varies in duration (depending on demand) and costs around KD 50 per person. You can also charter the Wanderer, a 26 foot twin keeler yacht, from KOSA – the cost for a day charter is KD 35. Contact Marc Horn (973 1859) for more information.

Step Forward

The meek may inherit the Earth, but they won't make it into this chapter! Don't be shy... if you are the organiser or member of a club that isn't in here, we need to hear from you. Send us an email (Info@Explorer-Publishing.com) and see your name in print in our next edition.

Shooting

Other options → **Paintballing [p.139]**

National Ranges Company

Location → 6th Ring Rd · Subhan | 475 9999
Hours → 17:00 - 21:00
Web/email → www.nrckuwait.com   Map Ref → na

This shooting club incorporates three indoor ranges with 30 lanes - perfect for pistol and rifle practice. The club is internationally recognised and has in-house instructors who are highly qualified. A shooting session costs between KD 4 and KD 7, depending on the type of weapon used, and it costs KD 5 for 20 bullets. The cost of a shooting session includes weapons, ammunition, targets (moving and fixed) and safety equipment, but if you just want to spectate, entrance is free

Snooker

300 Club Bowling and Billiard

Location → Opp Safir Int Htl · Bneid al-Gir | 244 8000
Hours → 10:00 - 03:00
Web/email → na   Map Ref → 4-A2

The 300 Club has five snooker tables and the cost for playing is KD 2 per hour. Booking is definitely required if you want to go in as a large group of people, and on Thursday afternoons when the club is particularly busy. The club also has a six-lane bowling alley, and a cafeteria selling snacks and soft drinks.

Cozmo Entertainment

Location → Souq Salmiya · Salmiya
Hours → 11:00 - 01:00 Thu & Fri 10:00 - 01:00
Web/email → www.cozmobowling.com | 574 4975   Map Ref → 8-D4

Cozmo houses nine snooker tables and charges KD 3 per hour of play. It also offers 16 bowling lanes, a games arcade and a coffee shop. It is the ideal location for a birthday party or other special occasion, and special party packages are available which include billiards or bowling, food, invitations and soft drinks.

Hunting & Equestrian Club, The

Location → Nr Military Hosp, Wista · Subhan
Hours → Timings on request
Web/email → www.tec.com.kw | 473 9199   Map Ref → 17-D4

This exclusive club offers an exhaustive list of leisure activities for members, including equestrian sports, swimming and a health club. It also has a billiard hall, where you can play a game for 250 fils. Snooker costs KD 1. To become a member (membership is available to Kuwait residents only), you need to complete the application form and pay the fees (KD 100 per couple plus KD5 per child; and there is an additional joining fee of KD 120 per couple, payable in the first year only). For further information, call the above number or dial 471 7271 ext. 181.

Explore the GCC

If you want to drop in on your neighbours then go prepared with one of the Explorer Insider Guide series. Be it for a shopping spree in Dubai, a luxury holiday in Abu Dhabi, a get-back-to-nature trip to Oman, a long weekend to Qatar or a sporting event in Bahrain, don't leave Kuwait without an Explorer!

Snorkelling

Other options → **Diving [p.133]**

Dive Caroline

Location → Fahaheel Sea Club · Fahaheel
Hours → Timings on request
Web/email → www.horn3.com | 371 9289   Map Ref → 2-D3

Due to calm waters and good weather, snorkelling in Kuwait is as easy as popping on your mask and snorkel and plunging right in. But if you want snorkelling with a bit of guidance, Dive Caroline offers it as just one of its many offshore activities. Call the above number for further information.

KIM Centre

Location → Hilton Kuwait Resort · Fahaheel
Hours → Timings on request
Web/email → http://kimcenter.selmob.com | 371 6002   Map Ref → 1-C3

For further information contact Mr Ali.

Softball

Mens & Ladies Softball

Location → beh Governorate Bldg · Al Ahmadi
Hours → Timings on request
Web/email → na | 976 5773   Map Ref → 1-C4

For further information contact Mr Johnny Baker on the above number.

Squash

Other options → **Sports & Leisure Facilities p.148**

Apart from the two entries below, squash can also be played at many of the sports clubs (such as the Al-Salmiya Club – 575 5052) and hotels (such as the Kuwait Regency Palace – 572 8000).

Duffers Squash League

Location → Various locations
Hours → Timings on request
Web/email → na | 983 3297   Map Ref → na

The league currently comprises of about 25 players of varying standards, split into groups of four who play three games every month. Matches are best of five and are arranged by mutual agreements. Standard rules apply. Contact Mr Mike Ling for further details.

Hunting & Equestrian Club

Location → Nr Military Hosp, Wista · Subhan
Hours → Timings on request
Web/email → www.tec.com.kw | 473 9199   Map Ref → 17-D4

This members-only leisure club has a long list of facilities, including several air-conditioned squash courts. A session costs KD 3 per hour. Professional coaching is available. Membership of the club costs KD 220 per couple for the first year, and KD 100 per couple for each subsequent year. Membership for accompanying children (younger than 18) costs KD 5 per child per year.

Kuwait Squash Federation

Location → Various locations | 263 4618
Hours →   Timings on request
Web/email → na   Map Ref → na

Contact Mr Youssef Hussain Mohsen on the above number for further information.

Nautilus Fitness Center

Location → Crowne Plaza · Farwania | 474 2000
Hours →   24 hrs
Web/email → www.kuwait.crowneplaza.com   Map Ref → 16-C3

This specialist health club has five squash courts. Squash lessons are offered to members and hotel guests by the in-house professional instructor at just KD 5 per half-hour lesson (KD 7 for non-members). There is also a quarterly squash tournament, which separates the men from the boys! Call Nautilus for more information.

Swimming

Other options → **Sports & Leisure Facilities [p.148]**
Beaches [p.112]

With hot, sunny weather for most of the year, swimming is an activity that everyone enjoys. Whether it's a lazy soak in the pool at your nearest hotel, or 50 brisk lengths in an Olympic-size pool, you can find the ideal watery facilities in Kuwait.

Nautilus Fitness Center

Location → Crowne Plaza · Farwania | 474 2000
Hours →   24 hrs
Web/email → www.kuwait.crowneplaza.com   Map Ref → 16-C3

Nautilus is a top-class fitness centre, full of workout choices and packed with the very latest fitness equipment. They offer swimming lessons with trained instructors. A package of six lessons (each lasting half an hour) costs KD 20 for members and KD 30 for non-members. Call to confirm timings.

The Swimming Complex

Location → Arabian Gulf Sreet · Maiden Hawally | 562 2600
Hours → 09:00 - 21:00   Sat closed
Web/email → na   Map Ref → 7-D1

The Swimming Complex, built by the Touristic Enterprises Company, houses five swimming pools in total. There is an Olympic-size pool and a diving pool, although children are not allowed to use these. There is a special pool just for children, monitored by professional swimming trainers (who also offer lessons at reasonable rates). There is also a covered, heated pool so you can swim all through the year, and a family pool.

Entrance to the complex costs KD 1 per person.

A day on the beach

Tennis

Other options → **Sports & Leisure Facilities [p.148]**

A tennis court is available at the Ras Al-Ardh Club (574 7023). The entrance fee is KD 1 during the week and KD 2 over the weekend. Kuwait Regency Palace Hotel (572 8000) has a court that can be used free of charge by members and hotel guests. Non-members can play for KD 3.

Volleyball

For a casual game of volleyball, you can play at the Ras Al Ardh Club (574 7023) or the Al Sha'ab Club (561 3777) by simply paying the entrance fee. The entrance fee at Ras Al Ardh is KD 1 for weekdays and KD 2 for weekends, and they are open from 08:00 to 24:00 (in summer) and from 08:00 to 23:00 (in winter). The entrance fee for Al Sha'ab Club is KD 3, and it has the same opening hours as Ras Al Ardh.

Activities

Swimming • Volleyball

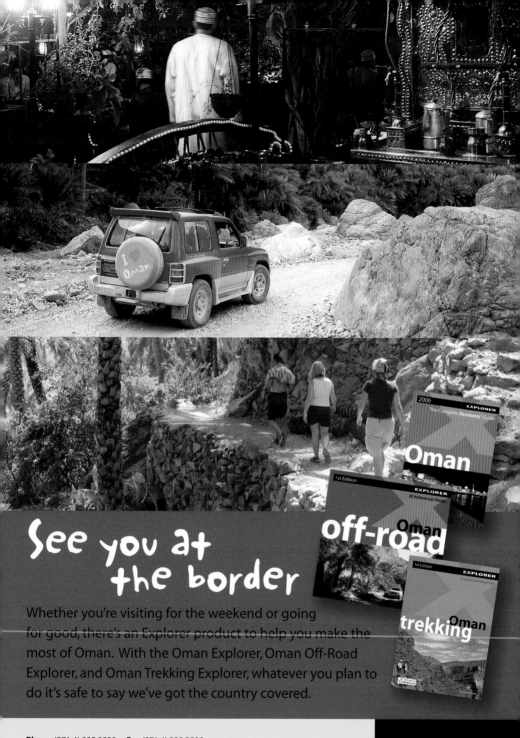

Water Skiing

Other options → **Beach Clubs [p.148]**

KIM Center

Location → Hilton Kuwait Resort · Fahaheel **371 6002**
Hours → Timings on request
Web/email → www.kimcenter.com Map Ref → 1-D3

KIM Center is a one-stop shop for a variety of watersports including waterskiing. All sports (except diving) take place between 10:00 and 17:00 at the Hilton Kuwait Resort. Waterskiing costs KD 5 for 15 minutes.

Water Sports

Most watersports can be enjoyed along Kuwait's beaches. A good place to start is at the beach hotels (try Kempinski Julai's Hotel & Resort or the Palms Beach Hotel & Spa) or the dive centres (try KIM Centre or Dive Caroline). Unfortunately for jet skiing fans, this activity is not allowed in Kuwait.

Windsurfing

Other options → **Water Sports [p.144]**
Kitesurfing [p.138]

KIM Center (371 6002) and Dive Caroline (371 9289) offer windsurfing. Prices vary from KD 5 to KD 12.500 per hour.

Well-Being

There are several excellent companies in Kuwait that can transport your body and mind to heavenly places. So in between working, sleeping and making new friends, make sure you find time to fit in a bit of pampering.

Beauty Salons

Other options → **Beauty Training [p.150]**
Hairdressers [p.79]
Perfumes & Cosmetics [p.174]

Being beautiful is big business in Kuwait, with ladies, both local and expat, reserving a considerable amount of time to pampering. Whether it's your hair, face, nails or general top to toe you'll find a number of beauty salons ready and willing to give you the star treatment for a reasonable cost.

Beauty Salons

Chateau VIP	253 0546
Cutting Edge	571 8001
Glamour Salon	262 6277
Images Salon & Day Spa	563 9388
Italian American Institute	263 4038
Jacques Dessange	264 1111
New La Fem Salon & Beauty Co. Training Institute	572 2507
Salon Dior	572 4524
Stay Young Hair & Beauty Salon	573 9266
Strands Hair & Beauty Co	572 6442

Club Membership Rates & Facilities

Beach Clubs				
Beach Club The Palms	Palms Beach Hotel & Spa, The	Salwa	13-D3	82 4060
Hiltonia Beach Club	Hilton Kuwait Resort	Fahaheel	1-D3	372 5500

Health Clubs				
Flex Health Club for Men	Azhar St	Bneid Al Gir	4-A3	252 2006
Flex Health Club for Women	Al Istiqlal St	Sha'ab Al Bahri	4-B4	261 6661
Dandy Body Health Club	Nr Sultan Centre	Salmiya	8-C2	573 2437
Pineapple Fitness Centre	Al Istiqlal St	Sha'ab Al Bahri	4-A3	262 2100
Nautilus Fitness Center	Crowne Plaza	Farwania	16-C3	474 2000

Health Spas

Other options → **Sports & Leisure Facilities [p.148]**
Massage [p.146]

Ayur Mana Ayurveda Health Centre

Location → Al Bishr & Al Kazmi Tower B · Bneid al-Gir | 240 2535
Hours → Timings on request
Web/email → www.ayurmana.com   Map Ref → 4-A3

Ayurveda is an ancient approach to healing that originated in India. Using organic herbs and oils, ayurvedic treatments can effectively treat a range of illnesses and complaints. At Ayurmana, you can get natural, gentle treatments for stress, arthritis, water retention, dandruff and more. They have special treatment packages for beauty (such as facials and hair treatments) and health (such as stress-busting massages and weight loss programmes).

Elysium Health Spa

Location → Arabian Gulf Street · Central Kuwait | 240 0865
Hours → Various timings
Web/email → na   Map Ref → 3-D1

More of a sanctuary for the body and mind than just a spa, Elysium boasts the latest spa technology and a team of highly trained professional staff to make it one of Kuwait's premium spas. Apart from the usual treatments, Elysium also offers ancient Chinese techniques to provide relief for rheumatism, muscle pain or back problems. And special Chinese massages can even help you lose weight or give up smoking. The spa also houses two separate gyms stocked with the latest fitness equipment, as well as four swimming pools, and tennis and squash courts. Fitness programmes can be drawn up, under medical supervision, especially for those with high blood pressure, diabetes or heart disease.

Various membership options are available – membership lasts a year and includes regular medical check-ups and a list of monthly treatments that might include aromatherapy massage, hand and nail care, facials and body care. For more information on membership options and costs, contact the spa directly.

Orchid Spa

Location → Palms Beach Hotel & Spa · Salwa | 564 6266
Hours → 08:00 - 22:00
Web/email → www.thepalms-kuwait.com   Map Ref → 13-D3

Orchid Spa offers over 40 treatments in a relaxing environment. The spa has seven treatment rooms and special sections for men and women. All therapists are internationally qualified, and treatments range from facials and massage to hydrotherapy and pedicures. Special packages are available.

Activities

health Spas

Membership Rates					Gym						Activity				Relaxation				
Male	Female	Couple	Family	Non-Members (peak)	Treadmills	Exercise bikes	Step machines	Rowing machines	Free weights	Resistance machines	Tennis courts	Swimming Pool	Squash courts	Aerobics/Dance Exercise	Massage	Sauna	Jacuzzi	Plunge pool	Steam room
750	650	900	1100	10	10	8	2	✔	✔	✔	2	✔	3	✔	✔	✔	✔	✔	✔
450	400	690	890	20	6	6	1	1	✔	✔	2	✔	–	✔	✔	✔	✔	✔	✔
350	–	–	–	5	10	10	–	✔	✔	✔	–	✔	–	✔	✔	✔	✔	✔	✔
–	525	–	–	15	✔	✔	✔	✔	✔	✔	–	✔	–	✔	✔	✔	✔	✔	✔
140	180	–	–	2	5	7	4	–	✔	✔	–	✔	–	✔	✔	✔	✔	✔	✔
–	450	–	–	3	10	2	1	✔	✔	✔	–	✔	–	✔	✔	✔	–	–	✔
290	290	480	630	7.5	20	20	10	5	✔	✔	–	✔	5	✔	✔	✔	✔	✔	✔

Softtouch Ayurvedic Centre

Location ➜ Kempinski Julai'a Hotel & Resort · Julai'a | 84 4444
Hours ➜ Timings on request
Web/email ➜ www.kempinski-kuwait.com   Map Ref ➜ 1-D4

The center is run by professional Keralan doctors from Softouch, world leaders in this ancient holistic healing science.

The Spa

Location ➜ Hilton Kuwait Resort · Fahaheel | 372 5500
Hours ➜ 10:00 - 21:30   Thu & Fri 10:00 - 22:00
Web/email ➜ www.hilton.com   Map Ref ➜ 1-D3

This luxurious spa at the Hilton Kuwait Resort has some of the most up-to-date facilities ensuring that you will leave refreshed and relaxed at the end of your treatment. There is a sauna, steamroom, turkish bath, a thalassotherapy pool and a variety of spa treatments from around the world. For more information call 372 5500 ext. 7118.

Massage

Other options ➜ Health Spas [p.145]
Sports & Leisure Facilities [p.148]

Kottakal Health Massage

Location ➜ Beh Amiri Hosp · Sharq | 240 8370
Hours ➜ 09:00 - 13:00 16:00 - 22:30
Web/email ➜ www.kottakal.org   Map Ref ➜ 3-E1

India's finest natural treatments are accessible at this massage centre behind the Amiri Hospital. Treatments are effective in detoxing the body, re-establishing your body's biochemistry and reducing stress. There are many treatments to choose from, including facials, massage and hot oil treatments in line with Ayurvedic medicine.

Reiki

Reiki has become a popular spiritual healing practice around the world and not only do many people desire the benefits of the enlightenment that comes with a Reiki session but also wish to acheive a higher level of comittment to the art by training to become a Reiki Master.

Synergie-Maha Nammour's

Location ➜ Bneid al-Gir | 247 0200
Hours ➜ Timings on request
Web/email ➜ www.synergie-mahanammour.com   Map Ref ➜ na

If you want to know how to perform Reiki, Maha Nammour is the only teaching Reiki Master in Kuwait, and Synergie offers various degrees of Reiki training for Reiki Jin Kei Do. For more information on these lessons and other spiritual healing practices check out the Synergie website listed above.

Yoga

Ayur Mana Ayurveda Health Centre

Location ➜ Al Bishr & Al Kazmi Tower B · Bneid al-Gir | 240 2535
Hours ➜ Timings on request
Web/email ➜ www.ayurmana.com   Map Ref ➜ 4-A3

Through the gentle exercise of yoga, you can enjoy better flexibility and well-being. Special yoga sessions are available to target specific health problems; for example those who spend lots of time staring at a computer screen or who have diminished eyesight can benefit from a package of special yoga exercises designed to improve vision.

Individual and group classes are available. An introductory session costs KD 5, and a one-hour private session costs KD 10. A package of 30 group sessions costs KD 100.

Yoga Breath Studio

Location ➜ Bl 5 St. 14 Villa 94 · Jabriya | 711 0909
Hours ➜ Timings on request
Web/email ➜ www.yogabreathstudio.com   Map Ref ➜ na

Yoga has become an internationally recognised practice, both for its calming spirituality as well as fitness benefits, and Terri Alexander has been practicing Ashtange Yoga, Yoga Therapy and Iynegar for the last 20 years. The founder of the Yoga Breath Studio, Terri offers a wide range of classes including Yoga Power, Hatha Yoga, Yoga for Teenagers, Yoga Fit and a weightloss yoga programme. Call the studio for more unformation and timings of the various classes.

Activities

Massage • Yoga

Unleash the secret agent within.

www.cinescape.com.kw

Let Go!

© 2005 Kuwait National Cinema Company

Yoga Private Lessons

Location → Various locations | 951 9386
Hours → Timings on request
Web/email → na | Map Ref → na

Dr Naaz has a BSc in Preventative Medicine and specialises in therapeutic yoga (Hatha and Shivananda). She works from various locations throughout Kuwait.

Yoga4Santhi

Location → Al Qatami Rd · Salmiya | 634 9235
Hours → Timings on request
Web/email → www.geocities.com/santhirajeev | Map Ref → na

Yoga is the ideal exercise because it can be done by both young and old, and it doesn't matter what your level of physical fitness is. People who have committed to yoga report benefits such as improved fitness and flexibility, better concentration and an overall sense of well-being. Yoga4Santhi offers a variety of yoga classes, including gentle yoga, ladies' yoga and kids' yoga. If you are suffering from any health problems like migraine, stress, diabetes, high blood pressure, obesity or back pain, Santhi may be able to help you.

Sports & Leisure Facilities

The weather in Kuwait is beautiful throughout most of the year, so is great for outdoor activities. In those summer months when the weather becomes unbearable there are however a wide variety of indoor sports and activities to keep you from suffering total cabin fever!

Beach Clubs

Hiltonia Beach Club

Location → Hilton Kuwait Resort · Fahaheel | 372 5500
Web/email → www.hilton-kuwait.com | Map Ref → 1-D3

The Hilton has the best beach club in Kuwait. The 1.75km beach is divided into three areas (the beaches furthest from the main building are the quietest) and there are two pools. Regular family days are held on Fridays. There is a great jogging/walking track which winds its way through the grounds; additional facilities include a fully equipped gym with professional instructors and a spa.

Kempinski Julai'a Beach Resort

Location → Kempinski Julai''a Hotel & Resort · Julai''a | 84 4444
Web/email → www.kempinski-kuwait.com | Map Ref → 1-C4

Equipment available for hire includes jet skis, banana boats, kayaks and water skis. Facilities include a children's playground and a Kids Club. There is also an entertainment centre with various arcade games, etc.

The Palms Beach Hotel & Spa

Location → Palms Beach Hotel & Spa · Salwa | 82 4060
Web/email → www.thepalms.com.kw | Map Ref → 13-D3

The Palms has six pools, five of which are outside (3 for adults; 2 for children) and one indoor pool which is used for dive training. There is a small private beach, a fully equipped gym with qualified instructors, tennis, squash and volleyball courts, saunas and stream baths, a play area for children and a junior care centre.

Shiik Flamingo Beach Resort & Hotel

Location → Rumaithiya | 572 5050
Web/email → www.shiik-flamingo.com | Map Ref → 8-D4

Shiik Flamingo is located on a private beach. Facilities include an outdoor swimming pool, fitness centre (with separate facilities for men and women), water skiing, scuba diving, sailing, and boating (leisure & fishing). There is a Pirates Club for young children, and a Teens Club.

Sports Clubs

Other options → **Beach Clubs [p.148]**

Al-Sha'ab Sea Club

Location → Arabian Gulf Street · Maiden Hawally | 564 1953
Hours → Timings on request
Web/email → www.tec.com.kw | Map Ref → 7-E2

Located on Arabian Gulf Street and spread over 7,300 square metres, the Al-Sha'ab Sea Club offers various services to match all interests. Its marina can hold up to 200 boats. It also has tennis courts, basketball and volleyball courts, a beautiful beach and two swimming pools. Instruction is available in tennis, swimming and karate. Annual membership for a family with up to three children is KD 150 (KD 15 per additional child). Students pay KD 60 (student ID required) and individuals pay KD 120. An additional KD 10 is payable as a one-off joining fee.

The club is open every day and non-members can enter the club after paying an entrance fee of KD 3 per person.

Flex Health Club for Men

Location → Azhar St · Bneid al-Gir | 252 2006
Hours → 06:00 - 23:30   Fri 10:00 - 23:00
Web/email → www.flexq8.com | Map Ref → 4-A3

Flex has a separate club for men. Facilities include free weights and stationary weights, cardiovascular equipment, a squash court, a sauna, a steam room, massage, physiotherapy, a swimming pool and a health food cafe. Special aerobics classes are offered for men, such as martial arts aerobics and spinning.

Flex Health Club for Women

Location → Beh Villa Fairoz Cafe, Istiqlal Rd · Dasma | 261 6661
Hours → 08:00 - 22:00   Fri 12:00 - 22:00
Web/email → www.flexq8.com | Map Ref → 4-B4

Flex Health Club has a separate club for women, in which there are several aerobics classes as well as facilities such as a cardio room, a gym, a sauna, jacuzzi, swimming pool, massage room and steam room. For a daily fee of KD 15, you can use all the club's facilities and attend the classes. For further information on the aerobics timetable and membership costs, please call the club.

Ras Al-Ardh Club

Location → Salmiya | 574 7023
Hours → 08:00 - 23:00
Web/email → www.tec.com.kw | Map Ref → na

Covering an area of over 9,000 square metres, the Ras Al-Ardh Club offers diverse services and facilities. There are play gardens for children and a huge, multi-purpose hall, as well as karate schools, a swimming club, volleyball, basketball and tennis courts, a walking track and two swimming pools. Annual membership costs KD 150 (for a family – parents and up to three children), KD 120 (for an individual) and KD 60

(for a student – valid student ID is required). There is an additional KD 10 administration fee, payable when you first apply for membership. The club is open every day, and non-member daily rates are available.

Expand Your Horizons

One of the best things about an expat posting is the community feeling among other expats. You'll find a lively network of social clubs and hobby groups who welcome new members of all nationalities. Alternatively, you could try your hand at something new and do a course in a variety of topics. Whether it's learning a new language, taking a dance class or going to a cooking workshop, you'll have plenty of opportunities to do it in Kuwait.

Art Classes

Other options → **Art & Craft Supplies [p.164]**
Art Galleries [p.104]

Artezan

Location → Artezan Studios · Salwa | 786 0054
Hours → na
Web/email → www.artezan.com | Map Ref → na

Folk art and decorative painting studio where you can develop your skills at your own pace. The courses are project based and incorporate various skills and techniques. Women of all nationalities regularly attend. Subscribe online to receive the regular newsletter. If you are new to Kuwait this is a great way to make friends.

Bayt Lothan

Location → Salmiya | 575 5866
Hours → Timings on request
Web/email → baytlothan@hotmail.com | Map Ref → 8-D2

Bayt Lothan is a community art centre that organises various creative workshops for members of the public in Kuwait. There are courses on painting and drawing, photography, pottery, jewellery making, Arabic calligraphy and more. For more information visit the website www.baytlothan.org or send an email to the address listed above.

Activities

Art Classes

Color Me Mine

Location → Gulf Rd · Salmiya
Hours → 10:00 - 22:00   Mon – Sun
Web/email → www.kuwait.colormemine.com

224 4604

Map Ref → na

Colour Me Mine, situated in the picturesque Marina Crescent, offers creative classes for both adults and children. Classes are available in topics as diverse as French Interior Painting, Ceramic and Glass Painting, and Decoupage. All instructors are experienced artists. Every Thursday morning there is a Kids' Club from 11:00 to 12:30, designed to bring out young creative talent and keep little ones busy. The schedule of classes is available from the studio.

Creative Art

Location → Nr La Baguette · Salmiya
Hours → Timings on request
Web/email → na

573 2757

Map Ref → na

Creative Art offers various art classes on topics such as drawing, painting (both water-colour and oil), glass painting, ceramics decorating, greeting card design and more. For more information, call Anita on 955 7876.

Kuwait Textile Arts Association

Location → Various locations
Hours → Timings on request
Web/email → na

390 3462

Map Ref → na

During the monthly meetings of the Kuwait Textile Arts Association, presentations are given by experts on contemporary textile themes such as national costume, carpets, weaving, quilting and needle arts. Membership costs KD 10 per year, but non-members are welcome to attend the presentations as guests, for a fee of KD 2 each time. The association also gives various lessons in textile arts at beginner, intermediate and advanced levels. Topics covered include embroidery, crochet, quilting, silk painting and weaving. For more information on classes, you can email ktaaworkshop@yahoo.com. A special craft day for children is also arranged regularly. A quilting group meets once a month to share expertise (q8quilters@yahoo.com).

Meetings of the assocation are usually on the third Saturday of every month, at the Dar El Cid Exhibition Hall.

Beauty Training

Other options → **Beauty Salons [p.144]**

New La Fem Salon & Beauty Co.Training Institute

Location → Hamad Al Mubarak St · Salmiya
Hours → Timings on request
Web/email → www.lafemkuwait.com

572 2507

Map Ref → 8-B3

Apart from being one of Kuwait's popular salons, New La Fem also offers training in beauty and haircare procedures. Students learn through a combination of practical lectures, theory sessions, training on models, and video workshops. Courses are available in hairdressing, beauty, advanced treatments and equipment.

Bridge

Bridge

Location → Various locations
Hours → See below
Web/email → na

395 0116

Map Ref → na

Duplicate Bridge is played on Sundays and Tuesdays at 20:00. Additional ladies games take place on Sundays at 09:30. Newcomers are very welcome.

Clubs & Associations

Other options → **Scouts & Guides [p.154]**

There are many clubs and associations for you to join, and since you are an expat, a good place to start is to find a club based on your nationality. It can be reassuring to mingle with your fellow country-folk, who will probably be able to pass some of their Kuwait experience on to you. Or you can just get together and share memories of your homeland. Check with your embassy whether there is a group you can join.If you organise or are a member of a club or association, we would love to hear from you. Send us an email (Info@Explorer-Publishing.com), let us know who you are and what you do, and we will happily spread your message for free in the next edition of the *Kuwait Explorer*.

Clubs & Associations

Clubs & Associations	
American Women's League	925 9878
The British Ladies Society	732 7596

Cookery Classes

AWARE Centre

Location → Villa 84, Surra Street, Block 3 · Surra | 533 5260
Hours → Timings on request
Web/email → www.aware.com.kw   Map Ref → 11-E2

To help westerners and other expats settle in and understand more about Kuwaiti culture, the AWARE Centre organises various cultural activities. Classes in Kuwaiti cooking cover the traditions and cultures relating to the preparation of food, and each student will help to prepare a three-course meal. Some of the appetisers you can expect to learn how to prepare are tabbouleh, fattoush, foul, hummus and malfoof salad. For main courses, you might learn how to make murabyan, stuffed zuchinni, kibbeh, shawarma or kushari. And for desserts, you'll learn the secrets of making umm ali, tamriyah, warba or baklawah. Students are given a folder of recipes with full-colour pictures, so that they can practise at home.

Dance Classes

Other options → Music Lessons [p.153]

British School of Dance

Location → British School of Kuwait · Salwa | 561 1701
Hours → Timings on request
Web/email → www.bsk.edu.kw   Map Ref → na

Offers a wide range of dance styles for girls and boys between the ages of 9-20. Latin American dance courses for adults.

Kuwait School of Dance

Location → Various locations | 562 2136
Hours → Timings on request
Web/email → na   Map Ref → 13-B3

In operation for over 30 years this school offers various courses including classical ballet, jazz ballet, contemporary and modern dance and choreography. Open to all ages.

The Swingers

Location → Nr Midas Furniture · Salmiya | 575 9601
Hours → Timings on request
Web/email → www.swingersdance.com   Map Ref → na

Swingers offers classes in various dance forms including jazz, ballet and modern. Separate groups are available for different age groups (5 - 12, 12 - 25 and 25 and upwards). There are classes for beginner, intermediate and advanced students.

Drama Groups

Kuwait Elizabethans

Location → Various locations | 563 1725
Hours → Timings on request
Web/email → na   Map Ref → na

A theatre group for adults. Check the 'What's On' section of the Arab Times for details of productions.

Kuwait Little Theatre

Location → Main Street · Ahmadi | 398 2680
Hours → Timings on request
Web/email → www.theklt.com   Map Ref → 2-D3

Supported by the Kuwait Oil Company, the Kuwait Little Theatre has been around since 1948. It has staged over 48 annual productions, ranging from musicals and pantomimes to dramas and comedy. The theatre runs on the same principles as many amateur dramatics societies around the world – membership is open to anybody who is willing to pitch in and help with productions and fundraising.

The Kuwait Academy of Speech & Theatre (KAST)

Location → British School of Kuwait ,The · Salwa | 563 1725
Hours → Timings on request
Web/email → kast_kast@hotmail.com   Map Ref → 13-B3

This theatrical training company offers workshops by experts in the field, both local and international. The company accepts applications (including an audition) from young people over the age of 10 who want theatrical training. Members are entered for Performance and Communication exams with the London Academy of Music and Dramatic Art (LAMDA). For more information, use the above contact details or contact Gregan Davis on 564 3409, or dgregan@ hotmail.com).

Off-Road Explorer
Perfect for a weekend break with a little adrenalin thrown in - check out the excellent UAE Off-Road Explorer with detailed route maps and driving tips as well as interesting diversions.

Environmental Groups

Other options → **Voluntary & Charity Work [p.55]**

Kuwaiti Marine Turtle

Location → Various locations | **958 3646**
Hours → Timings on request
Web/email → na   Map Ref → na

This group was formed to raise public awareness about the fragile plight of these fascinating, but endangered, sea creatures. Development and pollution are both factors threatening the three species of turtle found in Kuwaiti waters. The group is always looking for volunteers, so please call Andy Wilson (958 3646) or Marc Horn (973 1859) for more information.

Protecting Animal Welfare Society

Location → Salmiya | **944 0089**
Hours → Timings on request
Web/email → www.paws-kuwait.org   Map Ref → na

Since forming in 2004, PAWS have re-homed more than 180 cats and dogs from Iraq and Kuwait. The PAWS shelter (which is the first officially licenced animal shelter in Kuwait) offers outreach education facilities, where school groups can learn more about responsible pet care and Kuwait's indigenous wildlife. They also offer private boarding for pets in their comfortable facilities. PAWS is always on the lookout for volunteers to help them continue their good work. So whether you can lend a hand at the shelter, or foster a homeless dog or cat for a while, they want to hear from you.

First Aid

Kuwait Red Crescent Society

Location → Safat | **481 8084**
Hours → Timings on request
Web/email → www.krcs.net   Map Ref → na

In an emergency, wouldn't you rather be the cool-headed person who knows exactly what to do than the crazy, screaming person running around with their hands over their eyes? Knowing the principles of First Aid, and how to administer them, could help you save someone's life. The Kuwait Red Crescent Society runs various training courses in First Aid, both for those who need to learn the very basics, and

those who need a refresher course. A beginner's course lasts for a week, and costs KD 250. The advanced course lasts for two weeks and costs KD 35. Both are available in English and Arabic.

Language Schools

Other options → **Learning Arabic [p.85]**

A new start in a strange country often encourages people to learn a new language, and in Kuwait there are several language schools offering courses in various languages. If you are learning a second language, or you already speak a second language and want to keep practising, you can join the Language Circle (see p.155).

AWARE Centre

Location → Villa 84, Surra Street, Block 3 · Surra | **533 5260**
Hours → Timings on request
Web/email → www.aware.com.kw   Map Ref → 11-E2

The AWARE Centre aims to make life easier for westerners and other expats in Kuwait, and with that in mind they offer Arabic classes. Kuwaiti instructors teach various Arabic skills, including everyday conversation, reading, writing and pronunciation. Classroom instruction is supported with cassettes and exercise books to work on at home. Plus there is the advantage of being able to interact with Arabic speakers on a daily basis at the AWARE Centre.

Berlitz Language Institute

Location → Al-Gadhir Bldg · Safat | **254 2212**
Hours → Timings on request
Web/email → www.berlitz.com   Map Ref → na

The Berlitz method of learning a language is to speak and think in the target language. They offer various courses for adults. English courses include Getting Around in English, Brush-Up Your English, Moving Ahead in English and Exploring the Issues. Apart from English courses, Berlitz also offers courses in other languages, including Arabic, French, Spanish and Italian.

British Council in Kuwait

Location → Al Arabi Street, Mansouriya · Safat | **251 5512**
Hours → 08:00 - 15:00   Thu & Fri closed
Web/email → www.britishcouncil.org/kuwait   Map Ref → 3-E2

The British Council offers various courses in English, including Basic English, Business

English, English as a Second Language and English for Teachers. Class times and fees vary according to each course, so check the website for more information.

Libraries

Other options → Books [p.164[
Second-Hand Items [p.175[

AWARE Centre

Location → Villa 84, Surra Street, Block 3 · Surra | 533 5260
Hours → Timings on request
Web/email → www.aware.com.kw   Map Ref → 11-E2

The library in the AWARE Cultural Centre houses a collection of books, magazines and audiovisual resources. The aim is to help westerners and other expats learn and understand more about life in Kuwait and about Arab culture in general. Each month the centre publishes a cultural magazine *Together*, which is a valuable source of information about culture in Kuwait. The centre also publishes and distributes free leaflets on Kuwaiti culture.

British Council in Kuwait

Location → Al Arabi Street, Mansouriya · Safat | 251 5512
Hours → 08:00 - 15:00 Thu & Fri closed
Web/email → www.britishcouncil.org/kuwait   Map Ref → 3-E2

The British Council, situated in Mansouriya, offers many services to the public. It houses a comprehensive English lending library, membership of which is open to all for a small fee. Apart from a wide range of books and journals, the library also has a collection of videos and software. For more information, call the above number or 253 3204 ext.121.

The library is open from Saturday to Wednesday (16:00 - 20:00) and on Thursdays (09:00 - 13:00).

Music Lessons

Other options → Singing [p.154]
Music, DVDs & Videos [p.174]
Dance Classes [p.151]

Michael Varghese offers private guitar lessons. Beginners will have a 45 minute lesson (costing KD 6), and intermediate or advanced players will have a one-hour lesson (costing KD 10). For more information, contact Michael by email (mivguitar@yahoo.com) or phone (939 3852). Music classes are also offered by the British School

of Music (562 1701) and the Cracovia Music Bureau (264 9357). The British School of Music offers classes in keyboards, guitar, wind instruments, classical piano and singing.

Bayt Lothan (www.baytlothan.org) offers tuition in a diverse range of musical instruments, including piano (both classical and electronic), lute, guitar and violin. All classes are on a private basis, and the cost is KD 60 for a package of 10 classes.

British School of Music

Location → British School of Kuwait · Salwa | 562 1071
Hours →
Web/email → www.bsk.edu.kw   Map Ref → 13-B3

10-week courses covering a wide range of instruments including violin, guitar, clarinet, saxophone and piano. Ages 6-adult. Various timings.

Orchestras/Bands

Other options → Music Lessons [p.153]
Singing [p.154]

Kuwait Chamber Philharmonia

Location → Dasman | 264 9357
Hours → Timings on request
Web/email → www.cracoviamusic.com   Map Ref → na

Formed in 1992, the Kuwait Chamber Philharmonia aims to bring classical music to the residents of Kuwait. Concerts are frequently played at some of Kuwait's top hotels, featuring both local and international artists.

Photography

Kuwait has its fair share of photo opportunities - whether morning sunrises, bullet torn buildings or traditional architecture, so photography is a great hobby to take up. A photography group meets every month in Bayt Lothan. All those who have a fair knowledge of photography can apply to join the group. If required, you can do a course in photography; a course of 20 hour-long lessons costs KD 60. For more information, contact Bayt Lothan (575 5866).

There is a strong online community of photographers in Kuwait. Log onto their website (www.kuwaitphotolab.com) to see examples of work, get photo tips or take part in online disccusions.

Activities

Libraries • Photography

Scouts & Guides

Other options ➜ Clubs & Associations [p.150]

Girlguiding BGIFC

Location ➜ Various locations	|563 6060
Hours ➜ Timings on request	
Web/email ➜ www.bgifc.org.uk	Map Ref ➜ na

British Guides in Foreign Countries (BGIFC) is part of the UK Girl Guide association. The local units maintain a minimum 50% of British girls but all nationalities are invited to join subject to places. Ages from 5-14. All voluntary uniformed leaders have received training and the association is a registered charity.

Singing

Other options ➜ Music Lessons [p.153]

Ahmadi Music Group

Location ➜ New English School (NES) · Jabriya	|650 8965
Hours ➜ See below	
Web/email ➜ na	Map Ref ➜ na

Regular Monday rehearsals (19:00) at the Mousetrap Theatre in the New English School in Jabriya. Two seasonal annual concerts; in December and at the end of April. Newcomers are always welcome.

Kuwait Singers

Location ➜ A'Takamul International School	|563 6062
Hours ➜ See below	
Web/email ➜ na	Map Ref ➜ na

The Kuwait Singers is an amateur, non-audition, mixed-voice choir comprising of many nationalities of like-minded people who enjoy coming together to sing and perform for audiences in Kuwait. The choir is a non-profit organization and all its members are volunteers.

The repertoire is wide and varied and includes music from many styles, including classical, operatic, stage musicals and easy listening.

The choir performs two main concerts each year; a seasonal concert in December and a spring concert in May or June.

The choir currently meets every Sunday from 19:30 – 21:30 at the A'Takamul International School in Sabah Al-Salem. If you are interested in joining, contact Mike Kempster on 563 6062 or 668 3770, or e-mail kuwaitsingers@yahoo.com

Social Groups

Other options ➜ Clubs & Associations [p.150]
Support Groups [p.80]

Life as an expat can get lonely and you need a long list of activities and social gatherings to keep those homesick feelings at bay. Below are just some of the social groups available in Kuwait. If you organise a social group that you think deserves a shout-out in our next edition, then send an email to Info@Explorer-Publishing.Com

American Women's League

Location ➜ Various locations	|925 9878
Hours ➜ Timings on request	
Web/email ➜ www.awlkuwait.org	Map Ref ➜ na

A non-political, non-profit organisation which provides friendship and support among American women living in Kuwait. Regular meetings, special events and activities are held throughout the year. Members meet to make friends, share ideas and interests, participate in social and cultural activities and learn about the cultures and customs of their host country.

Aunkar Cultural Yard

Location ➜ Various locations	|955 7614
Hours ➜ Timings on request	
Web/email ➜ na	Map Ref ➜ na

A Bangladeshi cultural organisation

British Ladies Society

Location ➜ Various locations	|732 7596
Hours ➜ Timings on request	
Web/email ➜ na	Map Ref ➜ na

This group of expat women have regular social gatherings including a weekly coffee morning for newcomers and a mother and toddler group as well as monthly evening events. The network is constantly growing and members also benefit from special discounts with certain retail outlets.

Canadian Women's League

Location ➜ Various locations	|na
Hours ➜ Timings on request	
Web/email ➜ www.canadiansinkuwait.com	Map Ref ➜ na

The CWL is part of the Canadians in Kuwait group, a very active organisation which meets regularly and engages in various interesting activities throughout the year. Check out their regularly updated website for event listings.

Desert Pioneers Toastmasters

Location → Indian English Academy · Salmiya | 902 1502
Hours → Timings on request
Web/email → na   Map Ref → na

Desert Pioneers meets on the second and fourth Tuesday of every month at the Indian English Academy (commonly known as the Don Bosco School) in Salmiya. All nationalities and age groups are welcome. If you've never been to a Toastmasters meeting, attend as a guest and see for yourself how things work. To find out more about Toastmasters in general, visit www.toastmasters.org.

Kuwait Caledonian Society

Location → Various locations | 971 6840
Hours → Timings on request
Web/email → na   Map Ref → na

If you want to be part of this Scottish society you need to either be a Scot, married to one or have at least one Scottish parent, although you may be able to gain an associate membership if you have a vested interest in Scottish culture. Their annual events are some of the most popular on the Kuwait expat calendar and raise money for local and international charities.

Kuwait Toastmasters

Location → AMIDEAST · Salmiya | 571 7401
Hours → Timings on request
Web/email → na   Map Ref → na

This cosmopolitan group of men and women meet twice a month in a fun and supportive environment.

Language Circle

Location → Various locations | 538 7353
Hours → Various timings
Web/email → na   Map Ref → na

Some people learn a second language, only to lose it because they don't get the opportunity to practise it. The Language Circle meets once a month, so that people can converse in their second language with others. Current languages in the circle are French, Italian, German and Spanish, although new languages are always welcome.

Razan Club for Creative Writing

Location → Abdulla al-Salim | na
Hours → Timings on request
Web/email → www.razan.com   Map Ref → na

Whether you are a professional writer, an aspiring poet or you just like writing your thoughts down on paper, this creative writing club provides an encouraging atmosphere for creative writers to come together and share their work. You can

Activities

Social Groups

The Kuwait Towers at night

submit your own poems or short stories online (www.razan.com), or do one of the courses offered by Razan's founder, Haifa Al Sanousi (a Kuwaiti woman who teaches literature and language at Kuwait University).

Royal Society of St George

Location ➜ Various locations
Hours ➜ Timings on request
Web/email ➜ www.kuwaitsaintgeorge.k9.com   Map Ref ➜ na
| 627 2240

The Royal Society of St George has recently been resurrected after a period of inactivity for British expats. The society arranges various social events and is always looking for new members. Contact Nick Hasch on the above number for more information.

The Welsh Society

Location ➜ Various locations
Hours ➜ Timings on request
Web/email ➜ na   Map Ref ➜ na
| 390 4908

The Welsh Society has been active in Kuwait for many years and has slowly grown with new events and functions but they are always looking for new members.

Kids Activities

Kids

Even in normal circumstances it can be a challenge to keep little ones busy and stimulated. But in Kuwait, when summer temperatures mean that going outside is not an option, it becomes even harder to combat boredom. Fortunately, the city is well equipped to keep young minds and bodies active throughout the year.

Al Sha'ab Leisure Park

Location ➜ Off Arabian Gulf St · Salmiya
Hours ➜ See below
Web/email ➜ www.shaabpark.com   Map Ref ➜ 7-E2
| 561 3777

Spread over 100,000 square metres, this expansive park has a host of facilities and attractions that will keep your little ones busy for ages. From rides and games to indoor sports and a cinema, it's all available here. Kids can even go roller skating or ice skating on the specially

designed rinks. During winter they can play in the huge, shaded gardens, and when it is too hot to go outside there is a range of indoor games and activities to enjoy.

During summer (May to October), the park is open from 17:00 to 01:00. During winter (November to April), it is open from 16:00 - 24:00. On weekends and public holidays, the park opens at 10:00 and stays open until 24:00 (but it closes for one hour on Friday for prayers).

British School of Gymnastics

Location ➜ British School of Kuwait · Salwa
Hours ➜ Timings on request
Web/email ➜ www.bsk.edu.kw   Map Ref ➜ 13-B3
| 562 1701

Certified beginners, imtermediate and advanced courses (weekly, for one hour) for girls and boys aged 4-12. British Amateur Gymnastics Award Scheme. For further information contact Sharon Owen on the above number.

Color Me Mine

Location ➜ Gulf Rd · Salmiya
Hours ➜ 10:00 - 22:00   Mon – Sun
Web/email ➜ www.kuwait.colormemine.com   Map Ref ➜ na
| 224 4604

Colour Me Mine, in the Marina Crescent, is a ceramics painting outlet where people of all ages can go to express their creativity. There is a special focus on children though, and there is a kids' club every Thursday morning from 11:00 to 12:30. After choosing a 'blank' item, such as a mug, vase, ornament or plate, children can stencil on their designs, paint them and leave them at Colour Me Mine for firing. After a week, items can be collected.

The Thursday morning classes are designed to stimulate children's imaginations. They will learn various painting techniques on both ceramics and canvas. Each class is limited to 15 children, so book in advance.

Entertainment City

Location ➜ 20km from Kuwait City · Doha
Hours ➜ 15:30 - 22:00   Fri 10:00-22:00 Sat closed
Web/email ➜ na   Map Ref ➜ 1-C2
| 487 9545

Entertainment City is located about 20km from Kuwait City. There is a huge range of activities for the whole family to enjoy, based on various themes from around the world. One of the major advantages of Entertainment City is that once you have paid the KD 3.500 entrance fee, you can enjoy most of the rides at no extra cost.

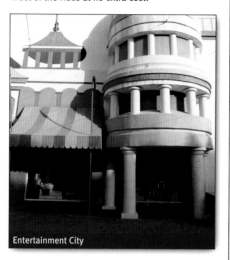
Entertainment City

Little Jungle

Location ➜ Off Fahaheel Expressway No. 30 · Bayan | 390 2635
Hours ➜ See Below
Web/email ➜ www.littlejungle.net   Map Ref ➜ 1-C3

Since opening in 1998, Little Jungle has made the fascinating world of animals easily accessible to thousands of young children in Kuwait.

It is a great opportunity for kids to see animals like leopards, jaguars, crocodiles, kangaroos, foxes, chimps, zebras, giraffe and several species of deer. They can even start the day by having breakfast with a chimpanzee! Ponies and camels are available for rides, and there is also a jungle train, bumper cars and inflatable games.

It is a lovely venue for children's parties, and they can help you make all the necessary arrangements. If you are having a party at home, they can bring their animals to you (for example, if you want to have pony rides at your party). Please call for more information on party services.

During winter, Little Jungle is open from 14:30 to 22:30 (16:00 - 24:00 on Fridays). But to keep the animals comfortable during the hot summer months, they only open at 16:30.

The Scientific Center

Location ➜ Ras Al-Ardh · Salmiya | 84 8888
Hours ➜ See below
Web/email ➜ www.tsck.org.kw   Map Ref ➜ 8-E1

The Scientific Center is a must-visit, especially for inquisitive minds both young and old. Apart from the largest aquarium in the Middle East, visitors can also learn about the natural habitats of the ocean and coastal areas, as well as the desert. It has a special section for children, called the Discovery Place, which houses oil and gas exhibitions and a puppet theatre. There is also an IMAX theatre, a dhow harbour and a gift shop.

The centre is open from Saturday to Wednesday from 09:00 – 12:30 and from 17:00 – 21:30, and on Thursdays from 09:00 – 21:30. On Fridays, the centre opens at 14:00 and closes at 21:30. Prices vary depending on what sections you want to visit; more details can be found on the website.

Scientific Centre

MARKS & SPENCER

Shopping
EXPLORER

Shopping

Highlights...

Here a Souk, There a Souk... [p.191]

You'll probably be amazed at how many shops from your home country, like Debenhams, Next, Mothercare and Bhs to name a few, have set up branches in Kuwait (the advantages of globalisation!). But one shopping experience that you'll definitely want to experience while you're in the region is souk shopping – from tin cabinets and hand-woven clothing to fascinating souvenirs and unique jewellery, you'll find it all in the dark, dusty alleyways of the city's many souks.

Catch of the Day [p.191]

Forget the sterile environment of the supermarket – for a truly fishy experience head down to the fish market early in the morning to pick up the freshest catches direct from the Arabian Gulf. Rows and rows of fish, ranging from the mundane (like salmon or tuna) to the exotic (shark, anyone?) are on display, and once you've selected the one you want, you can pay someone to descale and gut it for you. A word of warning though: all that fish makes for a pretty strong smell, so it's not for the weak of stomach!

Clothing Sizes

Women's Clothing							Women's Shoes						
UK	8	10	12	14	16	18	UK	5	6	7	8	9	10
US	6	8	10	12	14	16	US	6.5	7.5	8.5	9.5	10.5	11.5
Europe	38	40	42	44	46	48	Europe	38	39	40.5	42	43	44

Men's Clothing							Men's Shoes						
US/UK	32	34	36	38	40	42	UK	5	6	7	8	9	10
Europe	42	44	46	48	50	52	US	6	7	8	9	10	11
							Europe	38	39	40.5	42	43	44

Shopping

Kuwait has many shopping opportunities as well as the added benefit that you don't pay any tax. There are several shopping malls, souks and independent stores for your everyday needs, as well as special items. The prices are generally cheaper than in Europe and during the many sales you can find real bargains (some stores offer up to 85% off the regular prices). Gold is pretty cheap in Kuwait, as are textiles, carpets and curtain accessories. In the souks, bargaining is not only expected but welcomed, but department stores and many individual stores have a fixed-price policy. When bargaining in the souks it is common practice to walk away when the seller doesn't agree on the price you've offered. This usually results in the seller calling you back and giving in to your offer, although there are those stubborn sellers who will watch you and your money walk away, so if you really want the item be prepared to walk back and give in yourself! The staff are generally very friendly and offer you assistance whenever they can, and you are not made to feel obliged to buy. If you want to be polite then don't refuse if they offer you a drink (juice, coke, coffee or tea). This is a sign of respect from their side and should be generously accepted. Just remember that if you don't want any more coffee or tea, shake the cup as this means that you have had enough.

Each suburb in Kuwait has its own shopping street and Salmiya is the biggest shopping area. Most areas offer similar stores but keep an eye on the local paper or listen to the radio for the shops that are having sales.

Refunds and Exchanges

While most shops have a policy allowing refunds or exchanges within a specified amount of time, provided the original receipt is provided and the goods have not been used or damaged in any way, it is unlikely in souks and small independent stores that you will get your cash back once you have bought. Faulty goods will generally be replaced in the established stores but may require the original box/packaging. Generally each shop has its terms for refunds and exchanges displayed near the till areas, so remember to read them before you buy. Refunds and exchanges are not normally allowed on sale items. If you run into problems you can always ask to speak to the manager.

For items purchased or sent over from home from international chains, such as Marks & Spencer and Bhs, the store will generally allow an exchange as long as the item is part of the Kuwait range and is available locally.

Consumer Rights

The legal term 'caveat emptor' (let the buyer beware) applies in Kuwait as anywhere else and you should always check the goods before purchasing. However, should you run into problems the first right of recourse is the shop manager or owner. If that brings you no joy you can make a complaint to the police which normally does the trick. As a last resort complain to the Consumer Protection Department at the Ministry of Commerce and Industry, although this can be a tedious process. Generally shopkeepers in Kuwait are fair and reasonable and you'd be particularly unlucky if you ran into problems.

Shipping

It is possible to ship goods from Kuwait to your home country, but like in many Middle Eastern countries it can be quite an ordeal getting the necessary export paperwork and customs clearances in place. Fortunately, there are several reputable shipping and cargo organisations that can arrange this for you. It is definitely worth shopping around as prices can vary considerably. Some of the large furniture stores, art galleries and tailoring outlets will make the necessary arrangements to ship goods overseas, if required. Sea freight is generally quite a bit cheaper than airfreight but obviously takes more time. Some wood items may require treatment prior to import into another country. The most well-known and trusted shipping companies are Gulf Agency Company, who offer a wide range of specialised shipping options (both sea and air freight), for large corporations as well as individual needs (483 6465, www.gacworld.com) and Alghanim Freight, who also offer sea, air and land freight (245 1801, www.alghanim.com).

How to Pay

Kuwait is very much a cash society, although debit and credit cards are widely accepted. Cheques are hardly used at all these days and are not accepted in many places. Most credit cards, including Mastercard, Visa, American Express and Diners Club, are accepted in shopping malls, as well as in some independent shops. International debit cards accredited through Cirrus or Visa Electron are also acceptable when purchasing. When bargaining, cash enables you to secure a better deal, and cash is the only form of payment acceptable in many of the souks or at the 'Friday Market'. In some of the larger malls US dollars are sometimes accepted, but this is the exception rather than the rule. Most malls have currency exchanges should you need them. Many of the larger malls also have ATM machines available, and if not, there is always a bank close by.

Bargaining

Other options → Souks [p.191]

Bargaining is an acceptable practice in Kuwait's many souks. Department stores have a set price, but you can usually negotiate a 'special price' in the independent stores. Instead of bargaining, many of the larger malls/shops offer set discounts and have regular sales to move old or excess stock. In general, the more expensive the shop the less chance for any discount. A good rule is to walk away when bargaining as the price will generally come down, but you must have your own maximum price in mind beforehand. Try to have cash on you in various denominations so that if possible you can give the exact amount that has been agreed upon. Some sales staff use calculators when giving you a price, and you can use the calculator to offer your price too.

What & Where to Buy

From traditional items in souks, to the latest international brand names in shopping malls, all types of shopping are available in Kuwait. The traditional souks are an interesting shopping experience, whereas today's 'mod-cons', from the latest electronic gadgets to this season's high fashions, are available in the many modern malls. Salmiya is a popular shopping area, and several of the larger malls like Fanah and Marina mall, as well as Marks & Spencer and Bhs, are located there. Another popular area is Kahaleel, about 25km south of the city. Particularly good buys include gold, textiles and electronic items.

Alcohol

As Kuwait is a 'dry' country, alcohol can't be purchased and it is illegal to consume alcohol anywhere (even in hotels and restaurants), in any form.

Art

Other options → Art Classes [p.149]
Art Galleries [p.104]
Art Supplies [p.164]

Kuwait is certainly not artistically barren, quite the opposite in fact. There are a number of talented local artists and the main galleries regularly have exhibitions of both Arabic and international artist's work. The two largest galleries are Boushahri (see page 104) and Dar Al-Funoon (see page 106), which are both located in the city. The art on display is

Souk Sharq

تسوق مع الأهلي

برنامج مزايا الأهلي يمنحك الكثير من المكافآت القيمة لاستخدامك بطاقات الأهلي-الإمارات الائتمانية. إجمع نقاط سكاي واردز عند استخدامك بطاقاتنا الائتمانية في أي مكان حول العالم واحصل على خصومات، تذاكر سفر مجانية أو خصم على الإقامة في أفخم الفنادق حول العالم.

لا تفوتك الفرصة، أطلب بطاقات الأهلي الائتمانية الآن.

أهلاً أهلي ...
899 899
www.abk-kuwait.com

culturally unique and diverse and collectors from around the world often snap up the rare pieces. There are a number of very large private collections in Kuwait which also have items for sale in between the monthly exhibitions. Keep an eye on the local press for details or contact the British Council (251 5512) for more information.

Art		
Bangkok Art Studio	653 7823	Safat
Boushahri Art Gallery	572 9000	Salmiya
Dar Al Athar Al Islamiyyah	563 6528	Hawalli
Dar Al-Funoon	243 3176	Watiyya
Karizma Art Gallery	246 1249	Sharq

Art Supplies

Other options → Art Galleries [p.104]
Art Classes [p.149]
Art [p.162]

Serious artists may find that they have to hunt high and low to find specialist art supplies in Kuwait, so it might be worth stocking up when you next travel back to your home country. However, there are many frame shops where you will find every type of frame imaginable, in all shapes, sizes, colours and materials. Some of the larger bookshops also sell the more basic art supplies.

Art Supplies		
Al-Bader Stationery	571 3232	Salmiya
Art Center	240 9151	Safat
Color Me Mine	224 4604	Salmiya
Rima Art Interior Design	224 1544	Salmiya
The Sultan Center	434 3155	Safat

Beachwear

Other options → Sporting Goods [p.176]
Clothes [p.167]

Being a coastal country where the sun shines virtually all year round, swimwear is always easy to find. Most resorts and hotels sell swimwear and other equipment such as snorkels and masks. Speciality shops, such as Beyond the Beach and La Perla (located at the Hilton Beach Club) are fully stocked throughout the year, but department stores tend to only sell swimwear during the lead-up to summer. Prices are a little on the high side so it's worth shopping around. The City Center Mall offers affordable beachwear and accessories at reasonable prices. Unfortunately UV protected swimwear is not widely available.

Beachwear		
Beyond the Beach	372 5500	Hilton Resort
Debenhams	240 1500	Sharq
La Perla	372 5500	Hilton Resort
Marks & Spencer P.158	571 3304	Salmiya

Bicycles

Recreational cycling in Kuwait is not really recommended, unless you are out in the desert or on a suburban street with very little traffic. Surprisingly though there are still a number of bicycle shops selling everything from children's bikes to the latest lightweight mountain and racing bikes. Many stores will also order from overseas for buyers looking for a specific model. Prices do vary according to your needs, but a normal bike is not too costly. Safety equipment, however, is a little harder to come by. Bike shops, and some department stores, do sell helmets but buy one when you find one, as you can't be sure when they will have stock again. The range of accessories is also somewhat limited.

Bicycles		
ACE	476 9100	Shuwaikh
Al Sharq	244 2619	Salmiya
Al-Hadiah Exchange	246 7460	Salmiya

Books

Other options → Libraries [p.153]
Second-Hand Items [p.175]

There are several very good bookshops in Kuwait offering an extensive range of bestsellers, reference books and international newspapers (usually around one or two days old). If you can't find what you want on the shelves, most stores will order books or some magazines for you. Bookshops can be found in most major shopping malls or in some of the large department stores. Virgin Megastore and The Kuwait Bookshop offer a wide range of books from all around the world, as well as current western magazines. Bear in mind that due to censorship some magazines will be marked with a 'black pen' on certain photographs. Books are not as pricey as you may expect considering they have been brought in from abroad, but unfortunately magazines are, and you

What & Where to Buy

Shopping

vmeganews
.com

can expect to pay at least double what you are used to paying back home. If you are after second hand books or want to donate books, then Q8, located in Kuwait City, is a great bookshop. A good website to check out is www.araboo.com/dir/kuwait-books-shopping if you like shopping online.

Books		
Al Bader Stationery	571 2250	Salmiya
	245 5442	Central Kuwait
Jarir Book Store	261 0111	Hawalli
Q8 Books	245 7505	Central Kuwait
Star Books	431 2029	Shuwaikh
The Sultan Center	434 3155	Safat
The Kuwait Bookshop	242 4289	Safat
Virgin Megastore P.165	224 4555	Salmiya

Camera Equipment

Other options → Electronics & Home Appliances [p.169]

Most of the latest gadgets and technology are readily available in Kuwait, and it is not unusual for new cameras to be available here before they are in Europe. Prices are definitely cheaper but it's worth checking whether you get a worldwide or just a GCC warranty. Digital cameras are very good value, and many residents and visitors take advantage of the tax-free environment to grab a bargain. All of the leading brands including Nikon, Canon, Olympus and Minolta are readily available. The best place to check out prices are Alghanim Electronics (with several branches throughout Kuwait) and Eureka (branches in Salmiya and at the airport). Keep an eye on the local press for any special sales. All Kodak stores (located in Old

Shopping Spree in the UAE

In Kuwait you're just a hop, skip and a jump (and a plane ride) from the modern malls and super souks of Dubai, the retail Mecca for Middle East shopaholics. But when planning the mother of all shopping trips, your first purchase should be the Dubai Explorer – it's got more info on how to spend your cash than you could cram into a hundred shopping bags!

Camera Equipment	
A.A.B	572 0624
Alghanim Electronics	484 7244
Ashraf & Co Ltd	240 1530
Boushahri Art Gallery	572 9000
Eureka	575 1133
Panasonic	261 0590
Sony	80 4477

Salmiya and other areas of Kuwait) sell film, lenses and other camera accessories.

Cards & Stationery

Other options → Art Supplies [p.164]
Books [p.164]

Greetings cards can be found in Hallmark shops and the large supermarkets, including the City Center malls and The Sultan Center. Most local and Middle East festivities are catered for as well as the normal birthday and special occasion cards. Although the selection of humorous cards is a little limited you may find some gems if you have a good rummage. Western festive cards, including Christmas and Easter, can also be found although the range is not too extensive. Costs are a little higher than back home.

Many card shops also sell little gifts such as souvenirs and ornaments, as well as children's toys and wrapping paper. Special personalised cards, for weddings and the like, can be arranged through the local printing shops. As can be expected the more risqué cards are not available.

Cards & Stationery		
Al Bader Stationery	571 2250	Salmiya
Hallmark	484 9478	Shuwaikh
The Sultan Center	434 3155	Safat
The Kuwait Bookshop	242 4289	Safat
True Value	483 3168	Shuwaikh

Carpets

Other options → Bargaining [p.162]
Souvenirs [p.176]

Carpets of varying quality and price are plentiful in Kuwait and good bargains on Persian carpets can be had, especially if you know what you are looking for. For the more expensive, higher quality carpets, insist on a certificate of authenticity so that you can be sure you are buying the genuine article. There is a souk in Qurain that is dedicated to selling carpets and there are also several other outlets in the old souk downtown. Generally it's best to start by offering around 50% of the asking price. The price of Iranian carpets varies considerably and depends on the size, region of origin, weavers signature and the knots per square inch. Turkish carpets with intricate patterns of flowers, motifs and birds are also popular. Some of the better quality silk carpets show a different colour shade when viewed from different angles. There is also a carpet souk in Kuwait City, just north of Safat Square, where there are six shops all together in one street – it's a great place to bargain between the different sellers. Arabic carpets can be found in the newly built 'old style' souk opposite the Ahalhi Bank in Kuwait City.

For more basic household carpets you can try the Friday Market or the Iranian Market where the prices are quite a bit lower, but so is the quality. Some of the best deals are from salesmen driving around with a mini carpet souk in the back of their pickup, so you can literally pick up a really cheap local carpet that 'fell off the back of a lorry'!

Carpets

Alia Gallery Iranian Carpet	575 1508	Salmiya
Persian Carpet Exhibition	573 1431	Salmiya

Colourful carpets

Cars

Other options → Buying a Vehicle [p.186]

Cars are definitely one of the best buys in Kuwait, and are much cheaper than most other places. There is also no shortage of banks or finance companies willing to lend you the money to buy that dream car you never thought you would be able to afford. From Minis to Maseratis, Fords to Ferraris, everything is available, be it for the family or the flash Harry!

The second-hand market is a buoyant industry in Kuwait, and it seems there are more cars than people. Most households in Kuwait own two or three cars and regularly trade them in for a newer one or simply one in a different colour. Good deals can definitely be had but it's worth shopping around and bargaining is essential.

Most of the dealers are fair but if possible it's always best to see the service records or check the chassis/engine number with the local dealer to avoid any hidden surprises. Also, it's not a bad idea to have the car checked out by an independent garage. Good areas to go browsing for your dream car are Shuwaikh and Ras Al Ardh. Most finance companies put ads in the local paper, so you can shop around for car finance without leaving the house!

Clothes

Other options → Shoes [p.175]
Lingerie [p.172]
Sporting Goods [p.176]
Tailoring [p.176]
Kids' Items [p.172]
Beachwear [p.164]

Kuwait may not be Paris, London, Milan or New York but international fashion still finds its way to the racks here. You will find most of the malls and boutiques carry the latest designer fashions as well as locally influenced designs. Salmiya Street is the busiest area and there are more shops worth browsing nearby in the Old Salmiya area. The prices are relatively cheap compared to Europe, but during the half yearly sales you can get some real bargains. If you can wait until the prices drop you may save up to 50% or even 75% for the final clearance. If you can't find what you need in the shops, one of the many tailors in Kuwait can easily make up a suit, dress, trousers or shirts for you. Some tailors prefer that you bring in an item that you like so they can copy it, but some will create a design from a catalogue picture or a description. Tailors are not difficult to find and you will see a tailor sign on virtually every shopping street corner.

Al Muthana Center, opposite the JW Marriot, has a lot of clothes shops and Mexx For Less is a good place to find a bargain as they carry clothes from the international brand, Mexx, with up to 50% discount. It's a good tip to check the clothes size carefully as they can vary depending on where they were made. The shopping outlets in the souks generally offer clothes of varying quality although there are some real bargains to be had. It's good to shop around but you must check the item carefully before buying as refunds or exchanges are almost impossible.

What & Where to Buy

Shopping

Clothes

Anotah	242 1614	Sharq
	371 0620	Kuwait Magic
Calvin Klein	571 7502	Salmiya
Giordano	264 6501	Salmiya
Hugo Boss	574 7840	Salmiya
Jashanmal	242 0071	Central Kuwait
Karen Millen	571 9116	Salmiya
Mango	243 5232/3	Sharq
Marina Mall	572 2299	Salmiya
Marks & Spencer P.158	571 3304	Salmiya
Mexx	241 6619	Central Kuwait
Moschino	572 6677	Salmiya
Ralph Lauren	575 4260	Salmiya
Splash	473 4160	Salmiya
Stradivarius	571 9115	Al Fanar Cmplx
Union Trading Company	571 8511	Salmiya
United Colors of Benetton	571 5883	Salmiya
Valentino	572 6677	Salmiya
Yves Saint Laurent	572 6677	Salmiya
Zara	571 5540	Salmiya

Strut your stuff in style!

Clothes – Nearly New

If you are interested in second-hand clothes, head down to the Friday Market. During the winter months there will be endless stalls selling fur-lined and leather jackets, and lighter clothes during the summer months. The range of clothes is really quite interesting and is definitely worth a good browse.

There are no charity shops as such, so if you want to dispose of your used clothes it's better to pass them on to your housemaid, and who knows, they may turn up at the Friday Market!

Computers

Other options → **Electronics & Home Appliances [p.169]**

If you're a computer geek, then spare some time and wander around in the computer area of Hawalli. Hundreds of small shops offer computers, software programs, accessories, technical advice or DVDs (some of them not yet seen on the screen in America). If you're thinking of taking the goods overseas, just be aware that you might need an adaptor as Kuwait has three-pin plug sockets.

Alghanim Electronics and Eureka also offer a good range of computers, so keep an eye on the local press for sales. Most of the leading brands, and some lesser-known ones, are available. Remember to check the warranty coverage and duration on all purchases (especially if you are taking it overseas as you will need an international warranty).

Computers

Alghanim Electronics	484 7244	Shuwaikh
Cameo Computers	482 6692	Shamiya
Cameo Mega Computer Store	262 3637	Hawalli
Eureka	575 1133	Salmiya

Costumes

For those who like dressing up, or indeed down, there are not too many places where you can get that special costume. Some of the larger department stores offer a limited range of costumes. For the more adventurous costumes you could try Party Land in Shuwaikh (481 4485) where various costumes, from silly to elaborate, can be rented or bought. It is located close to the Harley Davidson shop so you can get your leathers there too! They also have an outlet in Marina Mall.

Discount Cards

Some of the clothes stores and department stores offer customer cards and also some supermarkets like The Sultan Center have a loyalty scheme that enables you to accumulate points and ultimately use them for purchases. At IKEA and Landmark you can also find loyalty cards that offer you a point system on the items that you're purchasing.

Electronics & Home Appliances

Other options → Camera Equipment [p.166]
Computers [p.168]

Plasma screens, the latest digital cameras and bachelor pad stereos, every electronics, home entertainment system or everyday appliance is available in Kuwait in the many outlets. Items can either be found in individual stores, supermarkets or department stores. The street behind the Old Heritage Souk is dedicated to electrical items, and here you can find international brands such as Bosch, Philips and Sony as well as lesser-known brands. The two biggest stores selling electronics and home appliances are Alghanim and Eureka. If you are buying an item from these two stores to take to Europe then you can trust it will be compatible with the European market. Many items come with adaptors or multi functional plugs. Prices are generally very reasonable compared to abroad.

Electronics & Home Appliances

Al Babtain Electronics	472 6170	Farwania
Al Mulla Electronics	242 3250	Shuwaikh
Alghanim Electronics	484 7244	Shuwaikh
Bang & Olufsen	575 3929	Salmiya
Casio	242 9700	Central Kuwait
Eureka	575 1133	Safat
Kenwood	242 0071	Central Kuwait
Mohamed Abdulrahman Al-Bahar	261 9476	Hawalli
Sony	224 1101	Shuwaikh
Supplying Store Co	392 2771	Fahaheel
	571 6085	Salmiya
True Value	483 3168	Shuwaikh
Virgin Megastore p.165	224 4555	Salmiya

Eyewear

Other options → Sporting Goods [p.176]
Opticians [p.179]

Pearl, located in the Marina Mall, is the biggest optician in Kuwait and has the best range to choose from whether glasses or sunglasses. Most opticians offer the latest fashion frames and shades from all the leading brands, and they will do an eye test for you for free. If you use contact lenses most international brands are available as well as coloured or throw away lenses. Virtually all of the brand name sunglasses can be customised to your prescription. Most opticians

are located in Salmiya area, however there are also many others dotted around Kuwait. Al Muthana Center in Safat also has many opticians lined up on ground floor.

Dedicated sunglasses shops are normally located close to the clothes shops in the malls. Prices are generally reasonable but some name brands can be a little expensive. Check the local paper or radio if there are any special deals going on.

Eyewear

Gulf Optical Co.	240 2068	Safat
Hassan's Optician Co.	80 6080	Central Kuwait
International Optique	299 7657	Sharq
	571 4007	Salmiya
Kefan Optics	240 9244	Salhiya
Pearl Opticians	224 4771	Salmiya

Flowers

Other options → Gardens [p.170]

You will find a wide selection of flowers available, from the exotic to the traditional. Flowers can be bought in most supermarkets and hotels, although there are a number of flower shops hidden away in most residential suburbs. If you're looking for a bargain then try the nursery district (located on the 4th Ring Road between Roads 55 and 60) or the Iranian Market (just behind the nursery district, which also offers a wide selection of large imitation flowers and plants). The flowers are quite seasonal, can be very colourful, and many are ideally suited to the harsh climate. The sellers can normally give good advice on the types of plants and how to look after them.

Most florists in the larger shopping malls do provide international deliveries, although these can just as easily be arranged on the internet through www.interflora.com. If you are shopping for flowers online you can also try www.sufloreria.com or www.flora2000.com.

Flowers

Al Arzah Flowers	571 4785	Salmiya
Al Fanar Flower Shop	574 9900	Salmiya
Lopaz Flowers	538 0525	Mishrif
Munira Flowers	240 4441	Hawalli
Richou Flowers	572 8857	Safat
Roots Flowers	265 9530	Hawalli
Sultan Center,The	434 3155	Safat

What & Where to Buy

Shopping

Food

Other options → Health Food [p.171]

Going grocery shopping in Kuwait is not a million miles away from what you will be used to in your home country. Most International brands are available and if the supermarket doesn't carry the brand, they will order it in for you. A handy hint is to stock up on a few extra cans of your favourite brand when you shop, as stocks do seem to disappear quickly and are not always immediately replenished. Most reputable brands are available. Pork products are not sold anywhere. Al Muthana Center has an Asian Grocery Store stocking imported spices and other exotic foods.

The ubiquitous corner shop is alive and well in Kuwait and known as a 'bakala'. These can be found all over the city, in the basement of apartment blocks or even in the back of parked trucks when you are driving out to the desert. A bakala sells a wide variety of groceries including milk, juice, bread, soft drinks and of course sweets for the kids.

There are also a number of very good fresh food markets in Kuwait, and The Sultan Center chain (www.sultan-center.com) operates the biggest food markets, located beside the Sharq Souk and in Fahaheel.

Food

Food		
City Center Shuweikh	80 5222	Shuwaikh
The Sultan Center	434 3155	Safat
The Sultan Center Bakery	571 9620	Salmiya

Food shopping in the souk

Gardens

Other options → Flowers [p.169]
Hardware & DIY [p.170]

Between Airport Road (Road 55) and Gazali Road (Road 60) on the 4th Ring Road is the nursery district. From rows of palm trees to much smaller plants, you'll find a good variety depending on the season. There are some outdoor plants that are surprisingly resilient, so you should be able to keep your garden green even as the summer hots up. The Iranian Market sells garden furniture as do some of the smaller furniture shops around Shuwaikh. Coming into spring and summer, supermarkets and larger hardware stores (such as ACE and True Value) sell a good selection of garden furniture and ornaments.

Gardens

Gardens		
ACE	476 9100	Shuwaikh
Landmark	473 4160	Shuwaikh
Nursery District	na	Shuwaikh
Sears	434 1791	Farwania
True Value	483 3168	Safat

Hardware & DIY

Other options → Outdoor Goods [p.174]

Jotun, Hempel and other paint companies will give the DIY interior designer enough ammunition to do a complete villa makeover. Apart from a wide range of colours, they also offer a blending process so you can get the exact colour you need. Brushes, stencils and virtually any painting accessory are available and if you can't find it at ACE, you probably won't find it! If you don't feel like doing the hard labour yourself, Hempel can help you find a painter that will do the job at a reasonable cost. Many companies offer home delivery, but if not then its easy to hire a driver with a pick-up. Most paint shops are located in the Shuwaikh area. If you need wood or any other DIY material the Shuwaikh area is also good and you will certainly find what you are looking for at a cheap price.

Hardware & DIY

Hardware & DIY		
ACE	476 9100	Shuwaikh
Hempel Paint	481 3366	Shuwaikh
Jotun	474 3014	Shuwaikh
Sears	434 1791	Farwania

DIY dream

Health Food

Other options → Health Clubs [p.148]
Food [p.170]

Most supermarkets have a health food section, but more and more independent health shops are opening in Kuwait. There is a particularly good place in Souk Salmiya offering a wide selection of vitamins, supplements and more. The staff are efficient and will give you good advice on what to use for various ailments.

The Sultan Center stocks lactose-free and gluten-free products, as well as a range of items for diabetics. If they don't have it on the shelves it is worth asking whether they will order it for you. Most general pharmacies can offer help with your dietary requirements or refer you to somewhere that can.

Health Food

Al Farwaniya Pharmacy	476 3566	Farwania
International Clinic	574 5111	Salmiya
Mervat	517 2550/249	Salmiya
The Sultan Center	571 9620	Salmiya

Home Furnishings & Accessories

Other options → Hardware & DIY [p.170]
Furnishing Accommodation [p.68]

'Out with the old and in with the new' is a very true cliché in Kuwaiti as many families buy new furniture every year. It's not surprising then that there are many home furnishing companies

catering to many different tastes. IKEA is one of the bigger furniture companies and the Kuwait branch was in fact the first IKEA in the Middle East. A few blocks away is Sun City which has many home furnishing shops. It's also possible to get furniture made to order, and the mechanical souk area (in Fahaheel) has a street dedicated to carpenters.

Other home furnishing stores include The One, Midas and Landmark, and some furniture shops have designers available.

Good bargains can be found when buying second-hand furniture from people leaving Kuwait – if you are in the market for second-hand furniture keep an eye on supermarket noticeboards or have a browse round the Friday Market.

Home Furnishings & Accessories

A 2 Z Home Store	481 3142	Shuwaikh
Al-Ghanim	431 4000	Shuwaikh
BO Concept	224 4511	Salmiya
Daiso	571 2250	Salmiya
Debenhams	240 1500	Sharq
Emporium	475 1555	Al Rai
Ethan Allen	471 0020	Al Rai
Homes R Us	482 2180	Shuwaikh
IKEA	481 0477	Shuwaikh
Landmark	473 4160	Salmiya
Midas	431 7852	Farwania
THE One	224 4511	Salmiya

Jewellery & Watches

Other options → Souks [p.191]

Most shopping malls have at least one jewellery or watch shop. Behind the Old Souk you can find the Gold Souk with aisles and aisles of gold, so keep your credit card, or even better cash, handy. The souk behind the Sheraton Hotel also has a lot of jewellery shops or you can head down to Hawalli which has its very own 'Jewellery Street'. Hawalli offers mostly European designs, while the gold market behind The Sheraton displays the more ornate Indian and Arabic designs. Even a trip to the souk opposite the Marina Mall is worth a try, but remember to bargain hard. Gold is generally sold by weight and jewellers will usually issue an authentication certificate on all purchases. Specific jewellery designs can be tailor-made to suit your own individual requirements. Paying by cash enables you to get the best discounts.

Watches come in all shapes, sizes and brands and can be purchased from as little as KD 1 up to the 'if you need to know the price you can't afford it' variety!

What & Where to Buy

Shopping

Jewellery & Watches

Al Abdulla	246 4817	Central Kuwait
Al Arbash	573 1150	Salmiya
Al Fanar Jewellery	245 9844	Salmiya
Al Maarawi Jewellery	264 5765	Hawalli
Al Malaika	391 2737	Fahaheel
Cartier	484 4352	Salmiya
Classic Jewellery	264 6222	Hawalli
Damas	571 8684	Salmiya
	481 8114	Safat
Gulf Crown	263 5299	Hawalli
Hamed Jewellery	392 2185	Fahaheel
Oris	244 9925	Salmiya
Payal Jewellers	244 0414	Central Kuwait
Rana Al Kuwait	242 7401	Central Kuwait
Swatch	573 0132	Safat
Swiss Jewellery	244 0865	Hawalli
Tala Jewellery	240 7017	Central Kuwait
Tiffany & Co	240 8449	Salhiya

Gold – the more the better

Kids' Items

Other options → Clothes [p.167]

Landmark, Jashanmal and The Sultan Center have items for the newborn up to school age. Bhs and Marks & Spencer, in Salmiya, also stock clothes and baby equipment for newborns and children, while Party Land is perfect when you need to get children's party essentials. Compared to Europe, the prices are really low. Shoe Mart, located within Landmark in Salmiya and Al Rai, have shoes for children who are just starting to walk and upwards.

Shoe prices are very reasonable. Okaidi also has two excellent stores in Al Kout Mall and Arraya Mall, and Next Kids is also located in Al Kout Mall in Fahaheel.

Kids' Items

Arraya	294 7999	Sharq
Bhs	263 2160	Hawalli
	571 7187	Salmiya
Chicco	244 8186	Salhiya
Confetti	266 1352	Hawalli
Debenhams	270 1500	Sharq
IKKS	263 4129	Hawalli
Jashanmal	242 0071	Central Kuwait
Junior Puzzle	572 6677	Shaab
Juniors	264 5081	Hawalli
Landmark	473 4160	Shuwaikh
Lego	571 3921	Salmiya
Luxemburg	372 1219	Abu Halifa
Marks & Spencer P.158	571 3304	Salmiya
Mothercare P.179	573 0822	Salmiya
	391 7095	Fahaheel
	539 1398	Mishrif
	476 5856	Farwania
	564 2242	Rumaithiya
Next	224 4777	Salmiya
Okaidi	299 7633	Sharq
OshKosh B'Gosh	266 0803	Hawalli
Party Land	481 4485	Shuwaikh
Petit Boy	263 4693	Hawalli
Sears	434 1791	Farwania

Lingerie

Other options → Clothes [p.167]

Department stores and individual lingerie stores (Marina Mall or Souk Sharq) offer the latest styles from abroad, in addition to your everyday essentials from Bhs and Marks & Spencer. From the frilly to the flimsy, all tastes and styles are catered for. Prices vary but are generally cheaper than abroad, and most of the leading designer brands are available. During sales you can get some real bargains.

Lingerie

Bhs	263 2160	Hawalli
	571 7187	Salmiya
Debenhams	270 1500	Sharq
La Senza	261 1124	Hawalli
Landmark	473 4160	Shuwaikh
Marks & Spencer P.158	571 3304	Salmiya
Oysho	224 4566	Salmiya
Triumph	224 4830	Salmiya
Women's Secret	263 4711	Hawalli

Luggage & Leather

Other options → Shipping [p.161]

Due to the large expatriate population and the high disposable incomes of the locals it's no surprise that shops and malls sell a good range of luggage and travel goods. There are some dedicated shops, but a good place to start is the larger malls.

Kuwait can get a little chilly in winter and you will be surprised at the range of leather clothes and coats from Pakistan, Iran and Turkey. It is a good idea to shop around as the quality can vary.

From handbags to glad rags, everything (well almost everything – wink, wink) is available in leather. Designer copies are also available in some of the souk areas and the City Center malls.

Luggage & Leather		
Hamoud R. Al-Omar General Trading Est	240 8125	Central Kuwait
Jashanmal	393 0857	Safat
Leather Palace	572 0500	Salmiya
Louis Vuitton	243 1337	Salhiya
Samba	572 9610	Salmiya
Samsonite	484 4352	Salmiya
Sana	575 3556	Salmiya
Tosca Blu	571 8535	Salmiya

Maternity Clothes

For mums-to-be the range is a little limited. Although the basics are available, for high fashion you may have to consider looking further afield. Bhs and Marks & Spencer are good starting points and prices are reasonable. Jashanmal also has a good range of maternity clothes, as do Next and Mothercare. There are several maternity and children's shops on the ground floor of the Plaza Complex.

Maternity Wear		
Bhs	263 2160	Hawalli
Jashanmal	393 0857	Safat
Marks & Spencer P.158	571 3304	Salmiya
Mothercare P.179	573 0822	Salmiya
	391 7095	Fahaheel
	539 1398	Mishrif
	476 5856	Farwania
Mothercare/Bhs	573 0822	Salmiya
Next	224 4777	Salmiya
Plaza Complex	263 3191	Hawalli

Medicine

Other options → General Medical Care [p.76]

Some of the pharmacies in Kuwait are open 24 hours and many are staffed by good pharmacists who can recommend various medicines for mild complaints. Each suburb and mall has its own pharmacy and many others are located close to a hospital or clinic. Commonly used medicines can be bought over the counter but stronger medications and scheduled drugs will only be given if a doctor's prescription is presented.

Most pharmacies also carry a range of dental, health and beauty products as well as sunscreens – essential in the hot summer months.

Kuwait pharmacies have a rotation system so that there is at least one open 24 hours a day in all the major areas. Names and telephone numbers of pharmacies that are open 24 hours on each day are given in the newspapers and announced on TV after the 20:00 news.

Mobile Telephones

Other options → Telephone [p.73]

Kuwait is well and truly part of the mobile generation with many people owning more than one phone, for different moods! So it makes sense that there is a mobile phone shop on almost every corner. If you are into one particular brand such as Ericsson or Nokia, head for the malls or Sun City as you are sure to find a shop there. The prices of phones tend to be much cheaper than Europe and America. With the high use of mobile phones in Kuwait the latest models make it on the market pretty quickly after their release including cutting edge models with Bluetooth and camera technology. Getting a faulty mobile fixed is not a problem as most shops are very cooperative as long as you have your guarantee.

Future Communications Company (FCC) and Axiom have branches in most, if not all, malls. Phones are not sold with a contract, this is a separate process and the two service providers are MTC and Wataniya. Prepaid cards are available in the malls and some of the small stores offer second-hand phones.

Mobile Telephones		
Axiom	904 8101	Lulu Center
CelluCom	571 0801	Salmiya
Ericsson	484 4352	Central Kuwait
Future Communications	224 4822	Salmiya

What & Where to Buy

Shopping

Music, DVDs & Videos

Whether it's Hindi, Arabic or English blockbusters you're after, Kuwait has an excellent range of CDs, DVDs and Videos. The not so legitimate DVD market is also in operation and if you head down to Hawalli or Fahaheel you can pick up some copy DVDs for KD 1. Most of the latest releases in America are available before they even make it to Europe. The quality is generally good, but if you're not happy they'll change it for you without a fight. As technological developments continue, the video is somewhat extinct, and although there are still some video rental shops around, most shops now have DVDs. Many supermarkets have a video section with cartoons and early learning programs. Virgin Megastore in Salmiya has a wide selection of CDs, DVDs and videos, as well as books.

Music, DVDs & Videos		
The Sultan Center	434 3155	Safat
Virgin Megastore **P.165**	224 4555	Salmiya

Musical Instruments

Other options → Music Lessons [p.153]
Music, DVDs & Videos [p.174]

Though few and far between, there are some stores selling musical instruments in Kuwait. Although it works out to be quite expensive if you factor in the shipping costs, you can order from Europe or America if you can't find what you're looking for locally. Sometimes in the evenings young musicians will jam in one of the local musical instrument stores. A number of department or electronics stores also sell some instruments, but these tend not to be specialised.

Musical Instruments		
Adawliah Universal Electronics	264 3764	Hawalli
Easa Husain Al Yousifi Est.	261 0590	Hawalli
	571 9499	Salmiya
Panasonic	224 4579	Salmiya

Outdoor Goods

Other options → Sporting Goods [p.176]
Camping [p.132]
Hardware & DIY [p.170]

Camping equipment is predominantly available in the spring, in The Sultan Center or City Center.

Shops like ACE Hardware and True Value will have a collection of camping and outdoor gear throughout the year. Director-style chairs, with built-in drink holders, are a good buy. Sometimes Landmark also has camping chairs for a good price. Tents and small stoves are readily available, as are disposable barbecues – suitable for overnight trips.

Outdoor Goods		
ACE	476 9100	Al Rai
City Center	80 5222	Shuwaikh
The Sultan Center	434 3155	Safat
True Value	483 3168	Shuwaikh

Party Accessories

Party accessories are available although the selection isn't as good as you might find at home. Most major supermarkets and stationery outlets sell cards, candles, balloons, sprays, and napkins, among other party paraphernalia. Many hotels offer catering services if you're having a party at home; they will arrange glasses, crockery and waiters as well as food if required. They will even clean up afterwards! A few independent restaurants also offer this facility. Party Land (481 8766, 481 4485; www.partyland.com), located at the intersection of Gazali Road (Ring Road 60) and Canada Dry Street is the best one-stop shop for party accessories. They also have a branch in Marina Mall.

Perfumes & Cosmetics

Other options → Souks [p.191]

Most shopping malls, department stores and souks have a perfume shop or counter. A popular local perfume is the Bashara (more expensive than gold), which is perfumed roots that are lit like incense. It is purchased per gramme. It is an interesting experience to go into a Bashara shop – shopkeepers are usually happy to show you the various types of Bashara and explain the background of the different scents. Another local perfume to look out for is Kashka. You can even create your own unique perfume by mixing various fragrances together. Also available is the world's most exclusive (and expensive) perfume Amouage. The famous Muscat born perfume is the perfect symbol of Arabian luxury and heritage and different sized bottles suit different budgets!

Perfumes & Cosmetics

Amouage **p.vi** ▶	372 3931	Kuwait Magic
	265 9060	Beidoun Plaza
	243 8200	Sharq
	471 6256	Farwniya
	391 4789	Fahaheel
	457 8606	Jahra
Debenhams	240 1500	Sharq
Jashanmal	242 0071	Central Kuwait
Lifestyle	473 160	Salmiya
M.A.C	224 4706	Salmiya
	573 5903	Salmiya
	261 5113	Hawalli
The Body Shop	575 9316	Salmiya
	224 4688	Salmiya
	240 9588	Sharq

The sweet smell of luxury perfume

Pets

Other options → Pets [p.70]

Animal lovers may find the animal market at the Friday Market somewhat upsetting. The market has all kinds of animals including crocodiles and monkeys but their care is pretty sub-standard. If you want a pedigree pet check the noticeboards in the supermarkets, or visit the Veterinarian Hospital. If you want to adopt or foster a pet, Paws (www.paws-kuwait.org, 944 0089) will give you a helping hand. Most vets, ACE Hardware in Shuwaikh (476 9100), True Value in Shuwaikh (483 3198) and The Sultan Center all sell leads, collars and other pet accessories, including food. They do run out of stock sometimes so buy extra when you see it. There is no formal local tax or registration required for keeping an animal. The only dedicated pet store in Kuwait is Fantasy Island (246 5925), located in Al Muthana Center, which offers a variety of birds, reptiles, fish and accessories.

Portrait Photographers/Artists

There are a number of photographers and artists who will do family portraits, but their services aren't cheap. You'll find many photography shops around Kuwait; this comes in handy when you have to have up to 12 passport photos for each government procedure! If you are looking for a photographer for a special occasion or more serious requirement, there are a number of freelance photographers, many of whom have produced work of a high standard which has been displayed in some of the hotels (for example Teatro at the Hilton Kuwait Resort). For more information on photography and links to the websites of some of Kuwait's best freelance photographers, visit www.kuwaitphotolab.com.

Second-Hand Items

Other options → Furnishing Accommodation [p.68]
Books [p.164]
Cars [p.167]

The best place for second-hand items has to be the Friday Market and even if you're not in the market for buying it is worth a trip just for the experience. If you don't want to go for the full-on hectic experience then Thursday afternoons may be preferential. A lot of the second-hand items are little more than junk from old computers, used washing machines, lights, telephones and even kitchen sinks! However, there are some hidden gems like brass and copper items, many of which have come from old ships or colonial hotels in India. There is no real structure or organisation to the market – things are all over the place so you can easily spend half a day walking around rummaging. The Friday market and the Second-Hand Souk are side by side in an area called Khaldiya in Al Rai. It is located west of Road 55, off the 4th Ring Road. Any taxi driver should know the way.

Shoes

Other options → Sporting Goods [p.176]
Clothes [p.167]
Beachwear [p.164]

Finding shoe shops in Kuwait is not difficult. Malls, department stores and independent shops have a good selection. If you are in the Marina Mall, cross the street and you will find many small shoe shops with the latest European fashions (this is the area the local Kuwaiti ladies go to to get their shoes). The prices vary and might not always be cheaper than Europe, but bargains can be found now and then. Shoe Mart has stores inside each of the Landmark outlets and has a large and reasonably priced range. You may struggle to find your size if you have abnormally large or small feet. Unfortunately shoe repair shops are few and far between so it's worth inquiring when you buy your shoes if they can recommend anywhere. Some shoe repair shops are attached to malls or in little huts in carparks, like the one alongside Fintas Co-operative.

Shoes

Arraya Center	294 7999	Souk
Birkenstock	240 7125	Hawalli
Debenhams	240 1500	Souk
Jashanmal	242 0071	Safat
Jimmy Choo	241 1131	Salhiya
Landmark	484 5995	Shuwaikh
Marina Mall	572 2299	Salmiya
Marks & Spencer P.158	571 3304	Salmiya
Nine West	572 0594	Salmiya
	574 6108	Salmiya
	265 6942	Hawalli
Sears	434 1791	Farwania
Shoe Mart	473 4160	Salmiya
The Athlete's Foot	240 9317	Souk

Souvenirs

Other options → Carpets [p.166]

From Kuwait T-shirts and stuffed camels to wooden furniture and incense, the range of souvenirs is wide and varied. The main shopping malls are a good place to start, as is the Heritage Souk. Shops within hotels are another good source of souvenirs and have plenty of trinkets. At the souvenir shop in the airport you can even get the notorious 'most wanted' deck of cards made famous during the 2003 Iraqi conflict – each card bearing the image of a person wanted by the US Forces, including Saddam himself and his two sons. Another popular souvenir is gold necklaces bearing the wearer's name in Arabic; they are available at souks and are quite reasonable, depending on how hard you can bargain!

Souvenirs

Heritage Souk	na	Central Kuwait
Hilton Resort	372 5500	Fahaheel
SAS Hotel	575 6000	Salwa
Souq Salmiya	na	Salmiya
Sultan Centre	na	Central Kuwait

Pick up a souvenir

Sporting Goods

Other options → Outdoor Goods [p.174]

From ice-hockey skates to squash rackets, most sporting goods can be found in Kuwait. Many of the larger supermarkets and malls like City Center and the Sultan Center sell sports goods as do some dedicated sports shops like Nasser Sports in Al Rai. Football and fishing equipment are plentiful as these are two of the main sports in Kuwait, and Salmiya is a good area for general sporting equipment.

Sporting Goods

Nasser Sports Centre	266 5411	Al Rai
Orient Sport	574 8683	Safat
Sears	434 1791	Farwania
Sportsman	573 1686	Salmiya
Sun & Sand Sports	224 4845	Salmiya

Tailoring

Other options → Clothes [p.167]
Souvenirs [p.176]
Textiles [p.178]

Tailors seem to be everywhere in Kuwait so the best way to find a good one is to ask around for recommendations. Many tailors copy from existing clothes, but if you find a good tailor he will be able to create a design from your instructions. The best place to buy fabric is in the Textile souk and it is quite cheap compared to Europe, but quality can vary. The shopkeepers can recommend how many metres you have to buy if you ask them.

Seek out a souk and bag a bargain!

Textiles

Other options → Souvenirs [p.176]
Tailoring [p.176]

If you go to the Textile Souk you can find textiles at decent prices, although the quality does vary. Alghanim also sells textiles from Europe and Asia and will make up curtains and re-cover sofas. There are often sales and special offers throughout the year, so it pays to shop around. Companies will send someone to your house to take measurements, and Alghanim will even pick up a sofa should you require it to be re-covered. IKEA also sells a range of textiles suitable for home decor and they provide a sewing service for curtains and bedding.

Textiles		
Alghanim	392 7814	Safat
IKEA	481 0477	Central Kuwait
Textile Souk	na	Central Kuwait

Toys, Games & Gifts

A few dedicated shops sell toys, including Kids Town in Fahaheel, but you can find a good range of toys at Landmark or in the large supermarkets. City Center also has a good range at very reasonable prices, and the toy shop in Souk Sharq is worth checking out. If you are looking for computer games, head down to either Fahaheel or Hawalli where you will find plenty of computer and DVD shops. Other toy shops are Waleed Toys & Gifts in the Shuwaikh industrial area (484 5489) and H&F Centre, Salmiyah (574 6856).

Psychedelic shopping

Places to Shop

If you love shopping and are always after a bargain, then you won't be disappointed with the opportunities in Kuwait. There are modern shopping malls like Marina Mall, Al Fanar, Mahalab and Souk Sharq as well as large department stores like Marks & Spencer, Debenhams, Sears and Jashanmal, all offering a wide variety of clothes, shoes, perfume and accessories. If you're looking for cultural items then head for the souks. The most famous is The Old Souk in downtown Kuwait, which can occupy you for hours. Alternatively, visit the Friday Market where you can easily spend a whole day wandering around. Out of Kuwait City there are plenty of other souks and malls, as well as the newly opened Madinat Al Fahaheel in Fahaheel. Kuwait Magic in Mangaf is another mall worth visiting.

Shopping Malls

Kuwaitis love shopping and spend hours wandering around the many malls. Most malls are well equipped with restaurants, food courts, coffee shops, children's play areas, and most have a cinema. Many of the malls are very lavish in design with marble flooring, fountains, high ceilings, and of course air-conditioning. Parking is mainly outside and is free, although some malls now have a valet service due to the limited spaces available. Most malls are open all day (some close between 13:00 and 16:30) but tend to get busy after 20:00 and close at around 22:00. Most malls don't open until 16:00 on Fridays. During Ramadan the timings change and its best to check the local paper as many stay open later. Individual shops have sales but the biggest sales are usually in February and during the summer.

Shopping Malls		
Al Bustan	571 1660	Salmiya
Al Fanar P.181	572 0297	Salmiya
Al Kout P.183	393 0144	Fahaheel
Al Mohallab Centre	266 2020	Hawalli
Al Muthanna Centre	241 4081	Central Kuwait
Al Othman Complex	266 3366	Hawalli
Arraya Centre P.v	294 7999	Sharq
City Center Shuweikh	80 5222	Shuwaikh
City Centre Salmiya	571 2250	Salmiya
Kuwait Magic	371 0866	Abu Halifah
Laila Galleria	574 8524	Salmiya
Marina Mall	572 2299	Salmiya
Salhia Complex P.v	242 1260	Central Kuwait
Sharq Shopping Complex	245 1821	Sharq
Zahra Complex	574 1548	Salmiya

Shopping

Places to Shop

mothercare

Shopping Malls – Main

Listed below are Kuwait's main malls, all of which have a good range of shops from the cheap and cheerful to the designer boutiques. They also have parking facilities and coffee shops.

Al Fanar Shopping Centre

Location ➜ Salem Al Mubarak Street · Salmiya | 571 2284
Hours ➜ 10:00 - 22:00
Web/email ➜ www.tamdeenrealestate.com   Map Ref ➜ 8-C2

The Al Fanar Complex opened in 1997 and has since become a popular location in Kuwait for shopping and recreation. The mall itself, despite being eight years old is relatively modern and with 24,000m² of retail space in the centre of Kuwait's busiest commercial district, New Salmiya, it is an excellent location for a day's shopping spree. An added bonus is the fact that on the same street, Salem Al Mubarak Street, you will find a number of other shopping options such as Zahra Complex, Leila Gallery, Salmiya Plaza and the Sultan Centre. Al Fanar has an excellent range of fashion stores, the ground floor has a number of exciting brands as well as a delightful French restaurant where you can take a well-deserved lunch stop. There is also a large Zara on the Mezzanine floor and a multi-screen cinema on the first floor. The complex has two basement level car parks which can get a bit busy at weekends as well as a ground level VIP parking area.

Al Fanar Shopping Centre

Accessories
Claire's Accessories
Dora Fashions
Swarovski

Clothes
Anotah
Boushiya
Concorde
Dananeer
Dice
Elite
Evans
Fabricasa
Gant
Gas
Gucci
Koton
La Senza
Laura Ashley
Liu Jo
Mango
Moments Avenue
Motivi
Paul Smith

Pretty Woman
Primo Emporia
Pull & Bear
Ralph Lauren
River Island
Stefanel
Stradivarius / Confetti
Tally Weijl
Violette
Way of Life
Zara

Cosmetics & Perfumes
Al Qurishi
Atyab Al Marshoud
Fruits and Passion
Body Shop
Mac
Al Shaya Perfume
Tanagra

Electronics
Bang & Olufsen

Food
Godiva

Home Accessories
Claire De Lune
Le Village
Sadeel

Kids' items
Adams
La Senza Girl
Little House
Sergent Major

Lingerie
Asrar

Mobiles
Nokia

Opticians
Al Noor Opticals
Hasan Opticians

Shoes
Athelete's Foot
Bagatt
Clarke's
Manzoni
Milano
Milano Square
Nine West
Stephanie Klien
Steps
Toscana

Watches & Jewellery
Al Arbash
Al Qatoof
Al Sayegh
Barthelay Watches
Damas Jewellery
Louis Feraud
Swatch
Tiffany
Trafalgar

SHOP & RELAX

- Selective range of premium brands
- Cinema theatres
- Cafes and restaurants

ال فـنـار

AL FANAR

Salmiya - Salem Al Mubarak Street, Tel. 5712284.

Managed by: Tamdeen Shopping Centre Development Company

Al Kout Shopping Centre

Location → Nr Waterfront · Fahaheel
Hours → 10:00 - 22:00
Web/email → www.tamdeenrealestate.com

393 0010

Map Ref → 1-D3

This relatively new mall opened in 2004 and extends from the waterfront into the Arabian Gulf via two piers. It has fast become a popular choice with residents and visitors especially as it is situated on the coast and is an excellent setting with good parking facilities. There is a fantastic range of stores selling local and international names such as Zara, Next, Giordano, and Calvin Klein lingerie. The Okaidi shop sells a range of funky kids' clothing. There are several restaurants and cafes in the mall for that relaxing snack or hot coffee, as well as a yacht club nearby and a 1.6km public beach. In addition the North Pier has a four screen cinema showing various international films. The South Pier includes the Vegetable, Meat and Fish Market and a Sultan Supermarket.

Al Kout Shopping Centre

Accessories
Accessories
Tanagra

Clothes
Al Mothahajiba
Amazon
Anwar Collections
Arena
Camaie
Camaiaux
Calvin Klein
Evans
Gaz
Giordano
L'Echarpe
La Senza
Mexx
Next
Oasis
Polo Jeans
Promode
Pull&Bear
Springfield
Samba

Rene Derhy
Zara

Electronics
Future Communications
(Nokia)
Jashanmal

Entertainment
Cinescape

Food
Al Mukbil
Al Refai Roastery
Al Qerqaa Honey
Al Watan Sweets Co.
Burger King
Cafe Supreme
Cinnabon
Coffee Break
Costa Cafe
Columbus Cafe
GNC Co.
Janaht Al
Tomoor/Grocery
Kudu

Marina Thai
Mijana Restaurant
Natural Land
Nadec
Paul's Restaurant
Pizza Hut
Santino's Restaurant
Shamiana Restaurant
Sara Cake
The Sultan Centre
Supermarket
Wadi Al Zaafaran
Rostery/Grosery
Waffles House
Zaatar

Cosmetics & Perfumes
Ajmal
Al Shaya Perfume
Arabian Oud
Faces
Harn National Home Spa
Rituals
Tola Perfumes
Qurashi

Kids' Items
Adams
Athletes Food (kids)
La Senza Girl
Next Kids
Okaidi
Pumpkin Patch
Zara Kids

Optics
International Optic

Shoes
ALDO
Atheletes Foot
ECCO
Nine West
Verona Shoes

Watches & Jewellery
New Diamond
Swatch
Al Arbash Jeweller
Behbehani Watches
Damas Jewellery
Trafalgar

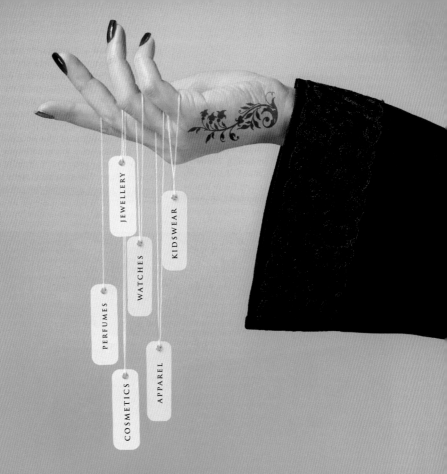

INCREDIBLE SHOPPING

AND SO MUCH MORE AT AL KOUT.

AL KOUT الكوت

واجهـة الفحـيـحـيـل البحـريـة
FAHAHEEL WATERFRONT

مدينة الفحيحيل
MADINAT AL FAHAHEEL

Over 100 of the finest brands in the world are now in Al Kout – the retail multi-centre of Madinat Al Fahaheel.

Featuring a relaxing shopping and waterfront leisure experience, Al Kout welcomes you to the new city centre in Fahaheel.

Over 100 leading brands of fashion, apparel, kidswear, leather, footwear, watches, jewellery, perfumes, cosmetics, sports and more

Fresh fish, vegetable, meat and chicken market

Food court, restaurants and waterfront cafés

Cineplex and supermarket

Luxurious yachting club and beachfront

Al Kout, Madinat Al Fahaheel. Tel: 3930010.

Managed by:
Tamdeen Shopping Centre Development Company

Arraya Centre

Location → Courtyard Marriott · Sharq
Hours → 10:00 - 21:00
Web/email → www.arrayacentre.com

299 7000

Map Ref → 3-E2

Upmarket, modern and fashionable, the Arraya shopping mall consists of three levels and targets the high end of the market. The Centre has many designer shops including Burberry (299 7622), Giordano (299 7604), Furla (299 7755), Damas Jewellery (249 0757), Gerry Weber (299 7644) Charles Jourdan (299 7721) and more. Parking is easy in the two-storey carpark located next to the mall and accessible via a pedestrian bridge. The complex also has several small but attractive coffee shops including Richoux, Cafe Supreme, Waterlemon, Haagen-Dazs and Burger Boutique. This meticulously designed mall is a credit to the modern architecture of Kuwait, placing it at the forefront of the country's luxury market. In addition to the shopping mall the centre also houses a grand ballroom, a spacious outside plaza and the exquisite Courtyard Marriott Hotel. The shopping malls three floors have nine public accesses for convenience and are connected to the car park via air-conditioned fly-over bridges.

Arraya Centre

Clothes
Al Mothahajiba
Amazon
Anwar Collections
Arena
Calvin Klein
Camaie
Evans
Gaz
Giordano
La Senza
La Senza Girl
L'Echarpe
Mexx
Next
Oasis
PoloJeans
Promod
Pull & Bear
Rene Derhy
Samba
Springfield
Zara

Entertainment
KNCC-Ci

Food
Burger King
Café Supreme
Cinnabon
Coffee Break
Costa Coffee
Dalloyau
Gelatini
Kudu
Marina Thai
Mijana restaurant
Paul's Coffee
Pizza Hut
Silk & Spice

Kids' items
Adams
Catimini Fashions
Next Kids

Okaidi
Pumpkin Patch
Zara Kids

Perfumes & Cosmetics
Al Ajmal
Al Shaya Perfume
Arabian Oud
Harn National Home Spa
Qurashi
Rituals
Tola Perfumes

Services
ATM
Future Communications
Wataniya Telecom

Shoes
ALDO
Athelete's Foot

Atheletes Foot (kids)
ECCO
Nine West
Verona Shoes

Watches & Jewellery
Al Arbash Jeweller
Al Sawani
Behbehani Watches
Crystal
Damas Jewellery
Harley Davidson
Jashanmal
New Diamond
On Time Plus
Swatch
Trafalgar

Salhia Complex

Location → Beh JW Marriott Htl · Central Kuwait | 299 6000
Hours → 08:00 - 13:00 16:30 - 22:00 Fri 16:00 - 22:00
Web/email → www.salhiacomplex.com   Map Ref → 3-C4

The Salhia Complex is located right in the heart of Kuwait City's commercial centre and is one of Kuwait's most well-established and much-loved malls. For the past 25 years the complex has been attracting residents and visitors because it has an excellent mix of affordable high-street style shops as well as exquisite designer brands and boutiques. In some of the stores you will find that bargaining is welcomed and don't be surprised if they offer you tea or coffee mid-negotiation – remember it would be impolite to refuse. The shops and the shopkeepers definitely have character, adding to the pleasure of a well-deserved shopping spree. And after a long hard day treading the shopping mall boards you can enjoy a delicious meal on the ground floor's popular Cafe Royal

There are also some luxury brands available in this mall, so you can spend a small fortune on beautiful things from Chanel, LaCoste, Louis Vuitton, Tiffany & Co, Rolex, Jimmy Choo and Cartier.

Designer names at Salhia

Places to Shop

Shopping

Accessories
Al Hidaa
Al Moda
Duomo
Fashion House
Gold Pfeil
Home Leathers
Leather Palace
Louis Vuitton
Palermo
Rocco Line
Sergio Rossi
Stephane Kelian
Vicini
Zenia (opening soon)

Clothes
Aigner
Al Aouj Fashion
Al Ostoura
Alta Moda
Black Bouchiya
Boutique Stars
Chanel
CoCo Ribbons
Dananeer
Dinar Trading
Discount
Escada
Fashion Corner
Fular
Gerard Daret

Givenchy
In Bond
Kenzo
Lacoste
Luisa Spognoli
Marc'O Polo
Mariage
Mariella
Marina Rinaldi
Marriala Burani
MaxMara
Miss Dalal Fashion
More & More
Mosaic
Moustache
Niveau Elevee
Philosophy Di Alberta
 Ferretti
Raina
Rena Launge
Sonia Rykiel
The Golden Chance
Thoub Zaman
Toul
Trends
Triumph
Valentino

Food
Café Royal
Starbucks Coffee

Home Accessories
Art Shop
Beit Al Athari
Ben Nekhi Textiles
Casa Bella
Decorama
Porcelain
Princes Textiles
Ricamo
Sommer

Kids' items
Chicco

Opticians
Opti Life

Perfumes & Cosmetics
Al Foudari Perfumes
Al Shaya Perfumes
Amal Al Kuwait
Atyab Al Marshood
Lazord
Tanagra
Wahran

Shoes
Bruno Magli
Charles Jordan
Jimmy Choo
Tod's

Services
American Express
Bouquet
Commercial Bank of Kuwait
Dar Al Tharwa for
 translation
Munira Flowers

Watches & Jewellery
Al Arbash Jewellery
Al Mutairi Watches
Audemars Piaguet
Behbehani Watches
Bvlgary
Cartier
Chopard
De Grisogono
Flawless
Fuad Jewellery
Ghadah Jewellery
Habiba Jewellery
Jawhara for Jewels
Korloff
La Dauphine
La Moda Jewellery
La Ruby
Majestic Palace
Piaget
Rolex
Swatch Group
The New Modern Jewellery
Tiffani & Co

Marina Mall

Location → Salmiya
Hours → 10:00 - 22:30
Web/email → na

| 572 2299

Map Ref →8-B2-

Marina Mall is one of the latest malls in Kuwait and is located along the Arabian Gulf Street in Salmiya. It is one of Kuwait's most modern malls with cutting edge design, a warm, tree lined interior with glass roofs and a stunning fountain right in the middle of the mall. The Mall is divided into two sections, connected by a bridge over the road: a shopping centre with a food court and coffee shops, and the Marina Crescent with restaurants and coffee shops surrounding the marina in a beautiful setting. The mall has mostly clothes shops including Tommy Hillfiger, Next and Zara. But you can also find opticians, perfume and cosmetics, Hallmark, Virgin Megastore, Harley Davidson and much more. The shops get quite crowded on a Wednesday, Thursday and Friday evenings when as well as the usual crowd you will find lots of young Kuwaitis catching a coffee or browsing in Virgin for the latest releases . The mall has a wide variety of dining options, whether you want to indulge in coffee and cake or have a more substantial meal.

The modern Marina Mall

Accessories

Accessorize
Claire's Accessories
Foular
Reminiscence
Ultra

Clothes

123
Camaleu
Cacharel
Diesel
Echo
Elina Miro
Rite
Energie
Etam
Escada Sport
French Connection
Givenchy
Guess
Hugo Boss
Harley Davidson
Jade Fashion
Liz Clairborne
Massimo Dutti
Mexx
Morgan
Next
Netiya
Oltre
Persona
Polo Jeans

Promod
Pull & Bear
Renee Derhy
Signatures
Tommy Hilfiger
T-Store
Vero Moda
XOXO
Zara
Zerbaft

Food

Burger King
Dip'n Crunch
Fatoosh
Great Steak
Gulf Royal Chinese
Hardees
KFC
Kurdo
Mc Donalds
Mrs. Vanellis
Mughal Mahal
Pastamania
Domino's Pizza
Teriyaki
Za'atar
2nd Cup
Cinnabon
JAX Cafe
Jamaica Blue Cafe
Le Notre
Pauls Restaurant
Pauls Cafe

Richoux Cafe
Starbucks
5th Avenue Lounge

Home Accessories

THE One

Kids' items

Catamini
Chipie
Exit
Lego Wear
Tammy

Lingerie

Oysho
Triumph
Wolford

Mobiles

FONO
Nokia
Wataniya Telecoms

Opticians

Hassan's Optician
Pearle Vision
Sunglass Hut

Perfumes & Cosmetics

Molton Brown

Wahran Gallery
The Body Shop
Vavavoom

Services

Burgan Bank
SHOWTIME
Global Direct
Al Bustan Al Wardi

Shoes

5th Avenue
Aldo
Faith
Pablosky
Steve Madden
Stride Rite
The Comfort Shoe Co.
Verona

Watches & Jewellery

Al-Nibras
Damas Jewellery
Marafie
On Time
Omega
R&H Al Arbash Jewellery
Swatch
Tabaa
Tag Heur
Trafalagar
Ultra

Sharq Shopping Complex (Souk Sharq)

Location → Souk Sharq
Hours → 10:00 - 22:00
Web/email → na

241 5645

Map Ref →3-D1

Souk Sharq is one of the busiest malls in Kuwait so if possible it is best to avoid Thursday afternoon and Friday evening as the mall is packed and finding a parking space can sometimes be difficult.

Shops include Debenhams, Body Shop, Mango and The Sultan Center. The mall is built on two levels with a food court dividing the mall into two sections. It also houses a cinema and play area for kids. The Sultan Center restaurant, overlooking the Marina, is a popular spot for Friday brunch. Or you can just pass the time watching the world go by at one of the many coffee shops (including two branches of Starbucks). The unique water clock in the atrium is both accurate and fascinating!

Sharq attack

Accessories
Al Sawani
Ara
Claire's Accessories
Michael Angelo
Nooran Sharq

Banks
National Bank of Kuwait

Clothes
Al Taher
Anotah
Choise
Energie
Guess
Jack & Jones
Jeans Stop
Kenneth Cole
Kookai
Mango
Monsoon
Montania
Motivi
Next
Oasis
Primo Emporio
Riva
River Island
Zara

Department Stores
Debenhams

Electronics
Casio
FCC Nokia
Fono
MTC Vodafone
Sony

Food
Baskin Robbins
Burger King
Bredz
Caboria
Chili's
Dora
First Shawarma
Fatoosh
Gloria Jeans
Great Steak & Potato
Haagen Dazs
Hardees
KFC
La Cava
La Marina Café
Marina Thai
McDonald's
Pasta Mania
The Pizza Company

Pizza Hut
Second Cup
Starbucks
Sweet Factory

Kids' Items
Adam's
IKKS
MotherCare
Reset

Music & Video
Al Nazaer
International Video Co.

Optics
Hassan's Optics
Insight Opticians
International Optics

Perfumes & Cosmetics
Al Qurashi Perfumes
Al Shayaa Perfumes
Red Earth
The Body Shop

Shoes
Aldo
Faith Shoes

Hush Puppies
Milano
Samba
Steps
The Athlete's Foot
Verona Shoes

Supermarket
Sultan Center

Watches & Jewellery
Behbehani Watches
Collier Jewellery
La Dauphine Watches
R&H Al Arbash Jewellery
Trafalgar

Places to Shop

Shopping

Shopping Malls – Other

Although most of the shopping malls are located in the city centre, or in the suburbs close by, good shopping is also available further afield. Most suburbs will have at least one mall, and they will all have similar facilities including food courts, coffee shops and of course designer shops. The better-known ones are Landmark in Al Rai and City Center in Shuweikh. South of the city you will find Kuwait Magic in Mahboula and the new Al Kout Mall in Fahaheel. Also scheduled to open in early 2006 will be The Avenue in Al Rai which will be one of the biggest malls in the Middle East.

Al Mohallab Centre

Location ➜ Hawalli | 266 2020
Hours ➜ 10:00 - 22:00   Fri 16:00 - 23:00
Web/email ➜ na | Map Ref ➜ 7-C2

Designed to look like a ship, and known to the locals as Titanic, this modern three-level mall in Hawalli has a wide range of shops and restaurants, as well as four cinema screens. The mall has clothes (Mango, Women's Secret, IKKS, Birkenstock and more), jewellery and photo shops (Ashraf & Co, 261 6599) and a number of nice coffee shops such as Costa. The foodcourt has a large variety of different food outlets making this a pleasant mall for prolonged periods of shopping.

City Center Salmiyah

Location ➜ Salmiya | 571 2250
Hours ➜ 10:00 - 22:00
Web/email ➜ na | Map Ref ➜ 13-A1

The City Center complex is more commonly known as Souk Salmiya as it more of a souk than a mall. The ground floor has that feeling of a souk with many small shops selling various things such as clothes, handbags, perfume, crockery and cutlery, toys and shoes. A large portion of the mall houses the huge City Center supermarket which includes a magazine/stationery shop. On the first floor is a foodcourt and a Chinese restaurant. Behind City Center is the Fish and Meat Market if you want to pop over to get something for dinner. City Center is pretty big so take your time to have a good wander around.

City Center Shuweikh

Location ➜ Shuwaikh | 80 5222
Hours ➜ 10:00 - 22:30
Web/email ➜ na | Map Ref ➜ 5-E3

Just outside the city is the City Center Shuweikh complex which is more of a huge department store than a mall. Its range is adequate and is a little cheaper than some of the other supermarkets and stores. A good place to go if you want to buy in bulk or get cheaper clothes. On the top level there is a Little Caesars pizzeria and a small amusement area for kids.

Kuwait Magic

Location ➜ Abu Halifah | 371 0866
Hours ➜ 10:00 - 13:30 17:00 - 22:00 Fri 15:00 - 22:00
Web/email ➜ www.kuwait-magic.com | Map Ref ➜ 1-C3

Looking like a fantasy castle, Kuwait Magic is a small mall based on the concept of a shopping village with separate streets. The mall is popular with locals. However there are still plenty of European brands including Riva for clothes, Shoe Talk and international designer sunglasses in Hassan's opticians. Upstairs there is an amusement arcade and fast-food area that tends to be a bit noisy, but offers good playing facilities for kids such as rides and interactive games. It also includes a small fun park next door. The mall has some interesting shops but the biggest draw is having a meal outside the mall on a quiet, palm-tree-filled terrace overlooking the Arabian Gulf. The easiest way to drive to the mall is to take Road 30 (Fahaheel Expressway), then turn off at Exit 211 and turn right at the T-junction, after which the mall is on your left side.

Zahra Complex

Location ➜ Al Fanar · Salmiya | 574 1548
Hours ➜ 10:00 - 22:00   Fri 19:00 - 22:00
Web/email ➜ www.zahracomplex.com | Map Ref ➜ 8-C2

This mall, located next to Eureka, is smaller and older than many of the other malls but is still worth a visit as it has a selection of smaller boutiques and shoe shops. There are also some great jewellery stores as well as an Areej, Fun Factory and the Leather Palace.

Places to Shop

Shopping

Department Stores

British Home Stores (Bhs)

Location → Salmiya | **573 0822**
Hours → 10:00 - 22:00   Wed & Thu 10:00 - 23:00
Web/email → na   Map Ref → 8-B2

Bhs is a good place to find a reliable source of reasonably priced clothes and household accessories. Clothes range from weekend leisure gear to formal wear and a great children's section. Shoes are also available but only a limited selection. Sizes are displayed in UK measurements only, while the clothes have European and USA sizes. The household section has the basics such as bedding, bathroom towels and homeware accessories such as photo frames. Although the range is not huge, it has enough to cater to most tastes, and the quality is pretty good. Mothercare is located in the same shop and has clothes for newborns and upwards. as well as maternity clothes and baby equipment including strollers, toys, cots, changing tables and accessories. A Starbucks inside can help you recharge your batteries if required, and has a special kids' theme to keep the little ones entertained while you unwind.

Debenhams

Location → Souk Sharq | **240 1500**
Hours → 10:00 - 23:00
Web/email → na   Map Ref → 3-D1

Debenhams is one of the bigger department stores in Kuwait. Located in Souk Sharq, the store provides clothes for men, women and children ranging from suits and shorts to evening dresses and lingerie. The kids' clothes include items for newborn up to 12 years. As you walk into the store, you will at first find yourself in the cosmetics section selling brands like Clinique, Chanel and Clarins. Something you might not find in the Debenhams in Europe is the perfume/bashora counter where you can have your own perfume created with the help of expert staff (just keep an eye on the cost). The home furnishing section includes bedding, bathroom items, kitchenware and interior accessories such as frames, vases and table top decorations.

Landmark

Location → Salmiya, Al Rai, Fahaheel, Awkaf | **571 1957**
Hours → 10:00 - 22:00   Fri 16:00 - 21:00
Web/email → na   Map Ref → na

Landmark stores are located around Kuwait in Al Rai (473 4160), Fahaheel (391 2485), Awkaf (247 2856) and Salmiya (above number). Here you will not only be able to shop for clothes and shoes, but also for furniture and accessories. Each Landmark store has a section called Junior that sells toys and clothes for babies and toddlers. For new parents, Junior has a good selection of strollers and other newborn items. Apart from Junior, each Landmark building usually has a Shoe Mart, Lifestyle (gifts, cosmetics, accessories and decorative household goods), Home Centre and Splash (affordable fashion). Shoe Mart sells shoes for men, women and children. Their selection includes running shoes, boots, slippers and more, and prices vary from great bargains to the 'expensive-but-worth it' kind. They also have a small selection of wallets, handbags and socks.

Marks & Spencer

Location → Salem Al Mubarak St · Salmiya | **571 3304**
Hours → 10:00 - 22:00
Web/email → www.marksandspencer.com   Map Ref → 8-D2

The huge green M&S sign on Salem Al Mubarak Street, perched on top of one of the tallest buildings in Salmiya, can be seen for miles. The basement floor is dedicated to ladies' clothes; sizes are the same as you'll find them at home and vary from small to extra large.

The lingerie section carries everything from glamorous, special-occasion items to the more practical, day-to-day gear. The selection in the ladies shoe department varies depending on the season with lots of boots in winter and plenty of sandals in summer. On the ground floor, men have their fair share of shopping with everything from suits and ties to jeans and T-shirts. The childrenswear section caters for newborns and upwards, and there is also a home furnishings area with a small but beautiful selection of frames, candle holders, cushions and towels. The food section, although a little on the pricey side, is hugely popular with expats who crave their favourite biscuits, sweets and tea from home. While Marks & Spencer itself has very few toys for kids (apart from a couple of books), the top floor of the building houses Toys R Us with an excellent range of games and toys for all ages.

Places to Shop

Shopping

Streets/Areas to Shop

The are a number of decent areas around Kuwait to shop. Al Mubarak Street in Salmiya is probably the most popular as it is home to many malls and runs parallel with the Arabian Gulf Street which is lined with shops. For a more authentic shopping experience head to Old Salmiya (further down on Al Mubarak Street) which has cultural appeal.

Al Mubarak Street

Location → Salmiya	na
Hours → 10:00 - 22:00	
Web/email → na	Map Ref → 8-B3

Al Mubarak Street is known as the trendy part of Kuwait city. Located in Salmiya, here you will find the latest designer fashion from Europe and the Middle East. Shopping malls are lined up one after the other and you can easily spend a day (the malls do not close during the afternoon) just shop-hopping from one to the next. And if you get hungry there are coffee shops, restaurants and fast food outlets everywhere. Parking can sometimes be a problem, but open fields behind the shopping malls are available for parking for a few hours (one good thing in Kuwait is that there are not too many parking meters). The biggest malls are Marina Mall and Al Fanar – which also has a cinema. This is a long street that could keep a dedicated shopaholic busy for days. There are also some arcades on the side of Al Mubarak Street that have some good shops.

Fahaheel

Location → Fahaheel	na
Hours → 10:00 - 12:30 16:30 - 21:00 Fri 16:00 - 21:00	
Web/email → na	Map Ref → 2-D3

Although it is a bit out of the city centre, Fahaheel is surprisingly good for shopping and with the new Madinat Al Fahaheel and Al Kout Mall it is definitely becoming a competitor to Kuwait City. Though the area is a bit older it still has its charms, and strolling around the streets is a pleasant way to pass the time. One option is to park your car at Madinat Al Fahaheel and walk around from there. Many bedouins come to Fahaheel for their weekly shopping (as they've done for decades) and there is always a interesting mix of people to watch. More and more of the shops are now staying open all day, but there are still many that have a lunch break between 13:00 and 16:30. If you're not

looking for clothes and shoes, then there are plenty of other shops selling DVDs, PlayStations, souvenirs and carpets to keep you busy.

Fahaheel

Hawalli

Location → Hawalli	na
Hours → 09:30 - 12:30 16:30 - 21:00 Fri 16:00 - 21:00	
Web/email → na	Map Ref → 7-B2

Hawalli is bustling, noisy and in the evenings there is an endless queue of cars and people but it is still the place to shop if you want jewellery, computers, DVDs, clothes and 'hubbly bubbly', all in one stop. The area is open in the mornings and during the evenings. The most famous street is Tunis Street, but while you will find a wide range of items, it is not the place for bargaining. Between the shops you'll find some small restaurants, but the area is more famous for the shopping than the food. Like everywhere else in Kuwait on Fridays the shops only open in the late afternoon. The area is also home to the Al Mahallab Mall.

Madinat Al Fahaheel

Location → Al Kout Shopping Centre	393 0511
Hours → 10:00 - 22:00	
Web/email → www.sultan-center.com	Map Ref → 1-D3

This is latest shopping mall in Kuwait, located right on the shores of the Arabian Gulf. There are not many malls where you can hear the waves crashing in the distance while you shop. Apart from clothes, shoes and bashora shops you will also be able to find restaurants, cafes and the newest branch of The Sultan Center.

Shuwaikh

Location → Between 4th and 5th Ring Road
Hours → 09:30 - 12:30 16:30 - 21:00 Fri 16:00 - 21:00
Web/email → na
na
Map Ref → 5-E4

If you can't find it elsewhere, you will be sure to find it in Shuwaikh. Interestingly enough, the area has no street names, but it is easy to find your way around when you're there. Here you will be able to find paint for your home, carpenters, wood, spare parts for the car and much much more – including a new kitchen sink. If you are looking for second-hand clothes then the Friday Market is the place. Despite the name, it's open on a Thursday too. Being part of the old trade area of Kuwait, most shops are closed for lunch between 13:00 and 16:00 although there are some shops that are open all day. The traffic getting into and out of Shuwaikh around lunchtime and in the evening can get pretty congested; if possible it's best to go shopping here in the mornings.

Souks

Other options → Bargaining [p.162]

Souks or markets are commonly found in Kuwait and are an important cultural reminder and steadfast tradition of the Arabian trading heritage. Most areas have at least one souk although the most renowned are the Gold Souk, Old Heritage Souk, Textile Souk and the Persian Carpet Souk. The Friday Market, Second-Hand Market, Iranian Market, and the Fish, Meat and Vegetable Markets are all very popular.

The fish sold in markets are usually freshly caught in the Arabian Gulf, but you can also find fish from neighbouring countries. Due to the hot temperatures and the desert climate, vegetables are hard to grow in Kuwait. Despite the climate there are two main markets and farming areas being developed in Wafra and Abdally. Here you can find vegetables that are locally grown and on Fridays many people drive the 45 minutes to buy fresh vegetables. Most souks and markets are open in the morning and later on in the afternoon, being closed between 13:00 and 16:30 for prayers and siesta. One exception is the Friday Market, which opens all day on Thursdays and Fridays. If you are interested in an item, don't forget that you can probably knock the price down if you have a go

at bargaining. Most of the sellers in the s[ ] very friendly and are more than happy to s[ ] what they've got in stock. If the price is no[t] for you, then walk away and you will most likely find that the seller runs after you to agree to your price. But be prepared to take your time and be patient if you really want to secure that real bargain.

Antique Souk

Location → Salmiya
Hours → 09:30 - 13:00 16:30 - 21:00
Web/email → na
na
Map Ref → 8-B2

Hard to find, but worth the trip, the Antique Souk is located on the right hand side of Marks & Spencer in Salmiya. Enter the building that sells beauty accessories and hair treatments, go down the stairs, and then only when you are outside the building will you see a signpost for the Antique Souk.

If you are interested in old Asian and Arab artefacts, then the Antique Souk is a must. It is full of trinkets, antique gems and souvenirs. Bargaining is expected so be prepared to haggle. You can, however, also find similar furniture and artifacts in either the Friday Market, in Fahaheel or in other wooden furniture shops around Kuwait.

Fish Market

Location → Sharq and Fahaheel · Central Kuwait
Hours → 07:00 - 14:00 16:00 - 20:00 Fri 12:00 - 20:00
Web/email → na
na
Map Ref → na

Being on the coast, Kuwait is a good place for fresh fish and although the main supermarkets sell all sorts of fresh catch the best place to go for a real

Savour the smell... the Fish Market

bargain is to one of the fish markets. The two main ones are located in Sharq, next to Souq Sharq, and in Al Kout Mall in Fahaheel. The range, all of which is caught locally, is generally fresh and reasonably priced, but get there in the mornings for the pick of the catch.

Friday Market

Location ➜ Off the 4th Ring Rd in Al Rai · Khaldiya | na
Hours ➜ 10:00 - 19:00   Sat – Wed closed
Web/email ➜ na   Map Ref ➜ 10-C2

The Friday Market (Suq Al-Jum'a) and the Second-Hand Souk are side by side in an area close to Al Rai, called Khaldiyah. Located west of Road 55 it is well known to all taxi drivers and sells everything from tin pots and old TVs to carpets and trinkets.

While the name suggests that it is only open on Fridays, it actually opens on Thursday afternoons, which tends to be a quieter time to visit. The market covers a large area so give yourself plenty of time to have a really good rummage. Good buys include wooden and brass artefacts, many from old colonial hotels or ships. Check that whatever you buy works before you leave as exchanges are generally not allowed.

Gold Souk

Location ➜ Souk Al Kuwait · Central Kuwait | na
Hours ➜ 09:00 - 13:00 16:30 - 22:00
Web/email ➜ na   Map Ref ➜ 3-C3

The central Gold Souk (Suq Al-Dahab Al Markazi) contains the government office where gold can be checked for purity and hallmark. The range of gold available is quite overwhelming and various styles of jewellery are on display. You can have your own design tailor-made but make sure you ask for a certificate of authenticity. Other gold hotspots to visit are Hawalli and Fahaheel. A new souk has recently opened behind the Chani Palace in Salmiya, and it has a good range of gold items.

Old Souk

Location ➜ Palestine St · Central Kuwait | na
Hours ➜ 00:00 - 13:00 16:00 - 22:00 Fri 16:00-22:00
Web/email ➜ na   Map Ref ➜ 3-C3

Just off Ahmad Al Jaber Street in downtown Kuwait you will come across the Old Souk on Palestine Street. The area really has an authentic, traditional feel to it and there are streets of densely packed

shops selling everything imaginable. The shopping area is covered and the atmosphere is full of the sights, sounds and smells of a traditional souk. It's a good place to buy Bashura (scented wood) and perfumes, and you can even design your own fragrance. Spices and gold are also very affordable. As with all souks bargaining will generally get you the best deal. Remember that not only can cash help you get a better deal, it is also often the only accepted method of payment in souks.

Second-hand Souk

Location ➜ Friday Market · Khaldiya | na
Hours ➜ 10:00 - 21:00   Thu and Fri only
Web/email ➜ na   Map Ref ➜ 10-C2

The second-hand souk is right next to the Friday Market in Shuwaikh and is open on Thursdays and Fridays. Fridays are quite a bit busier because of the Friday Market. The increase in people generally translates into an increase in prices, so if you can, go on Thursday.

Tin Market

Location ➜ Sharq | na
Hours ➜ 09:30 - 12:30 16:30 - 22:00
Web/email ➜ na   Map Ref ➜ na

The Tin Market is a hive of activity where you can see traditional tradesmen plying their skills. There is everything from silver coloured coffins, ovens, chimneys and boxes, or tailor-made pieces, as well as the mass-produced chests that line the roads. It is very much a male dominated area though so women should be prepared for the stares.

Women's Souk

Location ➜ Old Souk, The · Central Kuwait | na
Hours ➜ 10:00 - 13:00 16:00 - 22:00 Fri 16:00 - 22:00
Web/email ➜ na   Map Ref ➜ 3-C3

The Women's Souk, or Souk Al-Hareem, is so-called because all the sellers are women. It marks the entrance to the Old/Heritage Souk area in downtown Kuwait and is a popular attraction. The stalls sell all sorts of bits and bobs including clothing hand-woven by the women themselves. The area can get quite busy and definitely has that old traditional souk feel about it, making it worth a visit if only to soak up the cultural atmosphere.

Grocery shopping, Arabian style

BEACH HOTEL MUSCAT

BEACH HOT

Rooms & Apartm

A Home Away From Home

Going Out
EXPLORER

Going Out

Highlights...

Try the local cuisine
[p.200]

While Kuwait may be packed with as many cuisine types and menu styles as your stomach could dream of, dining on local dishes is a must. Whether it is fine dining Arabic restaurants or street side shawarma stands it won't take long until your taste for hummus, tabouleh, arabic breads, falafel, kofta and bakluva becomes a regularity. There are a plethora of Arabic restaurants to choose from so feeding your habit won't be a problem!

Sample the Shisha
[p.222]

When in Rome... or Kuwait...you have to sample the shisha. Not just for the sweet taste but also for the atmospheric experience of a shisha cafe. There are plenty of places where you can try it, from specific cafes to various restaurants that will serve shisha with or after a meal. Alternatively you can pick up your own shisha pipe and fruity selection and host a dinner/shisha party. Ifyou have family or friends in town it is also an excellent cultural experience for them.

Treading the boards
[p.224]

Just because Kuwait's social scene is not all about bars and nightclubs it doesn't mean that there isn't a whole host of entertainment to enjoy. Thanks to the Kuwait Little Theatre an evening out doesn't just have to be about dining, with a plethora of plays and a myriad of musicals there never need be a dull evening. Whether you want to be on stage or in front of it getting into the performing arts is a must in Kuwait.

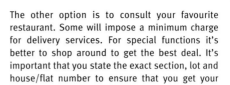

Going Out

Strict alcohol laws in Kuwait make going out a little different than in other GCC countries. Dining out is a very popular pastime, whether it's at a restaurant or going to friends' houses for dinner or a barbecue.

In addition going to the cinema is a popular evening out - regardless of what is showing! For a full evenings entertainment you can do a bit of shopping in one of the many malls, grab some dinner and then catch a movie!

Generally in Kuwait the evening starts quite late. It's not uncommon to be invited to dinner or a business meeting closer to your regular bedtime. Part of the reason is to avoid the blistering heat and a lot of people partake in a siesta to make better use of the cooler night hours.

Hotspots include the downtown area, the main shopping areas like Salmiya or even Fahaheel, south of the city, Marina mall and Marina Crescent.

Eating Out

Surprisingly, Kuwait has some excellent restaurants and eateries and a good variety of cuisines to keep you on your gastronomic toes. Eating out is a big deal and few people are aware that Kuwait has a remarkable amount of restaurants and cafes.

Kuwait is definitely different from some of its more 'liberal' GCC neighbours and despite alcohol restrictions, dining out is a sophisticated affair.

Your stomach will not be bored here, the variety and quality of food available is incredible and there's cuisines to suit all tastes and budgets. Even the standard buffets are excellent with a wide range of cuisines and live cooking stations.

Eating tends to be a late evening pastime and many restaurants are almost deserted until 21:00. With lots of people descending on the most popular restaurants at once it is a good idea to book.

Delivery

Life in Kuwait often revolves around entertaining friends and visitors at home. The good news is that most hotels offer full inside or outside catering services, including waiters to serve the drinks and canapes.

The other option is to consult your favourite restaurant. Some will impose a minimum charge for delivery services. For special functions it's better to shop around to get the best deal. It's important that you state the exact section, lot and house/flat number to ensure that you get your food on time, and the name of a local landmark can be useful.

Barbecues and takeaways are a popular part of the local way of life and most of the restaurants offer takeaway and delivery services for big events or just a quiet night in.

Drinks

Other options → Alcohol [p.162]

Alcohol cannot be purchased in Kuwait, nor can it be brought into the country legally. Kuwait wasn't always dry and there are always rumours that alcohol will be re-introduced as part of its drive to develop tourist attractions, but at this stage they are just rumours. However you shouldn't be put off by the lack of alcohol, no booze just means you have to be a little more creative with your entertainment.

Hunt and you may find alcohol for sale, but it will be expensive, up to KD 35 a bottle, and be warned, it is against the law and you run the risk of a stern word, slap on the wrist or worse. Needless to say the sale of white and red grape juice and sugar is quite high among the expats!

Both mineral water and mocktails can be very expensive. It is worth paying attention because the waiters here have a habit of opening a bottle of water without even asking you and just adding the fee to your bill.

Hygiene

Generally hygiene standards are high and it's reasonably safe to eat almost anywhere, including the small streetside shawarma stands, which are unbelievably delicious. The Municipality regularly checks on outlets and will issue warnings to those falling below standards. However, common sense should prevail when eating - or drinking - off the beaten track.

> ### Evening Entertainment
>
> *A night out in Kuwait doesn't automatically mean dining out. Although there are a wide variety of restaurants which are popular with locals and expats alike, people also spend their evenings doing the rounds at the many shopping malls, catching a film or visiting friends.*

Tax & Service Charges

Many restaurants, outside of hotels, do not have a specific charge for service, although it is generally acceptable to leave 5-10% as a tip.

In hotels and upmarket restaurants, the charge will be stated on the menu (check the small print at the bottom or back page), and is added to the bill at the end. This type of charge is generally not passed onto the staff, so leaving a cash tip can be the best practice to reward good service.

The good news is that there are no municipality or other indirect taxes levied in Kuwait.

Big Night Out

Kuwait may have its fair share of fine dining options but if you're looking for a different scene then why not pop on a short haul flight to Dubai for a big night out. Just pick up a copy of the delectable *Posh Nosh, Cheap Eats and Star Bars* which showcases some of the best locations on Dubai's social scene.

Tipping

Tipping is not generally expected but a cash tip of about 10% can be appropriate if service has been particularly good. Don't bother to add more to your bill if you are paying by credit card, this money rarely gets to those who deserve it. Make an effort to carry cash with you, even if it just enough for a tip. This way you'll be sure to thank the people that made your evening special.

Independent Reviews

We undertake independent reviews of all restaurants and bars that are included in this book. The following outlets have been visited by our freelance reporters and the views expressed are our own. However, if we have unwittingly led you astray, please do let us know. We appreciate all feedback, positive, negative and otherwise. You can email us at Info@Explorer-Publishing.com. Your comments are never ignored and you never know you may be a food reporter for the 2nd edition!

Restaurant Listing Structure

Explorer lists only the best selection of restaurants in each category, highlighting those that are recommended as must-dos.

Featuring reviews for up to 100 outlets, this chapter provides a comprehensive listing of the recommeded places to check out. Listed alphabetically by cuisine styles, as much information as possible is given on the individual outlets.

In order to categorise the restaurants by cuisine we have placed restaurants that serve varying cuisines or styles either under their prominent cuisine or under international if the mix is truly varied. If, however you want to know what outlets are in a particular hotel you can flip to the index at the back of the book and look up the hotel, under which there will appear a list of all the outlets with their corresponding page numbers.

To avoid any confusion concerning a particular restaurant's listing, as a rule, any non English names retain their prefix (ie, Al, Le, La and El) in their alphabetical placement, while English names are listed by actual titles, ignoring prefixes such as 'The'. Bon appetit!

Vegetarian Food

Kuwait is definitely not just a meat and potato state. Seafood and salads are on most menus irrespective of the food theme of the outlet. The many Arabic/Lebanese restaurants also offer an extensive selection of vegetarian mezzes, as well as a good range of salads and fresh vegetable dishes. We have yet to find a restaurant that did not have any vegetarian meals on its menu.

Sometimes you will have to explain vegetarian, since stocks and sauces aren't entirely meat free. If in doubt, check with the chef or Manager. For specific one-off dietary requirements you should call ahead and check that the kitchen can accommodate.

Quick Reference Explorer Icons	
	Explorer Recommended!
	NO Credit Cards Accepted
	Live Band
	Will Deliver
	Kids Welcome
	Outside Terrace

American

Applebee's

Location → Gulf Road · Bneid al-Gar
Web/email → www.applebees.com

240 7536
Map Ref → 4-A3

This international Tex-Mex chain has a refreshingly modern decor, is lively and well-stocked with young couples, singles and families. The menu is also packed with favourites guaranteed to leave you feeling well and truly satisfied and the free soft drink refills are all part of the excellent service. This is the kind of restaurant that you go hungry to and leave having eaten far too much! Kids will love the fun atmosphere too and the deserts are some of the most calorific in town.

Buffalo's Café

Location → Arabian Gulf St · Salmiya
Web/email → www.buffaloscafe.com

572 8989
Map Ref → 8-E1

This American chain is one hundred percent Wild West themed with various pieces of 'cowboys 'n indians' paraphenalia lining the walls and dictating the decor. No surprises that the menu also follows the same direction with gigantic portions of authentic chilli, nachos, fajitas, burgers and the signature Buffalo style chicken wings. They also have special deals so it is worth calling ahead if you're interested.

Chili's

Location → Arabian Gulf St, nr the Towers · Dasman
Web/email → www.chilis.com

245 2200
Map Ref → 4-A1

Chili's is well-established as one of the best-loved family restaurants in Kuwait. The menu is as you would expect from a Tex-Mex style menu - burgers, fajitas, steaks, cajun chicken, nachos and the like - but also has a wide variety of Italian options, sandwiches and salads as well as a few vegetarian options. As for the kids, they will love the menu, which doubles as a colouring sheet and comes with crayons, and is full of firm favourites such as chicken nuggets and pasta. The other big draw of Chili's is the tranquil terrace with views of the sea and Kuwait Towers.

Fresh 'n healthy!

Hard Rock Cafe

Location → Arabisn Gulf St · Salmiya
Web/email → na

571 0004
Map Ref → 6-A1

This franchise burger joint has built its reputation on regurgitating Americana to a T. From authentic-looking memorabilia (there's a suspended classic Cadillac over the bar) to the fun, old-school atmosphere courtesy of a juke-box and good ol' fashioned service with a smile. The food is served in generous portions so be careful when ordering, and consider the your eyes being bigger than your stomach syndrome. Think twice about starter and entrée but whichever way you go, you really ought to save space for the fudge brownie and ice cream, which by the way is ample for two, unless you're a greedy-guts! This is an ideal place to celebrate a birthday or anniversary – the staff will be only too pleased to make it a special occasion with embarrassing singing and extra attention.

> **GCC easy as ABC**
>
> *If you want to drop in on your neighbours, then go prepared with your Explorer. Be it for a shopping spree in Dubai, a luxury holiday in Abu Dhabi, to find tranquility in the wilderness of Oman, to watch the Asian Games in Qatar or to have a tipple with your tea in Bahrain!*

American

Going Out

Johnny Rockets

Location ➜ Marina Mall · Salmiya
Web/email ➜ www.johnnyrockets.com

| 575 0404
Map Ref ➜ 8-B2

If you really have to eat at a fast food joint, then this is by far the best around. For a start the food is actually tasty and reasonably healthy (well, there's some salad stuff on the burgers!). Another American styled eaterie, this place is all '60's diner with all of the décor, fun, playful staff and menu items to boot. The portions – just so you know – are also very American (ie huge). French fries are available with everything and the chilli cheese fries are definitely not to be missed. All of the burgers are good and the man-sized omelette can be filled with a vast range of tasty fillings. There's also delicious, creamy milk shakes or a float for a taste of the stateside.

Ruby Tuesday

Location ➜ Aqua Park Gulf Rd · Farwania
Web/email ➜ www.crowneplaza.com

| 244 4454
Map Ref ➜ 16-C2

Ruby Tuesday is normally packed with regulars and locals alike. The menu selection is huge and fantastically varied and the salad bar is tasty. The portions are more than ample and the staff are very friendly and welcoming, and on hand to help you with whatever you need. The thing is, it doesn't all mix-n-merge to make for a good night out, and you can't help feeling that something is missing considering the bill doesn't come cheap.

T.G.I Friday's

Location ➜ Arabian Gulf St · Dasman
Web/email ➜ www.tgifridays.com

| 254 4300
Map Ref ➜ 4-A1

Probably one of the most famous world-wide American restaurant chains, TGI Friday's is bold, bright and bursting with Hollywood memorabilia (mainly pre-millennium). The menu is as big as the restaurant's personality with stacks of massive burgers, sizzling Tex Mex fajitas, salads, pasta dishes, chicken platters, ribs and steaks and a whole host of naughty-but-nice deserts. The staff are very vibey and the atmosphere a little frenetic but this is definitely a fun restaurant and a particular favourite with the kids.

Arabic

Al Berdawny

Location ➜ City Center Salmiyah
Web/email ➜ www.alberdawny.com

| 566 1117
Map Ref ➜ 8-C4

This hugely popular restaurant is a must, not only for its excellent Lebanese food and added mediterranean dishes but also for its unique and spacious layout. The restaurant combines three dining rooms, each with their own individual style, with a central courtyard for outside dining which has a garden enclosed by a stream. The Al Qal'aa dining room has a cavenous interior with stone walls and dimmed lantern chaneliers, while the Byblos dining room is Egyptian in style and the Elessa dining room is totally non-smoking. The food is an eclectic mix of classic Lebanese dishes and inventive Al Berdawny creations.

Ayam Zamam Salmiya

Location ➜ Holiday Inn Kuwait
Web/email ➜ www.holiday-inn.com.kw

| 576 0000
Map Ref ➜ 8-E2

Set in the modern and stylish Holiday Inn, Ayam Zaman, offers a large selection of authentic Lebanese dishes, along with authentic Lebanese service, which – in case you didn't know – is very helpful, very chatty and really, very friendly. Don't be afraid to ask for some guidance navigating your way through the menu, especially if you're a novice at Lebanese cuisine. The place seems popular with

Fresh Bread

Arabic

Going Out

local residents, as well as the expat community, and once you've tasted their food you'll understand why. You can relax outside and indulge in a shisha to add to the experience. Alternatively sit inside, amongst the faux-Roman Temple décor, craning your neck to watch the chefs hard at work preparing your feast.

Ayam Zamam Farwania

Location → Crowne Plaza
Web/email → www.kuwait.crowneplaza.com
474 2000
Map Ref → 16-C2

A typically warm Lebanese welcome awaits you at the Ayam Zaman in the Crowne Plaza. The service is very helpful and friendly, without being too over the top. The cuisine is unashamedly authentic Lebanese, and the menu is packed full of traditional dishes, making it really hard to choose. The venue gives the impression you are eating al fresco even though you are smack in the middle of the hotel. The tables are arranged on different levels, and create quite a relaxed and intimate atmosphere, with each table having its own bell for the Waiter!

Cafe Blanc

Location → Marina Mall · Salmiya
Web/email → www.cafe-blanc.com
224 4644
Map Ref → 8-B2

A special occassion restaurant that perfectly infuses tradition and delivers superb cuisine with a dynamic and fresh approach, this place is deliciously intimate and not as pompous as you'd imagine. Café Blanc is perfect for a casual get together, a bite to eat or a quick coffee. The portions here are generous and dishes are impeccably presented with presentation rating almost as highly as the quality of the food itself. Lebanese fusion food, with Arabic music, makes even the briefest of sojourns here an interesting

Location, location

If you have a specific location in mind for dinner, such as a hotel where you have guests staying, then just flick to the index at the back of the book and look up that hotel. Listed with it will be all the outlets (with their page numbers) within the hotel that have been reviewed in this book.

event. Sit back, relax, order food or drink or both, and people watch till you can people watch no more.

Layali Al Helmeya

Location → Arabian Gulf St · Al Shamia
Web/email → na
263 8710
Map Ref → 6-A1

This restaurant/café hybrid is nicely located overlooking the Gulf with an uninterrupted view of the sea from the terrace, ideal for a coffee and shisha and perfect for watching the sunset. The menu is in Arabic and English with breakfast section for the early risers. Friendly and helpful waiters are on-hand to make your visit go smoothly. They also add to the whole ambience of Arabic leisure, only showing up when you need them to. The only downsides (or up, depending on your mood) are the plasma screens dotted about on the inside of the restaurant and a large television on the terrace, sometimes proving to be very distracting. A word of warning be sure to specify that each course come out separately, otherwise you'll end up with a great big table of grub.

Le Tarbouche

Location → Sheraton Kuwait Hotel & Towers · Qibla
Web/email → www.starwoodhotels.com
835 555
Map Ref → 3-B4

If you want good quality, traditional Lebanese food in a romantic setting, then you should definitely try Le Tarbouche. Located on the 7th floor of the Sheraton Hotel, the views at night over the city and adjacent Gulf Road compliment the cuisine. This restaurant offers a peaceful setting enhanced by the quiet strings of the lute playing in the background. The no-rush attitude of the courteous restaurant staff and the soft sound of live Arabic music, provide a pleasant atmosphere and an overall pleasant experience. The courses are generous but not excessive. The traditional Lebanese mezze starters are delicious with a good selection of meat and fish dishes to follow – all well flavoured but with sensible servings, leaving room for the sweet Arabic dessert and aromatic Turkish coffee.

Arabic

Going Out

Mais Alghanim

Location → Arabian Gulf St · Salmiya   246 0456
Web/email → na   Map Ref → 3-E1

Mais Alghanim is a hugely popular Arabic restaurant, not only because it is one of the longest standing restaurants in Kuwait but also because the traditional Lebanese menu may be simplistic but also happens to be simply excellent. The mezzes can be devoured as a main course if you should so desire as they are not only delicious but also generous in size. Whether you choose to sit in the air-conditioned inside (which obviously is a necessity in summer) or in the relaxed garden with a little kid's play area, you can soak up the casual family atmosphere. There are also some shisha tents for those wanting to enjoy the complete Arabic dining experience.

Mijana Restaurant

Location → Al Kout Shopping Centre   393 9393
Web/email → na   Map Ref → 1-D3

The view of the Al Kout harbour at Mijana makes for a stunning backdrop to the evening. Expect excellent Lebanese food with an international flair. Choose from a wide variety of starters, from the fancy to the homely – the grilled Haloumi cheese is simple but delicious. Service here is fast and fabulous and the staff are more than happy to make excellent recommendations. Specify if you want starters to be served separate because Mijana style is to get all the food on the table. The restaurant is very popular with locals, which is a good indication of how tasty the Arabic food is.

Shabestan

Location → Crowne Plaza · Farwania   473 2100
Web/email → www.kuwait.crowneplaza.com   Map Ref → 16-C2

This light and airy restaurant embraces the welcoming approach of Iranian dining. The traditional Persian cuisine is fabulously unique and a must for anyone who has yet to stray from the middle-of-the-road Arabic food of most hotel restaurants. Whether you want to fill up on the mystifying starters and share a main couse or go

straight for the kebab selection you will no doubt experience a whole new taste sensation. The decor is subtle and comfortable with interesting Iranian art adding to the atmosphere.

Shirin Banu

Location → Safir Int'l Hotel Kuwait · Bneid al-Gar   253 3000
Web/email → www.safirhotels.com   Map Ref → 4-A2

Walk towards the Shirin Banu - particularly when it is in full swing - and you'll notice the smell of bread thanks to the mighty bread oven in the corner of the room and that produces Kuwait's finest breads made to order. Serving Iranian cuisine the atmosphere is as relaxed as the food. The staff are friendly and the restaurant boasts two private tables that can seat up to 14 people. Seating is intimate but to guarantee a booth it is best to make a reservation (especially at weekends).

Jeans Grill

Location → Sultan Center · Salmiya   562 5811
Web/email → www.sultan-center.com   Map Ref → 8-C2

With so many cuisines featuring on the Jeans Grill buffet you will have a tough job deciding what delicious dish to try. American, Arabic, Indian, Chinese, Italian and European - versatility is the order of the day. There are calorific choices or more healthy options as well as excellent buffet breakfasts and daily specials. There is also the international al la carte menu should buffets not be your thing. The atmosphere is lively and the restaurant is also popular with children, with a special room you can hire for birthday parties. They also offer catering services. Other Locations: Sharq (240 9876), Waterfront (562 5811).

Villa Fairouz

Location → St 80, Block 8 adjoining Istaqlal St   265 2030
Web/email → na   Map Ref → 5-D3

This up market Lebanese restaurant is ideal for a special night out. The décor creates the atmosphere of an authentic Arabic courtyard with ample, well spaced seating. All the favourite

Arabic

Going Out

Lebanese dishes are present and accounted for, from assorted mezze & grills at a gloriously high standard with generous portions, to the grilled meats and tasty entrees. The hummous is especially good and served with a never-ending supply of hot, freshly baked bread. Also worth a try is the lentil soup and the grilled chicken - basically it's simple dishes that are hard not to love. Wash you meal down with anything from the wide range of refreshing fresh fruit juices. Smoking and non-smoking areas are provided and the shisha is definitely worth a puff.

Buffet

Other options ➜ Friday Brunch [p.223]

Al Ahmadi

Location ➜ Crowne Plaza · Farwania
Web/email ➜ www.kuwait.crowneplaza.com
474 2000
Map Ref ➜ 16-C2

A typical hotel restaurant that is mainly filled with hotel guests and families, Al Ahmadi is one of the most well-known, and well-visited, themed buffets. Every day of the week is a different flavour, Asian, Oriental, Italian or International, there's no room for bored tastebuds in this dining room. A la carte is available, but the live cooking station and varied selection makes it hard to avert your attention to the menu. Information on evening theme nights is available on the hotels website, where you can book a table and print yourself a promotion voucher discounting a buffet meal by 25%. The staff here are friendly and efficient, but being a self-service affair, there won't be much need for anything but an appetite and a will to keep on eating.

Al Bustan

Location ➜ Radisson SAS Hotels & Resorts · Salwa
Web/email ➜ www.radissonsas.com
575 6000
Map Ref ➜ 13-D3

If you can avoid spending your dinner money in the various shops on route to the Al Bustan, then you are doing well. The restaurant is versatile and caters for most tastes (and budgets) with starters ranging from prawn and mango tiam to the classic caesar salad. Entrees worth trying include the

chicken shawarma or grilled gulf prawns, or both. If you are spoilt for choice, try visiting the evening buffet that is as varied as it is large. The restaurant caters for carnivores and vegetarians alike, although there is no children's menu. In the winter Wednesday becomes BBQ night, where you can take advantage of the terraced area and eat as much food off the grill as your waistband will allow, while listening to live music. And all for a snip at 13 KD.

Al Hambra

Location ➜ Sheraton Kuwait Hotel & Towers · Qibla
Web/email ➜ www.luxurycollection.com/kuwait
242 2055
Map Ref ➜ 3-B4

They took the concept of a buffet and mixed in some international flavour called the place Al Hambra and set it inside the splendid Sheraton Hotel. The quality of the food is good with lots of variety and the presentation is the best a buffet place can offer. Live cooking areas will allow you to make plates to your personal fancy and the chef will even bring it over to your table. Al Hambra gives the other, similar restaurants a run for their money and does well to stand out with tasteful décor, professional service and an air of a quality eatery. Locals and expats flock in droves but it's never too packed for a pleasant night out.

Asseef

Location ➜ Four Points by Sheraton Kuwait · Qibla
Web/email ➜ www.starwoodhotels.com
241 5001
Map Ref ➜ 3-B4

On the second floor of the Four Points Sheraton, overlooking the Sheraton roundabout, is this fairly run-of-the-mill buffet restaurant. The food claims to be international, but has a definite Arabic bias. Nevertheless, the food is of a good standard and while a little limited the presentation is excellent and the flavours are delicious. The shawarma and cooking stations are a nice touch. The decoration is kept simple, with polished wooden walls, and plenty of natural light. There is somewhat of a business diners feel, but it does seem to get a little full on the weekend. The staff are very friendly, helpful and courteous.

Buffet

Going Out

Sea Breeze

Location ➜ Safir Int'l Hotel Kuwait · Bneid al-Gar | **253 0771**
Web/email ➜ www.safirhotels.com | Map Ref ➜ 4-A2

If the windows were open you probably would be able to feel the 'sea breeze', since the restaurant is situated on the top floor of the Safir International, and is blessed with the most of a beautiful panoramic view of the coast. The Sea Breeze offers guests the choice of an a la carte menu or buffet spread that changes enough to keep you guessing: pasta on a Wednesday, excellent seafood on Thursday before changing again to brunch on Fridays. Generally though, you can expect a happy mix of Arabic and European fare, with a hearty selection of both and a good start if you have not experienced Arabic food before.

Sea Breeze

Chinese

Foo Chow

Location ➜ Safir Al Bastaki Hotel · Bneid al-Gar | **255 5081**
Web/email ➜ www.safirhotels.com | Map Ref ➜ 3-E3

Llocated in the lobby of the Safir Al Bastika Hotel, Foo Chow is more of a convenience restaurant than a choice for a lingering dinner. That said the range of Chinese dishes, and international options, are deliciously served. What Foo Chow does best is takeaway so if you are in the area and stuck for what to have for dinner drop in and pick up a mouthwatering array of Chinese favourites.

Greens

Location ➜ Arabian Gulf Road · Bneid al-Gar | **251 6031**
Web/email ➜ na | Map Ref ➜ 4-A3

Stylish décor complemented by welcoming and attentive staff are a feature of this Chinese restaurant situated on the Arabian Gulf Road. The décor is modern with a tasteful 'hint' of the Chinese chintz about it. The ambience is kept up with well planned and spacious seating arrangements. Your meal is served with the minimum of fuss having been prepared by the talented Chef and delivered to your table by eager yet courteous staff. Greens successfully takes its cuisine-cues from all around China giving a varied and well balanced menu.

Gulf Royal Chinese Restaurant

Location ➜ Ibn Kahldoon St · Hawalli | **262 2770**
Web/email ➜ na | Map Ref ➜ 7-B3

As you can probably guess from the name, the Gulf Royal Chinese Restaurant is rather regal. The red-obsessed decor is somewhat overpowering but set the over-enthusiastic theme aside and the food is first-class. The menu, which favours seafood but has all the standard Chinese options, is extensive and satisfies all types of clientele from business dignentaries to families and couples on a romantic evening out. They also offer tempting and reasonably priced buffets at the weekend. Other Locations in: Salmiya: Al Mubarak St (571 0448), Marina Mall: (224 4795), Fahaheel: Al Wady St, Sanaa Market (392 5390).

The Peacock

Location ➜ Radisson SAS Hotels & Resorts · Salwa | **575 6000**
Web/email ➜ www.radissonsas.com | Map Ref ➜ 13-D3

The red interior of The Peacock is possibly one of the main reasons you'll remember a night here, but it's well worth it because the dim lighting and fabulous cuisine will make sure you keep coming back for more. This place is nearly always busy, filled with a charming blend of locals, expats and hotel guests. Keep in mind you have the choice of small or large portions to satisfy any appetite, and a varied menu of starters and entrees is bound to fill you up without damaging your wallet. Prices

range from an average of KD 5 for a small portion up to KD 18 for a large. Take your time to savour this venue from the light background Oriental music to good food, good atmosphere.

professional and accommodating approach. Take your time to linger lunch along with some of the hippest city or seal a deal over dinner later in th Whatever the occasion, the main eve always the food.

The Peacock

Tang Chao

Location ➜ Holiday Inn Kuwait · Salmiya
Web/email ➜ www.holiday-inn.com.kw

| 84 7777
Map Ref ➜ 8-E2

A meal in the Tang Chao will always be a memorable occasion as the food is exquisite. The Chinese decor and background music create an ambiance that is quiet and graceful. The executive chef and his team are so proud of their skills that a large glass window at the entrance gives a view of all the preparations in the spotless kitchen. The food is light and delicate, garnished with spices specially imported to ensure an authentic Chinese taste. The fragrant Jasmine tea is an ideal accompaniment. If you like Chinese cuisine Tang Chao could become your favourite restaurant.

French

Le Notre Paris

Location ➜ Nr Kuwait Towers, Gulf Rd · Safat
Web/email ➜ na

| 80 5050
Map Ref ➜ 4-A1

To dine here is to experience some of the finest food with a backdrop of one of the finest views in Kuwait – across the bay to the Kuwait Towers. The food is international, of the highest quality and beautifully presented. The staff are excellent,

Lina's Cafe

Location ➜ Marina Mall · Salmiya
Web/email ➜ www.linascafe.com

| 224 4966
Map Ref ➜ 8-B2

If you want a good sandwich before a stroll around the Marina Mall shops, Lina's Café is a good option for a tasty and healthy sandwich or salad. Situated in Marina Crescent away from the hustle and bustle and linked to the Marina Mall escalators. Admittedly, depending on your table, its locale may feel like you are eating in a passage way. The terrace overlooking the Marina is a better choice if it's not too hot outside. A perfect pit stop for the avid, hungry shopper.

Greek

Zorba's Greek Taverna

Location ➜ Al Blajat St, Nr Al Beda'a RA · Salmiya
Web/email ➜ na

| 571 5124
Map Ref ➜ 8-D4

As the only Greek restaurant in Kuwait, Zorba's offers a unique dining experience. On entry the traditional decor sets the scene but looses its authenticity when you realise the food is an international buffet. The al a carte menu, however, does offer traditional Greek cuisine and is on the whole of a high standard, although depending on your tastes and experience with Greek food may disappoint some. The Mousaka and Kleftiko are particular favourites and the starters may be more enticing than the main courses. In its favour the restaurant has good views of the sea and also includes a shisha area and a big TV screen showing sport.

> **Any Cuisine Will Do!**
>
> *While the reviews within this chapter are catagorised by their cuisine type if you are more interested in visiting a specific hotel for dinner because of its location then simply flick to the index at the back of the book. Look up the hotel in question and it will be listed with all its outlets underneath.*

French • Greek

Going Out

Indian

Asha's

Location ➜ Marina Crescent, Marina Mall · Salmiya | 224 4502
Web/email ➜ na   Map Ref ➜ 8-B2

Asha's describes itself as contemporary Indian cuisine and a quick scan of the menu will attest. This is a very happy marriage, a mixture of traditional Indian dishes with a nouvelle cuisine twist. The starters are very well presented and full of subtle Indian flavour without being overpowering. The chicken tikka selection is delicious, the prawn curry dishes exceptional, and the chicken biryani served in an individual earthenware pot, will definitely delight. Main courses are generous, and in fact not one of the dishes will fail to please. The service is friendly and the staff knowledgeable and more than happy to chip in with recommendations. This is not an inexpensive night out – but for a special occasion it would be difficult to beat.

Bukhara

Location ➜ Sheraton Kuwait Hotel & Towers · Qibla | 242 2055
Web/email ➜ www.starwoodrestaurant.com   Map Ref ➜ 3-B4

This is a high priced, top class Indian restaurant on the top floor of the Sheraton. The food is north Indian Mughali and Punjabi cuisine, and no matter what you choose from the extensive menu, you can rest assured that it will be prepared and served to the highest standard. The biryani dishes are delicious and the korma subtle and creamy – both made with quality meat or vegetables depending on which way you sway. The staff on hand are well informed and attentive, taking the time to explain the wide variety of dishes available. The menu also features a wide range of fresh fruit juices, but these can be expensive.

Caesars

Location ➜ Nr Sheraton Kuwait Htl · Qibla | 243 1100
Web/email ➜ na   Map Ref ➜ 3-B4

It might take a low-key, casual approach to its decor, but Caesars is still one of the best cheap-and-cheerful restaurants in town. Fabulously authentic, the food is a delicious array of Indian favourites as well as a few surprising signature dishes including the steak with cheese and the mandarin hammour. As for those looking for meat-free options there is a wholly vegetarian branch in Kuwait City (242 4228). Caesars is popular with families, couples and singles and if you have never been it is likely that after your initial visit you will become one of the many regulars. Other locations: Salmiyah, Al Mubarak St (573 3044); Al Farwaniya, beh Farwaniya Co-Op (473 8777); Fahaheel, Al Daboos St (392 0343).

Darbar Indian Restaurant

Location ➜ Kuwait Continental Hotel · Bneid al-Gar | 252 7300
Web/email ➜ www.kcontl.net   Map Ref ➜ 13-D1

As far as Indian buffets go, Darbar's Wednesday and Thursday offering has to be one of the best in Kuwait. The food is of the same a la carte standard as during the rest of the week, with all the mild to spicey favourites making an appearance along with an excellent live music performance. The open display kitchen adds a bit of flair to the festivities and allows you to see the master chefs at work. The decor is subtle, and families, business diners and couples can be found enjoying an evening out and a rather fine curry!

Bukhara

Dawat Restaurant

Location ➜ Bneid al-Gar
Web/email ➜ na

| 241 1728
Map Ref ➜ 4-A3

This place is fantastic value, which coupled with good service, and very tasty Indian food, gives you a delectable dinner out. Dawat Restaurant feels like a little bit of India, and the soft lighting, friendly waiters and the Bollywood-style music makes it a place worth visiting. The menu is bursting with authentic Indian dishes, with a splash of Chinese thrown in for good measure. The Chinese food is pleasant but this isn't why you should visit, this is an Indian restaurant after all, so don't be tempted away from what they do best. From the different sizzlers, to the selection of many curries, without the assistance of the friendly waiters, it's easy to be spoilt for choice.

Kuwait Kohinoor

Location ➜ Al Sinan St, Nr Ajial Mall · Fahaheel
Web/email ➜ www.kuwaitkohinoor.com

| 391 1856
Map Ref ➜ 1-C4

It may be a long haul from downtown Kuwait to Fahaheel where this new restaurant is located but despite the long journey you will not be disappointed. The stylish decoration and the attentive service matches the interesting selection of oriental Indian dishes. The menu is not too extensive, but look out for new additions and specials. If you don't understand something, then don't be shy to ask, as the waiters are on hand and only too happy to explain as well as recommend favourites. This place is definitely different from the mainstream Indian outlets, and while it's still quiet, without doubt word will spread and this will become a popular spot.

Mughal Mahal

Location ➜ Jaber Al mubarak St · Sharq
Web/email ➜ www.mughalmahal.com

| 242 5131
Map Ref ➜ 3-D2

This is the original restaurant of a well-known chain of Indian/Chinese eateries in Kuwait. There's something to be said about combination menus but Mughal obviously does it well enough to warrant more locations. So far it has proven to be the people's choice for good food at reasonable

prices with excellent service. This Sharq restaurant is Mughali Indian only, with an extensive menu of curried and grilled dishes. Sizzlers are especially popular. The naan bread is delicious, the chicken korma almost has the status of a signature dish, and the prawn massala is well worth a try. You really can't go wrong, as all dishes are of a high standard. Lemon with mint is a favourite drink but all fruit juices are fresh and tasty. Great value – a must visit.

Mughal Mahal No 2

Location ➜ Opp Farwania Co-op · Farwania
Web/email ➜ www.mughalmahal.com

| 474 0003
Map Ref ➜ 16-B2

This restaurant is part of the famed Indian and Chinese eateries in Kuwait. The main cuisine here is Indian but you can also order a wide variety of Chinese dishes, which makes fussy eaters easy to cater for. The group of restaurants is well known for it superb value for money as well as its great service and this branch is no exception. The wide selection of Chinese and Indian dishes are all well prepared with ample portions. The dining room layout is well thought out, with plenty of space, even when it gets really busy. There are also private rooms that can be pre-booked for special occasions or just for a quiet night with friends. More often than not the restaurant is filled with locals and residents from the sub-continent, which is always a good sign for a curry house.

Mughal Mahal Restaurant

Location ➜ Salem Ak Mubarak St · Salmiya
Web/email ➜ www.mughalmahal.com

| 572 2223
Map Ref ➜ 8-B3

The third of a chain of restaurants that offers both Indian and Chinese cuisine, this particular branch favours Chinese but still keeps the signature Indian fare. It's done very well, but should temptation overcome you go ahead and browse the Indian dishes which are still very good. As with the chain's other outlets, the food is of a high standard, portions are plentiful, and the service is spot on. The vegetable spring rolls are especially good. A typical array of fruit juices is on offer and the coffee is very strong and surprisingly good. The view from certain tables is phenomenal, and if you intend to visit for a

Indian

Going Out

special occasion be sure to mention that you'd like to make the most of the backdrop.

International

Other options ➜ Buffet [p.203]

Atlantis

Location ➜ Marina Hotel Kuwait · Salmiya | 224 4970
Web/email ➜ www.marinahotel.com   Map Ref ➜ 8-B2

Atlantis is special for many different reasons, such as its nautical theme (there's a clue in the name – after the lost city), and its seafaring decor in 1930s cruise ship style, with live music to boot. The novelty is enough to cheer anyone up and surprisingly it doesn't wear thin. It helps that it's actually situated overlooking the bay and that the ambience is perfect. The menu is Eurasian and at the helm of this great kitchen is a fabulous in-house European executive chef promising to keep your taste buds tingling with pleasure. The salad buffet is extensive and presentation of the entrees and seafood is first class.

Atrium Lounge & Restaurant

Location ➜ The Courtyard by Marriott · Kuwait City | 299 7001
Web/email ➜ www.courtyard.com   Map Ref ➜ 3-E2

This all day restaurant serves an excellent international buffet for breakfast, lunch and dinner combining dishes to suit all appetites and palates. Situated in the centre of the hotel's lobby the restaurant is surrounded by high glass windows with a mesmerising view of the Liberation Tower. Popular for hearty breakfasts, business lunches and smart or casual dinners, Atrium is modern, vibrant and has a nice buzz. Cuisines include Asian seafood, Spanish paella and everything you could imagine in between.

They also offer a fine dining a la carte menu between 11:00 and 23:00.

Alternative Nights

Due to the lack of alcohol people may feel a little negative about Kuwait's social scene - but don't. There are a range of fantastic restaurants and cafes where you can appreciate good food and don't forget the Kuwait Little Theatre for some alternative entertainment!

Avenue

Location ➜ Kempinski Julai'a Hotel & Resort | 84 4444
Web/email ➜ www.kempinski-kuwait.com   Map Ref ➜ 1-D4

It may be another all-day hotel restaurant but Avenue has just the right amount of gourmet options to make this a cut above Kuwait's many other offerings. Whether you choose to dine outside with a view of the pool or within the elegant and spacious interior of the restaurant you can expect relaxed dining at its best. Three meals a day, seven days a week rarely disappoint and the theme nights, such as Asian night and American night, as well an excellent Friday Brunch make this a popular choice for any occasion.

Bays

Location ➜ Mövenpick Hotel Kuwait · Shuwaikh | 461 0033
Web/email ➜ www.moevenpick-hotels.com   Map Ref ➜ 5-B2

The nicest thing about buffets, particularly for the indecisive diner, is that you can have a little of everything. The other nice thing about buffets is that you can have a lot of everything and no one will think you're greedy because no one will notice! The selection here is phenomenal, with the dishes on offer including sushi, Indian, Lebanese, salads, soups and a very nice display of tasty looking desserts. Wednesday night is BBQ night around the pool, and children eat for free on Fridays. The location of the restaurant is pleasant and well thought out, overlooking the pool at one end and the fountain garden at the other, along with pretty panoramic views of the bay and wonderful sunsets when the time is right. A nice little touch is the Henna station, so you can feast and be fashionable all in one night.

L'Aroma Café

Location ➜ Holiday Inn Kuwait · Salmiya | 84 7777
Web/email ➜ www.holiday-inn.com.kw   Map Ref ➜ 8-E2

L'Aroma Café is in the reception lobby but has enough wood paneling and typical cafe decor to at least stand out a little and not seem like another check-in counter. The place is open all hours making it a good little spot to stop, take the weight off your feet, have a bite or quench your thirst. The menu is small but still intriguing. With snacks like

MARRIOTT IN KUWAIT, TWO HOTELS, ENDLESS POSSIBILITIES

Choose the JW Marriott approachable luxury or the Courtyard's bright and fresh surroundings.

Whether it's business or leisure, a grand launch or a high profile conference, family dining or catering, Marriott hotels in Kuwait bring a world of possibilities within your reach. GOING ABOVE AND BEYOND.

IT'S THE MARRIOTT WAY.[SM]

جي دبليو ماريوت الكويت

JW MARRIOTT.
KUWAIT CITY

KUWAIT CITY

Marriott International - Kuwait
Al Shuhada Street - P.O. Box 1216
Dasman 15463 - Kuwait

Room reservation center:
Tel: +965 2997000
Fax: +965 2997041
Email: sales@marriotthotels.com

L'Aroma Cafe

salads and sandwiches to bigger main course meals, you'll find something on the menu whatever your appetite. Being slap-bang in the hotel's reception makes this an excellent place to people watch too.

La Brasserie

Location → JW Marriott Hotel Kuwait City · Safat   **245 5550**
Web/email → www.marriott.com   Map Ref → 3-B4

Located in the JW Marriot Hotel, La Brasserie is a conventional hotel buffet serving a suitable selection of salads, entrees and desserts. The international fare is certainly of notable quality for a standard buffet without being pretentious, so at least satisfying a healthy appetite. It's perfect for a low and slow dinner night out, so if you are looking for a traditional buffet dining experience then La Brasserie should please, with appropriately attentive service. For a themed buffet option, Monday nights feature Spanish cuisine and Wednesdays are perfect for seafood lovers.

Layali Al Helmeya

Location → Arabian Gulf St · Salmiya   **263 8710**
Web/email → na   Map Ref → 6-A1

This restaurant is in a very nice location overlooking the Gulf, with an uninterrupted view of

the sea from the terrace. It's a perfect little spot to sip one of their tasty coffees and watch the sunrise (if you're a very early bird) or sunset (if you're not). The shisha is of excellent quality here and definitely worth a puff, even if it's not really your thing. Popular with Arabic clientele, it certainly makes a good spot to refuel while enjoying a nice day out in Kuwait. The menu is in Arabic and English with a comprehensive breakfast section. Everything on the menu is well prepared and the presentation is reasonable. The friendly and helpful waiters also add to the whole ambience of Arabic leisure. Plasma screen TVs are scattered throughout the premises, inside and out, so small talk is entirely unnecessary!

Shook

Location → Swiss Inn Kuwait Plaza Hotel · Safat   **243 6686**
Web/email → www.swissinnkuwait.com   Map Ref → 3-B4

Shook is pretty much your standard hotel buffet restaurant, serving international cuisine that includes the usual suspects of Indian, Chinese, Arabic and European dishes. The restaurant is open to all, but generally caters to in-house guests. However don't overlook Thursday's buffet as not only does the food tend to get a little more exciting so does the atmosphere with a spot of live entertainment. The daily buffet breakfast is also good but again is unlikely to attract anyone other than hotel guests.

Six Palms Lounge

Location ➔ Marina Mall · Salmiya | **224 4970**
Web/email ➔ www.marinahotel.com | Map Ref ➔ 8-B2

Situated right at the very end of Marina Mall, behind Marina Crescent, the Six Palms Lounge offers incredible value for money. It gets busy quickly and since it is located on the basement level in the middle of the hotel, seating can be a little cramped. The international buffet is kept simple, but with a wide selection of good quality food, including two cooking stations. The glass roof ensures the seating area is flooded with natural light during the day, and no matter what time of day you visit, there is always an incredibly relaxed atmosphere, though it could be said this has rubbed off slightly onto the staff. It takes a while to get and keep their attention. Luckily this is a buffet, so starving does not have to be an option. Nevertheless, if it's no fuss, good value, good food you're after, then this is the right place for you.

Teatro

Location ➔ Hilton Kuwait Resort | **372 5500**
Web/email ➔ www.hilton.com | Map Ref ➔ 1-C3

Five star quality in a five star hotel. The informal buffet that operates alongside this restaurant's a la carte offerings provides a delightful opportunity to 'eat your way around the world' with culinary cues

Teatro

taken from the best authentic Indian, Chinese, American and European cuisines. Take as much or as little as you like. Beautifully presented, freshly prepared and served by some of the best and most knowledgeable staff you will ever have the pleasure to meet in Kuwait. Eat outside by the beach during cooler months for an added dimension. Though most of the clientele seem to be hotel guests, there is always an added mix of local and expat families enjoying the food.

Italian

Other options ➔ Pizzerias [p.215]

Al Dente

Location ➔ Mövenpick Hotel Kuwait · Shuwaikh | **461 0033**
Web/email ➔ www.moevenpick-hotels.com | Map Ref ➔ 5-B2

A truly authentic Italian trattoria, Al Dente is perfect for a casual family dinner, a lingering lunch with friends or a romantic evening. The interior is intimate yet not cramped, thanks to the added space of the balcony. The decor is as you would expect from an Italian restaurant, terracotta villa-style walls, low wooden ceilings and dark wood tables and chairs. The a la carte menu is packed with delicious pasta dishes, pizzas, salads and various other tempting Italian delights, especially in the dessert section. You can also enjoy the traditional live band and rather impressive opera singer!

Il Forno

Location ➔ The Courtyard by Marriott Kuwait City Htl | **299 7000**
Web/email ➔ www.marriot.com | Map Ref ➔ 3-E2

Il Forno is located on the second floor of the Marriott Courtyard Hotel and is well worth a visit even if it is lacking the traditional Italian decor & Chianti bottles. A fresh fruit cocktail – on the house – is presented to guests as they arrive and wait to be seated. From there, your evening can just keeps getting better. The ambience of this hotel gives you the feel-good factor before you even get to experience the culinary delights that await you. The food is served to please the eye well before your stomach since the presentation is a delight. Delicious Italian fare is prepared in the open kitchen, so you can steal a peak at the chefs. Choose from a varied menu that covers all bases well: meat, fish and chicken main courses, along with all the well-loved pastas dressed in simple, or for the more fancy, intricate sauces. This restaurant is a delight from start to end.

Il Forno

La Piazza

Location ➔ Wattiyah
Web/email ➔ na

242 6639
Map Ref ➔ 3-B4

Authentic Italian food prepared and presented in great surroundings – is the best way to sum up La Piazza. It's located in an old traditional-style Arabic villa, admittedly as far from old Italy as you can get, but La Piazza has stylishly recreated Italian cuisine in Kuwait. From simple pastas to pizzas, meat and

La Piazza

fish, this is good food at its best. Your time will be fruitfully spent among appreciative fellow diners along with all the noise and commotion that is always associated with the finest Italian cooking. Eccellente! Semplicemente il la cosa migliore!

Pizza Express

Location ➔ Hilton Beach Resort
Web/email ➔ www.pizzaexpress.com

372 5500
Map Ref ➔ 1-C3

If you're looking for a quick bite or have an attack of 'the munchies' whilst out shopping, then one of Pizza Express's tasty pizzas could be just what you need. Freshly cooked and served in double quick time (hence the 'Express' of Pizza Express), this franchised pizzeria is tasty, quick and affordable. And lest we forget, the pasta options are equally as good. This may not be gourmet cuisine, but for fast food, its mouth-wateringly delicious.

Riccardo

Location ➔ Sheraton Kuwait Htl & Towers · Wattiyah
Web/email ➔ www.starwoodhotels.com

242 2055
Map Ref ➔ 3-B4

If you're looking for the kind of Italian food that 'Mama used to make' you'll be disappointed with Riccardo. However, if you're looking for the kind of food 'Mama wished she'd paid attention for long enough to learn how to make' then this could be just the place for you. In terms of depth of menu and plate presentation there are few better Italian restaurants in Kuwait. Just remember that this IS a five star hotel so lacks some of the personal warmth, individuality and charm of a Tuscan 'trattoria', but its romantically subdued lighting, first class presentation, top quality food and attentive staff will make any night a special occassion.

Japanese

Cuts Steakhouse & Sushi Bar

Location ➔ Mövenpick Hotel Kuwait · Shuwaikh
Web/email ➔ www.moevenpick-hotels.com

461 0033
Map Ref ➔ 5-B2

Refer to the review under Steakhouses, p.216

Edo

Location ➜ Arabian Gulf Rd · Sa'ab
Web/email ➜ www.edorestaurant.com

265 9590
Map Ref ➜ 7-C1

A real oriental jewel in Kuwait, the Edo restaurant offers the very best in Japanese cuisine. The decor is modern, but still manages to create a calm and relaxed atmosphere, with additional seating outside if the temperature permits. There is an enormous selection for you to attempt to choose from. Be warned, it all sounds so good that making a decision won't be easy so don't hesitate to ask the staff. Helpful and friendly, they to have tried everything on the menu, and are more then able – and willing – to assist you in anyway they can. All of the dishes here are beautifully presented, high quality and fabulously tasty. If you want to try something a little different, or you just love Asian cuisine, you are going to adore Edo.

Kamikaze

Location ➜ Palms Beach Hotel & Spa, The · Salwa
Web/email ➜ www.thepalms-kuwait.com

82 4060
Map Ref ➜ 13-D3

A small slice of Japan right here in Kuwait, this is a very swanky sushi bar with a super swanky big, flat screen TV behind the bar and the friendliest staff you are ever likely to find. The TV gets a bit loud but the sushi always stays fresh, tasty and innovative. Skip a meal because dining here during happy hour (19.00 – 20.00) will see your sushi bill cut in half. Beyond the sushi, the rest of the menu is equally as divine. The Teppanyaki al a carte is worth writing home about and you shouldn't leave without trying the scallops. Go with a small gathering (four to six people) and you'll be given a nice Japanese room where you can sit in private.

Kei

Location ➜ JW Marriott Hotel Kuwait City ·
Web/email ➜ www.marriott.com

245 5550
Map Ref ➜ 3-B4

A peaceful enclave in the busy world of the JW Marriott Hotel, Kei is a great place to savour the delights of Japanese cuisine. Designed to emulate a slice of the orient, from the tastefully traditional welcome and serene background music to the wide array of menu choices. Don't be shy, the staff are very friendly and will gladly talk you though the dishes that seem less common to the non-Japanese. This is no fast food joint, so be sure to allow time between courses to make the most of your dinner here. The portions are more than generous so watch your waistband.

Sakura

Location ➜ Crowne Plaza · Farwania
Web/email ➜ www.kuwait.crowneplaza.com

474 2000
Map Ref ➜ 16-C2

This traditional Japanese restaurant serves a mouth-watering array of sushi, sashimi, yaki-niku, teppanyaki and tatami. The menu has a few international touches to suit the novice diner and the decor is suitably authentic to create a relaxed dining experience. The traditionally garbed staff are not only pleasant but will also help you with your menu selection. They hold many special promotions such as a two for one sushi happy hour, so it is worth calling beforehand to check what deals are available. Also located at the Crowne Plaza is the Sakura Xpress, a sushi bar that offers quick, efficient service and has become popular for working lunches.

Wasabi

Location ➜ Al Mashura Bld· Wattiyah
Web/email ➜ na

249 4000
Map Ref ➜ 3-B4

Your entrance across a small bridge over running water (a tradition in Japan where it is believed this will bring good fortune) is your first hint to the fact that your visit to Wasabi may turn out to be a truly auspicious occasion. The chic, yet comfortable, interior is as welcoming as the thought of the gastronomic delight that lies ahead. The appetisers, salads, sushi, maki, sashimi and teppanyaki are beautifully prepared and are served to you as 'art-forms on a plate'. But it's not all style over substance at this restaurant, the food here is very good and the flavours are appetising without being overpowering. This place is favoured by Kuwait's 'smart set' and with the decor, ambience and chic factor, along with the good food and happy staff, you can see why.

Pizzerias

Other options → Italian [p.211]

Pizzas are a very popular part of the local staple diet, particularly with the younger generation. The range is good and not too expensive, and most outlets will make to order. Delivery is not a problem, although sometimes it can arrive a little late and can be cold. However, the quality is generally of a high standard. From thick to thin to cheese stuffed crusts, the extensive range will ensure that you never go hungry, and some are remarkably tasty and authentic. Most malls and all the main shopping areas like Salmiya have a good selection of pizza outlets, and Pepe's Pizza (574 4442) is a particular favourite for delivery.

Ciro's Pomodoro

Polynesian

Kontiki

Location → Radisson SAS Hotels & Resorts · Salwa | 575 6000
Web/email → www.radissonsas.com   Map Ref → 13-D3

Built on what used to be (many years ago) a dry dock, Kontiki is situated around the hull of an old Kuwaiti trading dhow. The space of the restaurant will grab you, as will the colourful reproductions of the French Polynesian art that adorn the walls. The food is truly excellent and ahead of its time in Kuwait. The staff know the menu inside out and are good at making suggestions that are guaranteed to have you thanking them later. At the end of the night, if you ask nicely, the chef may even show you a picture of his ancestor – a tribal Polynesian – that hangs in the kitchen.

Seafood

Al Boom

Location → Radisson SAS Hotels & Resorts · Salwa | 575 6000
Web/email → www.radissonsas.com   Map Ref → 13-D3

This magical restaurant is situated within a real Arabian dhow (although mercifully for those landlubbers amongst us it now sits firmly on dry land). The beautiful carvings and richness of the wood complement the outstanding quality of the food served. The menu features prime US beef steaks, tender chicken specialities, lobster and giant Gulf shrimps as well as local fish specialities and a rich and varied mezze buffet. And lest we forget, the delicious sesame seed bread baked in traditional clay ovens is worth a trip in itself. The romantics may decide to take their after dinner 'qahwa' (Arabic coffee) in the traditional 'diwania' out on the deck... what finer end to an outstanding meal?

Al Boom

Al Noukhaza

Location → Crowne Plaza · Farwania | 474 2000
Web/email → www.kuwait.crowneplaza.com | Map Ref → 16-C2

This specialist fish buffet offers so much variety that it is virtually impossible to leave hungry or unsatisfied. The cold buffet has unlimited smoked salmon, prawns, crab meat and other cold fish specialties with a dazzling assortment of accompanying salads. You can choose your main course ingredients from the display board and the live cooking station will prepare it as you like it. This is 'all you can eat' on a grand scale - a must for fish lovers and they will even bring a steak from the kitchen if one of you has a hankering for red meat. The dessert table is limited but tasty, and the fruit juices expensive, but this buffet is well worth the price.

Sea Shell

Location → Kempinski Julai'a Hotel & Resort | 84 4444
Web/email → www.kempinski-kuwait.com | Map Ref → 1-D4

It's worth a trip to the Kempinski Resort just to visit this superb seafood restaurant. Despite the name, there are a variety of meat dishes on the menu too, and all are very tasty. But if you've come here on a Thursday then it really ought to be for the seafood buffet, because it is simply excellent. With a large selection of fresh fish cooked to your specification, as well as the a la carte menu, you really will be spoilt for choice. The restaurant is placed at the heart of the resort, right on the coast, and is the perfect backdrop for a quiet, relaxed and romantic evening.

Steakhouses

Other options → American [p.199]

Cuts Steakhouse & Sushi Bar

Location → Mövenpick Hotel Kuwait · Shuwaikh | 461 0033
Web/email → www.moevenpick-hotels.com | Map Ref → 5-B2

Modern decor and fine dining is the order of the day at Cuts, combining dark wood, leather and minimalist artwork that adorns the softly lit walls. The a la carte menu combines a variety of dishes to suit the ravenous meat eater and delicate seafood lover. The atmosphere is particularly conducive for a romantic evening, but is spiced up by the energetic live cooking stations. They also have various theme nights and buffet nights too, so it is worth calling ahead. As for the sushi, it is pretty standard but delicious nonetheless.

The Gaucho Grill

Location → The Palms Beach Hotel & Spa · Salwa | 82 4060
Web/email → www.thepalms-kuwait.com | Map Ref → 13-D3

This upmarket grill restaurant is located in a dark cavern within the Palms Hotel, with cool jazz music playing in the background. The attentive staff are well qualified to advise on the different cuts of meat and accompaniments, and once you've made that tough decision you can watch your steak being prepared to your liking in the open kitchen. The prime cuts of beef are cooked to perfection, making this venue a favourite for Kuwait's carnivores. The appetizers are tasty too, and you'd better go hungry if you plan on making it to the desserts.

Rib Eye Steak House

Location → Crowne Plaza · Farwania | 474 2000
Web/email → www.kuwait.crowneplaza.co | Map Ref → 16-C2

This wild west themed restaurant comes complete with low-key country music plus upbeat and fun 'cow-garl' waitresses. The food is served swiftly and with a smile. The starters are varied, the salads are good, but the steaks are the reason people come. Great big hunks of juicy meat are served whichever way you like them. Choose the cut, the sauce and the side dish and the portions are so generous, your doggy bag will last you well into a midnight snack. Indulge in the delicious starters, but it is unlikely you'll have room for dessert, which is a shame because their puddings are a marvel and well worth pacing yourself for.

> ### GCC easy as ABC
>
> If you want to drop in on your neighbours, then go prepared with your Explorer. Be it for a shopping spree in Dubai, a luxury holiday in Abu Dhabi, to find tranquility in the wilderness of Oman, to watch the Asian Games in Qatar or to have a tipple with your tea in Bahrain!

Going Out · **Seafood · Steakhouses**

simply unique...
feel the difference

Radisson SAS Hotel Kuwait, the only 5 star hotel located on the beach front near the fashionable and central ▪iya district with a unique choice of restaurants, recreation club and 300 meters private beach.

▪isson SAS Hotel
Box 26199, Safat 13122, Kuwait
+965 575 6000, Fax: +965 565 2999

to book. Easy to find. Easy to use.
▪ait.radissonsas.com

HOTEL, KUWAIT

Terrace Grill

Location → JW Marriott Hotel · Kuwait City
Web/email → www.marriott.com

245 5550
Map Ref → 3-B4

A meat lovers' paradise! The range of juicy, tender, mouthwatering cuts of meat you are able to choose from is staggering. Never has there been a 10 ounce fillet that has just melted the way the Terrace Grill's steaks seem to. The service is provided by a very professional and friendly team, who take great care to ensure you enjoy your meal. Put this together with the perfect atmosphere from the live band and you will be very hard pushed to find better places to eat in Kuwait. Be warned though, everything comes at a price.

Terrace Grill

Thai

Bamboo Shoot

Location → Safir Int'l Hotel Kuwait · Bneid al-Gar
Web/email → www.safirhotels.com

253 0771
Map Ref → 4-A2

If you like Thai food then you will love Bamboo Shoot. It boasts a postcard view of the Kuwaiti towers (especially at night) and a comprehensive menu. Add to the equation your own goldfish in a bowl on your table and a relaxed ambience and you have all the ingredients for a good night. Each month has a different theme (call ahead for more details). The menu caters for all tastes ranging from

Bamboo Shoot

the mild to the hot. Try the Tom Yam Goong – a spicy soup, followed by Geang Kiew Wan Gai – a fiery green duck curry. This is a restaurant that will satisfy all appetites.

Blue Elephant

Location → Hilton Kuwait Resort
Web/email → www.hilton.com

372 5500
Map Ref → 1-C3

The Blue Elephant has a reputation and while this particular version may not be franchised from the same brand, its quality of fare certainly ranks highly. A dinner or lunch here is very nearly a substitute for a trip to Thailand – gastronomically speaking at least. The ambience, decor (there are actual palm trees involved) and beautifully uniformed and friendly staff are a brilliant taste of the Far East. Complimentary starter snacks will get your stomach begging for more and anything on the exquisite menu will finish off a fabulous evening of traditional, tasty Thai food.

Dinner Cruises

Other options → Boat & Yacht Charters [p.218]
Dhow Charters [p.218]

Dinner cruises are gaining in popularity in Kuwait and there are several organisations and travel agencies offering such services. They are very popular for corporate entertaining and for special occasions and can be chartered for any length of time required. At this time there are no specific scheduled evening dinner cruises, although several companies are planning to start again soon. Kuwait Bay is an enchanting sight in the evening and should be enjoyed from the water if you get the chance.

Nuzha Touristic Enterprises

Location ➔ Al Bustan Mall · Safat | 575 5825
Web/email ➔ www.nuzhatours.com   Map Ref ➔ 3-C3

Nuzha touristic enterprises have several boats that offer private tours and charters rather than a scheduled dinner cruise service. Ideal for private parties or corporate functions. They also offer a boat service to the islands.

Cafes & Coffee Shops

People watching and hanging out in cafes is a very popular pastime in Kuwait, and there are plenty of cafes and coffee shops from which to choose. From modern and upmarket international chain outlets like Starbucks, Costa Coffee, Second Cup and Gloria Jeans, to the more traditional shisha places and coffee houses around the authentic heritage area in the city – one thing's for sure, you will never run out of choices!

Although popular throughout the day, the cafes are even more alive in the evenings, and as the tables can't be booked you need to be there early if you want to get one of the prime slots. Most coffee houses tend to offer some food, although generally it is fairly basic consisting of some sandwiches and cakes.

Internet cafes are still not that common but have become more popular in recent years. The range of food, however, is generally very basic. For a list of net cafes see the table on p.222.

The Palms Beach Club

Location ➔ The Palms Beach Hotel & Spa · Salwa | 82 4060
Web/email ➔ www.thepalms-kuwait.com   Map Ref ➔ 13-D3

Thanks to ceiling to floor windows, minimalist modern decor and splashes of orange, this bright and airy cafe, located next to the Beach Club, instantly lifts your spirits. You have the option of dining inside or out, overlooking the pool and beach, and the menu is an enticing combination of healthy options as well as hearty selections. Private parties can also be catered for and their mocktails are a must for a truly rejuvenating experience.

Café Royal

Location ➔ JW Marriott Hotel Kuwait City · Wattiyah | 245 5550
Web/email ➔ www.marriott.com   Map Ref ➔ 3-B4

This popular venue is a smart upmarket foodcourt-style cafe, located in one of the more expensive shopping malls adjacent to the JW Marriott hotel in the centre of Kuwait City. Ideal for a quick lunchtime or early evening casual get-together. The menu offers typical cafe style eats like fish & chips, salads, or sandwiches, there is even a few Arabic dishes worth considering and the mezze and oriental dishes make for a nice change if you have a bit of time on your hands. This cafe is a pleasant pit stop for refueling between shopping spurts or even a lunch away from the office. The people-watching potential is excellent and the service is fast enough should you need to get in and out in a hurry.

Blue Elephant

Dinner Cruises

Going Out

Casper & Gambini's

Location → Old Arabic Houses · Watiyah
Web/email → www.casperandgambinis.com
| 243 0054
Map Ref → 3-B4

Located in one of the few traditional Arabic villas that remain in Kuwait City, its contemporary interior style combines fast and friendly service with good Italian food in great surroundings. An excellent choice during the day for a quick lunch due to its location and ease of parking, in the evening it is a favoured hangout for the young and trendy. Where better to while away the time with friends over a coffee and some good food? Pick the right time of year and eating outside is a must-do.

The terrace at Casper & Gambini's

Chocolates

Location → Marina Cresent, Marina Mall · Salmiya
Web/email → na
| 224 4880
Map Ref → 8-B2

A small, casual and pleasant cafe located at the Marina Crescent. Indoor and outdoor seating is available. Expect a limited selection of breakfasts and light meals, but the name is the main reason for coming here: a huge selection of delectable treats. If you are willing to share, try the fondue, which comes with an assortment of fruits, biscuits and cakes for dipping. At KD 5.900 it's the most expensive item on the menu, but when it comes to decadence, money is no object. If money is an object then fret not, other prices average around KD 3. The service is friendly but don't be in a hurry.

Take time to just sit and look at all that lovely chocolate and then look out at the lovely harbour. Diet starts tomorrow!

Espresso Lounge

Location → Safir Int'l Hotel Kuwait · Bneid al-Gar
Web/email → www.safirhotels.com
| 253 3000
Map Ref → 4-A2

Situated in the lobby of the Safir International, you may be excused for thinking that this is just another coffee shop, but look past the tables and you realise that it is not. The large cake display counter an is indication of something so much greater. Sure you can get a cappuccino and a tasty sandwich while listening to live music (there is often a pianist or violinist) but the cakes are the icing on the cake for this coffee shop. With a wide variety to choose from if you are eating in, the coffee shop also specialises in making cakes to order, whether it be wedding, birthday or just because you like cakes!

Le Pain

Location → The Palms Beach Hotel & Spa · Salwa
Web/email → na
| 563 3684
Map Ref → 13-D3

Le Pain is a continental style bakery (Belgian, to be specific) where 'fresh' is the buzzword. From the endless varieties of freshly baked bread to the salads and bigger meat dishes, all are fresh and freshly prepared for your gastronomic pleasure. Bare wooden tables and floors give Le Pain a very laid back and relaxed European feel. The breads are worth writing home about and if you can't resist then just ask for a loaf or two to take home. The bakery will only be too happy to oblige.

Paul

Location → Marina Mall · Salmiya
Web/email → na
| 224 4588
Map Ref → 8-B2

Walking into Paul gives you the feeling you've stepped back in time. This is in no way due to the service, because the staff are very helpful to say the least, but rather because of the typically French olde worlde decor that surrounds you as you eat. Whether it's just a stop off for coffee, or if you're ready to take on something more from the menu, Paul never fails to please, which is why it is one of the most popular places to eat in Kuwait. Other locations: Al Kout Mall.

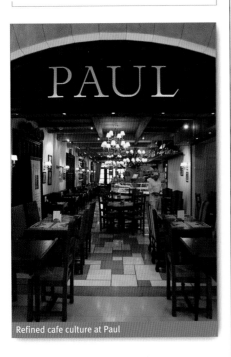

Refined cafe culture at Paul

Six Palms

Location → Marina Hotel Kuwait · Salmiya
Web/email → www.marinahotel.com

224 4970
Map Ref → 8-B2

Situated right at the very end of the Marina, behind Marina Crescent, the Six Palms Lounge offers incredible value for money. The international buffet is kept simple, but with a wide selection of good quality food, including two cooking stations to keep you on your culinary toes. Considering its home in the basement level of the hotel, the large glass roof works wonders to keep the place light, bright and airy. Ambience and atmosphere are very relaxed and this seems to have rubbed off on the staff, who are a little on the slow and nonchalant side but still friendly. Nevertheless, if it's no fuss, good value and good food you're after, then this is the right place for you.

Song Bird Cafe

Location → Hilton Kuwait Resort
Web/email → na

372 5500
Map Ref → 1-C3

Open all hours, this songbird will leave many night owls very happy. The interior is pleasantly spacious and comfortable, perfect for a late night munchie session. If the weather permits, make the effort to sit outside under one of the colourful parasols and enjoy the sea view. The menu is pretty straightforward and caters for the snack hankerers tas well as those who fancy a full-on, substantial mixed grill. The staff are helpful and courteous and make the cafe a perfect little spot to meet, greet and while away the hours.

Tiramisu

Location → The Courtyard by Marriott · Kuwait City
Web/email → www.courtyard.com

299 7001
Map Ref → 3-E2

Tiramisu may be a coffee lounge but its emphasis is on luxury with a fabulous gourmet selection of Italian blends and Arabic coffees as well as a mouthwatering selection of pastries, mini snacks, cakes and delectable deserts that you just cannot ignore. Whether you want to savour some well deserved sustenance after a shopping spree in the Arraya Mall or catch up with friends, Tiramisu is simply a sublime solution. After you've been once, expect to keep coming back for more.

Villa Moda Test & Taste

Location → Kuwait Free Zone · Shuwaikh
Web/email → www.villa-moda.com

482 7010
Map Ref → 5-C2

Tucked away on the ground floor of the Villa Moda Shopping Mall (at the Shuwaikh Free Port), you will find this fashionable restaurant as classy as the clothing sold in the neighbouring stores. The cuisine is delicious and the food expertly prepared and presented. Choose from an international menu offering pasta, fish and everything in between, although the vegetarian choices are a little limited. On the whole the place gets a thumbs up and if you have the space then you ought to finish your meal with the Swedish Ice Berries & White Chocolate – divine!

Cafés & Coffee Shops

Going Out

Shisha Cafes

Other options → Arabic/Lebanese [p.220]

Shisha cafes are common throughout the Middle East, offering relaxing surroundings, often with authentic decor, where you have the chance to smoke a shisha pipe (also known as 'hookah', 'hubbly bubbly' or 'narghile') with a variety of aromatic flavours. Traditionally the preserve of local men while playing backgammon and gossiping with friends, shisha cafes are now popular with all ages and nationalities.

There are various shisa cafes around Kuwait, some of the most popular ones are listed in the table below. However, in addition there are various restaurants, especially those in the Arabic category, which will also have shisha available for after your meal. If you have guests in town it is always worth taking them to a shisha cafe or a restaurant with shisha as it is a truly Arabic experience. Also if you like the sweet taste then you can always invest in a shisha pipe for your home and host your very own Arabic dinner parties. Check out the shops listed in the shopping section under Souvenirs [p.176] for where to pick up a shisha.

Shisha Cafes	
Balbak Café & Restaurant	575 0588
Beit Lothan	575 5866
Classical Café & Restaurant	574 0077
Garden Restaurant	563 4200
Puerto Banus Café & Restaurant	245 6650
Song Bird Café	372 5500
Veranda Café & Restaurant	572 7120

Afternoon Tea

Other options → Cafés & Coffee Shops [p.219]

The English Tea Lounge

Location → Sheraton Kuwait Htl & Towers · Wattiyah | 242 2055
Web/email → www.starwoodhotels.com   Map Ref → 3-B4

For traditional English 'high tea' you need look no further. The room is wonderfully furnished in a traditional English Country House style. The choice of teas is wide but not overwhelming. The finest china is brought out to complement the subtle flavours of your choice of infusion. A selection of tasty bites is served, such as scones with cream and jam, tiny triangular sandwiches (yes - the crusts have been cut off!), and much more. The overall feeling is one of 'Little England abroad'. Almost quaint.

Tea Lounge

Location → JW Marriott Hotel Kuwait City · Wattiyah | 245 5550
Web/email → www.marriott.com   Map Ref → 3-B4

This is an elegant and relaxing lobby lounge serving exquisite light snacks, the finest teas, and gourmet coffees. As with any lobby lounge it's ideal for the hotel's guests, but this particular venue shouldn't be overlooked by everyone else. With their good range of freshly prepared food and beverages, the Tea Lounge is an ideal place to gather pre-dinner, to arrange an informal afternoon meeting, or to catch up with friends.

The Tea Lounge

Location → Mövenpick Hotel Kuwait · Shuwaikh | 461 0033
Web/email → www.moevenpick-hotels.com   Map Ref → 5-B2

A little bit of Blighty in the hot house that is Kuwait. The Tea Lounge is sheer English bliss with sophisticated decor, spacious seating and tea. Light snacks will lure you through the Mövenpick (which you'll have to wade through to get to this island of tea and crumpets) and crumbly, finger-licking pastries will ensure that you add this place to your top favourites. The light piano music will have you feeling like the royalty that you truly are, or at least wish you could be!

Internet Cafés

Other options → Internet [p.73]

If you want to surf the net, email your friends or just check out the latest international news then there are a number of internet cafes around town, although they are not always easy to find as they may be hidden inside a shopping mall. Prices range from around 250 fils to KD 1 per hour and there are censorship rules whereby certain sites may be blocked. Sometimes it is difficult to understand why certain sites are blocked and if you can be bothered you can contact your ISP and issue an enquiry.

Internet Cafes	
American Internet Café	392 3203
Café Olé	571 5595
Cozmo	574 4983
Intersat	265 3420
Kuwait Internet Café	240 5005
Platinum	88 0008

Friday Brunch

Although not as popular as other GCC countries, in part possibly due to the lack of champagne, several outlets offer a Friday brunch with the usual limitless supply of heavy food in a help-yourself buffet style. Jeans Grill is very popular and has three good locations inside the Sultan Centre in Salmiya, Souq Sharq and the Arabian Gulf Street. Several hotels also offer a good Friday brunch, but these tend to be at inflated local prices. Most restaurants in Kuwait are family friendly, and sometimes entertainment is provided to keep the kids busy so the parents can truly unwind.

On the Town

Kuwait is somewhat unique in the GCC. Having earlier had alcohol available, the sale of booze was stopped in the 70s, and like Saudi, Kuwait is now a dry state. This means that you'll have to take a little more time to come up with something entertaining, but don't be put off – consider it a challenge instead.

The main social activities revolve around the late shopping malls and the late evening meal scene. The coffee shops and shisha houses are also very popular and can stay open until the wee hours. Functions and balls held at hotels will also stay open till late, so there's still no excuse to not stay up past your bedtime.

Coffee shops normally close at around midnight but stay open longer in Ramadan. At the start of the weekend and particularly on Wednesday and Thursday evenings (considered the weekends for most people here) the traffic can be very bad and some of the malls extremely busy, so keep that in mind if you're planning to move around. If possible, wait until a little later in the evening before you hit the road.

The standard of driving is generally suspect at best, but the driving etiquette deteriorates later on in the evening and is more suited to drag racing. It's an interesting concept, but hold on to your hats because these drivers aren't messing around.

Bars

Other options → Pubs [p.223]
Nightclubs [p.223]

Alcohol is strictly prohibited in Kuwait, so there are no pubs and bars of which to speak. Instead, the nightlife tends to revolve around food and socialising (without booze – which is actually entirely possible!)

Shisha bars and the large chain coffee shops like Starbucks are very popular with the local community and tend to be the hub of activity. They also double up as excellent places to people watch, a fabulous pastime.

Dress Code

Most cafes and restaurants have a reasonably relaxed attitude to their customers' dress sense. Some places, however, especially smart restaurants in the hotels, insist on no shorts or sandals, while others require at least a shirt with a collar and no jeans.

Pubs

Other options → Bars [p.223]

Without any alcohol, it's difficult to say there is any real pub scene in the country. Most of the activities tend to revolve around BBQs or dinner parties at people's residences, or the balls that are held throughout the year.

Despite the lack of traditional pubs, Kuwait does actually have quite a big sporting following and Plasma screen TV's are everywhere – including cafes – for you to catch whatever game happens to be playing. There are also a number of social activities worth sniffing out and trying, including darts (which is very popular here), bowling leagues, and the Hash House Harriers, with runs every Tuesday and Saturday. All provide a great way to meet and mingle with other visitors and expats. However, the most popular form of socialising is to get a group of people together in a private residence.

Nightclubs

Other options → Dinner Cruises [p.218]

There are no formal nightclubs in Kuwait, although live entertainment is provided in some of the hotels and larger restaurants. These generally provide a live band or at least a DJ but still no sign of a bar. However, house parties seem to double up as nightclubs, and people generally dress up well to venture out. Although not banned, discos are kept very low key. The Hard Rock Cafe on the Arabian Gulf Street is probably the closest venue with a nightclub feel.

Entertainment

Live entertainment in Kuwait is somewhat limited. There are the occassional special events held in the larger hotels but they are – unfortunately – not held on a regular basis. Most balls and functions have live entertainment laid on and this normally includes some genre of music and sometimes even a belly dancer. Special one off events will be published in the media but tickets sell out fast so move quick if you are interested.

Concerts

Large-scale music concerts are not a big part of life here, and so Kuwait doesn't feature very highly on the world circuit when it comes to big name tours. Oddly, the country does have several large stadiums and the facilities to host big concerts, so perhaps this is an indication of things to change. There are a few exceptions, the Kuwait Jazz festival is one of these. Normally held in April at the Radisson SAS hotel, be sure to watch the local press for details. There are a few live concerts held during the year but these are mainly visiting Arabic artists, or more specifically, Lebanese artists, both of which still happen to be on a small scale in comparison to some of the other GCC countries.

There are several bands in the country that tend to be booked up for the many society balls held throughout the year, but these are normally only through word of mouth. On occasions the embassies may bring out international artists from their country and promote these concerts to the public. So while it's not handed to you on the silver platter, the lesson here is to seek and ye shall find!

Theatre

Kuwait is not a dearth of thespian activity and there are several theatres operating throughout the year. The most popular is the Kuwait Little Theatre (398 2680), located in a small intimate theatre in Ahmadi with at least six or so productions each year.

The performance normally runs for a week, and the annual Christmas Pantomime (yes, they do Panto here) is very popular and often highly entertaining. Also popular is the Kuwait Players (5625316) and the Kuwait Elizabethians (5631725), both put on several very good Shakesperian productions scheduled. Check local press for details.

In addition to these local productions, BA Playhouse productions are also held a couple of times a year. These are normally at the Hilton Resort Hotel in Mangaf and are as close to a professional evenings theatre production as you are likely to get here in Kuwait, with a three course meal thrown in to boot. Normally they only run for 2-3 days with their productions also playing in other GCC countries.

Kuwait Little Theatre

Cinemas

Going to the movies is very popular in Kuwait, although you can expect a selection of blockbuster mainstream films, some of which for obvious reasons will not make it here, but don't hold your breath for any art house offerings. Cinemas get pretty busy, especially when a new big name movie debuts so its worth getting your tickets early and then going for dinner or to do a bit of shopping if you're in one of the mall cinemas. Cinema timings can be found in the local newspaper.

You may find that some of the cinemas are a little on the chilly side thanks to the over exhuberant air conditioning so it is always worth taking a jumper. Also be warned that chatting is not uncommon during the film so pick your seat carefully.

Kuwait National Cinema Company has a number of Cinescape cinemas located around Kuwait. To find out what's showing call 80 3456 and a customer service advisor will provide you with screening and timings for your chosen cinema or specific film. The Cinescape cinemas are located in Ajial, Al Fanar, Al Kout, Al Muhallab, Al Sha'ab, Al Sharqia, Gernada, Laila, Marina, Metro and Plaza.

A square book but not for squares

Explore Dubai's decadent range of restaurants, bars, cafes and clubs in this beautiful book with stunning images and informative reviews. More than just a guidebook, it's at home on a coffee table while you're out on the town.

Maps

Maps

User's Guide

To further assist you in locating your destination, we have superimposed additional information, such as main roads, roundabouts and landmarks, on the maps. Many places listed throughout the guidebook also have a map reference alongside, so you know precisely where you need to go (or what you need to tell the taxi driver).

While the country overview map on this page is at a scale of approximately 1:1,000,000 (1cm = 10km) and the Kuwait city and surrounding area map is at a scale of approximately 1:500,000 (1cm = 5km) all other map pages scale is 1:20,000 (1cm = 200m).

Technical Info - Satellite Images

The maps in this section are based on rectified QuickBird satellite imagery taken in 2005.

The QuickBird satellite was launched in October 2001 and is operated by DigitalGlobe(tm), a private company based in Colorado (USA). Today, DigitalGlobe's QuickBird satellite provides the highest resolution (61 cm), largest swath width and largest onboard storage of any currently available or planned commercial satellite.

MAPS geosystems are the Digital Globe master resellers for the Middle East, West, Central and East Africa. They also provide a wide range of mapping services and systems. For more information, visit www.digitalglobe.com (QuickBird) and www.maps-geosystems.com (mapping services) or contact MAPS geosystems on (+971 0) 6 572 5411.

Online Maps

If you want to surf for maps online, a good starting point is www.map24.com. This site has detailed maps of countries throughout the Arabian Peninsular (as well as Europe and North America), and allows you to search by street name, hotel name, or by points of interest.

Kuwait Towns and Cities

The following is a list of the main towns and cities in Kuwait, which can be found on the Kuwait map (Map pages 1 & 2).

Town/City	Map Ref	Town/City	Map Ref
Ahmadi	1-C4	Jahra	1-A2
Fahaheel	1-C4	Kuwait City	1-B2
Farwaniya	16-B2	Salwa	13-C4
Hawalli	7-B3	Wafra	2-C4
Jabriya	12-C1		

Kuwait City	Map Ref	Kuwait City	Map Ref
Abbasiyah	15-E4	Rabiya	10-E4
Abdullah As Salem	6-D1	Rihab	15-E1
Abraq Khaitan	11-D4	Rawda	6-E3
Andalus	9-D3	Ray Industrial Area	10-E2
Ardiya	15-A1	Riggage	10-B3
Bayan	13-A3	Rumaithiya	13-C1
Bneid Al Gar	4-A3	Sabah Al Salem	18-C4
Central Kuwait	3-C3	Safat	3-C3
Da'iya	7-A1	Salam	12-B3
Dasma	4-A4	Salhiya	3-C4
Dasman	4-A1	Salmiya	8-C3
East Hawalli	7-E3	Salwa	13-C4
East Maqwa	3-E2	Sawabeer	3-D3
Faiha	6-D3	Sha'ab	7-C1
Firdous	14-D1	Shamiya	6-B1
Gornata	9-C2	Sharq	3-D2
Hitteen	17-C1	Shuhada	17-D2
Industrial Area	5-E3	Shuwaikh	5-D3
Industrial Area 2	14-A3	Shuwaikh Port	5-D1
Jleeb Al Shuyoukh	15-d3	Siddiq	11-E4
Khaldiya	6-B4	South Khaitan	16-D2
Madain Hawalli	8-A3	South Rabiah	15-E2
Mansouriya	3-E4	South Surra	12-B4
Messilah	18-C3	Sabah Al Nasser	14-D2
Mirqab	3-D4	Sulaibiya	14-A1
Mishref	18-B1	Surra	12-A1
Nuzha	10-E2	Umm Seddah	3-D4
Omariya	11-B4	Wattiyah	3-B4
Qadsiya	7-A2	Yarmouk	11-C2
Qibla	3-B3	Zahra	16-E1
Qortuba	11-D1		

Introduction

Maps

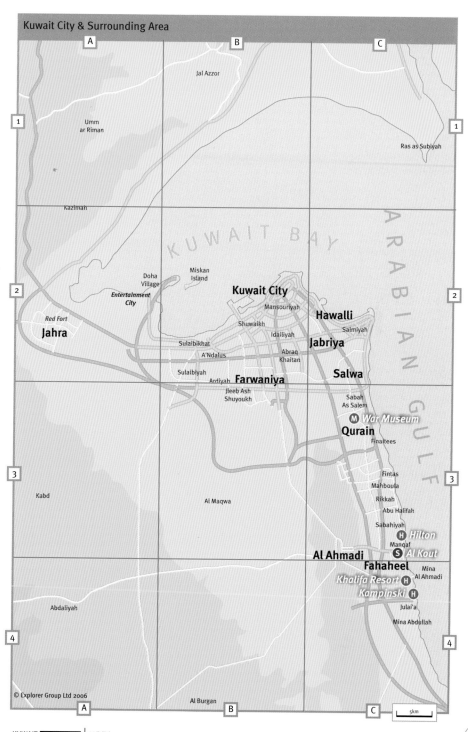

Kuwait City & Surrounding Area

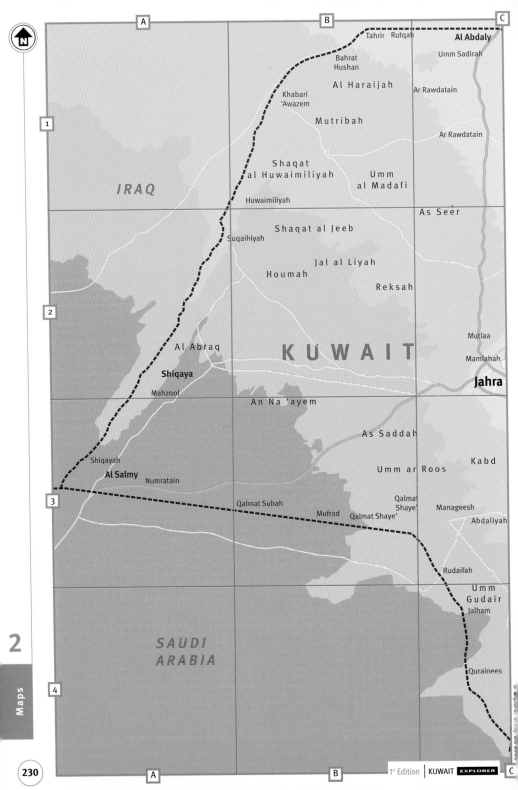

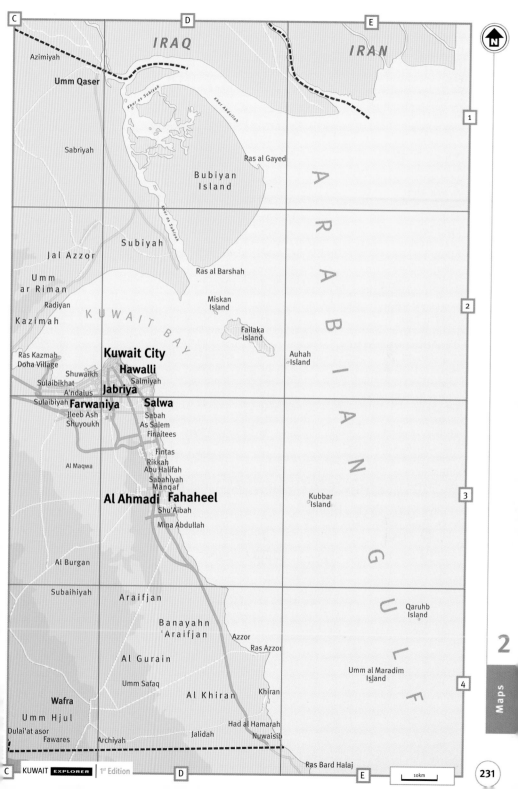

IRAQ

IRAN

Azimiyah

Umm Qaser

Khor as Subiyah

Khor Abdullah

Sabriyah

Ras al Gayed

B u b i y a n
I s l a n d

A
R
A
B
I
A
N

Khor as Subiyah

S u b i y a h

Ras al Barshah

Miskan
Island

Jal Azzor

U m m
a r R i m a n

Radiyan

K U W A I T   B A Y

Failaka
Island

Kazimah

Ras Kazmah
Doha Village

Kuwait City

Hawalli

Auhah
Island

Shuwaikh

Salmiyah

Sulaibikhat

A'ndalus

Jabriya

Farwaniya

Salwa

Sulaibiyah

Jleeb Ash
Shuyoukh

Sabah
As Salem
Finaitees

Fintas

Al Maqwa

Rikkah
Abu Halifah
Sabahiyah
Manqaf

B
I
A
N

Al Ahmadi **Fahaheel**

Kubbar
Island

Shu'Aibah

3

Mina Abdullah

Al Burgan

Subaihiyah

Araifjan

G
U

Banayahn
'Araifjan

Azzor

Ras Azzor

Qaruhb
Island

Al Gurain

Umm Safaq

Khiran

Umm al Maradim
Island

L
F

Wafra

Al Khiran

U m m H j u l

Dulai'at asor

Fawares

Archiyah

Jalidah

Had al Hamarah

Nuwaisib

Ras Bard Halaj

Street Name	Map Ref	Street Name	Map Ref
Abdul Kareem Al Khattabi Street	8-D4	Khalid Bin Al Waleed Street	3-D2
Abdulla As Salem Street	3-C4	King Fahad Ben Abdul Aziz Road	12-C3, 17-E2
Abdullah Al Ahmed Street	3-C2	King Faisal Motorway	11-D4, 16-E3
Ahmad Al jaber Street	3-D2	Maghreb Street	6-E1, 7-A3, 12-B1
Airport Road	5-E2, 6-A3, 11-B2, 16-C1	Masjid Al Aqsa Street	13-C2
Al Blajat Street	8-E3	Mohammad Ibn Kassem Street	10-D2
Al Ghaws Street	18-B1, B3	Mugheera Street	8-A3
Al Jahith Street	5-B4	Nasser al Mobarak Street	13-B1
Ali As Salem Street	3-C3	Riyadh Street	6-C3
Amman Street	8-A4	Road No. 1	18-A3
Arabian Gulf Street	3-B3, 3-E1,4-A3, 7-E2, 8-B2	Road No. 200	15-C4
Baghdad Street	7-E2, 8-A3	Road No. 250	15-C4
Beirut Street	7-B3	Road No. 3	18-D4
Cairo Street	3-E4, 7-A1, C2	Road No. 30	13-A4, 18-A1
Canada Dry Street	5-E4, 6-A4	Road No. 302	13-A3
Damascus Street	6-D3, E4, 11-E1	Road No. 40	14-E1
Fahaheel Expressway	7-D3, 13-B3, 18-C1	Road No. 5	18-D4
Fahed As Salem Street	3-C3	Road No. 50	15-B1
Fifth Ring Motorway	8-B4, 9-A4, 10-B3, 11-A3	Road No. 64	15-A2
First Ring Road	3-D4, E3	Salem Al Mubarak Street	7-E3, 8-B3
Fourth Ring Road	7-C4, 9-E2, 10-B2	Salwa Street	13-C3
Gamal Abdul Nasser Street	5-A4, 9-B1, 6-A1	Seventh Ring Road	14-B4
Ghazali Street	5-C2, 10-E1, 11-A4, 16-A1	Second Ring Road	4-A4, 6-B2, 7-A1
Hamad Al Mubarak Street	8-C3, D2	Sixth Ring Road	14-B3, 15-A3, E3, 17-B3
Istiqlal Street	4-A3	Soor Street	3-E2, C4, D4
Jaber Al Mobarak Street	3-E2	Street No. 103	15-D1
Jahra Road	5-C4, 6-B1, 9-A2	Ta'awen Street	13-D2, D4, 18-C1
Jordan Street	10-D4	Third Ring Road	6-B3, D3, 7-A2
Khalaf al Ahmar Street	14-B2, D2	Tunis Street	7-B2, C3
Khalid Ben Abdul Aziz Street	13-B4		

Map Legend

E Embassy/Consulate   **S** Souk/Shopping Centre   ▨▨▨ Motorway

H Hotel   **O** Hospital   ═══ Main Road

M Museum   DASMAN Area Name

Map page 1 is at a scale of 1:1,000,000 (1cm = 10km)
Map Page 2 is at a scale of 1: 500,000 (1cm = 5km)
Kuwait City Map sheet index at a sclae of 1: 150,000 (1cm = 1.5km)
Map pages 3-18 are at a scale of 1:20,000 (1cm = 200m)

Community & Street Index

Maps

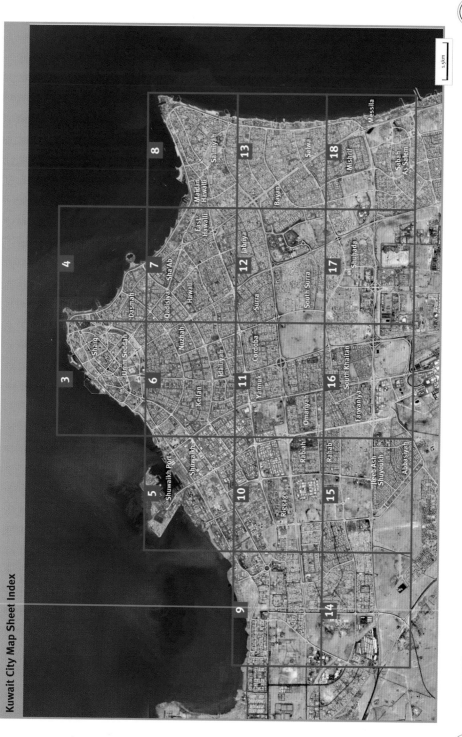

1.5km

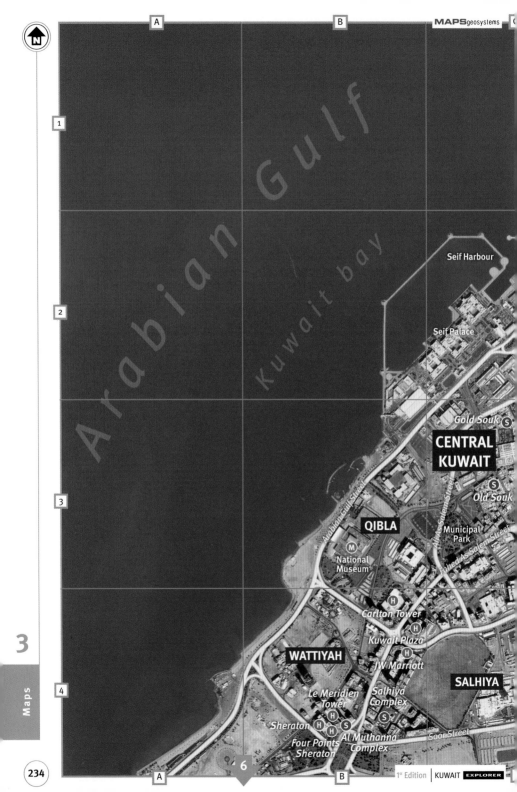

Arabian Gulf

Arabian

Kuwait bay

Seif Harbour

Seif Palace

Gold Souk (S)

CENTRAL KUWAIT

Old Souk (S)

QIBLA

Municipal Park

Arabian Gulf Street

Ali Al-Salem Street

Fahed As Salem Street

National Museum (M)

Carlton Tower (H)

Kuwait Plaza (H)

JW Marriott (H)

WATTIYAH

SALHIYA

Le Meridien Tower

Salhiya Complex (S)

(S)

Sheraton (H)(H)(S)

Soor Street

Four Points Sheraton

Al Muthanna Complex

6

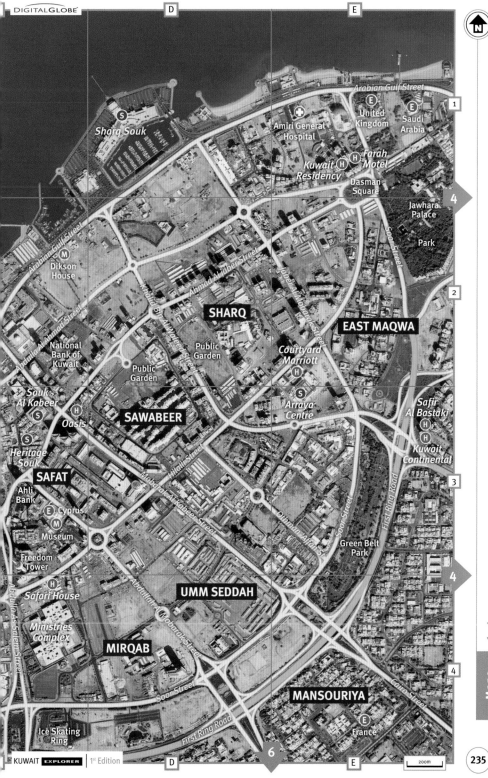

DIGITALGLOBE

N

1

4

Arabian Gulf Street

United
Kingdom

Saudi
Arabia

Sharq Souk

Amiri General
Hospital

Kuwait (H) *Farah
Residency* (H) *Motel*

Dasman
Square

Jawhara
Palace

Park

Arabian Gulf Street

(M) **Dikson
House**

Ahmad Al Jaber Street

Jaber Al Mubarak Street

SHARQ

EAST MAQWA

Soor Street

2

National
Bank of
Kuwait

Public
Garden

Public
Garden

*Courtyard
Marriott*
(H)

SAWABEER

*Souk
Al Kabeer*
(S)

Oasis (H)

(S)

*Heritage
Souk*

(S)

*Arraya
Centre*
(S)

*Safir
Al Bastaki*
(H)

(H)
*Kuwait
Continental*

SAFAT

Ahli
Bank

(E) Cyprus

(M)
Museum

Freedom
Tower

Hilali Street

Mohamed Al Kabeer Street

Othman Street

UMM SEDDAH

Soor Street

First Ring Road

Green Belt
Park

3

4

Safari House (H)

*Ministries
Complex*

MIRQAB

Abdulla Al Mubarak Street

Abdulla Al Salem Street

Soor Street

MANSOURIYA

Cairo Street

4

3

Maps

Ice Skating
Ring

First Ring Road

(E)
France

6

D   E

1

Aqua Park
Paintball Kuwaith
Kuwait Towers

Dasman
Palace

DASMAN

3

Public
Beach

2

Officers
Club

(H)
Safir Intl.

(H) *Ritz*

(H)
*Second Home
Hotel*

BNEID AL GAR

3

*Le Meridien
Kuwait* (H)

(E)
Iran (H)
Imperial (E) *Vatican*

3

(E)
Algeria (E) (E) (E)
Russia Turkey Sudan

(E)
India

DASMA

(E)
UAE (E)
Egypt (E) (E)
Qatar (E) Lebanon
(E)
Iran

*Dasma
Park*

4

4

Maps

7

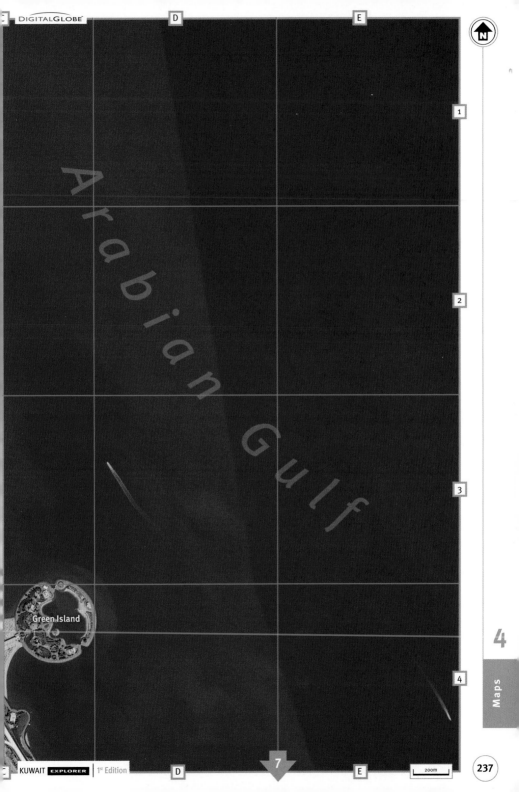

Arabian Gulf

Green Island

4

Maps

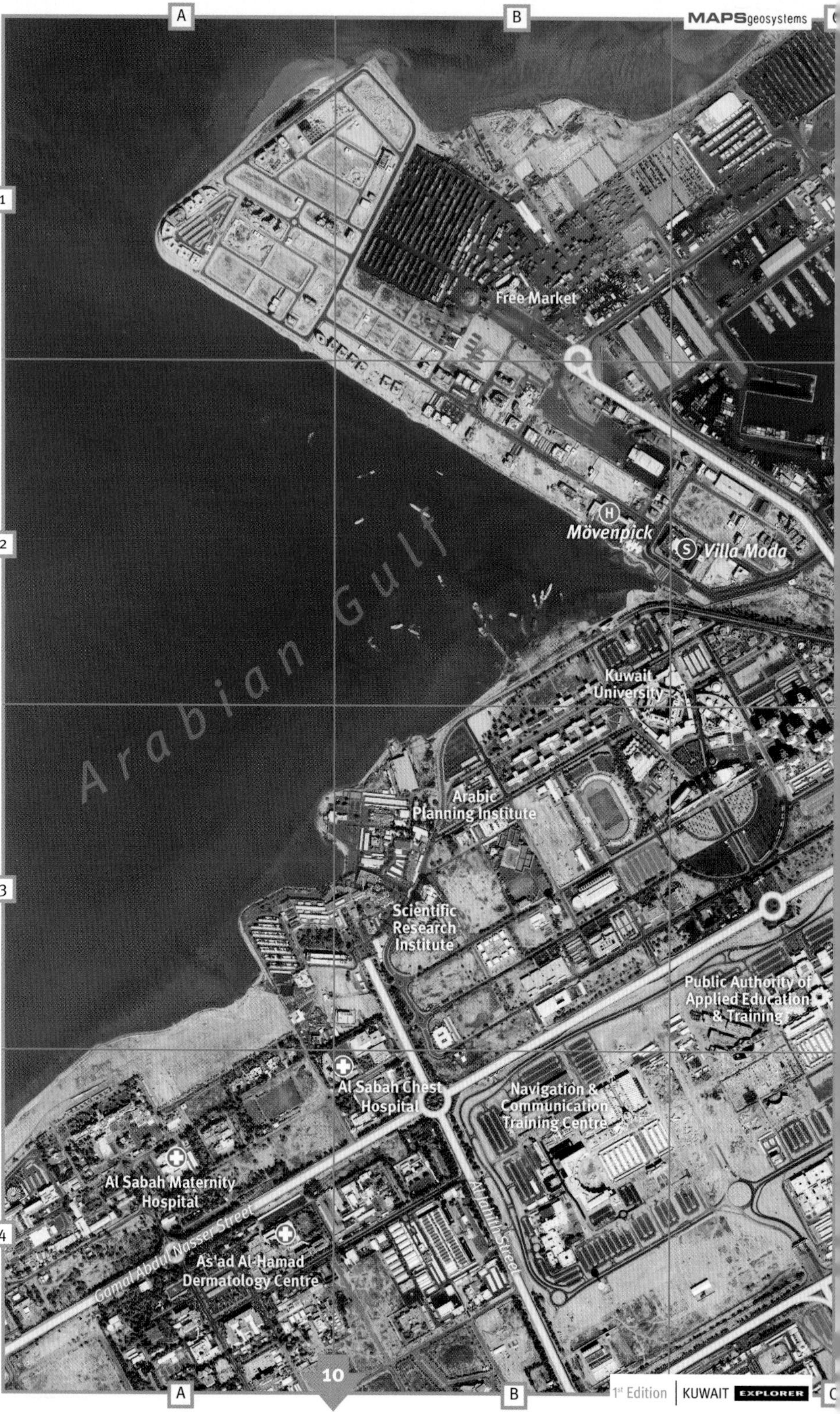

1

2

Free Market

(H) Mövenpick   (S) *Villa Moda*

A r a b i a n   G u l f

Kuwait
University

Arabic
Planning Institute

3

Scientific
Research
Institute

Public Authority of
Applied Education
& Training

Al Sabah Chest
Hospital

Navigation &
Communication
Training Centre

5

Al Sabah Maternity
Hospital

4

Gamal Abdul Nasser Street

As'ad Al-Hamad
Dermatology Centre

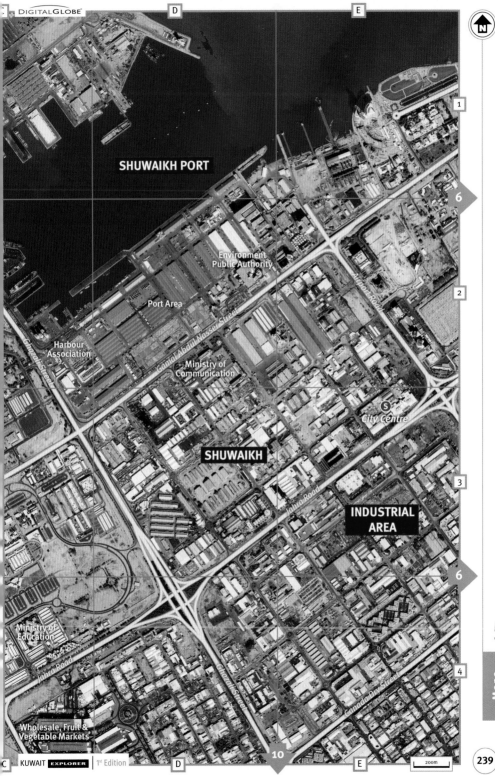

SHUWAIKH PORT

Environment
Public Authority

Port Area

Harbour
Association

Ministry of
Communication

SHUWAIKH

City Centre

INDUSTRIAL
AREA

Ministry of
Education

Wholesale, Fruit &
Vegetable Markets

Ghazali Street

Gamal Abdul Nasser Street

Airport Road

Jahra Road

Jahra Road

Ghazali Street

Canada Dry Street

5

Maps

Arabian Gulf Street

Salam Palace

Gamal Abdul Nasser Street

Yugoslavia

Wahran Garden

Police Station

Ministry of Interior

SHAMIYA

International Labour Office

Second Ring Road

Kuwait Red Crescent Society

Kuwait Sports Club

Ministry of Telecommunication

Collage of Education

Indonesia

Park

Romania

Airport Road

Third Ring Road

Riyadh Street

Bangladesh

Press House

Canada Dry Street

KHALIDIYA

Kuwait Automobile Association

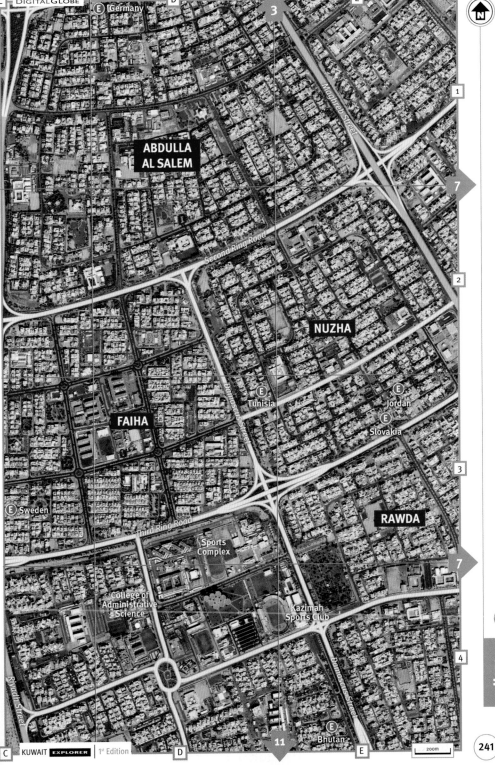

DIGITALGLOBE

Germany

ABDULLA
AL SALEM

Second Ring Road

NUZHA

Tunisia

Jordan

FAIHA

Slovakia

Sweden

Third Ring Road

RAWDA

Sports
Complex

College of
Administrative
Science

Kazimah
Sports Club

Bhutan

N

A

B

C

4

DA'IYA

Arabi Sports Club

Canada

Libya

Austria

City Park

SHA'AB

Cairo Street

QADISIYA

Third Ring Road

HAWALLI

Police Station

Hawalli Post

Beirut Street

Maghreb Street

Senegal

Fourth Ring Road

12

7

Maps

© Explorer Group Ltd 2006

Arabian Gulf

Swimming Pool
Complex

Sha'ab Palace

Sha'ab Sea
Club

Arabian Gulf Street

College of
Business Studies

Al Sha'ab
Leisure Park

Al Muhalab
Centre

New Park

Baghdad Street

Qadisiyah
Sports Club

Beirut Street

EAST HAWALLI

Police
Station

Fahaheel Expressway

Salem Al Mubarak Street

Hawalli
Theatre

College
of Medicine

Mubarak
Al kabeer
Hospital

Bayan School

Hadi
Hospital

7

Maps

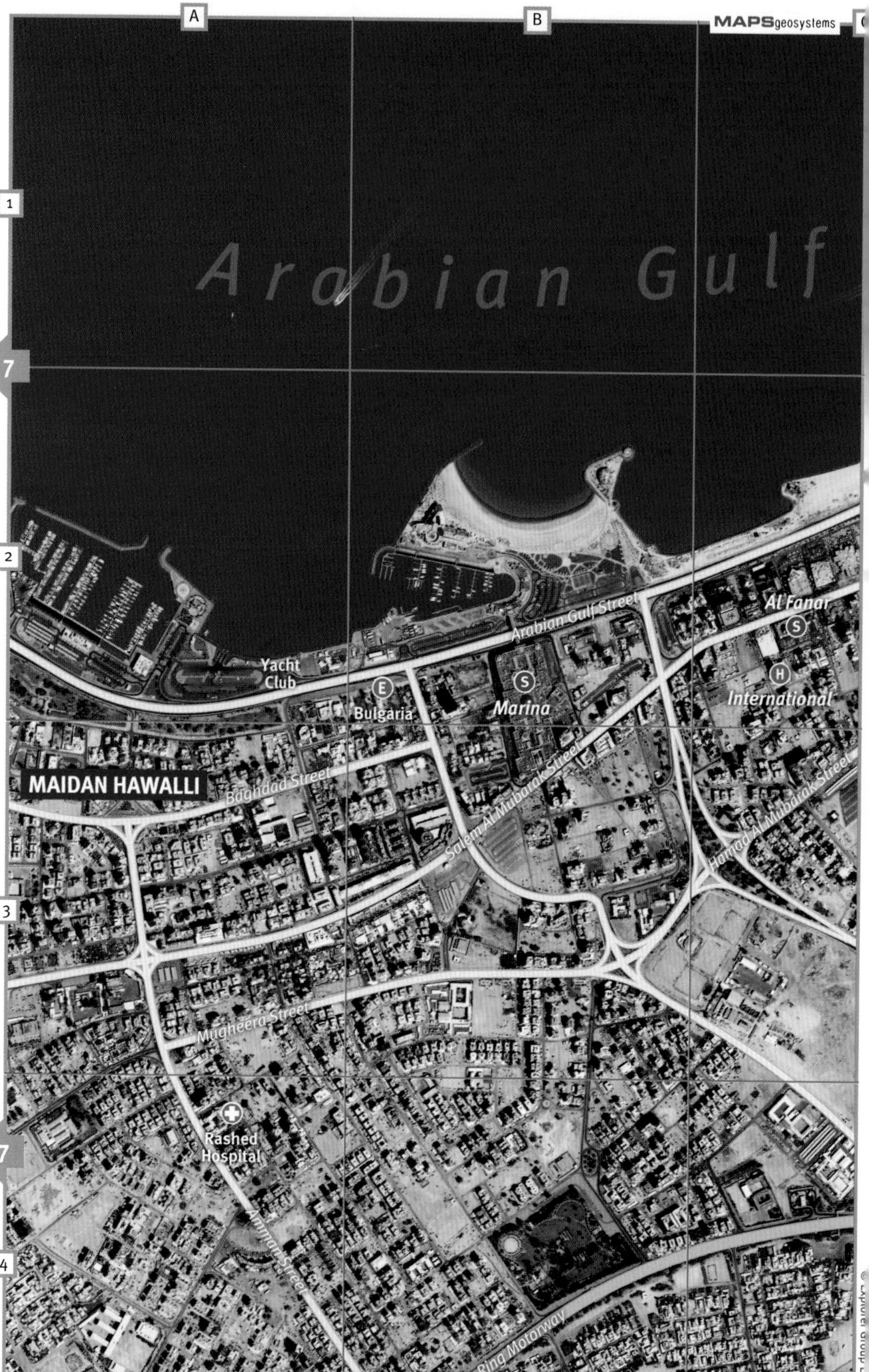

N

1

Arabian Gulf

7

2

Yacht
Club

E
Bulgaria   S
                    Marina

Arabian Gulf Street

Al Fanar
S

H
International

MAIDAN HAWALLI   Baghdad Street

Salem Al-Mubarak Street

Hamad Al-Mubarak Street

3

Mugheera Street

Rashed
Hospital

7

8

Maps

4

Fifth Ring Motorway

DIGITALGLOBE

1

Ras al Ardh

Scientific
Centre

Bus Station

Holiday Inn

Show Biz
Amusment Park

2

Sultan (S)

Salem Al Mubarak Street

Ghani
Palace

New Mowasat
Hospital

Kuwait
Sea Club

(S) Spring
Continental

Hamad Al Mubarak Street

Al Bustan

Salmiyah
Sports Club

(E) Belgium

Hawalli Park

3

SALMIYA

Al Bhon Street

Arabian Gulf

Qadar Street

City
Centre (S)

Fire Station

Immigration
Office
Jawazat R/A

Abdul Kareem Al Khattabi Street

Al Bida'
Sea Club

4

Shik Flamingo
Resort (H)

13

8

Maps

1

Arabian Gulf

Gamal Abdul Nasser Street

GHORNATA

2

Al Khalifa
Market

Jahra Road

Isolation
Hospital

3

Cemetery

Fifth Ring Motorway

4

Ministry
of Health

Psychiatric
Hospital

1

10

2

Gamal Abdul Nasser St

Jahra Road

Fourth Ring Road

Bus Station

Infectious
Diseases Hospital

ANDALUS

3

10

Fifth Ring Motorway

9

Maps

4

Water Towers

14

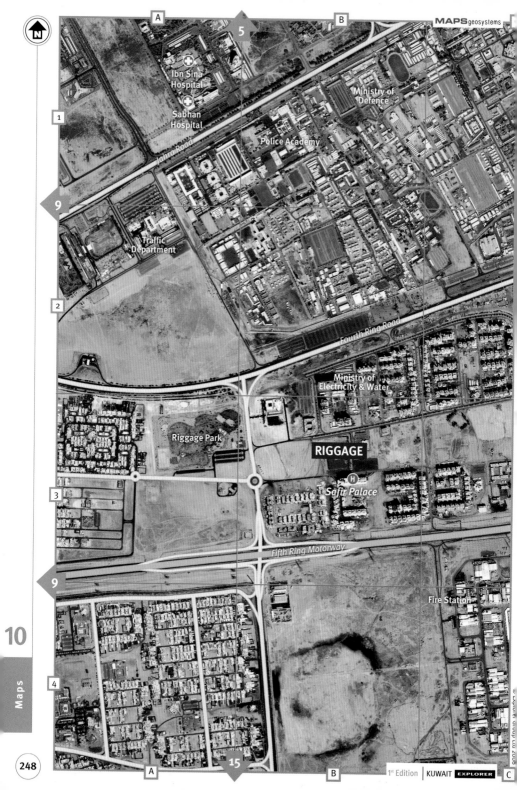

N

A 5 B

1

Ibn Sina Hospital

Sabhan Hospital

Ministry of Defence

Police Academy

9

Jahra Road

Traffic Department

2

Fourth Ring Road

Ministry of Electricity & Water

Riggage Park

RIGGAGE

3

Safir Palace

9

Fifth Ring Motorway

Fire Station

10

Maps

4

A 15 B C

1st Edition | KUWAIT EXPLORER

DIGITALGLOBE

D 5 E

N

Canada Dry Street

Ghazali Street

1

11

Fourth Ring Road

Ghazali Street

RAI INDUSTRIAL AREA

S

Landmark

2

Ministry of Awqaf & Islamic Affairs

Mohammad Ibn Qassim Road

Fifth Ring Motorway

3

Public Affairs for Agriculture & Fish

11

Experiment Farm

RABIYA

10

Maps

4

Jordan Street

15

200m

Police Station

E
Greece

1

Immigration &
Passport Dept.

Fourth Ring Road

E
China

10

Animal
Souk

**INDUSTRIAL
AREA**

Friday
Market

Airport Road

YARMOUK

2

Fifth Ring Motorway

3

Zoo

10

OMARIYA

Airport Road

Ghazali Street

Police
Station

4

Tadhamon
Sports Club

College of
Science &
Engineering

Kuwait University
Women's College

D

E

6

N

E
Tunisia

E
Oman

Fourth Ring Road

E
Cuba

1

E
Korea

12

QORTUBA

E
Switzerland

E
Denmark

2

E
Hungary

E
Morocco

E
Brazil

Fifth Ring Motorway

Water Tower

3

12

11

SIDDIQ

Maps

Park

4

ABRAQ KHAITAN

C

D

12

E

200m

MAPSgeosystems

7

White
Palace

American
School

(E)
Nigeria

(E)
Malaysia

Maghreb Street

SURRA

(E)
Bangladesh

(E)
Bahrain

1

(E)
Afghanistan

(E)
Sudan

11

(E)
Venezuela

(E)
Eritria

2

(E)
Spain

Fifth Ring Motorway

Electricity
Station

SALAM

3

11

SOUTH SURRA

12

Maps

4

252

17

1st Edition | KUWAIT EXPLORER

C

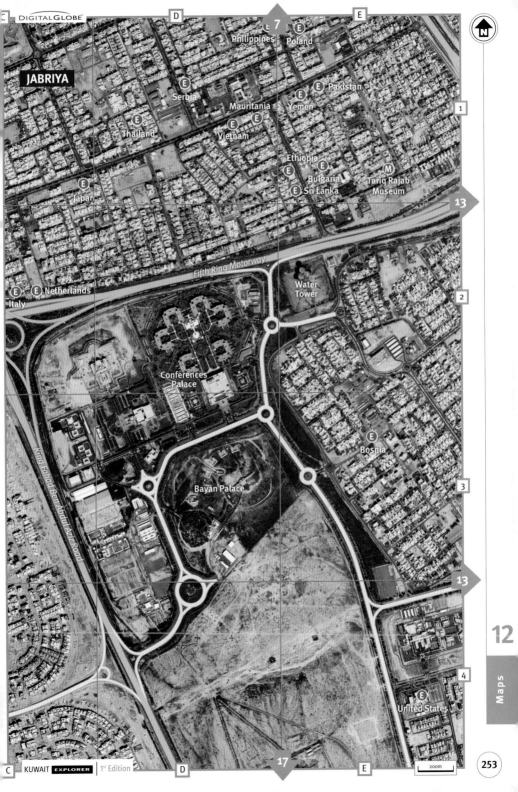

JABRIYA

7
Philippines   Poland

Serbia
Pakistan
Mauritania   Yemen

Thailand   Vietnam

Ethiopia
Bulgaria
Japan   Sri Lanka   Tariq Rajab Museum

13

Fifth Ring Motorway

Water Tower

Netherlands
Italy

2

Conferences Palace

Bosnia

3

Bayan Palace

King Fahed Ben Abdul Aziz Road

13

12

United States

4

Maps

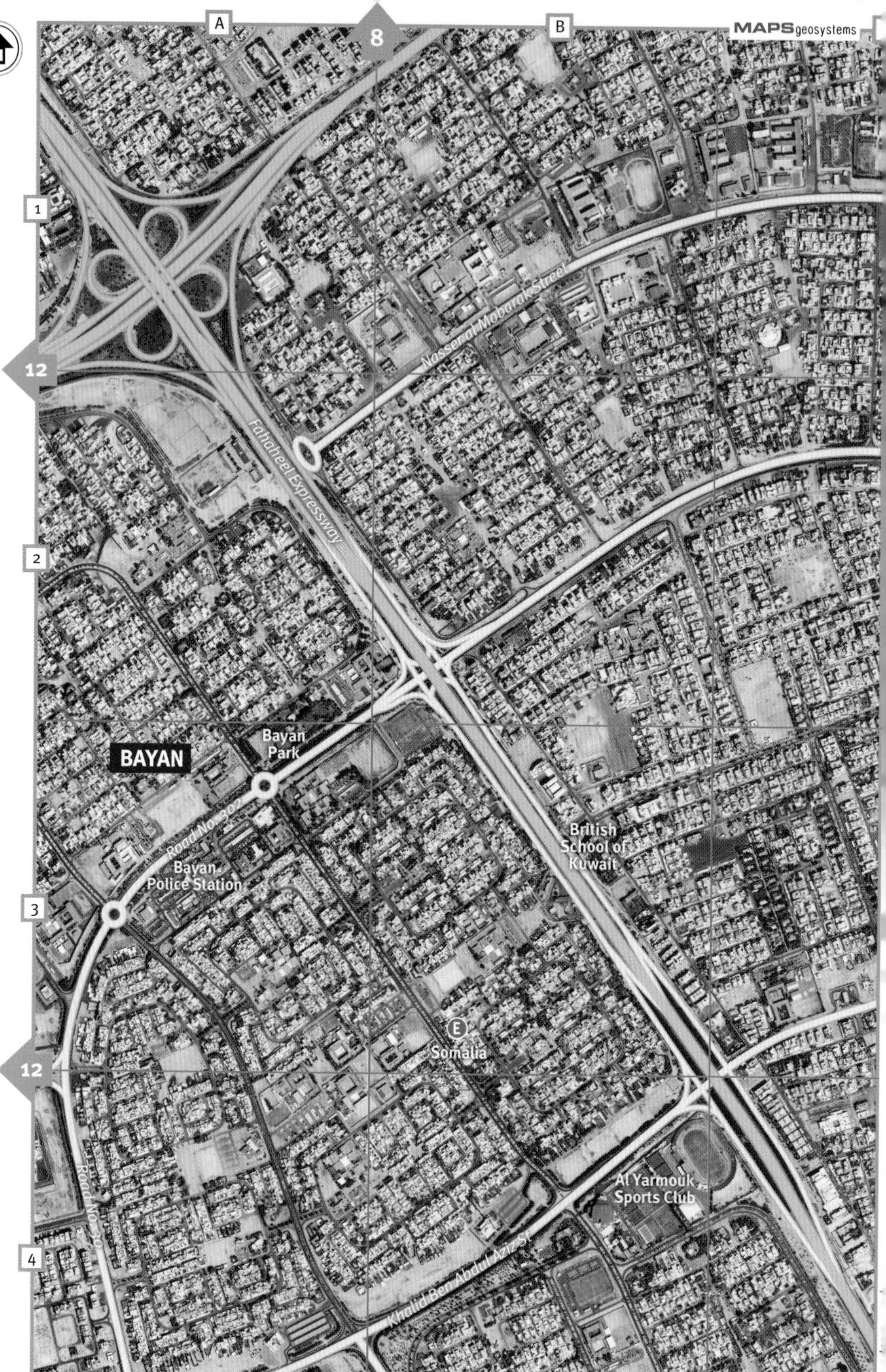

MAPS geosystems

1

12

2

BAYAN

Bayan
Park

Bayan
Police Station

3

British
School of
Kuwait

12

(E)
Somalia

Al Yarmouk
Sports Club

Nasseem Mubarak Street

Fahaheel Expressway

Qadi No Road

Khalid Ben Abdul Aziz

4

1st Edition | KUWAIT EXPLORER

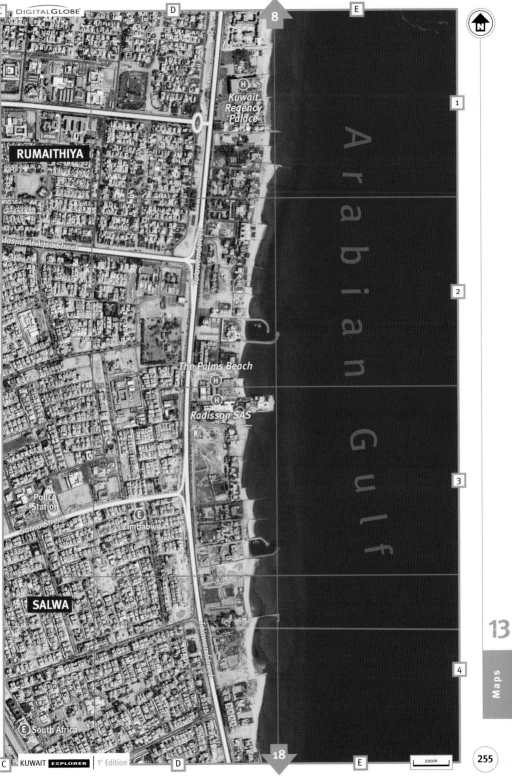

DIGITALGLOBE

H
Kuwait
Regency
Palace

1

RUMAITHIYA

A
r
a
b
i
a
n

Masjid Al Aqsa Street

2

The Palms Beach
H
H
Radisson SAS

G
u
l
f

3

Police
Station
Salwa Street
E Zimbabwe

SALWA

13

4

E South Africa

SULAIBIYA
IND. AREA 1

1

SULAIBIYA

Prison

2

Khalaf al Ahmar Street

SULAIBIYA
IND. AREA 2

3

Sixth Ring Road

Seventh Ring Road

FIRDOUS

Khalaf al Ahmar Street

SABAH AL NASSER

Sixth Ring Road

Zoo (Proposed)

14

Maps

200m

Sewage Works

ARDIYA

Road No. 39

Road No. 67

Farwaniya Hospital

Road No. 50

Sixth Ring Road

Road No. 106

Road No. 250

15

Maps

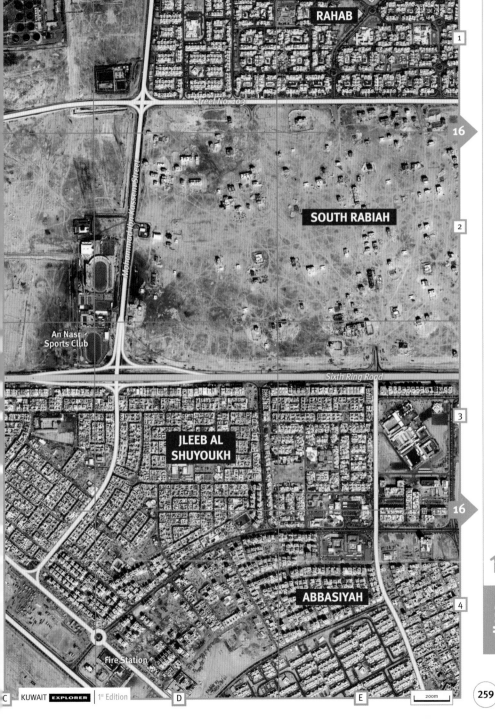

RAHAB

Street No. 103

SOUTH RABIAH

Mohammad Ibn Kassm Street

An Nasr
Sports Club

Sixth Ring Road

JLEEB AL
SHUYOUKH

ABBASIYAH

Fire Station

200m

15

Maps

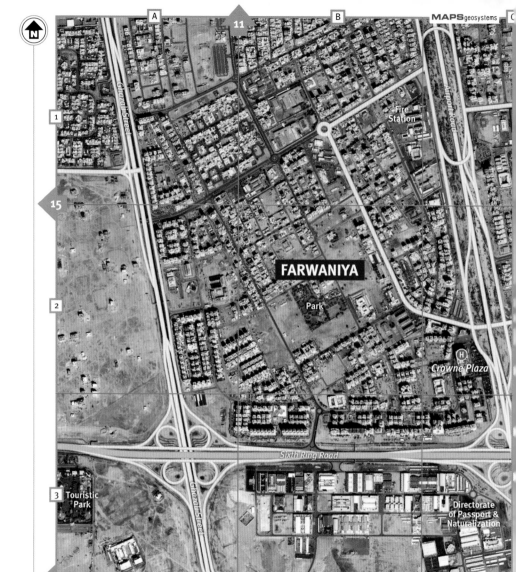

1

15

2

FARWANIYA

Park

3   Touristic Park

15

Ghazali Street

Airport Road

Fire Station

Crowne Plaza

Sixth Ring Road

Directorate of Passport & Naturalization

Kuwait Airways

Khaitan
Sports Club

ZAHRA

SOUTH KHAITAN

Drive in
Cinema

Sixth Ring Road

King Faisal Motorway

Water Towers

Airport Road

200m

16

Maps

Ministries Area

Sixth Ring Road

National Guard

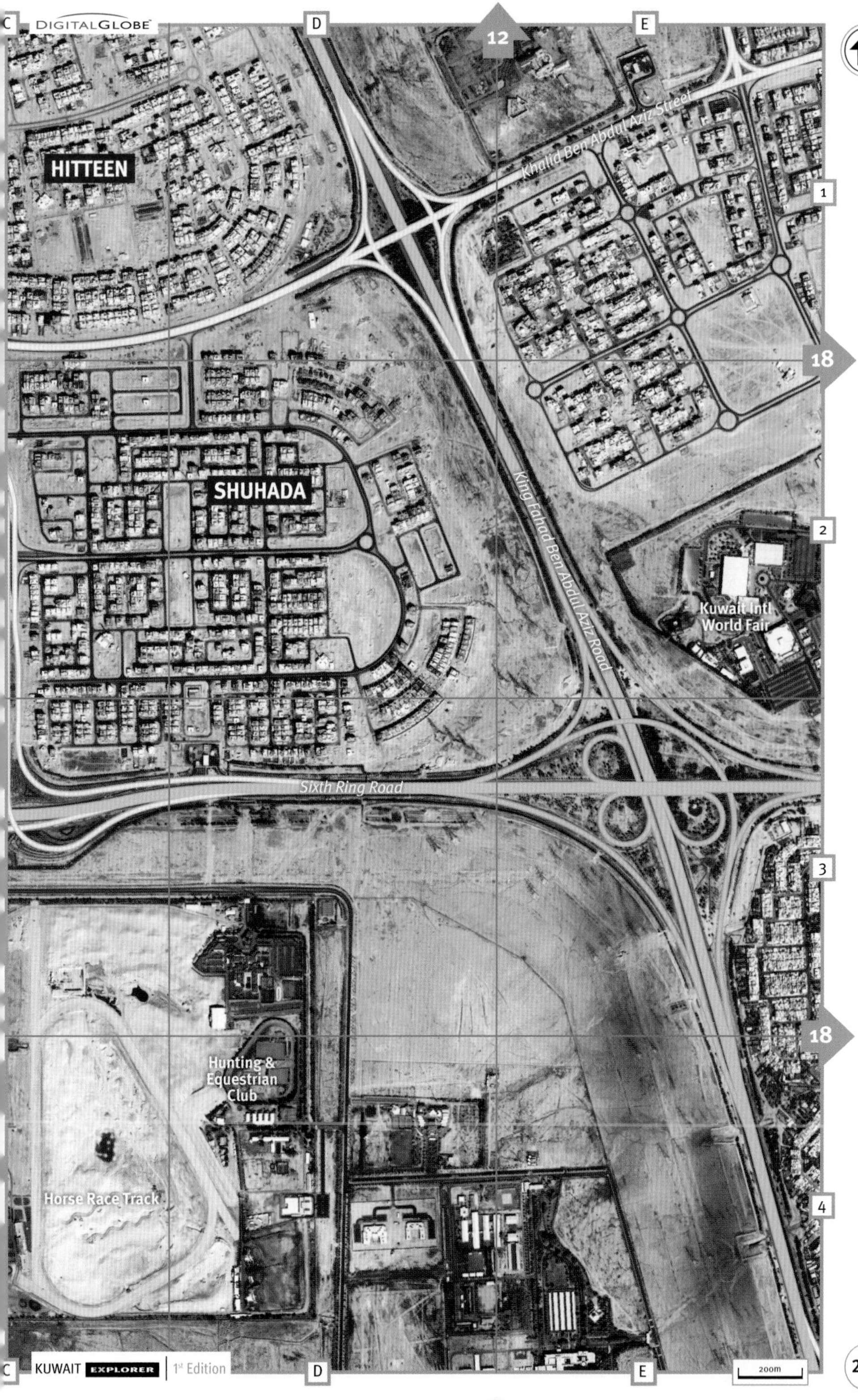

N

HITTEEN

1

Khalid Ben Abdul Aziz Street

18

SHUHADA

King Fahad Ben Abdul Aziz Road

2

Kuwait Intl
World Fair

Sixth Ring Road

3

18

Hunting &
Equestrian
Club

17

Horse Race Track

Maps

4

Mishrif
Centre

Syria

MISHRIF

Mishrif
Park

Radio
Station

SABAH
AL SALEM

18

Maps

13

1

2

3

4

Arabian Gulf

Fahaheel Expressway

Tariwean Street

Gulf English School

Messila Beach

Ⓗ

Messila Water Village

Messila Public Beach

MESSILA

Sixth Ring Road

Fahaheel Expressway

Sabal Al Salem Hospital

Road No.3

Road No.5

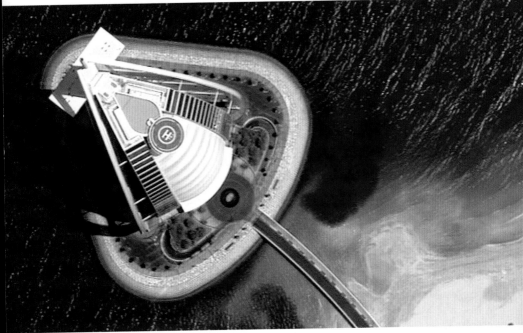

Index

EXPLORER

Index

Index

Index